Due Return	Due Return
Date Date	Date Date

POLITICAL SCIENCE
AND
PUBLIC POLICY

POLITICAL SCIENCE
AND
PUBLIC POLICY

edited by

AUSTIN RANNEY

sponsored by

**The Committee on Governmental and
Legal Processes of the Social Science Research Council**

MARKHAM PUBLISHING COMPANY · CHICAGO

MARKHAM POLITICAL SCIENCE SERIES
AARON WILDAVSKY, Editor

To Pendleton Herring
in the hope that our answers
are worthy of his questions

Preface

In 1964 the Social Science Research Council appointed the Committee on Governmental and Legal Processes to succeed its Committee on Political Behavior, which, under the successive chairmanships of Pendleton Herring, V. O. Key, Jr., and David B. Truman, had contributed so much to the "behavioral revolution" in political science since 1945. Support for the new committee's program was provided by the Ford Foundation. The committee's members considered at some length among themselves the question of what initiatives they should take in encouraging the study of governmental and legal processes in the United States. In June 1965 they held a conference on the question in New York City with Robert A. Dahl, James G. March, Richard E. Neustadt, James W. Prothro, and Aaron Wildavsky. Out of these discussions emerged a consensus that the most timely and urgent question now within the committee's purview is: What professional expertise and obligations, if any, have political scientists to study, evaluate, and make recommendations about the contents of public policies?

To explore this question in depth, the committee sponsored two conferences. The first, held at Princeton in June 1966, centered on papers by Lewis A. Froman, Jr., Ralph K. Huitt, Lucian W. Pye, Vernon Van Dyke, and Aaron Wildavsky, which were discussed by the members of the committee and staff and Bernard C. Cohen, J. Willard Hurst, Charles S. Hyneman, Herbert Kaufman, W. Duane Lockard, Theodore J. Lowi, Richard E. Neustadt, Nelson W. Polsby, H. Douglas Price, William H. Riker, John R. Schmidhauser, M. Brewster Smith, and Sidney G. Verba.

At the second conference, held at Cape Newagen, Maine, in August of 1967, papers were presented by Lincoln P. Bloomfield, James W. Davis, Jr., Kenneth M. Dolbeare, Vincent Ostrom, James M. Rosenau, and Robert H. Salisbury. The discussants included members of the committee, to which David J. Danelski had been added, and Thomas Dye, Oliver Garceau, Edward S. Greenberg, Pendleton Herring, Richard I. Hofferbert, Herbert Jacob, Ira Sharkansky, Gilbert Y. Steiner, Raymond E. Wolfinger, Bryce Wood, and Harmon Zeigler.

The papers given at the two conferences were revised in the light of the conference discussions, and their revised versions constitute ten of this book's twelve chapters. Two papers have been added. In the introductory chapter, I set forth what I believe to be the framework within which the broad problem of political science and public policy should be discussed and note the relation of each chapter to that framework. The concluding chapter is a revised version of a paper originally delivered by David B. Truman to a meeting of the American Association for the Advancement of Science. Its author, the long-time chairman of the Committee on Political Behavior and a distinguished political scientist and educator, is especially qualified to be given the last word. And his topic— the obligation of universities to train both practicing social scientists and administrators equipped to understand and use social science expertise— gathers in many of the themes developed by the other authors and relates them directly to the professional activity on which most political scientists spend a good deal of their time and energy: training the future producers *and* governmental consumers of political science.

All of us involved in this project wish to express our thanks to Bryce Wood for his staff support of the committee and its conferences. I also wish to thank Edward S. Greenberg for his careful summary of the Newagen discussions, and Mrs. Nancy Edgerton for her help in preparing the manuscript for publication. No thanks can be adequate for Pendleton Herring's stimulation and encouragement of this undertaking, but a small recognition of his contribution is presented elsewhere.

AUSTIN RANNEY

February 1, 1968

Contents

The Editor and the Authors

Austin Ranney, born in Cortland, New York, in 1920, is Professor of Political Science at the University of Wisconsin. Currently, he is Chairman of the Social Science Research Council's Committee on Governmental and Legal Processes and is Managing Editor of the *American Political Science Review*. He is author of *The Doctrine of Responsible Party Government, The Governing of Men,* and *Pathways to Parliament;* co-author of *Democracy and the American Party System;* and editor of *Essays on the Behavioral Study of Politics.*

Vernon Van Dyke, born in Idaho in 1912, is Professor of Political Science at the University of Iowa. He obtained a Ph.D. in International Relations at the University of Chicago and taught at DePauw and Yale before going to Iowa in 1949. He has been editor of the *Midwest Journal of Political Science* and is the author of: *International Politics; Political Science, A Philosophical Analysis;* and *Pride and Power: The Rationale of the Space Program.*

Lewis A. Froman, Jr., born in Buffalo, New York, in 1935, is Associate Professor of Political Science at the University of California, Irvine. He is the author of *People and Politics, Congressmen and Their Constituencies,* and *The Congressional Process,* as well as numerous articles in professional journals.

Aaron Wildavsky, born in Brooklyn in 1930, is Professor of Political Science and Chairman of the Department at the University of California, Berkeley. He is author of *The Politics of the Budgetary Process, Leadership in a Small Town, Dixon-Yates: A Study in Power Politics,* and *Studies in Australian Politics: The 1926 Referendum,* and is co-author of *Presidential Elections.*

James W. Davis, Jr., born in Chillicothe, Missouri, in 1935, is Associate

Professor of Political Science at Washington University. He is co-author (with Kenneth M. Dolbeare) of *Little Groups of Neighbors: The Selective Service System.*

Kenneth M. Dolbeare, born in Mineola, New York, in 1930, is Associate Professor of Political Science at the University of Wisconsin. He is author of *Trial Courts in Urban Politics* and co-author (with James W. Davis, Jr.) of *Little Groups of Neighbors: The Selective Service System.*

Vincent Ostrom, born in Nooksack, Washington, in 1919, is Professor of Government at Indiana University. He is author of *Water and Politics* and of numerous articles on water resource development and related policy problems.

Robert H. Salisbury, born in Elmhurst, Illinois, in 1930, is Professor of Political Science at Washington University where, since 1966, he has been Chairman of the Department. He is co-author of *State Politics and the Public Schools* and *American Government: Problems and Readings in Political Analysis* and is a contributor to *Politics in the American States, Planning for a Nation of Cities,* and a number of other volumes and scholarly journals.

Lincoln P. Bloomfield, born in Boston in 1920, has received three degrees from Harvard University. After eleven years in the U.S. State Department, he joined the M.I.T. Center for International Studies where he is Director of The Arms Control Project and Professor of Political Science. Consultant to government agencies and private industry, he wrote *The United Nations and U.S. Foreign Policy* and *Evolution or Revolution,* co-authored *International Military Forces* and *Controlling Small Wars,* and edited *Outer Space: Prospects for Man and Society.*

James N. Rosenau, born in Philadelphia in 1924, is Professor of Political Science at Rutgers—The State University and Research Associate at the Center of International Studies at Princeton University. He has also taught at Columbia and New York Universities and, in 1958–59, held a Ford Foundation International Relations Training Fellowship. He is author of *Public Opinion and Foreign Policy* and *National Leadership and Foreign Policy;* co-author and editor of *International Aspects of Civil Strife* and *Domestic Sources of Foreign Policy;* and editor of *International Politics and Foreign Policy.*

Lucian W. Pye, born in China in 1921, is Professor of Political Science at the Massachusetts Institute of Technology, is a Senior Staff member of the

Center for International Studies, and is Chairman of the Social Science Research Council's Committee on Comparative Politics. He has done field work in Southeast Asia and Hong Kong and has served in various capacities in the organizations of scholarly associations and government agencies. He is author of: *Spirit of Chinese Politics; Aspects of Political Development; Politics, Personality and Nation-Building;* and *Guerrilla Communism in Malaya;* co-author of *The Politics of the Developing Areas* and *The Emerging Nations;* and editor of *Communication and Political Development* and *Political Culture and Political Development* (with Sidney Verba).

Ralph K. Huitt, born in Corsicana, Texas, in 1913, is Professor of Political Science at the University of Wisconsin. In 1965 he was granted leave for an indefinite period to serve as Assistant Secretary for Legislation of the Department of Health, Education, and Welfare. He has been a member of the staffs of Senators Lyndon B. Johnson and William Proxmire and has been a member of the council and executive committee of the American Political Science Association. His articles on legislative behavior have appeared principally in the *American Political Science Review.*

David B. Truman, born in Evanston, Illinois, in 1913, is Professor of Government and Vice-President and Provost of Columbia University. He has been president of the American Association for the Advancement of Science. His publications include *The Governmental Process* and *The Congressional Party.*

Part One

CONCEPTS AND ISSUES

The Study of Policy Content:
A Framework for Choice*

AUSTIN RANNEY

This book is addressed to political scientists and to those outside the discipline who may look to political science for help in dealing with the great public problems and issues of our time. It proceeds from the conviction, documented below,[1] that at least since 1945 most American political scientists have focused their professional attention mainly on the *processes* by which public policies are made and have shown relatively little concern with their *contents*.[2] Its authors attack, from many angles and with a wide variety of weapons, the central question: Should political scientists in their research and teaching pay substantially more attention to policy contents than they have in recent years?

Our discussions mainly revolve about four component issues:

First, what is likely to be the net gain or loss from more study of policy contents for the theoretical sophistication and empirical validity of political science's special body of knowledge?

Second, what problems of conceptualization, data collection, and analysis must be solved if studies of policy contents are to meet high scholarly standards?

Third, what is likely to be the net gain or loss from more study of policy contents to the relevance and utility of political science for policy-makers and policy critics?

Fourth, what professional expertise and obligation, if any, have political

---

* I am grateful to all the members of the Committee on Governmental and Legal Processes for their contributions to our conferences and this book. My particular thanks go to Richard F. Fenno and John C. Wahlke for reading the first draft of this chapter and making many valuable suggestions.
[1] See pp. 9–13.
[2] For my definitions of these key terms, see pp. 7–8.

scientists to contribute directly to the formulation, implementation, and evaluation of public policies in the United States?[3]

My purpose in this introductory chapter is to prepare the stage (and perhaps also suggest some canons for evaluating the scripts and actors to come) by setting forth my conception of the intellectual and moral framework within which these questions should be pondered, discussed, and decided.

Let us begin with the last.

I. THE POLITICAL SCIENTIST AS EXPERT AND ACTIVIST

We should be clear at the outset that this book is concerned with the political scientist's proper scientific and professional approach to all aspects of public policies, whether he focuses on their contents or on the processes by which they are made, and whether he describes, analyzes, evaluates, or prescribes. It is *not* concerned with his *extra*professional attitudes, activities, or obligations toward policy-making.

By this I do not mean to imply that the latter are unimportant. Obviously they are of great importance for all Americans, whether they be political scientists or professional fullbacks or astronauts. The point is that the strategic and moral problems they raise for Americans who happen to work in the field of political science do not differ essentially from those they raise for Americans in other occupations. Any political scientist who feels the nation should get out of Vietnam or abolish the income tax has the same right and obligation as any other citizen to press his position as forcefully and persistently as his resources permit and the intensity of his feelings demands.

But that is not the question here. We are asking, instead, what are his skills and obligations *as a political scientist* to deal with policy contents? In my view, we can most relevantly and usefully consider this question if we always keep in sight the basic distinctions between the political scientist's scientific, professional, and nonprofessional obligations.

In this regard, I find Don K. Price's formulation most helpful.[4] In the American political system, he says, there are four "estates," each with its special function in and approach to the making of public policy. They are: (1) the *scientific,* which is concerned solely with discovering truth, not with its governmental application or social utility or moral effects; (2) the *professional,* which is concerned with "taking the abstractions of science (or other systematic knowledge) and applying them to the concrete and practical affairs of men"; (3) the *administrative,* whose members "must be prepared to understand and use a wide variety of professional expertise and scholarly

---

[3] We deal only with public policies and political scientists in the United States, but we believe that most of the questions we raise and many of the answers we suggest are equally relevant for political scientists and their present and potential clienteles in many other nations.

[4] As presented in his *The Scientific Estate* (Cambridge: Belknap Press, Harvard University Press, 1965), esp. pp. 122–35.

disciplines [to help their] political superiors attain their general purposes";
and (4) the *political*, whose practitioners "may make use of the skills of
administrators, and engineers and scientists," but in the end must "make their
most important decisions on the basis of value judgments or hunch or
compromise of power interests."[5]

A number of sciences provide the intellectual bases for well-established,
distinctive professions whose members apply the sciences' knowledge to the
solution of practical problems: e.g., engineering (physics and chemistry),
medicine (biology), and agronomy (botany). As David Truman correctly
points out in our concluding chapter,[6] political science has not yet bifurcated
into a distinctive basic science and a derivative profession. Many political
scientists move back and forth freely between "basic research," which seeks to
discover scientific truth regardless of its utility, and "applied research,"
which seeks solutions to practical problems.[7]

I shall return to Price's categories in a moment. The point here is that if
political science is in part a true profession, and not just an agglomeration of
persons interested in political affairs, then what qualifies political scientists as
professionals is their special knowledge and skills, not their common sense or
their goodwill or their passion for social justice. And if that is so, then the
political scientist, like any expert, may legitimately speak as a professional on
matters of public policy only when what he says rests on and accords with his
discipline's special body of knowledge.

To illustrate: If Dr. S. says, "I tell you *as a pediatrician* that we should
get out of Vietnam," he violates medical ethics, for pediatric science says
nothing about foreign policy one way or the other. By the same token, if
Professor S. says, "I tell you *as a political scientist* that we should continue to
fight in Vietnam," he violates scholarly ethics; for political science says
nothing directly about what we *should* do in Vietnam—or at least it evidently
says very different things to different political scientists of comparable professional achievement and repute.

To be sure, the present or potential relevance of political science expertise to what we should do in Vietnam is, in both nature and degree, a good
deal more difficult to estimate than the relevance of pediatrics. Indeed, much
of this book is concerned with making this and comparable estimates. But the
political scientist's professional obligation to make statements about public
policies and the expertise from which those statements should flow are those,
and only those, which are firmly rooted in the discipline's special body of
knowledge.[8]

Accordingly, this book will not deal with the host of important and
vexing questions about what public causes persons who happen to be political

---

[5] *Ibid.*, pp. 122, 134.

[6] See p. 283.

[7] For illuminating discussions of some of the dilemmas this sort of movement poses
for political scientists, see Chapters 5 and 8 below.

[8] Just as the pediatrician clearly has the professional expertise and obligation to
examine and treat sick children—though not, perhaps, to the extent of making house calls.

scientists should support and oppose, by what means, and to what ends. It will deal with the problem of what, if any, *professional* contribution political scientists can and should make to the formulation and evaluation of public policies in the United States. And that, as we shall see, is at least as tough a problem.

II. SOME KEY CONCEPTS

Few exercises produce so quick and deep a glaze in the eyes of nonprofessional readers of scholarly literature as the hairsplitting and logic-chopping of conceptualization. Yet some degree of conceptual clarity is essential for the most elementary communication, and the greater the confusion over concepts in any field, the less likely is any substantial improvement in its knowledge.

This truism applies strongly to discussions of the political scientist's proper role in the study of public policy. Wherever the issue is debated, in the literature or around the conference table, the only thing entirely clear is that the discussants do not all mean exactly the same things by such often used terms as "public policy," "policy process," "policy content," and "policy outcomes." Accordingly, it seems appropriate in this introductory chapter to suggest some meanings for these key concepts. I have no illusion that, once they have read these paragraphs, all political scientists or even all the authors of this book will employ them just as I do. But it may be helpful to make explicit at least one set of concepts, if only as an instrument for identifying the nature and degree of variation in the concepts used by others.

1. PUBLIC POLICY

Most of us sometimes use the term "policy" to refer to whatever is being done by some actor in a broad area of activity: "American foreign policy," "General Motors' styling policy," "California's educational policy." However, for purposes of designing, conducting, and reporting research it is probably better to give the term somewhat more limited referents: "American policy toward Vietnam," "Milwaukee's policy toward open housing," "the Selective Service System's policy toward draft deferments for college students."

In this more limited sense, it seems to me that what we generally mean by a "public policy" has the following main components:[9]

---

[9] This conceptualization is a modest elaboration of what seems to me implicit in such prominent definitions as those by Harold Lasswell and Abraham Kaplan: "*policy* is a projected program of goal values and practices" (*Power and Society* [New Haven: Yale University Press, 1950], p. 71); Wilfrid Harrison: "the most common social and political usage of the term *policy* refers to a course of action or intended course of action conceived as deliberately adopted, after a review of possible alternatives, and pursued, or intended to be pursued" (in *A Dictionary of the Social Sciences*, ed. Julius Gould and William L. Kolb [New York: Free Press of Glencoe, 1964], p. 509); and James Robinson: "'policy' refers to goals (objectives, ends) of any social system, the means chosen to effectuate those goals, and the consequences of the means, i.e., the actual distribution of values"

A particular object or set of objects—some designated part of the environment (an aspect of the society or physical world) which is intended to be affected.

A desired course of events—a particular sequence of behavior desired in the particular object or set of objects.

A selected line of action—a particular set of actions chosen to bring about the desired course of events; in other words, not merely whatever the society happens to be doing toward the set of objects at the moment, but a deliberate selection of one line of action from among several possible lines.

A declaration of intent—whether broadcast publicly to all who will listen or communicated secretly to a special few, some statement by the policy-makers as to what they intend to do, how, and why.

An implementation of intent—the actions actually undertaken vis-à-vis the particular set of objects in pursuance of the choices and declaration.

These, in my view, are elements of any kind of policy toward anything by any social actor. A *public* policy is one special case, albeit of central importance for political scientists. Its special character consists in the fact that it is adopted and implemented by what David Easton calls "the authorities" in a political system: those persons who, in his words, "engage in the daily affairs of a political system," are "recognized by most members of the system as having the responsibility for these matters," and whose actions are "accepted as binding most of the time by most of the members so long as they act within the limits of their roles"—that is, "elders, paramount chiefs, executives, legislators, judges, administrators, councilors, monarchs, and the like."[10]

2. POLICY CONTENT

Vernon Van Dyke correctly points out in the following chapter that there is no perfect Aristotelian dichotomy between a policy's "content" and the "process" by which it is adopted and implemented; for one can study "process" only by studying conflict over the "content" of an actual policy or proposed policy.[11] Moreover, Lewis Froman and others have suggested that the United States (and, by implication, every "developed" nation) has no single process that cranks out all policies, but several different processes, each of which operates in a particular policy-content arena.[12]

Without denying the validity of such comments, it is still possible (and,

---

(*Congress and Foreign Policy-Making* [Homewood, Ill.: Dorsey Press, 1962], p. 3). Robinson's last phrase I will refer to as a "policy outcome"; see below. For James Rosenau's concept of an "undertaking," which he prefers to "policy," see pp. 221–26. For Vernon Van Dyke's conceptualizations, see pp. 23–25, 27–29.

[10] David Easton, *A Systems Analysis of Political Life* (New York: John Wiley & Sons, 1965), p. 212.

[11] See pp. 25–27.

[12] See Chapter 3 below.

for scholarly purposes, desirable) to focus on certain aspects of reality's seamless whole at any given time—to abstract "process" from "content," say, and look mainly at one with only minimal attention to the other. Indeed, as I shall try to show later, many political scientists have done just that in their post-1945 concentration on "process" over "content." The operating distinctions between these two aspects of public policies implicit in our literature seem to me to be as follows:

Policy content, in terms of our prior discussion of "public policy," includes the particular object or set of objects the policy is intended to affect, the particular course of events desired, the particular line of action chosen, the particular declaration made, and the particular actions taken—in all cases as actually chosen from among the alternative objects, courses of events, lines of action, declarations, and actions that might have been chosen. This conception of "policy content" seems to me very similar to what David Easton calls a political "output": "a stream of activities flowing from the authorities in a system" which "set the goals toward which the energies and resources of the system may be directed."[13]

3. POLICY PROCESS

This concept includes the actions and interactions that produce the authorities' ultimate choice of a particular policy content over its rivals. It is very similar to the concept of "decision-making" developed most notably by Harold Lasswell and by Richard Snyder and his associates, which is said to include such elements as *intelligence* (gathering information, assessing relative desirability of conflicting values, setting goals), *recommending* (proposing a particular ordering of values and a course of action designed to promote the goals as arranged), *prescribing* (official promulgation of the chosen course of action), *invocation* (provisionally using a prescription to characterize a set of circumstances in which a person or group is thought to act contrary to policy, e.g., by an administrative official), *application* (employing the prescription with finality against transgressors, e.g., by a court), *appraisal* (evaluating the prescription's effectiveness and social costs), and *termination* (abandonment or alteration of the original prescription).[14]

4. POLICY OUTCOME

"Outcome" is a term suggested by Easton to distinguish the consequences of a political output (roughly equivalent, remember, to my conception of "policy") from the output itself. Thus a policy outcome includes the way or ways in which the course of events is in fact affected by the authorities'

---

[13] Easton, *Systems Analysis*, pp. 348–50.

[14] See especially Harold D. Lasswell, *The Decision Process* (College Park: University of Maryland Press, 1956), and Richard C. Snyder, H. W. Bruck, and Burton Sapin, eds., *Foreign Policy Decision-Making* (New York: Free Press of Glencoe, 1962), pp. 1–185.

FIGURE 1
THE "POLICY PROCESS"

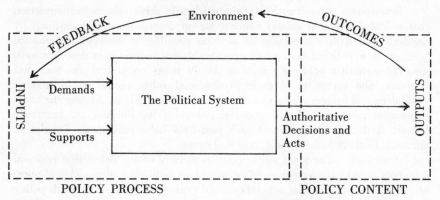

Adapted from David Easton, *A Systems Analysis of Political Life* (New York: John Wiley & Sons, 1965) diagram 2, p. 32.

actions in implementing the policy they have chosen. The consequences may be wholly or partially unintended by the authorities, and assessments of them play an important part in the "appraisal" stage of the policy process. But, as Easton argues convincingly, a useful increment of conceptual clarity results from distinguishing political outputs (public policies) from political outcomes.[15]

To summarize and further clarify the nature and interrelations of public policy, policy process, policy content, and policy outcome, I offer in Figure 1 an adaptation of Easton's simplified model of a political system.

The foregoing concepts and distinctions provide the basis for the following discussion of what political scientists have focused on in the past and should emphasize in the future.

III. "PROCESS" AND "CONTENT" AS FOCI FOR POLITICAL SCIENCE

1. FROM THE BEGINNING

The question of how much political scientists should focus on the study of policy processes or policy contents is not new. The useful short history of the discipline by Albert Somit and Joseph Tanenhaus shows that ever since its beginnings in the late nineteenth century American political science has encompassed three distinct and continuing strains, two of which took opposing stands on the desirability of studying policy contents. At various periods

---

[15] Easton, *Systems Analysis*, pp. 351–52.

one strain has predominated over the other, but neither has yet driven its rival beyond the limits of disciplinary respectability.

Scientism. Somit and Tanenhaus identify this strain as the conviction that political scientists should concentrate on describing and explaining, by methods and with a precision as near as possible to those of the natural sciences, how political systems *do* operate. Most who have held this view have also believed that political scientists should focus on policy processes, not contents, and certainly, in their professional roles, should avoid making evaluative and prescriptive statements about public policies. Among the more prominent advocates of this position are John W. Burgess, A. Lawrence Lowell, Arthur F. Bentley, and such post-1945 behavioralists as Gabriel A. Almond, Herbert Simon, and David B. Truman.[16]

Activism. The rival strain consists mainly of the belief that political scientists should concern themselves with how political systems *should* operate, and the corollary that scholars should evaluate and prescribe both policy processes *and* contents. Thus political scientists of this persuasion—e.g., Herbert Adams, Simeon Baldwin, John Fairlie, and such post-1945 scholars as Hans Morgenthau, Walter Berns, and James MacGregor Burns—were active and influential in movements for the direct primary, the council-manager form of municipal government, the short ballot, centralized budgeting, more disciplined and cohesive parties, and so on. Many were also active in the public debate of substantive policy issues: for example, in contrast to the *American Political Science Review's* silence on the merits of the Vietnam war in the 1960's, the *Political Science Quarterly* in the late 1890's published a number of papers severely critical of American policy before, during, and after the Spanish-American War, and others attacking the free-silver doctrine.[17]

A third strain of "education for citizenship" has also persisted: the belief that political science's main task is to develop "better minds for better politics" by training students for the responsibilities of democratic citizenship and by inspiring them to become active in public affairs. But this position, most prominently advanced by Thomas H. Reed, is only indirectly relevant to the process-versus-content dispute.[18]

2. IN THE BEHAVIORAL ERA

Few would dispute the characterization of political science since 1945 as increasingly dominated by "the behavioral persuasion"—partly in the growing number and prestige of its adherents, but even more in the fact that most post-1945 intradisciplinary controversies about where political science can and should go have been either expositions of or attacks on behavioralism.[19]

By no means have all behaviorally-oriented scholars ignored policy

---

[16] Albert Somit and Joseph Tanenhaus, *The Development of American Political Science: From Burgess to Behavioralism* (Boston: Allyn & Bacon, Inc., 1967), pp. 27–29.

[17] *Ibid.*, pp. 43–44.

[18] *Ibid.*, pp. 195–96.

[19] For a short but balanced summary of this dispute, see *ibid.*, pp. 183–94.

contents. As Robert Salisbury points out,[20] such works on domestic policies as Robert Dahl and C. E. Lindblom's *Politics, Economics and Welfare*, Vernon Van Dyke's *Pride and Power: The Rationale of the Space Program*, Gilbert Steiner's *Social Insecurity*, and Alexander Heard's *The Costs of Democracy* have not only dealt with policy contents, but evaluated present policies and offered suggestions for changing them. James Rosenau reminds us that many specialists on foreign policy have been not only willing, but eager (too eager, in his view) to advise the nation on the conduct of its foreign affairs.[21] And Lucian Pye makes clear that most scholars of politics in developing nations, many of whom are surely regarded as leading members of political science's behavioralist wing, have felt impelled by the urgency and difficulty of those nations' problems to evaluate and prescribe policies for them despite the absence of well-developed scientific theory as a basis for doing so.[22]

Nevertheless, I think it fair to say that the *dominant* mood of behavioral political science has been highly "scientistic." Somit and Tanenhaus, correctly in my view, give as one of the eight beliefs characteristic of the behavioral persuasion the conviction that:

> Political science should abjure, in favor of "pure" research, both applied research aimed at providing solutions to specific, immediate social problems and meliatory programmatic ventures. These efforts, as the behavioralist sees it, produce little valid scientific knowledge and represent, instead, an essentially unproductive diversion of energy, resources, and attention.[23]

Accordingly, most behavioralists have, in David Easton's words, viewed policy outputs

> as a terminal point in the intricate processes through which demands and support are converted into decisions and actions. To use the simple analogy of a manufacturing system . . . the outputs were viewed as the products forthcoming from the conversion operations performed on the mixture of items going into the system.[24]

There is considerable evidence for these judgments in what political scientists in recent years have and have not done in their professional journals and organizations. As to the first, Somit and Tanenhaus point out that

> if we take the really "big" issues of the past twenty years—foreign policy, nuclear policy, civil rights (including McCarthyism), the relationship of government to the economy—there is little in the pages of the [*American Political Science*] *Review* which suggests

---

[20] See Chapter 7 below.
[21] See Chapter 9 below.
[22] See Chapter 10 below.
[23] Somit and Tanenhaus, *Development*, p. 178.
[24] Easton, *Systems Analysis*, p. 344.

that American political scientists have had much to say about the direction which national policy should take.[25]

Substantially the same can be said of the other professional journals and more recent "big" issues, including the Vietnam war, black power, the Arab-Israeli conflict, and so on. Evidently, then, if political scientists have pressed their views on policy questions, they have not done so in the professional journals —or, it should be added, in the programs of their national and regional association meetings.

Moreover, the constitution of the American Political Science Association, adopted in its present form in 1953, stipulates:

> The Association as such is non-partisan. It will not support political parties or candidates. It will not commit its members on questions of public policy nor take positions not immediately concerned with its direct purpose [to encourage the study of political science].[26]

No doubt there are many reasons for the post-1945 behavioral emphasis on process over content. Let me mention two of the more obvious. First, many behavioral political scientists evidently feel that focusing on content is likely to lead to evaluations of present policies and exhortations for new ones; and evaluations and exhortations, they feel, not only have no place in scientific enterprise, but are likely to divert scholarly attention and energy away from true scholarship.[27] Second, many behavioral political scientists are concerned that the discipline may spread itself too thin by trying to do too much.[28] They feel that tackling policy content is bound to be too much; for, done properly, it would require the political scientist to become a subject-matter expert in his content specialty—a hydrologist to study water resources policy, an economist to study tax policy, an astronautical engineer to study space policy, and so on. Frederick Watkins summarizes this point of view thus:

> The important thing . . . is the necessary distinction between the *process* of decision-making and the *content* of the decisions made. If economics were the science of wealth-production, all knowledge would be its proper concern. If political science were the science of determining public policies, it would need to be at least as comprehensive. But political science, like economics, has a less ambitious purpose. It is concerned not with the potentially infinite

---

[25] Somit and Tanenhaus, *Development*, p. 200.

[26] Article II, Section 2.

[27] *Cf.* Robert A. Dahl, "The Behavioral Approach in Political Science: Epitaph for a Monument to a Successful Protest," *American Political Science Review*, 55 (December 1961) : 763–72, at 770–71; and Heinz Eulau, *The Behavioral Persuasion in Politics* (New York: Random House, 1963), pp. 135–37.

[28] *Cf.* Charles S. Hyneman, *The Study of Politics* (Urbana: University of Illinois Press, 1959), chap. 7, "Have We Tackled Too Much?"

content of all public decisions, but with the process by which those decisions are reached.[29]

3. PRESENT DISCONTENTS

In the past few years there have appeared signs of increasing discontent among political scientists of all persuasions with the discipline's post-1945 focus on process. A growing number of voices is heard urging more attention to policy contents.[30] But they are not all saying the same things. They disagree about *why* (that is, to what ends) political scientists should study policy contents, *how* they should be studied, and *what proportion* of the discipline's scarce resources of talent, time, energy, and research funds should be spent on such studies.

These, of course, are the critical questions for political scientists to ponder in deciding what, if any, scientific and professional effort they should give to the study of policy contents. Accordingly, I shall conclude this introductory chapter by summarizing and commenting on the principal answers now being given.

IV. WHY STUDY POLICY CONTENTS?

In the past few years I have read about, listened to, and participated in a number of discussions among political scientists about whether, how, and why our discipline should give more attention to policy contents. It seems to me important to recognize that the arguments of the growing number who advocate a change stem mainly from one or another of three quite distinct positions.

1. FOR SCIENTIFIC REASONS

A number of political scientists argue for more study of policy contents mainly or entirely on scientific grounds: they believe that such studies will add significantly to the breadth, significance, and reliability of the discipline's special body of knowledge. They expect one or both of the following contributions.

Improved Understanding of Policy Processes. All process studies —except those of such formal-mathematical theorists as Kenneth Arrow, Duncan Black, Anthony Downs, and William Riker—have investigated policy pro-

---

[29] In *A Design for Political Science: Scope, Objectives, and Methods,* ed. James C. Charlesworth (Philadelphia: American Academy of Political and Social Science, 1966), p. 31; emphasis in the original.

[30] One of the most forceful is that of Michael D. Reagan in "Policy Issues: The Interaction of Substance and Process," a paper presented at the Annual Meeting of the American Political Science Association, Chicago, 1967.

cesses mainly by observing the making of actual policies: the Employment Act of 1946, Medicare, foreign aid, racial desegregation of public schools, and the like. Typically, the policy content or "governmental output" has been the dependent variable, and scholars have sought to explain variations in policy outputs by such independent variables as the distribution of power among pressure groups and governmental agencies, the tactical techniques and skills of political actors, and so on. So they have identified the principal competing interests, groups, and actors; analyzed their objectives, techniques, support, opposition, and interactions; estimated their impact on the authorities; and thus accumulated materials for generalizations about factors determining the distribution of power in whatever part of the political system concerned them.

Few challenge this familiar approach to policy processes, and such studies are likely to continue in abundance and improve in technique. But some scholars, notably Theodore Lowi and Lewis Froman, have recently argued that we can greatly enrich our understanding of policy processes by reversing the orthodox explanatory relationships. They propose that we consider policy content as the *in*dependent variable and observe the differential impact of different contents on policy-making processes. As Lowi puts it, "There are three major categories of public policies . . . : distribution, regulation, and redistribution. . . . Each arena tends to develop its own characteristic political structure, political process, elites, and group relations."[31]

Lowi's particular categories may or may not be generally accepted, but his proposal that we approach policy processes through the different content areas with which they deal seems likely to be taken up by a number of scholars. But the objective of such studies, be it noted, is still to understand the nature of policy *processes*, and policy contents are considered interesting only insofar as they improve our understanding of the processes associated with them. Accordingly, the Lowi view is a change in technique, not in focus; and as such it represents no radical departure from what process-oriented political scientists have been doing.

Improved Understanding of Policy Outcomes. Some scholars have argued that we should use policy contents as independent variables to learn more about policy outcomes; that is, the impact of public policies on the political system's environment and on the system itself. Some—Aaron Wildavsky and Vincent Ostrom are notable examples[32]—propose that political scientists develop the vague notion of "impact" into some political equivalent of the economists' cost-benefit calculus. Ideally, they say, we should be able to calculate what a particular policy "costs," not only in dollars, but also in terms of other policies forgone or truncated, increases in internal social hostility and instability, increases in demands on and decreases in supports for

---

[31] Theodore J. Lowi, "American Business, Public Policy, Case-Studies, and Political Theory," *World Politics*, 16 (July 1964) : 677–715, at 689–90. See also Froman's discussion in Chapter 3 below.

[32] See Chapters 4 and 6 below.

the system, narrowing the range of future policy options, and so on. This is a broader notion than that of "political feasibility" analyzed by Ralph Huitt,[33] although the latter would certainly be a major element in it. After calculating the political "costs," we should calculate the policy's "benefits" in dollars, decreases in social hostility and instability, increases in supports, opening up new possibilities for future action, and so on. After all, some argue, policy processes and policy outputs are significant objects for study only as they influence the conditions of people's lives; and we need to know much more than we now know about the relation of process to outputs *and* of outputs to outcomes.

Unquestionably there are many great and unsolved problems in conceptualizing, operationalizing, and quantifying such a calculus of political costs and benefits. But some scholars believe that only if we solve these problems and construct such a calculus can political scientists make any serious contribution to the understanding—let alone a professional contribution to the evaluation—of policy contents. So, they conclude, rather than wasting our time on *a priori* disputations about whether it is possible, we should get on with the job of trying to work it out.

2. FOR PROFESSIONAL REASONS

Earlier in this chapter I borrowed Don K. Price's distinction between the scientific estate, which seeks only to discover knowledge, and the professional estate, which seeks to apply scientific knowledge to the solution of practical problems. I also noted that political science has not yet developed a distinct science and profession, and that many political scientists move freely back and forth between the two estates. It is therefore not surprising that some who advocate greater attention to policy contents give professional reasons as well as, or instead of, scientific reasons. They hope for major improvements in political scientists' technical skills for performing one or both of the following professional tasks.

Evaluating Present and Past Policies. The logical next step beyond political cost-benefit calculations is to strike a balance—to determine whether a policy's political benefits were or are "worth" its political "price." Nearly every scholar who discusses this possibility is acutely aware of how difficult it would be, even if we had an accurate and reliable way of assessing costs and benefits. The greatest difficulty is the fact that it would require the political scientist to make professional value judgments: whether an increased supply of water and electric power to the people of the Southwest is worth damaging the natural beauties of the Grand Canyon, for example, or whether increasing the number of artificial-kidney machines to keep some adults alive is worth decreasing public health measures to reduce infant mortality.

This, of course, plunges us into perhaps the most bitterly disputed issue of the controversy between behavioralists and antibehavioralists: what *profes-*

---

[33] See Chapter 11 below.

sional skills and obligations have political scientists to make and advocate value judgments? I have no illusion that I can settle that controversy, but I do want to suggest that empirical political scientists can make a substantial contribution to the study of values without going beyond their professional competence.

I see no general agreement as to whether political philosophers or historians of political philosophy have special skills beyond those of ordinary men to determine which values are good, better, and best. But I do see general agreement that empirical political scientists have *no* special skills for such determinations—that their skills relate solely to the framing and testing of hypotheses about the actual interrelations of observable phenomena. Hence they are professionally equipped to deal only with if-then statements: if A is introduced into situation X, then situation X will change in manner Y.

Quite true. But many, maybe most, value statements are instrumental rather than ultimate. That is, A is good, not in itself (ultimate), but because it maximizes X (instrumental). And any statement about the instrumental value of something has a major empirical component appropriate for the hypothesis-testing techniques of the empirical political scientist. As Robert Dahl puts the point:

> . . . the impatience of the empirical political scientist with the political philosopher who insists upon the importance of "values" arises in part from a feeling that the political philosopher who engages in political evaluation rarely completes all his homework. The topic of "consensus" as a condition for democracy is a case in point; when the political philosopher deals with this question, it seems to me that he typically makes a number of assumptions and assertions of an empirical sort without systematic attention to existing empirical data, or the possibility of gaining better empirical data.[34]

In addition to testing the empirical validity of instrumental value propositions, the empirical political scientist may, like the economist, simply postulate an overriding criterion equivalent to "productivity" or "economizing" and then evaluate policies according to whether they increase or decrease the political equivalent of the gross national product. Of course, such scholars would have to agree on what the political equivalent should be—stability, survival, social justice, popular participation, or whatever; and I offer no odds on the likelihood of any such agreement.

A third possibility has been suggested by Richard Snyder and James Robinson in their stimulating portfolio of ideas for future research: to develop and improve criteria for evaluating policy processes and contents. They suggest, among other things, that political scientists do case studies of policies generally agreed to be "good" (e.g., the Marshall Plan) and also of policies generally regarded as "bad" (e.g., the Bay of Pigs invasion). These

---

[34] Dahl, "Behavioral Approach," p. 771.

case studies should seek to discover what criteria were and are applied to these policies by decision-makers, nongovernmental policy elites, scholars, and so on, to arrive at these judgments. They also suggest sample-survey studies of the attitudes of governmental decision-makers and nongovernmental elites toward the values, notions about ends-means relations, and other criteria used in making and evaluating policy in general.[35] And I would add the suggestion that we press on with our survey studies of the mass public's value hierarchies so that we may gain a firmer basis for determining to what degrees and in what respects policies and policy proposals accord with the values of "the people."

In short, we can do a good deal more empirical study of value questions than we have yet done. The kinds of studies suggested here all involve the framing and testing of hypotheses about the interrelations of variables in the real world. Hence they are entirely appropriate for the methods and standards of empirical political science. And they do provide at least one way in which political scientists can make a truly professional contribution to the study of values and valuing beyond pushing their own personal preferences.[36]

Advising Policy-Makers. In some respects dispute over whether political scientists should advise policy-makers seems like a kind of scholasticism. The fact is that a number of political scientists *do* advise policy-makers and are seldom publicly charged with unprofessional conduct for doing so. Some serve as members of presidential commissions and task forces; some work on the staffs of commissions and congressional committees; some serve as consultants to various executive agencies; some testify before congressional committees; and so on.

We know all this in a general sort of way; but, surprisingly, we have no systematic or complete information on such questions as: How many political scientists are advising policy-makers today? In what capacities? In what subject-matter areas? What kinds of advice are they asked for? What do they give? What, if any, expertise do policy-makers think they have? What cognitive differences disturb their communications with policy-makers? What impact do they have on policy-making? Answers to these questions will not, of course, answer the question of whether and how political scientists *should* advise policy-makers; but they should certainly provide some highly useful materials for answering it.[37]

In my opinion, political scientists will—and should—be called upon to advise policy-makers to the degree that they are perceived to have special professional knowledge and skills. If all we can offer is common sense or a passion for social justice, then we have no claim to and will not receive any special attention not paid to any other citizen enjoying these admirable but

[35] Richard C. Snyder and James A. Robinson, *National and International Decision-Making* (New York: Institute for International Order, 1961), p. 29.

[36] For a careful description and analysis of various scientific techniques for evaluating governmental public service and social action programs, see Edward A. Suchman, *Evaluative Research* (New York: Russell Sage Foundation, 1967).

[37] *Cf.* similar suggestions in *ibid.*, pp. 102, 171–72.

widely diffused assets. And we can hardly hope to beat the subject-matter experts at their own games by becoming especially skilled hydrologists or welfare economists or astronautical engineers or whatever.

On the other hand, political science may develop, for example, a reliable and valid system for calculating political costs and benefits; an agreed and operationalized optimizing criterion of "gross political product"; and/or an extension of ends-means analysis to specify the interrelations and priorities of instrumental values. If it does, political scientists' professional knowledge and skills will become visibly useful in the identification, comparison, and evaluation of competing policy proposals; and, inevitably, policy-makers will call on us extensively for advice and quite possibly even pay it serious attention.[38]

3. FOR POLITICAL REASONS

A third group of political scientists urges the profession to write and talk more about the content of public policies, not primarily or at all for scientific or professional reasons, but for political purposes: to do all we can to see that the nation adopts the right policies to achieve the right goals. One strain has long argued that behavioralism, by its insistence on an "arid value-free stance" and its "obsession with techniques over substance," has rendered political science mute and impotent in the face of the great political and moral crises of our time.[39] It is not clear, however, what form of political activity these scholars advocate beyond publishing hortatory articles in journals of opinion.

Another strain, closely related to the "New Left" in American politics, is a good deal clearer about the line of political action political scientists should take. They do not want political scientists to *advise* policy-makers in any of the ways outlined above. They believe that much if not all of American society and the policy-making system it supports are hopelessly corrupt. Hence, if a political scientist lets himself be co-opted to work within the system, he can only be corrupted by it. The proper moral position for a political scientist, they feel, is outside the system, criticizing it, pressing for radical changes in it. Accordingly, they want political scientists to *make* policy, not by expert advice to the "power structure," but by direct political action to force the "power elite" to mend its ways, and to overthrow it if it does not.[40]

---

[38] For a similar conclusion presented nearly a quarter century ago, see Pendleton Herring, "Political Science in the Next Decade," *American Political Science Review*, 39 (August 1945) : 757–66.

[39] See in particular Herbert J. Storing, ed., *Essays on the Scientific Study of Politics* (New York: Holt, Rinehart, & Winston, 1962) ; the attack on the Storing volume by John H. Schaar and Sheldon S. Wolin in *American Political Science Review*, 57 (March 1963) : 125–50; and rejoinders by Storing and others in *ibid.*, 151–60.

[40] This appears to be one of the leading points of view, though not the only one, animating the Caucus for a New Political Science, formed in Chicago in 1967 under the chairmanship of H. Mark Roelofs. Its Statement of Objectives proclaims: "Whereas the American Political Science Association, at its conventions and in its journal, has consistently failed to study, in a radically critical spirit, either the great crises of the day

V. PRIORITIES IN POLITICAL SCIENCE

If one accepts the distinction, made earlier,[41] among the scientific, professional, and extraprofessional obligations of political scientists, then clearly the kind of political activism just described is not legitimate for political scientists *acting as political scientists*, though it may be entirely legitimate for them acting as citizens. No doubt colleagues of the activist persuasion will deny the validity of any such distinctions and judgments, and I am confident—though not happy—that little said in this or any other chapter of this book will make much sense to them.

But most political scientists, I believe, do accept these distinctions and try to conduct themselves accordingly. They are likely to agree with me that, while these political reasons for talking and writing about policy contents go beyond proper scholarly bounds, the scientific and professional reasons presented earlier do not. Accordingly, they are likely to ask whether the anticipated gains advanced as reasons for studying policy contents are likely to be forthcoming. They will want to know whether such studies will, in fact, improve our understanding of policy processes and policy outcomes, and/or enable us to evaluate past and present policies more objectively, and/or advise policy-makers, with high technical skill and reliability, about the effectiveness of means and the interrelations of goals. Perhaps many will feel, as do the authors of this book, that the study of policy contents is worth a good hard try before we make any final judgments about its utility.

Such a conclusion does not, however, solve all our problems. Like any other human endeavor, political science has limited resources of personnel, time, energy, research and teaching support, and, in shortest supply of all, talent. So each of us as an individual and all of us as a discipline have to face the question of priorities: what *proportion* of our resources should we spend on research and teaching focused on the contents of public policies and on advising policy-makers?

In my opinion that question is best decided according to the order of priorities so well stated by Charles Hyneman:

> . . . scholarship—which includes study, publication, and teaching
> —is the primary task of the political scientist. It is primary because
> it contributes more to the other activities of political scientists than
> those other activities contribute to scholarship. Participation in

or the inherent weaknesses of the American political system, be it resolved that this caucus promote a new concern in the Association for our great social crises and a new and broader opportunity for us all to fulfill, as scholars, our obligations to society and to science" (quoted in a letter dated October 3, 1967, from Professor Roelofs to the executive director of the American Political Science Association). For a brief account of the origins, membership, and purposes of the caucus, see Robert Samuelson's story in *Science*, 157 (September 22, 1967): 1414–17.

[41] See pp. 4–5.

public affairs informs the student and may provide him with understanding which redirects his scholarly effort. But scholarly study can be carried on effectively by political scientists who remain aloof from the public forum. The reverse is not true, however; the political scientist cannot take expertise as a political scientist to the public forum except as he carries with him the fruits of scholarship. He may personally refuse to engage in studious inquiry, even ignore the literature which others have produced, and participate effectively in public affairs as a citizen. But in this case his contributions are comparable to those of other citizens. In this case he does not bring to public policy and governmental activity the special gifts of a learned discipline.[42]

Of course, not all political scientists are equally skilled at designing, conducting, and reporting the kind of research most likely to improve our knowledge, nor are they equally skilled at evaluating, criticizing, or synthesizing the findings of others. But recognizing the primacy of scholarship over all our other professional activities gives us a sound basis for evaluating those other activities. In Hyneman's words:

> If other preoccupations are found to support and enrich the scholarly undertaking, they pass a high test of worthiness. If they are found only to be special outlets for the knowledge accumulated by the profession, neither contributing to nor setting obstacles to further study, one may view such activities with approval up to the point where indulgence in them is thought excessive because it too greatly diverts efforts from the scholarly enterprise. But if the other preoccupations, or any part of them, are thought injurious to scholarship, adversely affecting the amount and quality of serious study, for instance, it may be concluded that the social gains derived from these other preoccupations notably fail to balance the losses sustained from the impairment of scholarship.[43]

In sum, our professional skills and utility depend upon the scientific quality of our special body of knowledge. Hence, our primary obligation as

---

[42] Hyneman, *Study of Politics*, pp. 4–5. *Cf.* Pendleton Herring's plea fifteen years earlier that "students of government [give] due attention [to] the systematic study of governance. *This is the unique duty of the political scientist as such*" ("Political Science in the Next Decade," p. 765; emphasis added). See also Bertrand de Jouvenel's argument that one cannot evaluate the desirability of proposals for institutional change "unless one has acquired as much basic knowledge as possible about the elementary behaviors which are to be dovetailed in the new combination. *Thus we always come back to factual inquiry into the elements of political behavior*" ("On the Nature of Political Science," *American Political Science Review*, 55 [December 1961]: 773–79, at p. 779; emphasis added).

[43] Hyneman, *Study of Politics*, p. 5. Not all his colleagues agree. James C. Charlesworth, for example, argues that while "history, quantification, theory, observation, and documentation should be continued," they should be subordinated "to the main objective of prescribing governmental goals and designing governmental programs"; and he promises that "if this posture were adopted . . . our organization would lose its tax-exempt status, but we would all be more responsible, more masculine, and more adult. The country would be better off" (in *Design for Political Science*, p. 250).

scholars and teachers is to improve that knowledge. If frequent trips to Washington or the statehouse or city hall keep most of our best and most creative minds from that nuclear task, both political science and the students and policy-makers who hope to profit from it will be much the poorer.

My colleagues and I hope that this book will stimulate discussion of—and even shed some light on—the many difficult questions raised in this chapter and those to come. Of one thing we are certain: these questions are central to any serious discussion of what political scientists ought to be doing.

2

Process and Policy as Focal Concepts in Political Research

VERNON VAN DYKE

Process and *policy* have long figured in the dialogue about the nature of political science and the purposes of political scientists. Arthur F. Bentley, unhappy with the state of the discipline, urged concern with the *process* of government, and many others since he wrote have given a prominent place to process in their professional vocabulary. Harold Lasswell includes political science among the *policy* sciences, and he too is joined by many others whose interests are with matters of policy. At the same time, few have given specific attention to the meanings of these concepts and the purposes and implications of focusing upon them. Bentley emphasized the idea of the group much more than the idea of process, and the same is true of David Truman in *The Governmental Process*.[1] And the book on *The Policy Sciences* edited by Lerner and Lasswell is more about the scope and methods of research than about the nature and rationale of a policy orientation. This suggests the objects to be pursued here: clearer meanings of the concepts and an assessment of their usefulness and their limitations as focal concepts in political research.

I. PROCESS

WHAT A FOCUS ON PROCESS MEANS

The term "process" in political science becomes meaningful when we recall that we speak also of industrial processes. In this context, as Wilfrid

---

[1] *Cf.* Norman Jacobson, "Causality and Time in Political Process: A Speculation," *American Political Science Review*, 58 (March 1964) : 19.

Harrison indicates, the word "seems to refer to a system for turning out a product, a special way of inducing changes that works along fixed and predetermined lines and is repeatable."[2] Those who gave the term its prominence as a focal concept in political science accepted the connotation. They sought emphasis on what David Easton calls "situational" data, i.e., "those determinants which shape activity in spite of the kinds of personalities and motivations in the participants"; in other words, "the conditions which do not depend upon the feelings, attitudes, or motivations of an acting individual, but rather upon the form that the activity or presence of other persons or things, physical and non-human organic, take."[3] Later, according to Easton, when "behavioral" data were added to "situational" data, the pronounced tendency was to equate the behavioral with the psychological, that is, to stress the nonrational and the irrational, and to stress types of personality characteristics that would presumably condition responses to political problems.[4]

By and large, the connotation still holds. As we shall see later, political scientists who focus on process commonly also give attention to policies relating to the process, that is, relating to the characteristics and internal operations of government. Except for this, however, they seem to think of process quite apart from any specific policy or issue. They think of patterns of activity, patterns of behavior, which manifest themselves repeatedly in connection with different kinds of policies and issues. They tend to think in terms of groups whose interactions shape the course of events in an institutional setting; they stress the fact that groups have interests, but their concern is with generalizations about groups, which necessarily means that they can give little attention to the policies or the policy choices that the groups favor or oppose. When they think of the individual who participates in the process, they are likely to treat him as a type or as a statistic or as a ghostlike entity that plays a role rather than as a flesh-and-blood human being who is purposive and who reasons and argues in supporting or opposing a specific line of action.

The study of politics was once conceived differently. E. A. Shils points out in a very perceptive article that "the classic figures of social thought . . . were all involved in the consideration of the fundamental problems of policy. . . . The clarification of the standards for the judgment and guidance of public policy was always close to the centre of their attention."[5] According to Shils, a change occurred in the nineteenth century.

Even the study of politics adulterated its preoccupation with policy by concrete recipes of administration and the aproblematic description of governmental processes. . . . A peculiarly apolitical political

---

[2] Wilfrid Harrison, "Political Processes," *Political Studies*, 6 (October 1958) : 248.
[3] David Easton, *The Political System: An Inquiry into the State of Political Science* (New York: Alfred A. Knopf, Inc., 1953), pp. 194, 195; and *cf.* pp. 180, 191.
[4] *Ibid.*, pp. 201–18.
[5] E. A. Shils, "Social Science and Social Policy," *Philosophy of Science*, 16 (July 1949) : 219.

science grew up. Without a clear perception of the values to which it could be relevant, political science became a morally directionless and scientifically sterile descriptive discipline.[6]

Examples of the kind of writing to which a stress on process leads are numerous. J. Lieper Freeman's *The Political Process* is among them.[7] The book is suggestive of a cutaway model of an engine, mounted for exhibit. To use terms more common to political research, the book gives an abstract model of a system. In the background is a recognition of the fact that living human beings are active in the system, pursuing goals and employing strategies, but still the focus is on the features of the system and the interrelationships of its parts and not at all on the desires or reasoning of the participants or on the ends served. Freeman uses the Bureau of Indian Affairs and the problem of policy toward the Indians to illustrate the process, but one learns astoundingly little about substantive aspects of this problem. There is no attempt to inform the reader of different perceptions of it, different lines of reasoning concerning it, different prescriptions for its solution, and different consequences that are likely to follow different choices. The focus is on the general and enduring features of the process, not on the transient factors relating to mortal persons and their thoughts about a policy problem.

Is the Entire Process Covered?

Those who stress process rarely take up the question whether they are interested in all of its aspects and manifestations or only in some of them. The references usually are to both making and implementing policy, which suggests concern for the whole process of formulating and administering it. In principle, then, the range of concern is very extensive, for the governmental process includes a vast array of activities. When the National Institutes of Health make a grant to a medical school for research on cancer, they are at least implementing a governmental policy, if not also making it. When the Food and Drug Administration prevents the marketing of a drug or imposes requirements concerning the information that a label must give, its activities are parts of the policy process. When the Bureau of Internal Revenue checks income-tax returns or hails a man into court for failure to file a return, it is making or implementing policy. When a speeder is arrested or a jury impaneled, when land is acquired for a new highway, when the Government Printing Office sells a document, when the Bureau of Labor Statistics tells us about changes in the cost of living, when the Department of Defense lets a contract to Lockheed or issues a uniform to a new recruit, policy is being made or implemented. It is part of the governmental process that civil servants are recruited and the terms of their employment fixed. And it is part of the governmental process when the Treasury floats a short-term loan and

---

[6] *Ibid.*, pp. 219, 220.

[7] J. Lieper Freeman, *The Political Process: Executive Bureau–Legislative Committee Relations*, rev. ed. (New York: Random House, 1965).

when the Federal Reserve Board increases the discount rate. Obviously, however, few political scientists make their concern for process extend to such
matters as these. References to the *governmental* process and to the *policy*
process are thus likely to suggest a much greater range of concern than political scientists actually display, and thus raise a question about clarity of the
criteria of inclusion and exclusion. If the reference is to the *political* process,
then its appropriateness depends on the definition assigned to the term
"political."

Don K. Price in *The Scientific Estate* makes distinctions that are useful
here. He speaks of "the four broad functions in government and public affairs
—the scientific, the professional, the administrative, and the political." These
four, he says,

> are by no means sharply distinguished from one another even in
> theory, but fall along a gradation or spectrum within our political
> system. At one end of the spectrum, pure science is concerned with
> knowledge and truth; at the other end, pure politics is concerned
> with power and action.[8]

Price points out that "the process of responsible policy making is . . . a
process of interaction among scientists, professional leaders, administrators,
and politicians,"[9] and in a chapter on "The Diffusion of Sovereignty" he
makes it clear that the statement applies not only to the making of policy, but
also to its implementation. The National Science Foundation offers one of
many examples.

We do not have reliable data on the question of the extent to which
political scientists give attention to the various functions that Price identifies.
Certainly the greatest attention goes to the political—to functions in which
politicians play the central role. Students of public administration naturally
concern themselves especially with the administrative. Since the scientific and
professional functions are not sharply set apart, they also get some attention.
In fact, a look at the table of contents of a casebook in public administration
shows concern for a great many kinds of governmental activity.[10] Nevertheless, it is probably fair to say, most especially of the fields of political science
other than public administration, that relatively little attention goes to those
parts of the process in which the scientists and professionals in government
play central roles.

The above analysis reflects the common preoccupation with domestic
politics, but comparable problems in the international field should be recognized. If we say that there is an international system and process, with what

---

[8] Don K. Price, *The Scientific Estate* (Cambridge: Belknap Press, Harvard University Press, 1965), p. 135.

[9] *Ibid.*, p. 67. See also the discussion at pp. 23–25, above.

[10] *Cf.* Harold Stein, ed., *Public Administration and Policy Development, A Case
Book* (New York: Harcourt, Brace & Co., 1952). The Introduction to this book includes
sections on "Public Administration as Process" and "Public Administration as Politics,"
pp. xiii–xvii.

parts of it are political scientists concerned? Roughly, at least, Price's spectrum applies here too. Attention goes overwhelmingly to the political aspects of the process, and to a much lesser extent to its administrative aspects. It scarcely manifests itself at all where the process of making and implementing policy is to a very large extent a matter of professional and technical expertise. Few political scientists concern themselves with the process in the International Monetary Fund, the International Civil Aviation Organization, the World Meteorological Organization, and the World Health Organization. A high proportion of those employed by these and other intergovernmental organizations engage in welfare activities on the basis of some kind of specialized or professional expertise and are commonly thought of as nonpolitical. Secretary of State Rusk says that on every working day the United States takes part in from fifteen to twenty intergovernmental meetings throughout the world, dealing not only with such questions as Vietnam and the fate of NATO, but also with such problems as seed testing, hog cholera, the standardization of prunes, and the desalinization of water. Obviously, political scientists give scant attention to intergovernmental processes when the focus is on matters of these sorts. We do not concern ourselves with the entire process on either the domestic or the international level.

It might be added that the term "process" relates to the central interests of political scientists much more aptly in some cases than in others. Reference to the legislative process seems quite natural; and one can speak of such things as the electoral process, the judicial process, and perhaps even the administrative process. But if the focus is to be on a specific election, the idea of process may or may not be very helpful; and the same holds if the focus is to be, say, on the question of what the rules of constitutional law are rather than on the question of how they got formulated or adopted. Moreover, it is not at all clear that a focus on process would be helpful to one whose interest is in the powers of the President or in the foreign policies the President pursues.

II. POLICY

WHAT A FOCUS ON POLICY MEANS

According to the definition most commonly advanced, *policy* consists of several components: (1) goals; (2) a plan or strategy for achieving the goals, or rules or guides to action, or methods; and (3) action.[11] A policy is a

---

[11] James A. Robinson, "The Major Problems of Political Science," in *Politics and Public Affairs*, ed. Lynton K. Caldwell (Bloomington: Institute of Training for Public Service, Department of Government, Indiana University, 1962), p. 169, and *Congress and Foreign Policy-Making* (Homewood, Ill.: Dorsey Press, 1962), p. 6; Richard C. Snyder, H. W. Bruck, and Burton Sapin, *Decision-Making as an Approach to the Study of International Politics* (Princeton, N.J.: Organizational Behavior Section, Princeton University, 1954), p. 52; and Herbert A. Simon, *Administrative Behavior* (New York: Macmillan Co., 1960), p. 59. See also pp. 6–9, above.

product—perhaps a product of something called a process; it is an output of a system or subsystem. Sometimes the reference is to *substantive* policy, the contrast presumably being with policy of a procedural sort; but there is danger of confusion in the practice, for what is substantive from one point of view may be procedural from another. Most commonly, perhaps, a substantive policy in government is one designed to have consequences primarily outside the governmental system itself, whereas a procedural policy is designed to have consequences primarily within the system. It is substantive policy to have a graduated income tax, and procedural policy that the tax be collected through district offices of internal revenue.

A focus on policy requires choices, and each choice calls for others. The student of policy may focus on pending issues and thus on impending decisions, or on decisions that have been made and thus on policies that have been (or are being) pursued. He may focus on individual issues or policies, or on a class of issues or policies.

Assuming a focus on pending issues, Lasswell and Kaplan call attention to the need for a further choice between the intelligence function and the advisory function.[12] Similarly, Dahl identifies three possible roles for the policy expert by referring to the roles of a medical doctor. If the doctor makes the decision for you, there is "expert-authoritarianism." If he simply gives information and stops at that, there is "expert-neutrality." If he "helps you explore the various alternatives, calls your attention to consequences you have overlooked, and leaves the final decision to you, [there is] 'policy-advice.' "[13]

A more specific purpose must also be chosen when the focus is on actual policies of the past or present. For example, the purpose may be to explain the adoption of the policy, or to determine precisely what it is and to elucidate it, or to identify and perhaps assess consequences of various sorts.

We have noted that those who gave prominence to process as a focal concept aimed to rely on situational and behavioral data, avoiding dependence on data concerning the feelings, attitudes, or motivations of individuals. This is scarcely possible in connection with most kinds of policy studies. As the definition indicates, policies imply or reflect goals; and, in addition, they imply or reflect reasoning in the choice of plans or strategies or methods for promoting achievement of the goals. Moral judgments are involved; purposes, attitudes, and appraisals play their roles. The student of policy does not necessarily have to make moral judgments himself, or offer his own prescriptions, though he may do so. But he is likely to make descriptive analyses of the attitudes and motivations of others, their moral judgments and prescriptions. The actions that are a part of policy constitute the efforts of people to achieve their desires, which means that knowledge of their desires is likely to be helpful to anyone seeking to explain the adoption of the policy, to clarify

---

[12] Harold D. Lasswell and Abraham Kaplan, *Power and Society: A Framework for Political Inquiry* (New Haven: Yale University Press, 1950), p. 193.

[13] Robert A. Dahl, *Congress and Foreign Policy* (New York: W. W. Norton Co., 1950), pp. 150–51.

it, or to advise in connection with it. Studies of the consequences of a policy may or may not have so much to do with normative and prescriptive thought.

In sum, those adopting a policy orientation have a wide range of possibilities open to them. Focusing on the policy problem or policy of their choice, they can seek to identify the actors who are relevant to it, and to describe, analyze, and perhaps appraise the perceptions that the actors have of the environment, the actual characteristics of the environment, the causal conditions affecting behavior, the motivations or purposes or values or belief systems of the actors, the arguments that they employ, the actual or probable consequences of a decision, and so on. Or, without special reference to the actual actors, those adopting a policy orientation may call attention to conditions and considerations of many different sorts, whether descriptive, prescriptive, or normative, which they think ought to be taken into account. Though these statements are in the present tense, it is obvious that the policy-oriented may also focus on the decisions and policies of the past.

ARE ALL KINDS OF POLICIES TREATED?

Political scientists pay varying degrees of attention to policies falling in different categories.

We have already noted that some policies relate to the process itself, and in this area concern for policy overlaps concern for process. Political scientists pay a great deal of attention to policies of these sorts. Constitutions fix policies. It is a matter of constitutional policy to have a President, a Congress, and a Supreme Court. It is a matter of constitutional policy that the President and members of Congress shall gain office through elections, and that members of the Supreme Court shall be appointed for life. Further, within the constitutional system more policies operate, which we can call corollaries. For example, the two houses of Congress follow policies in assigning members to committees; the committees follow policies in handling bills referred to them. The President follows policies in his relationships with Congress. And so on. Whenever political scientists talk about constitutional or institutional arrangements for government, they are talking about arrangements that were adopted and are maintained as a matter of policy. If they implicitly or explicitly recommend a change in the process, this is a policy recommendation.

Political scientists also concern themselves with policies pursued by governments in relations with each other, at both the domestic and the international levels. The study of American politics, for example, includes the study of policies of the federal government toward or affecting the states and the policies of states toward or affecting the federal government; similarly, it includes the study of state-city relations, city-city relationships in metropolitan areas, and so on. The study of international politics includes considerable attention to the foreign policies of states and the factors that influence interstate political relationships.

Though I have not made a careful study of the question, my impression is that, so far as attention to policies and policy issues is concerned, political scientists have concentrated their efforts mainly in the above areas. To be sure, they do not entirely ignore policies and policy problems in other categories. I have already noted that case studies, especially in public administration, cover quite a range. The study of political philosophies and ideologies relates directly or indirectly to many kinds of policies. A fair number of books by political scientists have appeared in recent years having to do with problems and policies associated with urban affairs, and a few deal with policies falling in various other categories, e.g., those relating to natural resources, education, and civil rights. The book by Don K. Price quoted above relates to science policy. I have written one on the space program. The list of books and other pieces of writing oriented on policies and policy problems could no doubt be extended. But still, once you get away from policies having to do with governmental processes and intergovernmental relations, the coverage is rather scattered and scant.[14] Political scientists pay relatively little attention to policy outputs designed to have consequences in environments external to the system. They pay little attention to policies concerning such matters as transportation and communication; science, technology, industry, and agriculture; money and banking, currency and credit, taxation; employment and unemployment; health, education, welfare, and social security; the family; the conservation and utilization of natural resources; even law enforcement. Somewhat comparable statements apply to the study of foreign policies and international politics. Political scientists working in this field commonly concern themselves almost entirely with "high policy" —policy relating to the independence, sovereignty, and security of the state, to questions of peace and war. They rarely concern themselves with policies of other sorts, such as policies on international transportation and communication, international action on behalf of health and welfare, etc. Moreover, in the domestic field, when attention is given to the content of policy, the object is sometimes not so much to develop knowledge concerning the policy as to determine how the process of formulation and implementation differs with different kinds of policy issues,[15] or what the capabilities of the system are in connection with different kinds of measures.[16]

III. THE RATIONALE OF PRACTICES ON PROCESS AND POLICY

What is the rationale for the choices that political scientists make in selecting questions with which to be concerned? More specifically, why do they give so little attention to some aspects of the process and some kinds of policies?

---

[14] See Charles S. Hyneman, *The Study of Politics: The Present State of American Political Science* (Urbana: University of Illinois Press, 1959), pp. 38–39.

[15] *Cf.* Theodore J. Lowi, "Distribution, Regulation, Redistribution: The Functions of Government," in *Public Policies and Their Politics, Techniques of Government Control,* ed. Randall B. Ripley (New York: W. W. Norton Co., 1966), pp. 29ff.

[16] Gabriel A. Almond, "A Developmental Approach to Political Systems," *World Politics,* 17 (January 1965) : 195–203.

Many factors are no doubt involved. Three seem especially important: conceptions of the nature of the political, the practical need for limits, and the desire to make political science a science.

THE NATURE OF THE POLITICAL

Don K. Price's spectrum, encompassing the scientific, the professional, the administrative, and the political, is helpful here. If we say that we are mainly interested in "the political," what do we mean? Price identifies this part of his spectrum with politicians, as opposed to administrators, professionals, and scientists; but what distinguishes the politician? One of Price's answers is: concern for "power and action." This is unsatisfactory, especially in view of a fact that Price himself reaffirms: that power manifests itself, even within government, all along his spectrum. It manifests itself in many actions that we do not classify as political. The National Science Foundation and the National Institutes of Health have and exercise power in their respective fields. The Civil Aeronautics Board exercises power when it says that one airline can operate between New York and Miami whereas another cannot. The Department of Defense exercises power in letting the contract for the F-111 to General Dynamics rather than Boeing. The Food and Drug Administration exercises power when it bans the manufacture of antibiotic throat lozenges. The judge and jury exercise power when they convict a man for murder and order him hanged. The International Bank for Reconstruction and Development exercises power in granting a loan to one government and denying it to another. In other words, in government the scientists, the professionals, the administrators, and the politicians have and exercise power both separately and collectively, which makes it extremely difficult to use power as the distinguishing feature of the political.

The same kind of problem arises in connection with David Easton's conception of the political. He says:

> What distinguishes political interactions from all other kinds of social interactions is that they are predominantly oriented toward the authoritative allocation of values for a society. Political research would thus seek to understand that system of interactions in any society through which such binding or authoritative allocations are made and implemented.[17]

Now this conception obviously has merit. Many political scientists have found it helpful, and others yet to come will no doubt also find it helpful. But it has limitations. Though Easton's words leave some room for interpretation, I suppose it is fair to say that the National Science Foundation, the National Institutes of Health, the Civil Aeronautics Board, the Department of Defense, the Food and Drug Administration, the International Bank for Reconstruction and Development, and a host of other governmental and intergovernmental

---

[17] Easton, *A Framework for Political Analysis* (Englewood Cliffs, N.J.: Prentice-Hall, Inc., 1965), p. 50.

agencies make authoritative allocations of value. And I think it obvious that, though we regard some of the allocations as political, we do not by any means put all of them in this category. Political scientists and others commonly regard a great many of the actions of governmental agencies as nonpolitical, which means that Easton's statement is not descriptive of existing attitudes and practices. Of course, regardless of practice up to now, we could say that in the future we will regard all authoritative allocations of value as political, down to the decision of a draft board that one young man is to go into the armed forces and another is to be deferred. As I shall later indicate, I am inclined to believe that we ought to extend the conception of the political by which, in the main, we have been guiding our efforts. But if we do this, I wonder whether we should go as far as Easton's recommendation would take us. I am more inclined to accept Price's notion of the spectrum and to look further for a way of distinguishing between political interactions and those that, however authoritative, are nonpolitical.

Easton makes an additional suggestion: "The question that gives coherence and purpose to a rigorous analysis of political life as a system of behavior is as follows. How do any and all political systems manage to persist in a world of both stability and change?"[18] This suggestion assumes, of course, that we already know what kind of system is a political system; it does not help us identify the political. But it should help us in deciding what kinds of questions to ask about the political. Easton says that the search for an answer to his question

> will reveal what I have called the life processes of political systems
> —those fundamental functions without which no system could endure—together with the typical modes of response through which systems manage to sustain them. The analysis of these processes, and of the nature and conditions of the responses, I posit as a central problem of political theory.

The emphasis here is on process, but process is identified more with function than with procedures for formulating and implementing policies. I am not clear on the question of the extent to which Easton calls for a policy orientation. He provides for it in speaking of inputs that take the form of demands, the conversion of demands into outputs, the outputs themselves, and information feedback. Moreover, I would suppose that anyone who makes the persistence of the system the crucial problem would have to give great attention to policies and to some of the consequences of policies. But Easton directs attention much more to processes and functions considered in the abstract. At one point he asserts that his approach to the analysis of political systems "will not help us to understand why any specific policies are adopted. . . ."[19]

---

[18] Easton, *A Systems Analysis of Political Life* (New York: John Wiley & Sons, 1965), p. 17.

[19] Easton, *Framework for Political Analysis*, pp. 78, 89.

In the international field, a focus on conditions working for or against persistence may or may not be very useful. It is obviously useful in the study of foreign policies, for persistence (i.e., security, self-preservation) is normally the paramount goal of states. It is also useful in connection with such systems as NATO and the United Nations. Whether it is useful in connection with "the international political system" of which Easton speaks depends on the tests of existence and persistence that are employed. If the persistence of "the international political system" is simply the automatic consequence of the persistence of a number of states, and of interaction among them, then the focus becomes irrelevant.

Gabriel Almond's conception of the political suggests somewhat different principles of inclusion and exclusion.

> When we speak of the political system, we include all of the interactions—inputs as well as outputs—which affect the use or threat of use of physical coercion. . . . Political elites may be concerned with peace, social welfare, individual freedom and self-realization, but their concern with these values as politicians is somehow related to compulsory actions such as taxation, law-making and law-enforcement, foreign and defense policy.[20]

The thought has much to commend it. It at least contributes toward the explanation of a high proportion of the choices that fix the scope of the discipline. But it does not clearly explain them all. On the one hand, physical coercion is quite remote from many of the interactions that are commonly regarded as political, and may be only incidental or peripheral; for example, the fact that the President chooses one man rather than another for a Cabinet post normally has little or nothing to do with physical coercion. On the other hand, some interactions that clearly "affect the use or threat of use of physical coercion" may or may not be considered political; for example, a decision to equip a naval vessel with conventional rather than nuclear power, or a decision to get every possible state policeman out on the highways on Labor Day weekend.

The difficulties that people have in distinguishing the political warn against glib and confident assertions about the matter; and I do not claim to have a piece of litmus paper that provides an unerring test. But I endorse the idea that in determining whether to classify a governmental policy or a governmental decision as political or nonpolitical we concern ourselves with the relevant influencing factors. We say that a policy or decision is nonpolitical when it is based on generally accepted standards that are interpreted and applied by persons credited with special knowledge or expertise; otherwise we say that it is political. That is, we call a policy or decision nonpolitical when it is reached (or at least when we think it is reached) by the rational application of relevant knowledge on the basis of agreed values or principles; and we call a policy or decision political when it results from bargaining or struggle or

---

[20] Almond, *Developmental Approach*, p. 192.

arbitrary desire or judgment, and when power (coercive influence) plays a crucial if not determining role.

Illustrations are easy to offer. When the Food and Drug Administration decides that a drug can be sold only on the basis of a doctor's prescription, it presumably acts nonpolitically, rationally applying relevant knowledge on the basis of agreed values or principles. Similarly, a draft board or a local board of education presumably acts nonpolitically in applying generally accepted laws or rules or principles to specific circumstances to which it gives special attention. Policemen, judges, and juries are expected to act nonpolitically.

Even politicians sometimes act nonpolitically according to this conception. The point is illustrated by the favorable reaction of a member of the House of Representatives to President Johnson's proposal that elections to the House should be for four-year terms. "Instead of devoting every other year to politics," he said, "the House members could have three years for legislative work and only one for politics." Now the congressman may simply have been distinguishing in his own mind between two kinds of politics, partisan and legislative; obviously, some legislative work is political. But he also may have had in mind the fact that many kinds of legislative actions are commonly regarded as nonpolitical. In a great many instances Congress and other legislative bodies act as a kind of board of managers or as administrators, bringing knowledge and rationality to bear on the application of accepted principles to particular situations and making decisions on the basis of general consent. This implies, obviously, that politics and the political are far from synonymous with government and the governmental, though the meanings overlap.

As political scientists we concern ourselves with both politics and government, but the main emphasis is on politics. It is my impression that the extent to which we concern ourselves with an office or branch or activity or function of government (or of an international organization) varies directly with our conception of its relevance to the political. The point is easy to illustrate by citing the fact that we study the staffing of congressional committees, but not the staffing of the Government Printing Office. Public law and the courts provide a more ambiguous kind of illustration. Public law expresses widely accepted standards, and judges are credited with special expertise in applying these standards. On this basis we speak of the legal and the judicial as distinct from the political. But controversy over the law sometimes arises. Actual or aspiring political leaders may not be willing to leave a question to the courts. When judges disagree among themselves or reverse earlier decisions, they themselves tend to undermine the assumption that they are rationally applying expert knowledge on the basis of agreed principles. In other words, the legal and the judicial often border on the political, and sometimes become political.

Just as our concern for the political leads us to give attention to aspects of government that are highly relevant, so does it lead us to give attention to various nongovernmental problems or situations. For example, even when there was no serious controversy over voting rights for Negroes, the fact that Negroes were excluded from the polls in some states was politically significant; and so was the fact of the malapportionment of state legislatures.

Obviously, statements comparable to these have counterparts in the field of international politics.

In sum, conceptions of the political are helpful in varying degrees in indicating why political scientists stress some parts of the governmental process more than others and some kinds of policies more than others; but additional factors also need to be considered.

THE NEED FOR LIMITS

The tendency of political scientists to restrict themselves to parts of the process and to some kinds of policies probably also reflects a need to limit responsibilities and to arrange and respect an academic division of labor. If political scientists were to say that all parts of the process and all aspects of all public policies and policy issues are their meat, they would be adopting a field of inquiry without limits, and might soon find themselves shoulder to shoulder with professors and researchers of almost all other disciplines, trying to help solve all kinds of problems. They would need to be not only political scientists, but also economists, sociologists, pharmacologists, engineers, physicists, and so on. Particularly if they adopted an all-out policy orientation, they would need to be able to identify issues and discuss them on their merits in such areas as agriculture, education, natural resource development, transportation, public health, and international commercial relationships. Moreover, an all-out policy orientation would help take political scientists fully into the realm of normative problems and social engineering. The prospect is appalling, and it is no wonder that most members of the profession have steered sharply away from it.

The question is whether there is not an acceptable way of taking up policy matters without becoming complete academic imperialists and without losing identity as political scientists. I shall come back to this question later.

THE STRESS ON SCIENCE

Yehezkel Dror picks out what he calls "a physical-science-fixation" as a major barrier to the development of a policy science. Those suffering from this fixation, he believes, "tend to a narrow view of knowledge-seeking."

> More specifically, (a) their approach tends to seek relatively simple explanations, accepting Occam's Razor as applying to social phenomena, which encourages study of issues which can thus be dealt with; (b) empirical research susceptible to statistical tests of validity and reliability is regarded as the only legitimate source of knowledge, while problems not susceptible to such methods are excluded from the domain of investigation; (c) there is a strong striving for "factual" and "value-free" findings, normative recommendations being regarded as incompatible with the status of "scientists"; (d) general theories are regarded with suspicion.
>
> The net aggregative effect of these tendencies is a strong predisposition to concentrate on micro-issues. Macro-issues of social struc-

ture and dynamics—including most problems of high policy-signifi-
cance—are often regarded as subjects "at present" not susceptible to
"scientific" examination, and therefore not to be dealt with by
contemporary social sciences.[21]

Though Mr. Dror does not say so, the "fixation" of which he speaks would
presumably be somewhat less inhibiting where the focus is on process than
where it is on policy.

Not all of those who stress science would accept Mr. Dror's characterization of its implications, but their views are nevertheless likely to lead to
greater concern for process than for policy. To some, science and theory are
virtually interchangeable terms, and they aim at findings that have a fairly
high level of generality. Their object is descriptive theories giving more or
less abstract images of selected aspects of reality. The knowledge produced is
to be widely applicable and of enduring value, relating to much more than
fleeting circumstances and problems. This means a pronounced tendency to
focus more on categories of phenomena than on unique cases. The student
who aims at general, theoretical propositions likes to have data stemming
from many cases of the same kind or from repetitive patterns. Thus he may
study the pattern of actions involved in getting a bill enacted into law, or the
kinds of relationships existing between two branches of government, or the
factors that influence the outcome of elections.

As indicated above, attitudes and purposes of these sorts are more
conducive to a focus on process than a focus on policy, for policies so often
relate to the unique and the transient; and when attention does go to policy,
the fundamental purpose may be to enhance knowledge of the workings and
capabilities of the system. At the same time, some kinds of policy studies can
be at a fairly high level of generality, and can reflect concern for policy as
such. The comparative study of "The Politics of Taxation" in the states of the
United States suggests such a possibility.[22] Similarly, the comparative study of
foreign policies sometimes leads to the discovery of regularities and permits
the formulation of generalizations.

IV. COULD MORE ATTENTION APPROPRIATELY BE GIVEN TO POLICY?

I have no criticism of the stress on process or of the accepted limits within
which process is studied. The question is whether political scientists should

---

[21] Yehezkel Dror, "The Barriers Facing Policy Science," *American Behavioral
Scientist,* 7 (January 1965) : 4. *Cf.* Max F. Millikan, "Inquiry and Policy: The Relation of
Knowledge to Action," in *The Human Meaning of the Social Sciences,* ed. Daniel Lerner
(New York: Meridian Books, 1959), p. 161.

[22] Clara Penniman, "The Politics of Taxation," in *Politics in the American States, A
Comparative Analysis,* ed. Herbert Jacob and Kenneth N. Vines (Boston: Little, Brown &
Co., 1965), pp. 219–330; *cf.* other chapters in the same book on "State Politics and
Education," "The Politics of Welfare," and "State Politics and Highways."

not take a broader view of their tasks where policies are concerned—and I mean policies designed to have effects outside the governmental system itself as opposed to policies relating to the governmental process. I believe that they should; not that every political scientist should accept a policy orientation for himself, but that the proportion of those who do should increase and that everyone should regard a policy orientation as legitimate and proper.

The basis for the view is the proposition that our concern should be the promotion of human welfare. This is the overriding goal, the justification of the incomes we get. Dangers lurk in the proposition, to be sure. One is that human welfare will get translated into national welfare, and that national welfare will get translated into support for the existing system or even the existing government. Another is that we will get unduly preoccupied with day-to-day problems, seeking to apply what knowledge we have rather than trying to get more. But no course of action is without danger of some sort.

Our concern should also be with the development of general knowledge, with theory, with science, but this proposition should not supersede the earlier one. It states an instrumental value, not the goal value. We can have faith that general, theoretical knowledge will sooner or later contribute to human welfare, but we are not likely to exhaust our possibilities if we aim exclusively at the development of such knowledge. We ought to study some problems even if they are unique and regardless of the question of promoting general knowledge; we ought to study them simply because they are important.

As noted above, it is established practice for political scientists to concern themselves with foreign policies, that is, with "high policy" at the international level. And much of foreign policy concerns process; that is, depending on whether we say that an international political system exists and, if so, how we delimit it, much of foreign policy is analogous to the kinds of constitutional policies and their corollaries that we study at the domestic level. But, subject to check by scholars who use reliable methods, my impression is that students of foreign policies and international politics are more inclined than students of domestic politics to take up problems outside this realm. In other words, my impression is that we study the causes of war more than the causes of revolution, that we study the conditions of international peace more than the conditions of domestic peace, that we study the foreign aid program more than the various domestic tax and aid programs, that we study deterrence more in relation to nuclear weapons than in relation to municipal riots, and that we study national loyalty more as a problem in international relations than as a problem of domestic politics.

Those who say that our goal should be to identify the conditions working for or against the persistence of the system ought, it seems to me, to be especially concerned with policy issues. They now are to some extent; but they tend to focus on constitutional policies and their corollaries—on the characteristics of the system, on the conversion process, and on the way in which the output is administered. Quite obviously, however, other kinds of policies also affect persistence, e.g., policies having to do with the distribution of wealth, with social security, with education, with mass media, with societal attitudes and practices relating to race, with cultural values, and so on. In other words, the nature of the outputs affects persistence, and so do the nature of the feedback and the nature of the demands that endure or arise. The fate of governments and of men depends not so much on forms and processes as on the wisdom of the policies that are pursued.

Special stress can well be placed on the problem of purpose, closely associated with the problem of values and interests. Easton Rothwell had the problem very much in mind in writing the Foreword to *The Policy Sciences,* citing "the clarification of objectives" as an important task of these sciences.[23] Don K. Price, though identifying the political with "power and action," also holds that what distinguishes the political from the scientific estate is "a primary concern for purpose."[24] He cites an operations analyst who holds that we have too many " 'studies which try to determine the exact best way to perform an operation which shouldn't be performed at all.' "[25] McGeorge Bundy stresses a similar view:

> The heart of the matter . . . in all politics is to be found in power and purpose. . . . A technical, an economic, or a strategic problem will in the end become a problem of purpose. A recommended policy must have an object, and the object must be justified by standards of value or conviction. Behind all technical counsel there will be intent. . . . There is no escape from the problem of purpose. . . . The teaching of purpose is literally inescapable.[26]

Bundy goes on to say that "in the assumptions and behavior of our whole people there is today a question as to the clarity and coherence both of our purposes as citizens and the complementary purpose of our government. History has outrun thought, and our practice is no longer clearly based on our convictions."[27] He locates responsibility for the study of these matters in departments of philosophy and politics, indicating that if they reject the responsibility, other departments will take it up. Others in addition to Rothwell, Price, and Bundy have stressed the importance of purpose and of clarity of purpose.[28]

---

[23] Daniel Lerner and Harold D. Lasswell, eds., *The Policy Sciences, Recent Developments in Scope and Method* (Stanford, Calif.: Stanford University Press, 1951), p. ix.

[24] Price, *Scientific Estate,* p. 183.

[25] *Ibid.,* p. 127.

[26] McGeorge Bundy, "The Battlefields of Power and the Searchlights of the Academy," in *The Dimensions of Diplomacy,* ed. E. A. J. Johnson (Baltimore: Johns Hopkins Press, 1964), pp. 5–6.

[27] *Ibid.,* p. 7.

[28] Hyneman, *Study of Politics,* pp. 101–3; Kenneth E. Boulding, *Principles of Economic Policy* (Englewood Cliffs, N.J.: Prentice-Hall, Inc., 1958), p. 2; Millikan, "Inquiry and Policy," p. 167; Henry A. Kissinger, "Reflections on Power and Diplomacy," in *Dimensions of Diplomacy,* p. 38, and *The Necessity for Choice* (Garden City, N.Y.: Doubleday & Co., 1960), pp. 362–65; Mark S. Massel, "Regulation and Politics: An Overview," in *The Politics of Regulation,* ed. Samuel Krislov and Lloyd D. Musolf (Boston: Houghton Mifflin Co., 1964), pp. 258–60; and John Strachey, *The End of Empire* (New York: Random House, 1960), pp. 212–13, 229, 244, 246–47.

The reasons for a stress on purpose are not far to seek, for they play a central role in political behavior—in fact, in all behavior. Political leaders are expected to declare their purposes. The political measures taken are expected to be purposeful. Political parties and political movements gain in strength as they correctly identify and effectively serve the purposes of those whose support they seek. Political behavior without purpose is scarcely imaginable, though political actors (like others) are sometimes not fully conscious of the purposes they pursue. It is notable that the relative aimlessness of the Eisenhower years, climaxed by the shock of sputnik, was followed by anguished concern for American national purposes and by the appointment of the President's Commission on National Goals.[29] Action can become nonpolitical, as we have already seen, only when sufficient agreement on purposes exists to permit problems to be handled through the rational application of knowledge.

In suggesting greater concern for policy problems, I do not mean that all limits should be abandoned. Governmental policies, domestic and foreign, relate to matters falling within a number of different academic disciplines. Though it is part of my view that students of domestic politics need some interdisciplinary competence just as badly as students of international politics, I am not arguing that political scientists should try to range over all the fields of policy-related knowledge. What seems to me to follow from the above is that political scientists should give greater attention to the purposes—the values and interests—of politically relevant actors. What do they desire, and what are they likely to desire? What relationships exist among the desires of the same actor and of different sets of actors? What is the relative urgency or importance of the different desires of the same actor and of different actors, and on the basis of what standard of judgment? Where is conflict most likely to occur and how can it be either averted or handled in such a way as to minimize some consequences (presumably evil) and maximize others? I do not say that such questions have hitherto been ignored. But I believe that they deserve more stress than they have so far received.[30]

---

[29] U.S. President's Commission on National Goals, *Goals for Americans* (Englewood Cliffs, N.J.: Prentice-Hall, Inc., 1960).

[30] *Cf.* Bertrand de Jouvenel, "Political Science and Prevision," *American Political Science Review*, 59 (March 1965) : 29–38.

3

The Categorization of Policy Contents

LEWIS A. FROMAN, JR.

The emphasis on scientific technique in a discipline not previously accustomed to such rigor is likely to follow the line of least resistance. By and large I think this is what has happened in political science in recent years. Not only has there been a reaction against descriptive, historical, and normative analyses of political phenomena; there has also been an emphasis on research in those areas of politics where data are most easily available and where statistical data analysis may most easily apply.

As a consequence of the current emphasis on research on political processes and on methodological developments, certain potentially interesting subfields or topics within the discipline have been left relatively unaffected and unexplored. For reasons having to do both with the rejection of past ways of proceeding and with certain methodological problems, policy analysis may certainly be placed in the forefront of those areas of political interest which have yet to be intensely developed. Perhaps this book and the conferences preceding it will mark the beginning of a long road that will lead the profession, and the graduate students who will be the profession of the future, to the understanding that those who are interested in "policy" questions are no longer to be considered outside the mainstream of the discipline.

But to say this is simply to raise the question: How might it be fruitful for political scientists to attempt to answer some interesting questions about public policy? The answer to this question will not be settled here, but perhaps some tentative guidelines may emerge out of a discussion of the problems we face in conducting research in public policy.

I. SOME GENERALIZATIONS ABOUT PAST PUBLIC POLICY RESEARCH

The following generalizations are not meant to exhaust what might be said about research on public policy questions. They are, however, important topics that will mark the starting points for possible new departures.

1. Research on questions of public policy has, generally speaking, taken two directions.

The first, and older, tradition may be called "normative" studies of public policy. These studies attempt to analyze, usually in a critical fashion, a particular public policy (agriculture, labor, education, unemployment, etc.), and generally will also suggest either reforms in the existing policy or a new type of policy altogether. For example, there are numerous studies of our foreign aid program which describe in detail how it has failed in one way or another to live up to certain standards. These reports are accompanied by general or specific recommendations on how the program can be "improved."

The criteria for evaluating these critiques of ongoing programs are usually certain stated goals that the authors feel are, or ought to be, highly valued. Often authors will suggest that if certain steps are taken, programs can be developed which will lead to "solutions" of the problems under examination. The major point of argument, however, is generally the extent to which ongoing policies deviate from important values or goals.

Studies of this kind have now fallen somewhat into disrepute as being "value-laden" and lacking in scientific interest. Much of the dissatisfaction revolves around the point that such studies are argumentative and sometimes rhetorical, using data to score policy points rather than scientific ones. Almost anyone can think of values that current policies in almost any field are either slow in satisfying or not satisfying at all, and hence can criticize public policies on that basis.

The second, and newer, effort in the direction of policy analysis has been the attempt to think futuristically either about the consequences of ongoing policies or about the kinds of policies that would be appropriate given a world x number of years hence. These studies have taken impetus from governmental interest in social scientists' efforts to talk about the future in terms of population, disarmament, nuclear strategy, natural and human resources, and so on. Less concerned with past policy failures, these studies generally attempt to point out what may be a problem in the future, given certain hypothesized trends.

2. Each of these types of research on public policies may be classified as "problem-oriented" in that the concerns of each are usually some particular problem and the policies that are appropriate to dealing with it. There is, usually quite explicitly, a general notion that there is a problem, and that it is possible to take steps to "solve" it.

3. In the process-oriented literature that has been the main product of the interest in political science as a scientific discipline, when policies are

discussed they are often treated as "outcomes" of the process. Several researchers have suggested that certain political processes or aspects of political organizations have policy consequences. For example: the system of electing the President by means of the Electoral College tends to favor "liberal" interests; apportionment of state legislatures on bases other than population tends to have a "conservative" bias; the political activities of leaders will tend to have a greater pro–civil-liberties bias than will the political activities of nonleaders; wealthy, industrial states are more likely to have higher per capita expenditures on welfare than poorer, rural states.

The major point here is that policy has, by and large, been treated as a *dependent variable* that is affected in one way or another by political and socioeconomic processes.

These three generalizations about policy studies and policy analysis have undoubtedly served to impede the development of a more empirically and theoretically based analysis of public policies.

The reasons for this are relatively straightforward. First, problem-oriented research, whether it be past, present, or future, is likely to emphasize a single policy. Now it is certainly possible to generalize from case studies of particular policies,[1] but for the most part there are built-in constraints that prevent the case method from generating theory. Certainly this has been true in the field of constitutional law, where the case method has been most used. The emphasis is on a single policy, and the making of hypotheses that may hold true over many cases, and certainly the testing of such hypotheses, are severely limited. Ordinarily one of the purposes of case studies is to deal with a problem in its details, some of which may be quite irrelevant for theoretical purposes. Also, in dealing with single cases it is extremely difficult to isolate causal factors.

The emphasis on solutions to problems is also an impediment to theory building in that a good deal of effort is likely to go into proposing answers to action-type questions.

Second, viewing policy as something to be explained (that is, as a dependent variable) undoubtedly places less emphasis on the development of analytic categories than does viewing policy as an independent variable that helps to explain something else. For reasons that are not hard to analyze, researchers are likely to spend a good deal more time constructing explanations of phenomena than in becoming more sophisticated in the description of the behavior to be explained. Indeed, the history of social science is replete with examples of rather sophisticated developments of explanations (independent variables) rather than dependent variables. Psychoanalysts, for example, clearly find it easier to construct explanations (and rather elaborate ones) of human behavior than to classify the behavior to be explained. The

---

[1] For the best of these efforts, see Raymond A. Bauer, Ithiel de Sola Pool, and Lewis Anthony Dexter, *American Business and Public Policy* (New York: Atherton Press, 1963).

development of theories explaining why people vote the way they do clearly outdistances in sophistication the description and analysis of the behavior itself.

The way out of these impediments to theory building in the field of public policy I think is clear. If a new direction for policy analysis were to be suggested here, it would require no commitment to any particular policy, nor would it require an effort to provide solutions to problems. It would rather place heavy emphasis on the study of multiple policies, and it would allow for policy to be treated as an independent variable as well as a dependent variable.

This approach to policy analysis would require us to see what kinds of variables are related to policy variables. Policy could be treated as an independent variable. For example, we might ask and attempt to answer the question: Do political processes vary in accordance with the issue or stakes of the game? The answer to this question would clearly change the nature of the research enterprise. Rather than treating policy as an outcome of the political process, we are asking whether policy itself is a variable that may affect the political process. To answer this question we would certainly need some categories of policy which could then be related to variations in political processes.

It would also, of course, be useful to view policy as an independent variable. For example, research might be undertaken to explore the relationship between types of decision structures and types of public policy. Do different kinds of organizational structure facilitate or impede the handling of different kinds of policies?

The emphasis in this type of policy analysis would be on developing categories of policy which could allow us to test hypotheses about differences in policies as they relate to differences in other variables. This method of theory building has parallels in other disciplines and in other areas within our discipline.

II. DEVELOPING POLICY THEORY

In order to develop theory in any discipline, certain requirements must be met. Let us define "theory" as a logically related set of empirical propositions; let us define "empirical proposition" as a statement that relates one variable to another; and let us define "variable" as a concept that may assume different values. When we use this simplified model of a theory, it becomes clear that if we are to develop a theory or theories about public policy, we must begin at a relatively primitive level, the level of concepts. It would be most useful if "policy" were a variable. At the present time, for example, it makes little sense to assert that "the more the x policy, the more the y," or "the more the y, the more the x policy." "Policy" is simply not a word that has yet acquired the status of a variable.

Traditionally, one beginning step in developing variables is the development of typologies, classifications, or taxonomies. A typology (or classification, or taxonomy) is a set of concepts or categories which differentiates among various kinds of higher-order concepts. For example, at a very simple level, a typology of a concept like "government" might be "dictatorship" and "democracy." One may then ask a number of questions about such a typology, for example, whether the categories are exhaustive and/or mutually exclusive.

At a slightly different level, it is also possible to define a typology as a measure of a concept at the nominal level of measurement. When viewing it as a measurement problem, one can then ask additional questions, such as whether the typology has validity and reliability, and whether operational definitions are easy or difficult to construct.

Once a typology has been constructed, it may then be possible to go further to see whether there is an underlying factor that could join the discrete categories to form a continuous variable (increase the measurement power from nominal to ordinal or interval). If one can move in this general direction, it then becomes a good deal easier to talk of theory building.

One further problem is involved in theory building. It would be quite possible to solve all the prior problems of measurement, reliability and validity, and inclusiveness and mutual exclusiveness, and still not have contributed much to theory. The next obvious question is: Do the categories successfully differentiate other phenomena? That is, can the categories be related to some other set of categories in such a way that relationships can be observed which might then develop into the status of theory?

When one asks this question, a possible paradox comes immediately to mind. It may be the case, as we explore concepts that have been used in policy analysis, that the most interesting theoretical concepts have the greatest difficulties in terms of the other criteria, and that those categories that most easily satisfy the criteria of concept reliability, etc., are the least interesting theoretically. In the light of what we know of difficulties in social science research, such a result might be expected. Often the most intriguing theoretical work is the most difficult to operationalize, and *vice versa*. In fact, the development of interesting theoretical speculation may be held back by too close attention to concept problems. In any event, we may find that the introduction of measurement problems reduces the attractiveness of many speculative theories.

III. THE PROBLEM OF CONCEPTS

Once we take this posture toward theory building, it then becomes immediately apparent just wherein lies the difficulty in developing theory about public policy. The problem is clearly at the level of concepts. It is also interesting to observe that the reason the problem is at this level is that the profession has become increasingly sensitive to another problem, that of marshaling evidence in support of empirical statements at a high level of abstraction. If it were not for this concern, the problems of concept validity and reliability, ease or difficulty of operationalization, and inclusiveness and mutual exclusiveness would not be so important. Because we have developed a strong interest in seeing empirical evidence wedded to theory, the basic first steps of conceptualization have increased in importance. In other words, the profession has become increasingly intolerant of sloppy abstractions.

It might be useful, then, to take a look at some of the ways in which policy has been defined and the typologies that have already been developed. From such a brief survey we may then get some idea of what is already available and what may look promising.

The first set of categories which we might look at are what I shall call "traditional" categories. These categories have been relatively widely used, but for one reason or another have not led to theoretical development. They include the following:

1. Substantive categories (labor, education, business, welfare, civil rights).

2. Institutional categories (congressional policies, Presidential policies, bureau policies).

3. Target categories (farmers, lower class, businessmen, Negroes).

4. Time periods (ante bellum, postdepression, prewar, Eisenhower years).

5. Ideological categories (secular, capitalist, First Amendment, liberal, conservative).

6. Value categories (good, bad, dangerous).

7. Extent of support (consensus, divisive).

8. Governmental level (national, state, local, metropolitan).

These are some of the major categories that have been employed, usually in descriptive-normative-historical studies of public policy. One of the major disadvantages of the use of these categories, although this disadvantage is not necessarily inherent in the categories, is that only single issues have been used. That is, there has been a notable lack of comparative research on public policies such that the categories could be used to differentiate among other phenomena (used theoretically).

Table 1 evaluates these categories according to the criteria we have previously mentioned. Very briefly, these categories of evaluation may be defined in the following manner:

Inclusive. Are the categories comprehensive? May all policies be classified in one or another category of the proposed typology?

Mutually exclusive. May policies be placed in one and only one category, or is there overlapping?

Validity. Does the concept define what it purports to define?

Reliability. Is there a high level of agreement among independent researchers on what specific policies fall into what categories?

Level of measurement. Is the measurement nominal (naming dis-

TABLE 1

ANALYSIS OF TRADITIONAL POLICY CATEGORIES

Categories	Inclusive	Mutually Exclusive	Validity	Reliability	Level of Measurement	Ease of Measurement	Differentiation
Substantive	Can be, but usually single categories; open-ended	Not in all cases	Relatively high	Relatively high	Nominal	Easy	Probably low
Institutional	Same as substantive	No	Relatively low	Relatively low	Nominal, possibly ordinal	Difficult	Probably low
Target	Same as substantive	Not in all cases	Relatively high	Relatively high	Nominal	Easy	Probably low
Time	Yes	Yes, except perhaps at margins	Relatively high	Relatively high, except perhaps on content	Nominal, possibly ordinal and even interval	Relatively difficult, especially with regard to content	Could be high
Ideological	No	Not in all cases	Relatively high	Moderate	Same as Time	Relatively easy	Could be high
Value	Same as substantive	Not in all cases	Relatively low	Low	Nominal, possibly ordinal	Variable	Low
Support	Yes	Yes	High	High	Nominal, possibly ordinal and even interval	Difficult	Could be high
Level	Yes	No	Relatively high	Moderate	Nominal, possibly ordinal	Easy	Moderate

crete categories), ordinal (ranking by more or less), or interval (distances between ranks of known value)?

Ease of measurement. How easily may the categories be operationalized?

Differentiation. Do the categories correlate with other phenomena, and if so, to what extent?

There are, of course, no data that will allow precise evaluation by these criteria. The comments in Table 1, then, are judgmental.

By and large we find from the table that only three of the eight categories we have defined as traditional show some promise for theoretical development. These three are time, ideology, and support. We might expect to find, for example, that public policies (as well as other phenomena) may vary over time and that these variations may be linked to historical events and possible changes in other phenomena (such as processes) as a consequence. Defining policies by time periods and searching for explanations in differences in policies over time might develop some very interesting historical theories. Similarly, we might expect ideological policies to differ from one another and to be linked with other kinds of differences, and the same may be true for policies with different levels of support.

The other five categories seem less useful for theoretical development, although in many cases they are "easier" concepts to deal with. The reason for this is that there is less presumption that the definitions of the categories will be useful in differentiating other phenomena. However, the evidence for this presumption is not yet in, since most policy studies have been noncomparative.

In addition to these more traditional categories, several efforts have been made to distinguish among policies at a considerably higher level of abstraction. One thing that the traditional categories all have in common (with the exception of the value category) is that they are all very close to the data. The categories that will be discussed now have been formulated in an effort to define policy in terms of concepts a good deal more complex. We can therefore expect that the measurement problems will, by and large, be more serious, and that the payoff in using them is in the theoretical interest they generate.

Berelson, Lazarsfeld, and McPhee distinguish between "style" and "position" issues. Essentially this distinction has to do with whether the issues are concrete and specific or abstract and general. They then go on to suggest that this dichotomization helps to clarify certain relationships in election campaigns (for example, party preference varies more by position issues than by style issues).[2] Additional research suggests that campaign strategies and tactics may vary in emphasis on style and position issues in accordance with the nature of misperception among party identifiers on these issues.[3]

[2] Bernard R. Berelson, Paul F. Lazarsfeld, and William N. McPhee, *Voting* (Chicago: University of Chicago Press, 1954), p. 199.

[3] Lewis A. Froman, Jr., and James K. Skipper, Jr., "Factors Related to Misperceiving Party Stands on Issues," *Public Opinion Quarterly*, 26 (Spring 1962): 265–72; and

A major difficulty with this distinction is the question of whether the difference lies with the content of the issues, with the way in which they are discussed, or with the perceptions of the audience. Most issues seem to have both style and position features, and classifying issues unambiguously is likely to be difficult.

Edelman has suggested a somewhat different dichotomy in terms of "material" and "symbolic" satisfaction, and has hypothesized a most intriguing differentiation of political processes on the basis of this distinction (for example, "the interests of organized groups in tangible resources or in substantive power are less easily satiable than are interests in symbolic reassurance,"[4] or "the most intensive dissemination of symbols commonly attends the enactment of legislation which is most meaningless in its effects upon resource allocation").[5] An effort has also been made to analyze the American political system and its institutions by employing, along with other distinctions, both the Berelson and the Edelman variables.[6]

Edelman's distinction between material and symbolic satisfaction is probably less ambiguous than the distinction made by Berelson *et al.* between style and position issues, but the major difficulty that arises is the problem of operationalizing the distinction. Clearly, in the first proposition cited above, Edelman is referring to the attitudes and values of the groups that are making demands. Some method of survey analysis seems indicated to test the proposition. In the second proposition, however, "effects upon resource allocation" is the operation suggested, and some measure of distinguishing among policies on the basis of this distinction would have to be developed. It is quite possible that economists might be helpful in suggesting an appropriate measuring instrument. The theoretical power of the Edelman categories appears large enough, however, to justify more intensive and more rigorous analysis.

Huntington has attempted to analyze some aspects of military decision-making by distinguishing between strategic and structural issues.[7] Certain aspects of decision by the Joint Chiefs of Staff, for example, were related to this differentiation. As with other relatively abstract definitions, a major difficulty with these categories is in distinguishing which issues are to be called strategic and which structural. Huntington attempts to give some guidelines, but the problem of reliability among these classifying issues is quite severe.

The attractiveness of the Huntington categories is that they attempt to classify issues essentially by content. Those that are concerned with overall

---

Froman, "A Realistic Approach to Campaign Strategies and Tactics," in *The Electoral Process*, ed. M. Kent Jennings and L. Harmon Zeigler (Englewood Cliffs, N.J.: Prentice-Hall, Inc., 1966), pp. 1–20.

[4] Murray Edelman, "Symbols and Political Quiescence," *American Political Science Review*, 54 (September 1960) : 695.

[5] *Ibid.*, p. 697.

[6] Froman, *People and Politics* (Englewood Cliffs, N.J.: Prentice-Hall, Inc., 1962).

[7] Samuel P. Huntington, *The Common Defense* (New York: Columbia University Press, 1961), pp. 4–6.

strategy are strategic, those that implement strategy decisions are structural. With this kind of classification, however, one inevitably runs into the problem of one man's strategy being subsumed by someone else's strategy, which leaves the original strategy as structure.

Lowi suggests an interesting and potentially useful trichotomy: policies that are distributive, regulatory, and redistributive. Distributive issues are those that give things away (subsidies, pork); regulatory issues are those that restrict available alternatives (antitrust, acreage allotments); and redistributive issues are those that take from one group of people and give to another (progressive income tax). Political processes are hypothesized to vary according to the nature of the issue.[8]

The theoretical power of these categories appears to be very large, but the methodological problems present some difficulties. Lowi, for example, introduces the question of perception of issues. It is quite possible that a researcher might classify an issue in one way, but a political actor might perceive it as being something else. For example, liberals in Congress might view the Poverty Program as a distributive issue (which would be an accurate classification, given Lowi's categories); conservatives, on the other hand, might perceive such a program as redistributive. In this case, does the political process vary according to an "objective" definition of the issue or by the perceived definition of the issue?

The problem of perceptions also brings up a number of other knotty problems, such as the necessity of collecting data on actors' perceptions of issues before one is able to classify the issues. Although this is not impossible, it clearly requires research of a different order than simply classifying issues by their objective contents.

I have elsewhere suggested that city policies may be classified as "areal" or "segmental."[9] Essentially this distinction is between policies (such as the city-manager plan, nonpartisan elections, fluoridation) which affect the whole community at the same time (areal policies) and those (such as welfare and urban renewal) which affect something less than the total population, and also affect different people at different times (segmental policies). It was then hypothesized that areal policies would be associated with homogeneous communities, segmental policies with heterogeneous communities.

This set of categories has the virtue of referring only to policy contents and not to attitudes within the target group, perceptions of the actors, etc.; but it, too, suffers from reliability problems.

There is also, of course, the distinction between issues as zero-sum versus non-zero-sum. In political science this distinction has most profitably been employed by Riker, but unfortunately only zero-sum games are developed and little or nothing is said of non-zero-sum games, except to suggest an interest-

---

[8] Theodore J. Lowi, "American Business, Public Policy, Case-Studies, and Political Theory," *World Politics*, 16 (July 1964) : 677–715.

[9] Froman, "An Analysis of Public Policies in Cities," *Journal of Politics*, 29 (February 1967) : 94–108.

TABLE 2
ANALYSIS OF ABSTRACT POLICY CATEGORIES

Categories	Inclusive	Mutually Exclusive	Validity	Reliability	Level of Measurement	Ease of Measurement	Differentiation
Style–position	Yes	No	Low	Low	Nominal	Difficult	Could be high
Symbolic–material	Yes	No	Medium	Probably low	Nominal	Difficult	Could be very high
Strategic–structural	Yes	Not in all cases	Low	Low	Nominal	Difficult	Could be high
Distributive–regulatory–redistributive	No; excludes foreign policy	Not necessarily	High	Probably low	Nominal	Very difficult	Could be very high
Areal–segmental	Perhaps	Yes, except perhaps at margins	High	Medium	Nominal; could be ordinal and even interval	Medium	Medium
Zero-Sum, non-Zero-Sum	Yes	Yes	Low	Low	Nominal	Difficult	Could be high

ing distinction between economics and political science, the former being concerned with non-zero-sum games and the latter with zero-sum games.[10]

Table 2 evaluates these classification schemes on the basis of the criteria employed in Table 1.

Comparing Table 1 with Table 2, we find what we originally expected: that problems of measurement are most severe with categories that show the greatest theoretical power.

IV. CONCLUSION

Perhaps it would be useful now to stress a point that has cropped up from time to time, but which has not received extensive attention. If we are to develop theory in the public policy field, comparative research is needed. I have made some effort elsewhere to collect case studies on policies in cities and to relate them in a theoretical framework.[11] The difficulties in doing comparative research by putting together other people's case studies are enormous. Very often the data are simply not comparable, both because the policies studied are different and because the focuses of the questions being asked are quite different. One is simply left with a number of disparate studies with only the barest hint at interesting theoretical differences.

When one undertakes comparative research, one is generally struck immediately by differences and similarities among the units of analysis. When this occurs, the data are ripe for concept construction, hypotheses, and testing. It is difficult to imagine that the policy field will develop theory very quickly without comparative analysis as a major research tool.

---

[10] William H. Riker, *The Theory of Political Coalitions* (New Haven: Yale University Press, 1962).

[11] Froman, "Analysis of Public Policies."

Part Two

STUDIES OF DOMESTIC POLICIES

4

The Political Economy of Efficiency:
Cost-Benefit Analysis, Systems Analysis,
and Program Budgeting*

AARON WILDAVSKY

What contribution can political scientists make to the study of the content of public policy? As the profession has been increasingly concerned with the processes through which policy is made, various political scientists have become worried about the apparent neglect of the substance of the major policy choices made by governments. The authors of this book want to evaluate the available tools for making recommendations about the substance of public choices. It is particularly appropriate for political scientists to inquire about the impact on political life of different ways of arriving at and justifying public policies. In recent years economists have developed a number of important approaches to aid in the determination of public policy. The apparent success of cost-benefit analysis, systems analysis, and program budgeting in facilitating rational choice has led some high government officials and political scientists to champion their widespread adoption. Yet questions remain: Are these modes of analysis effective in making economic choices, and if so, are they equally helpful in making political decisions? In this paper I propose to describe cost-benefit analysis, systems analysis, and program

* I am more than ordinarily indebted to the people who have improved this paper through their comments. Win Crowther, John Harsanyi, John Krutilla, Arthur Maas, Arnold Meltsner, Nelson Polsby, William Riker, and Dwight Waldo saved me from errors and contributed insights of their own. The responsibility for what is said is entirely mine. The paper, written while I was a research political scientist at the Center for Planning and Development Research, University of California, Berkeley, was initially published in somewhat different form in the *Public Administration Review*, 26 (December 1966) : 292–310.

budgeting, analyze the strengths and weaknesses of each method for particular purposes, and estimate the utility of each approach for governmental officials and political scientists.

I. EFFICIENCY

There was a day when the meaning of economic efficiency was reasonably clear. An objective met up with a technician. Efficiency consisted in meeting the objective at the lowest cost or in obtaining the maximum amount of the objective for a specified amount of resources. Let us call this "pure efficiency." The desirability of trying to achieve certain objectives may depend on the cost of achieving them. In this case the analyst (he has graduated from being a mere technician) alters the objective to suit available resources. Let us call this "mixed efficiency." Both pure and mixed efficiency are limited in the sense that they take for granted the existing structure of the political system and work within its boundaries. Yet the economizer, he who values efficiency most highly, may discover that the most efficient means for accomplishing his ends cannot be secured without altering the machinery for making decisions. He not only alters means and ends (resources and objectives) simultaneously, but makes them dependent on changes in political relationships. While he claims no special interest in or expertise concerning the decision apparatus outside of the marketplace, the economizer pursues efficiency to the heart of the political system. Let us call this "total efficiency." In this vocabulary, then, concepts of efficiency may be pure or mixed, limited or total.

A major purpose of this paper is to take the newest and recently most popular modes of achieving efficiency—cost-benefit analysis, systems analysis, and program budgeting—and show how much more is involved than mere economizing. I shall try to show that *even at the most modest level of cost-benefit analysis, it becomes difficult to maintain pure notions of efficiency. At a higher level, systems analysis is based on a mixed notion of efficiency. And program budgeting at the highest levels leaves pure efficiency far behind its overreaching grasp into the structure of the political system. Program budgeting, it turns out, is a form of systems analysis, that is, political systems analysis.*

These modes of analysis are neither good for nothing nor good for everything, and one cannot speak of them as wholly good or bad. It is much more useful to try to specify some conditions under which they would or would not be helpful for various purposes. While such a list could not be exhaustive at this stage, or permanent at any stage (because of advances in the art), it provides a basis for thinking about what these techniques can and cannot do. Another major purpose of this paper, therefore, is to describe cost-benefit and systems analysis and program budgeting as techniques for decision-making. I shall place particular stress upon what seems to me the most characteristic feature of all three modes of analysis: the aids to calculation designed to get around the vast areas of uncertainty where quantitative analysis leaves off and judgment begins.

II. COST-BENEFIT ANALYSIS

> . . . One can view cost-benefit analysis as anything from an infalli-
> ble means of reaching the new Utopia to a waste of resources in
> attempting to measure the unmeasureable.[1]

The purpose of cost-benefit analysis is to secure an efficient allocation of resources produced by the governmental system in its interaction with the private economy. The nature of efficiency depends on the objectives set up for government. In the field of water resources, where most of the work on cost-benefit analysis has been done, the governmental objective is usually postulated to be an increase in national income. In a crude sense, this means that the costs to whoever may incur them should be less than the benefits to whoever may receive them. The time streams of consumption gained and forgone by a project are its benefits and costs.

The aim of cost-benefit analysis is to maximize "the present value of all benefits less that of all costs, subject to specified restraints."[2] A long view is taken in that costs are estimated not only for the immediate future, but also for the life of the project. A wide view is taken in that indirect consequences for others—variously called externalities, side effects, spillovers, and repercussion effects—are considered. Ideally, all costs and benefits are evaluated. The usual procedure is to estimate the installation costs of the project and spread them over time, thus making them into something like annual costs. To these costs are added an estimate of annual operating costs. The next step involves estimating the average value of the output by considering the likely number of units produced each year and their probable value in the marketplace of the future. Intangible, "secondary," benefits may then be considered. These time streams of costs and benefits are discounted so as to obtain the present value of costs and benefits. Projects whose benefits are greater than their costs may

---

[1] A. R. Prest and R. Turvey, "Cost-Benefit Analysis: A Survey," *Economic Journal,* 75 (December 1965) : 683–75. I am much indebted to this valuable and discerning survey. I have also relied upon Otto Eckstein, "A Survey of the Theory of Public Expenditure Criteria," in National Bureau of Economic Research, *Public Finances: Needs, Sources, and Utilization* (New York: Princeton University Press, 1961), pp. 439–504; Irving K. Fox and Orris C. Herfindahl, "Attainment of Efficiency in Satisfying Demands for Water Resources," *American Economic Review,* May 1964, pp. 198–206; Charles J. Hitch, *On the Choice of Objectives in Systems Studies* (Santa Monica, Calif.: RAND Corp., 1960) ; John V. Krutilla, "Is Public Intervention in Water Resources Development Conducive to Economic Efficiency?" *Natural Resources Journal,* January 1966, pp. 60–75; John V. Krutilla and Otto Eckstein, *Multiple Purpose River Development* (Baltimore: Johns Hopkins Press, 1958) ; and Roland N. McKean, *Efficiency in Government through Systems Analysis with Emphasis on Water Resources Development* (New York: John Wiley & Sons, 1958).

[2] Prest and Turvey, "Cost-Benefit Analysis," p. 686.

then be approved, or the cost-benefit ratios may, with allowance for relative size, be used to rank projects in order of desirability.

Underlying Economic and Political Assumptions

A straightforward description of cost-benefit analysis cannot do justice to the powerful assumptions that underlie it or to the many conditions limiting its usefulness. The assumptions involve value judgments that are not always recognized and, when recognized, are not easily handled in practice. The limiting conditions arise partly out of the assumptions and partly out of severe computational difficulties in estimating costs and especially benefits. Here I can only indicate some major problems.

Cost-benefit analysis is based on superiority in the marketplace,[3] under competitive conditions and full employment, as the measure of value in society. Any imperfection in the market works against the validity of the results. Unless the same degree of monopoly were found throughout the economy, for example, a governmental body that enjoys monopolistic control of prices or outputs would not necessarily make the same investment decisions it would under free competition. A similar difficulty occurs where the size of a project is large in comparison with the economy, as in some developing nations. The project itself then affects the constellation of relative prices and production against which its efficiency is measured. The assumption based on the classical full-employment model is also important because it gives prices special significance. Where manpower is not being utilized, projects may be justified in part as putting this unused resource to work.

The economic model on which cost-benefit analysis depends for its validity is based on a political theory. The idea is that in a free society the economy is to serve the individual's consistent preferences revealed and rationally pursued in the marketplace. Governments are not supposed to dictate preferences or make decisions. The Grand Inquisitor is out.

This individualist theory assumes as valid the current distribution of income. Preferences are valued in the marketplace where votes are based on disposable income. Governmental action to achieve efficiency, therefore, inevitably carries with it consequences for the distribution of income. Projects of different size and location and composition will transfer income in different amounts to different people. While economists might estimate the redistributive consequences of various projects, they cannot, on efficiency grounds, specify one or another as preferable. How is this serious problem to be handled?

Benefit-cost analysis is a way of trying to promote economic welfare. But whose welfare? No one knows how to deal with interpersonal comparisons of

---

[3] In many important areas of policy such as national defense it is not possible to value the product directly in the marketplace. Since benefits cannot be valued in the same way as costs, it is necessary to resort to a somewhat different type of analysis. Instead of cost-benefit analysis, therefore, the work is usually called cost-effectiveness or cost-utility analysis.

utility. It cannot be assumed that the desirability of rent supplements versus a highway or dam can be measured on a single utility scale. There is no scientific way to compare losses and gains among different people or to say that the marginal loss of a dollar to one man is somehow equal to the gain of a dollar by another. The question of whose utility function is to prevail (the analyst's or that of the people involved, the upstream gainers' or the down-stream losers', the direct beneficiaries' or the taxpayers', that of the entire nation or a particular region, and so on) is of prime importance in making public policy.

The literature on welfare economics is notably unable to specify an objective welfare function.[4] Ideally, actions would benefit everyone and harm no one. As an approximation, the welfare economist views as optimal an action that leaves some people better off and none worse off. If this criterion were applied in political life, it would result in a situation like that of the Polish Diet, in which anyone who was damaged could veto legislation. To provide a way out of this impasse, Hicks and Kaldor proposed approval of decisions if the total gain in welfare were such that the winners could compensate the losers. But formal machinery for compensation does not ordinarily exist, and most modern economists are highly critical of the major political mechanism for attempting to compensate: log-rolling in Congress on public-works projects.[5] It is a very imperfect mechanism for assuring that losers in one instance become winners in another.

Another way of dealing with income distribution is to accept a criterion laid down by a political body and maximize present benefits less costs subject to this constraint. Or the cost-benefit analyst can present a series of alternatives differing according to the individuals who pay and prices charged. The analyst must compute not only the new inputs and outputs, but also the costs and benefits for each group with which the public authorities are especially concerned. No wonder this is not often done! Prest and Turvey are uncertain whether such a procedure is actually helpful in practice.[6]

Income redistribution in its most extreme form would result in a complete leveling or equality of incomes. Clearly, this is not what is meant. A

---

[4] A. Bergson, "A Reformulation of Certain Aspects of Welfare Economics," *Quarterly Journal of Economics*, February 1938; N. Kaldor, "Welfare Propositions and Interpersonal Comparisons of Utility," *Economic Journal*, 1939, pp. 549–52; J. R. Hicks, "The Valuation of Social Income," *Economica*, 1940, pp. 105–24; I. M. D. Little, *A Critique of Welfare Economics* (New York: Oxford University Press, 1950); W. J. Baumol, *Welfare Economics and the Theory of the State* (Cambridge: Harvard University Press, 1952); T. Scitovsky, "A Note on Welfare Propositions in Economics," *Review of Economic Studies*, 1942, pp. 98–110; J. E. Meade, *The Theory of International Economic Policy*, vol. 2: *Trade and Welfare* (New York: Oxford University Press, 1954).

[5] For a different view, see James M. Buchanan and Gordon Tullock, *The Calculus of Consent: Logical Foundations of Constitutional Democracy* (Ann Arbor: University of Michigan Press, 1962).

[6] Prest and Turvey, "Cost-Benefit Analysis," p. 702. For a contrary view, see Arthur Maass, "Benefit-Cost Analysis: Its Relevance to Public Investment Decisions," *Quarterly Journal of Economics*, 80 (May 1966): 208–26.

more practical meaning might be the redistribution of income to the point where specific groups achieve a certain minimum. It is also possible that the operational meaning of income redistribution may simply be the transfer of some income from some haves to some have-nots. Even in the last and most minimal sense of the term it is by no means clear that projects that are inefficient by the usual economic criteria serve to redistribute income in the desired direction. It is possible that some inefficient projects may transfer income from poorer to richer people. Before the claim that certain projects are justified by the effect of distributing income in a specified way can be accepted, an analysis to show that this is what actually happens must be at hand.

Since the distribution of income is at stake, it is not surprising that beneficiaries tend to dominate investment decisions in the political arena and steadfastly refuse to pay for what they receive from government tax revenues. They uniformly resist user charges based on benefits received. Fox and Herfindahl estimate that of a total initial investment of $3 billion for the Corps of Engineers in 1962, taxpayers in general would pay close to two-thirds of the costs.[7] Here, greater use of the facilities by a larger number of beneficiaries getting something for nothing inflates the estimated benefits that justify the project in the first place. There may be a political rationale for these decisions, but it has not been developed.

In addition to redistributing income, public works projects have a multitude of objectives and consequences. Projects may generate economic growth, alleviate poverty among some people, provide aesthetic enjoyment and opportunities for recreation, improve public health, reduce the risks of natural disaster, alter travel patterns, affect church attendance, change educational opportunities, and more. No single welfare criterion can encompass these diverse objectives. How many of them should be considered? Which are susceptible of quantification? The further one pursues this analysis, the more impassable the thicket.

LIMITATIONS IN THE UTILITY OF COST-BENEFIT ANALYSIS

One possible conclusion is that at present certain types of cost-benefit analysis are not meaningful. In reviewing the literature on the calculus of costs and benefits in research and development, for example, Prest and Turvey comment on "the uncertainty and unreliability of cost estimates . . . and . . . the extraordinarily complex nature of the benefits. . . ."[8]

Another conclusion is that one should be cautious in distinguishing the degree to which projects are amenable to cost-benefit analysis.

> . . . When there are many diverse types of benefits from a project and/or many different beneficiaries it is difficult to list them all and to avoid double counting. This is one reason why it is so much

---

[7] Fox and Herfindahl, "Attainment of Efficiency," p. 200.
[8] Prest and Turvey, "Cost-Benefit Analysis," p. 727.

easier to apply cost-benefit analysis to a limited purpose development, say, than it is to the research and development aspects of
some multi-purpose discovery, such as a new type of plastic
material. . . . It is no good expecting those fields in which benefits
are widely diffused, and in which there are manifest divergences
between accounting and economic costs or benefits, to be as culti-
vable as others. Nor is it realistic to expect that comparisons between
projects in entirely different branches of economic activity are likely
to be as meaningful or fruitful as those between projects in the same
branch. The technique is more useful in the public-utility area than
in the social-services area of government.[9]

If the analysis is to be useful at all, calculations must be simplified.[10] The
multiple ramifications of interesting activities can be taken into account only
at the cost of introducing fantastic complexities. Prest and Turvey remark of
one such attempt, "This system . . . requires knowledge of all the demand
and supply equations in the economy, so is scarcely capable of application by
road engineers."[11] They suggest omitting consideration where (1) side effects
are judged not terribly large or where (2) concern for these effects belongs to
another governmental jurisdiction.[12]

If certain costs or benefits are deemed important but cannot be quantified, it is always possible to guess. The increasing use of recreation and
aesthetic facilities to justify public works projects in the United States is
disapproved by most economists because there can be a vast but hidden
inflation of these benefits. For example, to attribute the same value to a
recreation day on a reservoir located in a desert miles from any substitute
source of water as to a day on an artificial lake in the heart of natural lake
country is patently wrong. Economists would prefer to see recreation facilities
listed in an appendix so that they can be taken into account in some sense, or
alternatively, that the project be presented with and without the recreation
facilities, so that a judgment can be made as to whether the additional
services are worth the cost.[13]

Economists distinguish between risk, where the precise outcome cannot
be predicted but a probability distribution can be specified, and uncertainty,

---

[9] *Ibid.*, pp. 729, 731.

[10] David Braybrooke and Charles Lindblom, *A Strategy of Decision* (New York:
Free Press, 1963).

[11] Prest and Turvey, "Cost-Benefit Analysis," p. 714.

[12] *Ibid.*, p. 705.

[13] See Jack L. Knetch, "Economics of Including Recreation as a Purpose of Water
Resource Projects," *Journal of Farm Economics*, December 1964, p. 1155. No one living in
Berkeley, where a "view" contributes to the cost of housing, could believe that aesthetic
values are forever going to remain beyond the ingenuity of the quantifier. There are also
costs and benefits, such as the saving and losing of human life, which can be quantified
but can be valued in the marketplace only in a most peculiar (or ghoulish) sense. See
Burton Weisbrod, *The Economics of Public Health: Measuring the Economic Impact of
Diseases* (Philadelphia: University of Pennsylvania Press, 1961), for a creative attempt to
place a market value on human life. Few of us would want to make decisions about public
health by use of this criterion—not, at least, if we were the old person whose future
social-value contribution is less than his cost to the authorities.

where one does not even know the parameters of the outcomes. The cost-benefit analyst must learn to live with uncertainty, for he can never know whether all relevant objectives have been included and what changes may occur in policy and in technology.

It is easy enough to cut the life of the project below its expected economic life. The interest rate can be raised. Assumptions can be made that costs will be higher and benefits lower than expected. All these methods, essentially conservative, are also highly arbitrary. They can be made somewhat more systematic, however, by sensitivity analysis, in which length of life, for instance, is varied over a series of runs so that its impact on the project can be appraised.

Lessening uncertainty by hiking the interest or discount rate leads to greater difficulties, for the dominance of "higher" criteria over economic analysis is apparent in the frustrating problem of choosing the correct interest rate at which to discount the time streams of costs and benefits essential to the enterprise. Only an interest rate can establish the relationship between values at different periods of time. Yet people differ in preferences for the present versus the intermediate or long-run value. Moreover, the interest rate should also measure the opportunity cost of private capital that could be used to produce wealth elsewhere in the economy if it had not been used up in the form of tax income spent on the project under consideration. Is the appropriate rate the very low cost the government charges, the cost of a government corporation like TVA which must pay a somewhat higher rate, the going rate of interest for private firms, or an even higher rate to hedge against an uncertain future? As Otto Eckstein has observed, ". . . the choice of interest rates must remain a value judgment."[14]

If the efficiency of a project is insensitive to interest costs, then these costs can vary widely without mattering much. But Fox and Herfindahl discovered that if projects of the Corps of Engineers raised their interest (or discount) rate from $2\frac{5}{8}$ to 4, 6, or 8 percent, then 9, 64, and 80 percent of the projects, respectively, would have had a benefit-cost ratio of less than unity.[15] This single value choice among many has such large consequences that it alone may be decisive.

THE MIXED RESULTS OF COST-BENEFIT ANALYSIS

Although cost-benefit analysis presumably results in efficiency by adding the most to national income, it is shot through with political and social-value choices and surrounded by uncertainties and difficulties of computation. Whether the many noneconomic assumptions and consequences actually result in basically changing the nature of a project remains moot. Clearly, we have come a long way from pure efficiency, to verge upon mixed efficiency.

Economic analysts usually agree that all relevant factors (especially

---

[14] Eckstein, "Survey," p. 460.
[15] Fox and Herfindahl, "Attainment of Efficiency," p. 202.

nonmarket factors) cannot be squeezed into a single formula. They therefore suggest that the policy-maker, in being given the market costs and benefits of alternatives, is in effect presented with the market value he is placing on nonmarket factors. The contribution of the analyst is only one input of the decision, but the analyst may find this limited conception of his role unacceptable to others. Policy-makers may not want this kind of input; they may want *the* answer, or at least an answer they can defend on the basis of the analyst's legitimized expertise.

The dependence of cost-benefit analysis on a prior political framework does not mean that it is a useless or trivial exercise. Decisions must be made. If quantifiable economic costs and benefits are not everything, neither would a decision-maker wish to ignore them entirely. The great advantage of cost-benefit analysis, when pursued with integrity, is that some implicit judgments are made explicit and subject to analysis. Yet, for many, the omission of explicit consideration of political factors is a serious deficiency.

The experience of the Soil Conservation Service in lowering certain political costs may prove illuminating. For many years the Service struggled along with eleven major watershed projects involving big dams, great headaches, and little progress. Because the watersheds were confined to a single region, it was exceedingly difficult to generate support in Congress, particularly at appropriations time. The upstream-downstream controversies generated by these projects resulted in less than universal local approval. The SCS found itself in the direct line of fire for determining priorities in use of insufficient funds.

Compare this situation with the breakthrough that occurred when SCS developed the small watershed program. Since each facility is relatively inexpensive, many of them can be placed throughout the country, markedly increasing political support. Agreement on the local level is facilitated because much less land is flooded and side payments are easier to arrange. A judicious use of cost-benefit analysis, together with ingenious relationships with state governors, places the choice of priorities with the states and yet maintains a reasonable level of consistency by virtue of adherence to national criteria. Errors are easier to correct because the burden of calculation has been drastically reduced and experience may be more easily accumulated with a larger number of small projects.

Consider the situation in which an agency finds it desirable to achieve a geographical spread of projects in order to establish a wider base of support. Assume (with good reason) that cost-benefit criteria will not permit projects to be established in some states because the value of the land or water is too low. One can say that this is just too bad and observe the agency seeking ways around the restriction by playing up benefits, playing down costs, or attacking the whole benefit-cost concept as inapplicable. Another approach would be to recognize that federalism—meaning, realistically, the distribution of indulgences to state units—represents a political value worth promoting to some extent and that gaining nationwide support is important. From this perspective, a compromise solution would be to except one or two projects in each state or region from meeting the full requirement of the formula, though the projects with the highest benefit-cost ratio would have to be chosen. In return for sacrificing full adherence to the formula in a few instances, one would get enhanced support for it in many others.

Everyone knows, of course, that cost-benefit analysis is not the messiah come to save water-resources projects from contamination by the rival forces of ignorance and political corruption. Whenever agencies and their associated interests discover that they cannot do what they want, they may twist prevailing criteria out of shape: two projects may be joined so that both qualify when one, standing alone, would not. Costs and benefits may be manipulated, or the categories may be so extended that almost any project qualifies. On the other hand, cost-benefit analysis has some "good" political uses that might be stressed more than they have been. The technique gives the responsible official a good reason for turning down projects, with a public-interest explanation the congressman can use with his constituents and the interest-group leader with his members.

This is not to say that cost-benefit analysis has little utility. Assuming that the method will continue to be improved, and that one accepts the market as the measure of economic value, it can certainly tell decision-makers something about what they will be giving up if they follow alternative policies. The use of two analyses, one based on regional and the other on national factors, might result in an appraisal of the economic costs of federalism.

The burden of calculation may be reduced by following cost-benefit analysis for many projects and introducing other values only for a few. To expect, however, that the method itself (which distributes indulgences to some and deprivations to others) will not be subject to manipulation in the political process is to say that we shall be governed by formulas and not by men.

Because the cost-benefit formula does not always jibe with political realities—that is, it omits political costs and benefits—we can expect it to be twisted out of shape from time to time. Yet cost-benefit analysis may still be important in getting rid of the worst projects. Avoiding the worst when one can't get the best is no small accomplishment.

III. SYSTEMS ANALYSIS

The good systems analyst is a *chochem*, a Yiddish word meaning "wise man," with overtones of "wise guy." His forte is creativity. Although he sometimes relates means to ends and fits ends to match means, he ordinarily eschews such pat processes, preferring instead to relate elements imaginatively into new systems that create their own means and ends. He plays new objectives continuously against cost elements until a creative synthesis has been achieved. He looks down upon those who say that they take objectives as given, knowing full well that the apparent solidity of the objective will dissipate during analysis and that, in any case, most people do not know what they want because they do not know what they can get.

Since no one knows how to teach creativity, daring, and nerve, it is not surprising that no one can define what systems analysis is or how it should be practiced. E. S. Quade, who compiled the RAND Corporation lectures on systems analysis, says it "is still largely a form of art" in which it is not possible to lay down "fixed rules which need only be followed with exactness."[16] He examined systems studies to determine ideas and principles common to the good ones, but discovered that "no universally accepted set of ideas existed. It was even difficult to decide which studies should be called good."[17]

Systems analysis is derived from operations research, which came into use during World War II when some scientists discovered that they could use simple quantitative analysis to get the most out of existing military equipment. A reasonably clear objective was given, and ways to cut the cost of achieving it could be developed, using essentially statistical models. Operations research today is largely identified with specific techniques: linear programming, Monte Carlo (randomizing) methods, gaming and game theory. While there is no hard and fast division between operations research and systems analysis, a rough separation may perhaps be made. The less that is known about objectives, the more they conflict, the larger the number of elements to be considered, the more uncertain the environment, the more likely it is that the work will be called a systems analysis. In systems analysis there is more judgment and intuition and less reliance on quantitative methods than in operations research.

Systems analysis builds models that abstract from reality but represent the crucial relationships. The systems analyst first decides what questions are relevant to his inquiry, selects certain quantifiable factors, cuts down the list of factors to be dealt with by aggregation and by eliminating the (hopefully) less important ones, and then gives them quantitative relationships with one another within the system he has chosen for analysis. But crucial variables may not be quantifiable. If they can be reduced to numbers, there may be no mathematical function that can express the desired relationship. More important, there may be no single criterion for judging results among conflicting objectives. Most important, the original objectives, if any, may not make sense.

It cannot be emphasized too strongly that a (if not the) distinguishing characteristic of systems analysis is that the objectives either are not known or are subject to change. Systems analysis, Quade tells us, "is associated with that class of problems where the difficulties lie in deciding what ought to be done—not simply how to do it—and honors go to people who . . . find out what the problem is."[18] Charles Hitch, former comptroller of the Defense Department, insists that:

> . . . learning about objectives is one of the chief objects of this kind of analysis. We must learn to look at objectives as critically

[16] E. S. Quade, ed., *Analysis for Military Decisions* (Chicago: Rand McNally, 1964), p. 153.

[17] *Ibid.*, p. 149.

[18] *Ibid.*, p. 7.

and as professionally as we look at our models and our other inputs. We may, of course, begin with tentative objectives, but we must expect to modify or replace them as we learn about the systems we are studying—and related systems. The feedback on objectives may in some cases be the most important results of our study. We have never undertaken a major system study at RAND in which we are able to define satisfactory objectives at the beginning of the study.[19]

Systems analysts recognize many good reasons for their difficulties in defining problems or objectives. Quade reaches the core: "Objectives are not, in fact, agreed upon. The choice, while ostensibly between alternatives, is really between objectives or ends and non-analytic methods must be used for a final reconciliation of views."[20] It may be comforting to believe that objectives come to the analyst from on high and can be taken as given, but this easy assumption is all wrong. "For all sorts of good reasons that are not about to change," says Hitch, "official statements of national objectives (or company objectives) tend to be nonexistent or so vague and literary as to be non-operational."[21] Objectives are not only likely to be "thin and rarefied," according to Wohlstetter, "but the relevant authorities are likely to conflict. Among others there will be national differences within an alliance and within the nation, interagency, interservice, and intraservice differences. . . ."[22]

Moreover, even shared objectives often conflict with one another. Deterrence of atomic attack might be best served by letting an enemy know that we would respond with an all-out, indiscriminate attack on his population. Defense of our population against death and destruction might not be well served by this strategy,[23] as the Secretary of Defense recognized when he recommended a city-avoidance strategy that might give an enemy some incentive to spare our cities as well. Not only are objectives large in number and in conflict with one another, but they are likely to engender serious repercussion effects. Many objectives, like morale and the stability of alliances, are resistant to quantification. What is worth doing depends on whether it can be done at all, how well, and at what cost. Hence, objectives really cannot be taken as given; they must be made up by the analyst. "In fact," Wohlstetter declares, "we are always in the process of choosing and modifying both means and ends."[24]

Future systems analysts are explicitly warned not to let clients determine objectives. A suggestive analogy is drawn with the doctor who would not ignore a patient's "description of the symptoms, but . . . cannot allow the

---

[19] Hitch, *Choice of Objectives*, p. 19.

[20] Quade, *Analysis*, p. 176.

[21] Hitch, *Choice of Objectives*, pp. 4–5.

[22] Albert Wohlstetter, "Analysis and Design of Conflict Systems," in Quade, *Analysis*, p. 121.

[23] See Glenn H. Snyder, *Deterrence and Defense* (Princeton, N.J.: Princeton University Press, 1961).

[24] Wohlstetter, "Analysis and Design," p. 122.

patient's self diagnosis to override his own professional judgment."[25] Quade argues that since systems analysis has often resulted in changing the original objectives of the policy-maker, it would be "self-defeating to accept without inquiry" his "view of what the problem is."[26]

I have stressed the point that the systems analyst is advised to insist on his own formulation of the problem because it shows so clearly that we are dealing with a mixed concept of efficiency. Objectives are being changed. It may still be the case that if you build a better mousetrap the world will beat a path to your door. But it is apparently advisable for the wary sponsor to make sure he has not got a cheaper way to catch mountain lions in his basement.

Adjusting objectives to resources in the present or near future is difficult enough without considering future states of affairs which hold tremendous uncertainty. Constants become variables; little can be taken for granted. The rate of technological progress, an opponent's estimate of your reaction to his latest series of moves based on his reaction to yours, whether or not atomic war will occur, what it will be like, whether we shall have warning, whether the system we are working on will cost anything close to current estimates and whether it will be ready within five years of the due date—on most of these matters there are no objective probabilities to be calculated.

An effective way of dealing with uncertainty must be a major goal of systems analysis. Systems analysis is characterized by the aids to calculation it uses, not to conquer uncertainty, but to circumvent and mitigate some of its pervasive effects. Before a seemingly important factor may be omitted, for example, a sensitivity analysis may be run to determine whether its variation significantly affects the outcome. If there is no good basis for calculating the value of the factor, arbitrary values may be assigned to test for extreme possibilities. Contingency analysis is used to determine how the relative ranking of alternatives holds up under major changes in the environment, say, a new alliance between France and Russia, or alternations in the criteria for judging the alternatives, such as a requirement that a system work well against attacks from space as well as from earth. Contingency analysis places a premium on versatility, as the analyst seeks a system that will hold up well under various eventualities even though it might be quite as good for any single contingency as an alternative system. Adversary procedures may be used to combat uncertainty. Bending over backward to provide advantages for low-ranking systems and handicaps for high-ranking systems is called a fortiori analysis. Changing crucial assumptions in order to make the leading alternatives even, so that one can judge whether the assumptions are overly optimistic or pessimistic, is called break-even analysis.[27] Since all these meth-

---

[25] Quade, *Analysis*, p. 157. Quade attempts to soften the blow by saying that businessmen and military officers know more about their business than anyone else. But the import of the analogy is clear enough.

[26] *Ibid.*, pp. 156–57.

[27] Herman Kahn and Irwin Mann believe that *"More than any single thing*, the skilled use of a fortiori and break-even analyses separates the professionals from the amateurs" (*Techniques of Systems Analysis* [Santa Monica, Calif.: RAND Corp., 1957]).

ods add greatly to the burden of calculation, they must be used with some discretion.

A variety of insurance schemes may also be used to deal with uncertainty. In appraising what an opponent can do, for instance, one can assume the worst, the best, and sheer inertia. In regard to the development of weapons, insurance requires not one flexible weapon, but a variety of alternatives pursued with vigor. As development goes on, uncertainty is reduced. Consequently, basic strategic choice involves determining how worthwhile it is to pay for the additional information by developing rival weapons systems to the next stage. The greater the uncertainty of the world, the greater the desirability of having the widest selection of alternative weapons to choose from to meet unexpected threats and opportunities. Alchian and Kessel are so wedded to the principle of diversified investment that they "strongly recommend this theorem as a basic part of systems analysis."[28]

As a form of calculation, systems analysis represents a merger of quantitative methods and rules of thumb. First, the analyst attempts to solve the problem before he knows a great deal about it. Then he continuously alters his initial solution to get closer to what he intuitively feels ought to be wanted. Means and ends are continuously played off against one another. New objectives are defined, new assumptions made, new models constructed, until a creative amalgam appears which hopefully defines a second-best solution, one that is better than others even if not optimal in any sense. In the famous study of the location of military bases conducted by Albert Wohlstetter and his associates at the RAND Corporation, widely acknowledged as a classic example of systems analysis, Wohlstetter writes:

> The base study . . . proceeded by a method of successive approximations. It compared forces for their efficiency in carrying a payload between the bases and targets without opposition either by enemy interceptors or enemy bombers. Then, it introduced obstacles successively: first, enemy defense; then enemy bombardment of our bombers and other elements needed to retaliate. In essence, then, the alternative systems were tested for their first-strike capability and then they were compared for their second-strike capacity. And the programmed system performed in a drastically different way, depending on the order in which the opposing side struck. In the course of analyzing counter-measures and counter-counter-measures, the enemy bombardment turned out to be a dominant problem. This was true even for a very much improved overseas operating base system. The refueling base system was very much less sensitive to strike order. It is only the fact that strike order made such a difference among systems contemplated that gave the first-strike, second-strike distinction an interest. And it was not known in advance of the analysis that few of the programmed bombers would

They think that convincing others that you have a good solution is as important as coming up with one.

[28] Armen A. Alchian and Reuben A. Kessel, *A Proper Role of Systems Analysis* (Santa Monica, Calif.: RAND Corp., 1954), p. 9.

have survived to encounter the problem of penetrating enemy defenses which had previously been taken as the main obstacle. The analysis, then, not only was affected by the objectives considered, it affected them.[29]

The advantage of a good systems study is that when the analysis is run through in theory on paper, certain disadvantages of learning from experience may be avoided.

If the complexity of the problems encountered proved difficult in cost-benefit analysis, the burdens of calculation are ordinarily much greater in systems analysis. Many aspects of a problem simply must be put aside. Only a few variables can be considered simultaneously. "Otherwise," Roland McKean tells us, "the models would become impossibly cumbersome, and . . . the number of calculations to consider would mount in the thousands."[30] Formulas that include everything may appear more satisfactory, but those that cannot be reduced "to a single expression are likely to convey no meaning at all. . . ."[31] Summing up their experience, Hitch and McKean assert that:

> . . . analyses must be piecemeal, since it is impossible for a single analysis to cover all problems of choice simultaneously in a large organization. Thus comparisons of alternative courses of action always pertain to a part of the government's (or corporation's) problem. Other parts of the over-all problem are temporarily put aside, possible decisions about some matters being ignored, specific decisions about others being taken for granted. The resulting analyses are intended to provide assistance in finding optimal, or at least good, solutions to subproblems: in the jargon of systems and operations research, they are suboptimizations.[32]

Although admitting that much bad work is carried on and that inordinate love of numbers and machines often gets in the way of creative work,[33] practitioners of systems analysis believe in their art. "All of them point out how the use of analysis can provide some of the knowledge needed, how it may sometimes serve as a substitute for experience, and, most importantly, how it can work to sharpen intuition."[34] Systems analysis can increase explicitness about the assumptions made and about exclusions from the analysis. The claim is that systems analysis can be perfected; sheer intuition or unaided judgment can never be perfect.

---

[29] Wohlstetter, "Analysis and Design," pp. 125–26.

[30] McKean, "Criteria," in Quade, *Analysis*, p. 83.

[31] Quade, *Analysis*, p. 310.

[32] Charles J. Hitch and Roland N. McKean, *The Economics of Defense in the Nuclear Age* (Cambridge: Harvard University Press, 1961), p. 161.

[33] See Hitch on "Mechanitis—putting . . . machines to work as a substitute for hard thinking" ("Economics and Operations Research: A Symposium. II," *Review of Economics and Statistics*, August 1958, p. 209).

[34] Quade, *Analysis*, p. 12.

Yet there is also wide agreement that systems analysts "do philosophy,"[35] that they are advocates of particular policy alternatives. What Schelling calls "the pure role of expert advisor" is not available for the analyst, who "must usually formulate the questions themselves for his clients."[36] Beyond that, Wohlstetter argues that systems analysts can perform the function of integrating diverse values. New systems can sometimes be found that meet diverse objectives.[37] The politician who gains his objectives by inventing policies that also satisfy others, or the leader of a coalition who searches out areas of maximum agreement, performs a kind of informal systems analysis.

All these men, however, work within the existing political structure. While cost-benefit analysis may contain within it implicit changes in existing governmental policies, it poses no direct challenge to the general decision-making machinery of the political system. Program budgeting is a form of systems analysis that attempts to break out of these confines.

IV. PROGRAM BUDGETING

It is always important, and perhaps especially so in economics, to avoid being swept off one's feet by the fashions of the moment.[38]
So this new system will identify our national goals with precision . . .[39]

On August 25, 1965, President Johnson announced that he was asking the heads of all federal agencies to introduce "a very new and revolutionary system" of program budgeting. Staffs of experts set up in each agency would define goals using "modern methods of program analysis." Then the "most effective and the least costly" way to accomplish these goals would be found.[40]

Program budgeting has no standard definition. The general idea is that budgetary decisions should be made by focusing on output categories like governmental goals, objectives, end products, or programs, instead of inputs like personnel, equipment, and maintenance. As in cost-benefit analysis, to which it owes a great deal, program budgeting lays stress on estimating the total financial cost of accomplishing objectives. What is variously called cost-effectiveness or cost-utility analysis is employed in order to select "alternative approaches to the achievement of a benefit already determined to be worth achieving."[41]

Not everyone would go along with the most far-reaching implications of

---

[35] *Ibid.*, p. 5.

[36] T. C. Schelling, "Economics and Operations Research: A Symposium. V. Comment," *Review of Economics and Statistics*, August 1958, p. 222.

[37] Wohlstetter, "Analysis and Design," p. 122.

[38] Prest and Turvey, "Cost-Benefit Analysis," p. 684.

[39] President Lyndon Johnson, quoted in *Program Budgeting*, ed. David Novick (Cambridge: Harvard University Press, 1965), p. vi.

[40] *Ibid.*, pp. v–vi.

[41] Alan Dean, quoted in *ibid.*, p. 311.

program budgeting, but the RAND Corporation version, presumably exported from the Defense Department, definitely does include "institutional reorganization to bring relevant administrative functions under the jurisdiction of the authority making the final program decisions." In any event, there would be "information reporting systems and shifts in the power structure to the extent necessary to secure compliance with program decisions by the agencies responsible for their execution."[42] Sometimes it appears that comprehensiveness—simultaneous and complete examination of all programs and all alternatives to programs every year—is being advocated. Actually, comprehensiveness has been dropped (though not without regret) because "it may be too costly in time, effort, uncertainty, and confusion."[43] There exists considerable ambivalence as to whether decisions are implicit in the program categories or merely provide information to improve the judgment of governmental officials.

Programs are not made in heaven. There is nothing out there that is just waiting to be found. Programs are not natural to the world; they must be imposed on it by men. No one can give instructions for making up programs. There are as many ways to conceive of programs as there are of organizing activity,[44] as the comments of the following writers eloquently testify:

> It is by no means obvious . . . whether a good program structure should be based on components of specific end objectives (e.g. the accomplishment of certain land reclamation targets), on the principle of cost separation (identifying as a program any activity the costs of which can be readily segregated), on the separation of means and ends (Is education a means or an end in a situation such as skill-retraining courses for workers displaced by automation?), or on some artificially designed pattern that draws from all these and other classification criteria.[45]

> Just what categories constitute the most useful programs and program elements is far from obvious. . . . If one puts all educational activities into a broad package of educational programs, he cannot simultaneously include school lunch programs or physical education activities in a Health Program, or include defense educational activities (such as the military academies) in the Defense Program. . . . In short, precisely how to achieve a rational and useful structure for a program budget is not yet evident.[46]

---

[42] Roland N. McKean and Melvin Anshen in *ibid.*, pp. 286–87. The authors say that this aspect of program budgeting is part of the general view adopted in the book as a whole.

[43] Arthur Smithies in *ibid.*, p. 45.

[44] A look at the classic work by Luther Gulick and Lyndall Urwick, *Papers on the Science of Administration* (New York: Columbia University Press, 1937), reveals considerable similarity between their suggested bases of organization and ways of conceptualizing programs.

[45] Anshen in *Program Budgeting*, pp. 19–20.

[46] G. A. Steiner in *ibid.*, p. 356.

In much current discussion it seems to be taken for granted
that transportation is a natural program category. But that conclusion is by no means obvious.[47]

A first question one might ask is whether, given their nature,
health activities merit a separate, independent status in a program
budget. The question arises because these activities often are constituents of, or inputs into, other activities whose purpose or goal
orientation is the dominating one. Outlays by the Department of
Defense for hospital care, for example, though they assist in maintaining the health of one segment of the population, are undertaken
on behalf of national defense, and the latter is their justification.[48]

The difficulties with the program concept are illustrated in the space
program. A first glance suggests that space projects are ideally suited for
program budgeting because they appear as physical systems designed to
accomplish various missions. Actually, there is a remarkable degree of interdependence between different missions and objectives—pride, scientific research, space exploration, military uses, etc.—so that it is impossible to
apportion costs on a proper basis. Consider the problem of a rocket developed
for one mission and useful for others. To apportion costs to each new mission
is purely arbitrary. To allocate the cost to the first mission and regard the
rocket as a free good for all subsequent missions is ludicrous. The only
remotely reasonable alternative—making a separate program out of the rocket
itself—does violence to the concept of programs as end products. The difficulty is compounded because the facilities that have multiple uses, like
boosters and tracking networks, tend to be very expensive compared to the
items that are specific to a particular mission.[49] Simple concepts of programs
evaporate upon inspection.

Political realities lie behind the failure to devise principles for defining
programs. As Melvin Anshen puts it, "The central issue is, of course, nothing
less than the definition of the ultimate objectives of the Federal government as
they are realized through operational decisions." The arrangement of the
programs inevitably affects the specific actions taken to implement them. "Set
in this framework," Anshen continues, "the designation of a schedule of
programs may be described as building a bridge between a matter of political
philosophy (what is government for?) and . . . assigning scarce resources
among alternative governmental objectives."[50]

Because program budgeting is a form of systems analysis (and uses a
form of cost-benefit analysis), the conditions that hinder or facilitate its use
have largely been covered in the previous sections. The simpler the problem,

---

[47] Smithies in *ibid.*, p. 41.

[48] Marvin Frankel in *ibid.*, pp. 219–20. I have forborne citing the author who
promises exciting discussion of the objectives of American education and ends up with
fascinating program categories like primary, secondary, and tertiary education.

[49] See the excellent chapter by M. A. Margolis and S. M. Barro in *ibid.*, pp. 120–45.

[50] In *ibid.*, p. 18.

the fewer the interdependencies, the greater the ability to measure the consequences of alternatives on a common scale, the more costs and benefits that
are valued in the marketplace, the better the chances of making effective use
of programs. Let us take transportation to illustrate some of the conditions in
a specific case.

Investments in transportation are highly interdependent with one another
(planes versus cars versus trains versus barges, etc.) and with decisions
regarding the regional location of industry and the movements of population.
In view of the powerful effects of transportation investment on regional
employment, income, and competition with other modes of transport, it
becomes necessary to take these factors into account. The partial equilibrium
model of efficiency in the narrow sense becomes inappropriate and a general
equilibrium model of the economy must be used. The combination of aggregative models at the economy-wide level and interregion and interindustry
models that this approach requires is staggering. It is precisely the limited
and partial character of cost-effectiveness analyses, taking so much for
granted and eliminating many variables, that make them easy to work with
for empirical purposes. Furthermore, designing a large-scale transportation
system involves so close a mixture of political and economic considerations
that it is not possible to disentangle them. The Interstate Highway Program,
for example, involved complex bargaining among federal, state, and local
governments and reconciliation of many conflicting interests. The development of certain "backward" regions; improvement in the flow of defense
supplies; redistribution of income, creating countervailing power against
certain monopolies; not to mention the political needs of public officials—all
these were involved. While cost-utility exercises might help with small segments of the problem, J. R. Meyer concludes that, "Given the complexity of
the political and economic decisions involved, and the emphasis on designing
a geographically consistent system, it probably would be difficult to improve
on the congressional process as a means of developing such a program in an
orderly and systematic way."[51]

On one condition for effective use—reorganization of the federal government to centralize authority for wide-ranging programs—proponents of program budgeting are markedly ambivalent. The problem is that responsibility
for programs is now scattered throughout the whole federal establishment and
decentralized to state and local authorities as well. In the field of health, for
example, expenditures are distributed among at least twelve agencies and six
departments outside of Health, Education, and Welfare. A far greater number
of organizations are concerned with American activities abroad, with natural
resources, and with education. The multiple jurisdictions and overlapping
responsibilities do violence to the concept of comprehensive and consistent
programs. It "causes one to doubt," Marvin Frankel writes, "whether there
can exist in the administrative echelons the kind of overall perspective that
would seem indispensable if Federal health resources are to be rationally

---

[51] In *ibid.*, p. 170. This paragraph is based on my interpretation of Meyer's work.

allocated."[52] To G. A. Steiner it is evident that "the present 'chest of drawers' type of organization cannot for long be compatible with program budgeting."[53] W. Z. Hirsch declares that "if we are to have effective program budgeting of natural resources activities, we shall have to provide for new institutional arrangements."[54] Yet the inevitable resistance to wholesale reorganization would be so great that, if it were deemed essential, it might well doom the enterprise. Hence the hope is expressed that translation grids or crossover networks could be used to convert program budget decisions back into the usual budget categories in the usual agencies. That is what is done in Defense, but that department has the advantage of having most of the activities it is concerned with under the Secretary's jurisdiction. Some program analysts believe that this solution will not do.

Recognizing that a conversion scheme is technically feasible, Anshen is aware that there are "deeply frustrating" issues to be resolved. "The heart of the problem is the fact that the program budget in operation should not be a mere statistical game. Great strategic importance will attach to both the definition of program structure and content and the establishment of specific program objectives (including magnitude, timing, and cost)."[55] The implications of program budgeting, however, go far beyond specific policies.

It will be useful to distinguish between policy politics (which policy will be adopted?), partisan politics (which political party will win office?), and system politics (how will decision structures be set up?). Program budgeting is manifestly concerned with policy politics, and not much with partisan politics, although it could have important consequences for issues that divide the nation's parties. *My contention is that the thrust of program budgeting makes it an integral part of system politics.*

As presently conceived, program budgeting contains an extreme centralizing bias. Power is to be centralized in the Presidency (through the Budget Bureau) at the national level, in superdepartments rather than in bureaus within the executive branch, and in the federal government as a whole instead of state or local governments. Note how W. Z. Hirsch assumes the desirability of national dominance when he writes: "These methods of analysis can guide Federal officials in the responsibility of bringing local education decisions into closer harmony with national objectives."[56] G. A. Steiner observes that comprehensiveness may be affected by unrestricted federal grants in aid to the states because "such a plan would remove a substantial part of Federal expenditures from a program budgeting system of the Federal government."[57] Should there be reluctance on the part of state and local officials to employ the new tools, Anshen states "that the Federal government may employ familiar

---

[52] In *ibid.*, p. 237.
[53] In *ibid.*, p. 348.
[54] In *ibid.*, p. 280.
[55] In *ibid.*, pp. 358–59.
[56] In *ibid.*, p. 206.
[57] In *ibid.*, p. 347.

incentives to accelerate this progress."[58] Summing it up, Hirsch says that "It appears doubtful that a natural resources program budget would have much impact without a good deal of centralization."[59]

Within the great federal organizations designed to encompass the widest ramifications of basic objectives, there would have to be strong executives. Only the top executive, cutting across the subunits of the organization, could put the program budget together, as is done in the Department of Defense. A more useful tool for increasing the executive's power to control decisions vis-à-vis his subordinates would be hard to find.[60]

Would large-scale program budgeting benefit the Chief Executive? President Johnson's support of program budgeting could stem in part from his desire to appear frugal, and could also be directed at increasing his control of the executive branch by centralizing decisions in the Bureau of the Budget. In the case of foreign affairs, it is not at all clear whether it would be preferable to emphasize country teams, with the budget made by the State Department to encompass activities of the other federal agencies abroad, or to let Commerce, Agriculture, Defense, and other agencies include their foreign activities in their own budgets. Program budgeting will unleash great struggles of this kind in Washington. An especially interesting possibility is that the Bureau of the Budget might prefer to let the various agencies compete, with the Bureau coordinating (that is, controlling) these activities through a comprehensive foreign-affairs program devised only at the Presidential level.

Yet it is not entirely clear that Presidents would welcome all the implications of program budgeting. It is well and good to talk about long-range planning; it is another thing to tie a President's hands by committing him in advance for five years of expenditures. Looking ahead is fine, but not if it means that a President cannot negate the most extensive planning efforts on grounds that seem sufficient to him.[61] He may wish to trade some program budgeting for some political support.

In any event, that all decisions ought to be made by the most central person in the most centralized body capable of grabbing hold of them is difficult to justify on scientific grounds. We see what has happened. First pure efficiency was converted to mixed efficiency. Then limited efficiency became unlimited. Yet the qualifications of efficiency experts for political systems analysis are not evident.[62]

---

[58] In *ibid.*, p. 365.

[59] In *ibid.*, p. 280.

[60] See my comments to this effect in *The Politics of the Budgetary Process* (Boston: Little, Brown, 1964), p. 140. For discussion of some political consequences of program budgeting, see *ibid.*, pp. 135–42.

[61] See William H. Brown and Charles E. Gilbert, *Planning Municipal Investment: A Case Study of Philadelphia* (Philadelphia: University of Pennsylvania Press, 1961), for an excellent discussion of the desire of elected officials to remain free to shift their commitments.

[62] It may be said that I have failed to distinguish sufficiently between planning, programming, and budgeting. Planning is an orientation that looks ahead by extending costs and benefits or units of effectiveness a number of years into the future. Programming

We would be in a much stronger position to predict the consequences of program budgeting if we knew (a) how far toward a genuine program budget the Defense Department has gone and (b) whether the program budget has fulfilled its promise. To the best of my knowledge, not a single study of this important experiment was undertaken (or at least published) before the decision was made to spread it around the land. On the surface, only two of the nine program categories used in the Defense Department appear to be genuine programs in the sense of pointing to end purposes or objectives. Although strategic retaliation and continental defense appear to be distinct programs, it is difficult to separate them conceptually; my guess is that they are, in fact, considered together. The third category—general-purpose forces —is presumably designed to deal with (hopefully) limited war anywhere in the world. According to Arthur Smithies, "The threat is not clearly defined and neither are the requirements for meeting it. Clearly this program is of a very different character from the other two and does not lend itself as readily to analysis in terms either of its components or of its specific contribution to defense objectives."[63]

What about the program called airlift and sealift? These activities support the general-purpose forces. Research and development are carried on presumably to serve other defense objectives, and the same is true for the reserve forces.

No doubt the elements that make up the programs comprise the real action focus of the budget, but these may look less elegant when spread into thousands of elements than they do in nine neat rows. When one hears that hundreds of program elements are up for decision at one time,[64] he is entitled to some skepticism about how much genuine analysis can go into all of them. Part of the argument for program budgeting was that by thinking ahead and

---

is a general procedure of systems analysis employing cost-effectiveness studies. In this view program budgeting is a mere mechanical translation of the results of high-level systems studies into convenient storage in the budgetary format. No doubt systems studies could be done without converting the results into the form of a program budget. This approach may have a lot to recommend it, and it appears that it is the one that is generally followed by the Department of Defense in its presentations to Congress. But if the systems studies guide decisions as to the allocation of resources, and the studies are maintained according to particular program categories and are further legitimatized by being given status in the budget, it seems most unlikely that programming will be separated from budgeting. One is never sure whether too much or too little is being claimed for program budgeting. If all that program budgeting amounts to is a simple translation of previous systems studies into some convenient form of accounting, it hardly seems that this phenomenon is worth so much fuss. If the program categories in the budget system are meaningful, then they must be much more than a mere translation of previously reached decisions. In this case, I think that it is not my task to enlighten the proponents of program budgeting, but rather that it is their task to make themselves clear to others.

[63] In *Program Budgeting*, p. 37.

[64] See U.S. House Appropriations Committee, Subcommittee on Department of Defense Appropriations for Fiscal 1965, 88th Cong., 2nd sess., IV, p. 133. McNamara asserted that some 652 "subject issues" had been submitted to him for the fiscal 1965 budget.

working all year round it would be possible to consider changes as they came up and avoid the usual last-minute funk. Both Hitch[65] and Novick[66] (the RAND Corporation expert on defense budgeting) report, however, that this has not worked out. The services hesitate to submit changes piecemeal, and the Secretary wants to see what he is getting into before he acts. The vaunted five-year plans are still in force, but their efficacy in determining yearly decisions remains to be established.

One good operational test would be whether the Department's systems analysts actually use the figures from the five-year plans in their work or whether they go to the services for the real stuff. Another test would be whether or not the later years of the five-year projections turn out to have any future significance, or whether the battle is really over the next year that is to be scooped out as part of the budget. From a distance, it appears that the services have to work much harder to justify what they are doing. Since the Secretary's office must approve changes in defense programs, and he can insist on documentation, he is in a strong position to improve thinking at the lower levels. The intensity of conflict within the Defense Department may not have changed, but it may be that the disputants are or will in the future be likely to shout at a much more sophisticated level. How much this was due to McNamara himself, to his insistence on quantitative estimates, or to the analytic advantages of a program budget cannot be determined now. It is clear that a program budget, of which the Secretary alone is master, has helped impose his will on the Defense Department.

It should also be said that there are many notable differences between decision-making in defense and domestic policy that would render suspect the transmission of procedures from one realm to the other. The greater organizational unity of Defense, the immensely large amounts of money at stake, the extraordinarily greater risks involved, the inability to share more than minimal values with opponents, the vastly different array of interests and perceptions of the proper roles of the participants—these are but a few of the factors involved.

The Armed Services and Appropriations Committees in the defense area, for example, are normally most reluctant to substitute their judgment on defense for that of the President and the Secretary of the Department. They do not conceive it to be their role to make day-to-day defense policy, and they are apparently unwilling to take on the burden of decision. They therefore accept a budget presentation based on cavernous program categories even though these are so arranged that it is impossible to make a decision on the basis of them. If they were to ask for and to receive the discussion of alternative actions contained in the much smaller program elements on which the Secretary bases his decisions, they would be in a position to take the Department of Defense away from him.

---

[65] Hitch, *Decision Making for Defense* (Berkeley: University of California Press, 1965).

[66] Novick, *Program Budgeting*, p. 100.

There is no reason whatsoever to believe that a similar restraint would be shown by committees that deal with domestic policies. It is at least possible that the peculiar planning, programming, and budgeting system adopted in Defense could not be repeated elsewhere in the federal establishment.

V. POLITICAL RATIONALITY

Political rationality is the fundamental kind of reason, because it deals with the preservation and improvement of decision structures, and decision structures are the source of all decisions. Unless a decision structure exists, no reasoning and no decisions are possible. . . . There can be no conflict between political rationality and . . . technical, legal, social, or economic rationality, because the solution of political problems makes possible an attack on any other problem, while a serious political deficiency can prevent or undo all other problem solving. . . . Non-political decisions are reached by considering a problem in its own terms, and by evaluating proposals according to how well they solve the problem. The best available proposal should be accepted regardless of who makes it or who opposes it, and a faulty proposal should be rejected or improved no matter who makes it. Compromise is always irrational; the rational procedure is to determine which proposal is the best, and to accept it. In a political decision, on the other hand, action never is based on the merits of a proposal but always on who makes it and who opposes it. Action should be designed to avoid complete identification with any proposal and any point of view, no matter how good or how popular it might be. The best available proposal should never be accepted just because it is best; it should be deferred, objected to, discussed, until major opposition disappears. Compromise is always a rational procedure, even when the compromise is between a good and a bad proposal.[67]

We are witnessing the beginning of significant advances in the art and science of economizing. Having given up the norm of comprehensiveness, economizers are able to join quantitative analysis with aids to calculation of the kind described by Lindblom in his strategy of disjointed incrementalism.[68]

Various devices are employed to simplify calculations. Important values are omitted entirely; others are left to different authorities to whose care they have been entrusted. Here sensitivity analysis represents an advance because it provides an empirical basis to justify neglect of some values. Means and ends are hopelessly intertwined.

The real choice is between rival policies that encapsulate somewhat different mixes of means and ends. Analysis proceeds incrementally by succes-

---

[67] Paul Diesing, *Reason in Society* (Urbana: University of Illinois Press, 1962), pp. 198, 203–4, 231–32.

[68] Braybrooke and Lindblom, *Strategy for Decision.* See also Lindblom, *The Intelligence of Democracy* (New York: Free Press, 1965).

sive limited approximations. It is serial and remedial as successive attacks are made on problems. Rather than waiting upon experience in the real world, the analyst tries various moves in his model and runs them through to see if they work. When all else fails, the analyst may try an integrative solution reconciling a variety of values to some degree, though meeting none of them completely. He is always ready to settle for the second or third best, provided only that it is better than the going policy. Constrained by diverse limiting assumptions, weakened by deficiencies in technique, rarely able to provide unambiguous measures, the systems, cost-benefit, and program analyst is nonetheless getting better at calculating in the realm of efficiency. Alas, he is an imperialist at heart.

In the literature discussed above there appears several times the proposition that "the program budget is a neutral tool. It has no politics."[69] In truth, the program budget is suffused with policy politics, makes up a small part of President Johnson's partisan politics, and tends toward system politics. How could men account for so foolish a statement? It must be that they who make it identify program budgeting with something good and beautiful, and politics with something else, bad and ugly. McKean and Anshen speak of politics in terms of "pressures and expedient adjustments," "haphazard acts . . . unresponsive to a planned analysis of the needs of efficient decision design." From the political structure they expect only "resistance and opposition, corresponding to the familiar human disposition to protect established seats of power and procedures made honorable by the mere facts of existence and custom."[70] In other places we hear of "vested interests," "wasteful duplication," "special interest groups," and the "Parkinson syndrome."[71]

Not so long ago less sophisticated advocates of reform ignored the political realm. Now they denigrate it. And, since there must be a structure for decision, it is smuggled in as a mere adjunct of achieving efficiency. Who is to blame if the economic tail wags the political dog? It seems unfair to blame the evangelical economizer for spreading the gospel of efficiency. If economic efficiency turns out to be the one true religion, maybe it is because its prophets could so easily conquer.

It is hard to find men who take up the cause of political rationality, who plead the case for political man, and who are primarily concerned with the laws that enable the political machinery to keep working. One is driven to a philosopher like Paul Diesing to find the case for the political:

> . . . the political problem is always basic and prior to the others. . . . This means that any suggested course of action must be evaluated first by its effects on the political structure. A course of action which corrects economic or social deficiencies but increases political difficulties must be rejected, while an action which contrib-

[69] Anshen in *Program Budgeting*, p. 370.
[70] In *ibid.*, p. 289.
[71] *Ibid.*, p. 359.

utes to political improvement is desirable even if it is not entirely sound from an economic or social standpoint.[72]

There is hardly a political scientist who would claim half as much. The desire to invent decision structures to facilitate the achievement of economic efficiency does not suggest a full appreciation of their proper role by students of politics.

A major task of the political system is to specify goals or objectives. It is impermissible to treat goals as if they were known in advance. "Goals" may well be the product of interaction among key participants rather than some *deus ex machina* or (to use Bentley's term) some "spook" that posits values in advance of our knowledge of them. Certainly, the operational objectives of the Corps of Engineers in the water resources field could hardly be described in terms of developing rivers and harbors.

Once the political process becomes a focus of attention, it is evident that the principal participants may not be clear about their goals. What we call goals or objectives may, in large part, be operationally determined by the policies we can agree upon. The mixtures of values found in complex policies may have to be taken in packages, so that policies may determine goals at least as much as general objectives determine policies. In a political situation, then, the need for support assumes central importance. Not simply the economic, but the *political* costs and benefits turn out to be crucial.

A first attempt to specify what is meant by political costs may bring closer an understanding of the range of requirements for political rationality.[73] Exchange costs are incurred by a political leader when he needs the support of other people to get a policy adopted. He has to pay for this assistance by using up resources in the form of favors (patronage, logrolling) or coercive moves (threats or acts to veto or remove from office). By supporting a policy and influencing others to do the same, a politician antagonizes some people and may suffer their retaliation. If these hostility costs mount, they may turn into reelection costs—actions that decrease his chances (or those of his friends) of being elected or reelected to office. Election costs, in turn, may become policy costs through inability to command the necessary formal powers to accomplish the desired policy objectives.

In the manner of Neustadt, we may also talk about reputation costs, i.e., not only loss of popularity with segments of the electorate, but also loss of esteem and effectiveness with other participants in the political system and loss of ability to secure policies other than the one immediately under consideration. Those who continually urge a President to go all out—that is, use all his resources on a wide range of issues—rarely stop to consider that the price of success in one area of policy may be defeat in another. If he loses popularity with the electorate, as President Truman did, Congress may de-

---

[72] Diesing, *Reason in Society*, p. 228.
[73] I am indebted to John Harsanyi for suggestions about political rationality.

stroy almost the whole of his domestic program. If he cracks down on the steel industry, as President Kennedy did, he may find himself constrained to lean over backward in the future to avoid unremitting hostility from the business community.

A major consequence of incurring exchange and hostility costs may be undesirable power-redistribution effects. The process of getting a policy adopted or implemented may increase the power of various individuals, organizations, and social groups, which later will be used against the political leader. The power of some participants may be weakened so that the political leader is unable to enjoy their protection.

The legitimacy of the political system may be threatened by costs that involve the weakening of customary political restraints. Politicians who try to suppress opposition, or who practice election frauds, may find similar tactics being used against them. The choice of a highly controversial policy may raise the costs of civic discord. Although the people involved may not hate the political leader, the fact that they hate each other may lead to consequences contrary to his desires.

The literature of economics usually treats organizations and institutions as if they were costless entities. The standard procedure is to consider rival alternatives (in consideration of price policy or other criteria), calculate the differences in cost and achievement among them, and show that one is more or less efficient than another. This typical way of thinking is sometimes misspecified. If the costs of pursuing a policy are strictly economic and can be calculated directly in the marketplace, then the procedure should work well. But if the costs include getting one or another organization to change its policies or procedures, then these costs must also be taken into account.[74] Perhaps there are legal, psychological, or other impediments that make it either impossible or difficult for the required changes to be made. Or the changes may require great effort and result in incurring a variety of other costs. In considering a range of alternatives, one is measuring not only efficiency, but also the costs of change.

Studies based on efficiency criteria are much needed and increasingly useful. My quarrel is not with them at all, as such. I have been concerned that a single value, however important, could triumph over other values without explicit consideration being given these others. I would feel much better if political rationality were being pursued with the same vigor and capability as is economic efficiency. In that case I would have fewer qualms about extending efficiency studies into the decision-making apparatus.

---

[74] In the field of defense policy, political factors are taken into account to the extent that the studies concentrate on the design of feasible alternatives. In the choice of overseas basing, for example, the question of feasibility in relation to treaties and friendly or unfriendly relationships with other countries is considered. Thus it seems permissible to take into account political considerations originating outside the country, where differences of opinions and preferences among nations are to some extent accepted as legitimate, but apparently not differences internal to the American policy.

My purpose has not been to accuse economizers of doing what comes naturally. Rather, I have sought to emphasize that economic rationality, however laudable in its own sphere, ought not to swallow up political rationality—but will do so if political rationality continues to lack trained and adept defenders.

5

Selective Service and Military Manpower: Induction and Deferment Policies in the 1960's*

JAMES W. DAVIS, JR.
KENNETH M. DOLBEARE

More than twelve million Americans have enlisted or been inducted into the armed forces in the two decades since the end of World War II. The broad outlines of military manpower procurement policy have remained stable throughout this period: articulating with continuing direct recruiting efforts, conducted by the armed forces, is the selective conscription of men not qualifying for one of several deferred classifications, accomplished by a decentralized civilian agency. Within this basic framework, adjustments in policy applications (in response to changing circumstances) have resulted in a wide range of new accessions to the armed forces from year to year. Force levels have ranged from 1,460,000 in early 1950 to nearly 3,700,000 at the height of the Korean buildup, down to the post-Korean low of 2,476,000 in

* This paper is in every sense our joint product. The data are drawn in part from our study *Little Groups of Neighbors: The Selective Service System* (Chicago: Markham Publishing Company, 1968), and some of the tables have appeared in the *Wisconsin Law Review* (Fall 1967), to which we are indebted for permission to reprint them. The research was supported in part by the Institute for Research on Poverty pursuant to the provisions of the Economic Opportunity Act of 1964. We acknowledge our indebtedness to the Institute for its many forms of assistance, and to Barry Gaberman, James Thomas, and Marilyn Wenell for exceptional research assistance. We are also grateful for the opportunity to participate as consultants in the work of the National Advisory Commission on Selective Service, and for the very useful criticism of an earlier draft of this paper by the participants at the SSRC Committee on Governmental and Legal Processes Newagen Conference in August 1967.

1960, and back up to the mid-1967 level of 3,450,000. The rate of accessions has varied similarly, from 200,000 per year in fiscal 1950 to 1,270,000 in fiscal 1951, and from about 500,000 in 1965 to 1,200,000 in 1966. The proportions of new recruits obtained through enlistment and through induction have also varied sharply during this period, with inductions ranging from 15 percent of new accessions in 1961 to over 30 percent in 1966. The effects of conscription are felt not only by those inducted, of course: 340,000 men were inducted in 1966, for example, but of the 800,000 who enlisted, nearly half did so only after passing their preinduction physical examination.[1]

This military manpower procurement policy, including both conscription and varyingly induced enlistment, has clearly met the critical test of delivering substantial but fluctuating numbers of men to the armed forces. But this is only one effect of these policies, and many other dimensions of their impact remain to be explored. We seek to define the consequences of present conscription policies in more comprehensive fashion by asking such questions as: What happens to whom by virtue of these policies? What social and economic implications do their effects carry? To what extent are the stated goals of these policies actually realized? What would be the consequences of instituting alternative policies?

Our analysis of conscription policies will employ policy[2] as an independent variable, empirically assessing the impact of deferment and induction policies upon various types of registrants. We shall identify the effects of various components of present policy in such a manner as to permit description of the probable consequences of alternative policies for the society, economy, and polity. By taking policy as the focus of our inquiry, rather than as the dependent product of decision-making activity, we hope to indicate some possibilities of a policy-oriented approach to the study of politics. Two broad categories of potential utility seem to inhere in such an approach. First, analysis of the impact and effects of particular public policies may underscore the consequences of determinative features of the policy-forming process; it may shed new light on the reasons for the political behavior of those affected

---

[1] Lieutenant General Lewis B. Hershey, director of Selective Service, in testimony before the House Armed Services Committee, June 22, 1966, reported in *Review of the Administration and Operation of the Selective Service System, Hearings before the Armed Services Committee of the House of Representatives*, 89th Cong., 2nd sess., June 24–26, 28–30, 1966 (hereinafter cited as *Hearings*), p. 9626. Military force level and annual accessions data from Department of Defense totals (*Hearings*, p. 10001).

[2] The concept of policy is varyingly employed (as it already has been here) to cover anything from the grand outline of goals and directions of societal movement to specific day-to-day details of bureaucratic decision-making. Henceforth we use the term to signify the substance of the adjustment or accommodation by participants to a problem or goal in their political context, expressed by the actions (or conscious inaction) of governmental bodies. This still leaves a possibility of ambiguity as to scale (i.e., congressional decisions to draft the youngest men first versus a particular local board's decision to draft a specific registrant) and as to the distinction between tangible impact and secondary or symbolic effects. We trust that the context in which we use the term will provide clarity as to the particular referent intended.

(directly and indirectly) by the policies; and it may suggest some characteristics of the processes of feedback and support. Second, analysis of present policies which identifies those aspects of policy which produce particular effects may permit empirically defensible predictions concerning alternative policies. Under some conditions, such projections may greatly narrow the range of policy-makers' choices and permit professionally responsible recommendations by political scientists. In both cases, some incremental advances in theoretical development are also possible; in the first, because the output of the system has structuring consequences for popular support and for the nature of future inputs; in the second, because hypotheses may be tested and interpretations refined through experimentation under varying conditions. But these are long-range goals, and our present purposes extend only to the analysis of policy impact and the assessing of alternative policies.[3] We begin by examining the substance of present policies and the conditions under which they are applied.

I. PRESENT POLICY: GOALS, SUBSTANCE, IMPLEMENTATION, CONDITIONS

Conscription has been a part of all major American wars. The more recent peacetime draft laws (the Selective Service Act of 1948 and its direct descendants, the Universal Military Service and Training Act of 1951 and the Military Selective Service Act of 1967) follow the precedent of the act of 1940, itself based on the experience of 1917.[4] The intent of all these statutes has been to induct selectively those men who can best be spared from the civilian and defense economies, with the goal of achieving that equity in liability for military service which is consistent with the national health,

---

[3] The approach taken follows in general the statement of the concerns of the Committee on Governmental and Legal Processes, which were as follows: What principal problems are the policies intended to deal with? What principal policy alternatives have been seriously considered? Which ones have been chosen? How effectively have they dealt with the problems? What have been their economic, social, and political costs? How has their choice affected the range of policy alternatives presently available in this field? Where are we likely to go from here? Where *should* we go from here? Implicit throughout the paper is a further question: To what extent can the research skills and professional judgments of political scientists contribute to the resolution of these questions?

[4] For histories of Selective Service and comparisons of the various statutes, see Jack Franklin Leach, *Conscription in the United States: Historical Background* (Rutland, Vt.: Charles E. Tuttle Publishing Co., 1952); the Special Monograph Series of the Selective Service System (Washington: U.S. Government Printing Office, 1947–55), containing volumes on the background, organization, and administration of the system in the Second World War; *Selective Service under the 1948 Act Extended* (Washington: U.S. Government Printing Office, 1953); Clyde E. Jacobs and John F. Gallagher, *The Selective Service Act: A Case Study of the Governmental Process* (New York: Dodd, Mead & Co., 1967), particularly for the congressional debates; and *Hearings*, Appendix II, for the current statute with analysis and a brief description of the Selective Service System.

safety, and interest.[5] To accomplish this end, deferments have existed under the 1948 act, as extended, for fathers, students, hardship cases, reservists, certain occupations, and physically and mentally unacceptable men.[6] The availability of these deferments has led the Selective Service System to see "channeling" as an important secondary goal. Through the use of deferments, as General Hershey has indicated, men are "channeled" into jobs where they are needed:

> A complementary function [to inductions] is to insure, by deferment, that vital activities and scarce skills are protected, and that the patterns of civilian life generally are disrupted no more than necessary by exercise of the duty and privilege of military service. . . . I do not believe that we are so rich in human resources that we can afford deliberately to ignore opportunities we have to channel people into training and the application of training. . . . There are enough factors over which we have no control which interfere with the development of the potential of our citizens, and with the best utilization of that potential when it is developed. By deferment we can influence people to train themselves and to use the skills they acquire in work critical to the nation in civilian or military life.[7]

---

[5] The congressional statement of "Policy and Intent" at the outset of the Universal Military Training and Service Act (now called the Military Selective Service Act) declares (Sec. 1c), ". . . the obligations and privileges of serving in the armed forces and the reserve components thereof should be shared generally, in accordance with a system of selection which is fair and just, and which is consistent with the maintenance of an effective national economy." The President is authorized to provide for the deferment (Sec. 6h) of those whose employment or whose activity in study, research, or medical, scientific, or other endeavors "is found to be necessary to the maintenance of the national health, safety, or interest."

[6] Classifications established pursuant to the authority just cited fall into the following general groupings, with the proportions of the approximately 33 million living registrants indicated as of the close of fiscal 1966.

Available for service (I-A, I-A-O, I-O)	3.1%
Disqualified (I-Y, fit only in emergency; IV-F, unfit for service)	14.8
Students (I-S, II-S)	7.7
Occupational deferment (II-A, nonfarm; II-C, farm)	.8
Dependency and hardship (III-A)	10.9
All other deferred and exempt categories	.3
In service or completed service (I-C, I-D, IV-A)	18.1
Over age of liability (V-A)	44.3
	100.0%

Note that these proportions are based on the total number of registrants; because the overage group is nearly half the total, the proportions of the effectively available manpower pool represented by each deferment category is almost double the percentage shown. In subsequent analyses of classification performance in Wisconsin, we have used proportions of the eligible age group only.

[7] *Hearings*, pp. 9620, 9623. Other statements of the System have also emphasized the importance of channeling. For example, a press information bulletin says: "One of the

Implementation of the law is in the hands of the almost 4,100 local boards, which operate under the general supervision of 56 state (or comparable) Selective Service headquarters within the United States and its territories.[8] National headquarters issues policy guidelines for application by the local boards, with the reminder that they are "advisory only." More detailed interpretations of these general guidelines are provided (when deemed necessary) by the various state headquarters to the local boards under their respective jurisdictions. The state headquarters are manned by full-time personnel, chiefly National Guard or reserve officers, but the local boards are made up of civilian volunteers drawn from the local communities in which they sit. This unique design, first tried in World War I, is intended to mitigate local resistance such as was encountered in the Civil War. Local advisers and appeal agents and an internal appeals system consisting of ninety-five appeal boards provide the registrant, at least in form, opportunities for review of his local board's actions and compensate to some extent for the statutory insulation of the system from legal challenge in court.

The individual registrant first encounters conscription within five days of his eighteenth birthday, when he is required to register with his local board. From that day forward, for a possible term of seventeen years (if he ever accepts a deferred classification), and regardless of where his schooling or occupation may take him, he shares control of his life and career with the members of that local board. He will probably be classified and reclassified several times, as his situation changes and as the needs of the nation and the size of the available manpower pools shift over time. Deferment criteria are modified, and applied with varying rigor even if unmodified in formal fashion, as the level of induction needs rises and falls;[9] for any given individual, therefore, military liability rests on a complex of relevant factors including personal, societal, and international conditions.

---

major products of the Selective Service classification process is the channeling of manpower into many endeavors, occupations, and activities that are in the national interest. This function is a counterpart and amplification of the System's responsibility to deliver manpower to the armed forces in such a manner as to reduce to a minimum any adverse effect upon the national health, safety, interest, and progress. By identifying and applying this process intelligently, the System is able not only to minimize any adverse effect but to exert an effect beneficial to the national health, safety, and interest."

[8] For descriptions of the organization, see especially *Hearings*, Appendix II; National Advisory Commission on Selective Service, *In Pursuit of Equity: Who Serves When Not All Serve?* (Washington: U.S. Government Printing Office, 1967) (hereinafter cited as *President's Commission Report*), chap. 3; the operations of the system, together with their legal bases and the registrant's rights, are well summarized on a step-by-step basis by Charles H. Wilson, "The Selective Service System: An Administrative Obstacle Course," *California Law Review*, 1967.

[9] The Selective Service System has made clear that at different times deferments may be granted conservatively or liberally. "The opportunity to enhance the national well being by inducing more registrants to participate in fields which relate directly to the national interest came about as a consequence, soon after the close of the Korean episode, of the knowledge within the System that there was enough registrant personnel to allow stringent deferment practices employed during war time to be relaxed or tightened as the situation might require" (from a press information bulletin entitled "Channeling," p. 2).

The goal of conscription policy—provision of rapidly fluctuating numbers of men to the armed forces—is to be accomplished in a context of the twin values of efficiency and equity. By "efficiency" we mean deferment, if and when necessary, in order to utilize a man's services in a manner that maximizes his potential contribution to the nation's "defense effort." This is the system's rationale for the existence of all but hardship, dependency, and unfitness deferments. The *Annual Report of the Director* (1966) declares, for example, "It must be continually emphasized that the Selective Service System is no longer just a draft. . . . Its reason for being is to see that men are assigned to the military or retained in the civilian area so that the right man may be in the right place at the right time."[10] By "equity" we understand equalization of burdens. Obviously there may be tension between the two values, for burdens cannot be equalized if some men are deferred to employ their civilian skills while others are inducted. When mobilization is nearly complete, however, as it was in World War II, tensions are low. Full equity was not achieved, because service was not universal; men were deferred in the name of efficiency to work in shipyards, munition factories, mines, farms, and other places thought essential to the war effort and the civilian economy. But the conflict between efficiency and equity then was tolerable because most eligible men *did* go into the army, and those who did not were in apparently necessary jobs. In the Korean period, the armed forces required a high proportion of the relatively small available manpower pool, and military liability extended to nearly all strata of the society, once again reducing the inevitable tensions.

But conditions of manpower availability in the 1960's have radically altered the situation and given rise to sharp conflict between the two values. Only a fraction of the available manpower is currently needed by the armed forces—even with the Vietnam buildup of 1965–67—and only one out of every seven physically acceptable men will have to be drafted in the 1970's.[11]

Table 1 shows the proportions of twenty-six-year-old men who have had service experience in the last ten years and shows also the proportions that will see service in the future. Reduced force levels in the late 1950's and early 1960's are responsible for the early sharpness of the drop in service experience, but it is clear that the steeply rising manpower pool of the mid- and late 1960's would by itself cause the proportions shown from about 1968 on. At noncrisis levels, the proportion of men with service experience could drop even lower than the projected 34 percent. This surplus of available manpower over military needs creates conditions quite different from those existing when men were deferred during World War II and the Korean conflict.

Throughout the late 1950's and 1960's, the Selective Service System

---

[10] National Headquarters of the Selective Service System, *Annual Report of the Director* (1966) (Washington: U.S. Government Printing Office, 1967), p. 31.

[11] Testimony of Assistant Secretary of Defense (Manpower) Thomas D. Morris, April 12, 1967. See *Hearings before the Committee on Armed Services*, U.S. Senate, 90th Cong., 1st sess., p. 64.

TABLE 1
MILITARY SERVICE EXPERIENCE OF 26-YEAR-OLD MEN, SELECTED YEARS

Year	Total 26-Year-Old Men	Ever Entered Military Service	
		Number	Percent
Actual:			
1958 (Korean-period men)	1,100,000	770,000	70%
1962	1,110,000	640,000	58
1964	1,190,000	610,000	52
1966	1,250,000	580,000	46
Projected:			
1974			
3,000,000 strength	1,870,000	790,000	42
2,700,000 strength	1,870,000	640,000	34

SOURCE: Department of Defense estimates, contained in *Hearings*, p. 10005.

NOTE: Age 26 is used as the critical age for comparison because it is the practical upper age limit by which time service will have been experienced by all those who are likely to undergo military service at all (except doctors and dentists). The median age of induction dropped to below 20 years in 1966, so that there is considerable time lag before such experience will be reflected in such totals as are here employed; the current expansion in numbers of men in service, however, will probably hold the proportion for 1970–72 at around 44 or 45 percent, and only very large increases could arrest the decisive downward trend in service proportions.

sought to cope with the relatively low military manpower needs and rising manpower resources by relaxing the stringency of deferment criteria. The tight student deferment standards of the Korean War gave way to the assignment of a student deferment classification without regard to class standing or Selective Service Qualification Test scores,[12] and finally the test itself was abandoned in 1963. In 1956, fathers were placed in the last category in the order of call, with the result in most instances of revoking their Korean-necessitated eligibility. In 1963 they were transferred to a deferred category (III-A), and married men without children were granted the last place in the order of call, again for practical purposes removing them from availability. The purpose of these generous allocations of deferments was to maintain some sense of certainty for those men who remained liable for service (thereby preserving some impetus for enlistments) and to reduce the age at which men were actually called, partly to reduce the disruptive impact of conscription on the economy and society, and partly because the armed forces prefer younger men.

---

[12] For chronological summaries of changes in deferment practices and other relevant policies and events, see the chronology sections of *Annual Report of the Director of Selective Service* (Washington: U.S. Government Printing Office, 1951–67).

Deferments thus have clearly been shaped by military needs and man-power resources: strict criteria were applied during the years 1951–53, and then these gave way to liberal granting of deferments in the late 1950's and 1960's, with tightening beginning again in 1965. These effects can be clearly seen in Table 2, which compares the proportions of twenty-six-year-old men with service experience and deferred status in 1958 (a year that reflects Korean service levels) with those of 1962 and 1966. (Lest it be assumed that the American male has declined in physical and/or mental capacity since the Korean War, we should note that the Defense Department has modified its standards in the face of manpower surpluses, accepting only those men who meet the higher standards; a separate classification (I-Y) was established for men whose qualifications were such that they would be acceptable only in time of national emergency.) The table shows that the proportion of men who have entered service has steadily decreased, while the proportions in two important deferment categories have increased.

It is not too much to say that those who actually see military service are those who are left over after all possible deferments have been extended. Deferments, originally intended to maximize the efficient use of manpower resources, have been used in effect to reduce the pool of available men to manageable proportions. The obvious question is whether they can be so used without undermining their original justification, and/or creating unantici-pated consequences with significant social implications. The critical question becomes: Who gets drafted when many are deferred?

II. POLICY IMPACT: WHO IS DRAFTED?

There are substantial difficulties in the way of discovering the consequences of deferment practices. Neither Selective Service nor the armed forces maintain comprehensive records of the socioeconomic characteristics of registrants, draftees, or enlistees. Selective Service record-keeping is limited to those few items of information that concern a registrant's availability for service, and, in any event, files are confidential by law. There exists, therefore, no ready way to compare those who serve with those who do not, or to ascribe reasons

TABLE 2

MILITARY SERVICE STATUS OF 26-YEAR-OLD MEN, SELECTED YEARS

Status	1958	1962	1966
Entered service	70%	58%	46%
Not qualified	22	27	30
Dependency (including married nonfathers)	5	12	20
Other deferred and exempt groups	4	4	4

SOURCE: Department of Defense Estimates, 1966. See *Hearings*, p. 10006.

for such patterns. Problems are also introduced by some of the special features of Selective Service operation: because men may still enlist after passing their preinduction physicals or even after being ordered to report for induction, analysis of those *actually* inducted would reach only one-half to one-third of the men *ordered* for induction, probably producing a skewed picture of Selective Service actions. In addition, analyses of mental and physical rejections must provide for the Defense Department's changes of standards in response to manpower needs. But in spite of these difficulties it is possible to make an assessment, however rough, of the impact of deferment policies.

The Defense Department Draft Study of 1964 commissioned a national survey through the Census Bureau and the National Opinion Research Center as part of its effort to ascertain whether adequate force levels could be maintained without the aid of conscription.[13] One by-product of this inquiry was an analysis by educational level of the military service experience of men aged twenty-seven through thirty-four, and these data are presented in Table 3. The lowest and highest educational levels (before entering service) experienced the least military service, with high school graduates, college dropouts, and college graduates sharing liability in roughly equal proportions. The same pattern was repeated when father's education or father's occupation was used as the independent variable, and while no income measures were available, it may well be surmised that income would also correlate with service experience in this way. These data appear to suggest that liability for service is lower only for graduate students or for men with an eighth-grade education or less, and that college graduates serve at roughly the same rate as college dropouts, high school dropouts, and high school graduates. The National Advisory Commission on Selective Service presented a chart showing these

---

[13] The report of the Defense Department Draft Study of 1964, according to Thomas D. Morris, Assistant Secretary of Defense, consists entirely of his prepared statement to the House Armed Services Committee on June 30, 1966 (*Hearings*, p. 9923ff.), and supplementary data presented as Appendix I to *Hearings*. But others insist that they have examined other unreleased and revised portions of it; see Jean Carper, *Bitter Greetings* (New York: Grossman Publishers, 1967), chap. 11. The study was undertaken in April 1964 "to assess the possibility of meeting our military manpower requirements on an entirely voluntary basis in the coming decade" (Morris, *Hearings*, p. 9923). As part of the study, opinion sampling was undertaken by the Census Bureau in conjunction with the National Opinion Research Center of the University of Chicago. Self-administered questionnaire data were received from a total of 9,593 civilian male respondents (60 percent nonveterans, 31 percent veterans in the final weighting) between the ages of sixteen and thirty-four, and combined with the responses to a similar questionnaire from 102,000 men on active military service (9 percent in final weighting). The basic source in which these results are reported is Albert D. Klassen, *Military Service in American Life since World War II: An Overview* (Chicago: National Opinion Research Center, 1966), many aspects of which are included among the materials presented by the Defense Department in Appendix I, *Hearings*. Several other publications from the National Opinion Research Center draw on these data; see, for example, Karen Oppenheim, *Attitudes of Younger American Men toward Selective Service* (Chicago: National Opinion Research Center, 1966).

TABLE 3
MILITARY SERVICE OF MEN AGE 27–34 IN 1964, BY EDUCATIONAL LEVEL

Educational Level before Service	Percent Who Served
Eighth grade or less	41%
High school dropout	70
High school graduate	74
College dropout	68
College degree	70
Graduate school	27

SOURCE: Albert D. Klassen, *Military Service in the United States: An Overview* (Chicago: National Opinion Research Center, 1966), p. 15.

proportions in its report, with no further interpretation, and the *New York Times* used it as one of two illustrations of the findings of the Commission in its *précis* of that report.

Many of the arguments for the elimination of graduate-student deferment and the retention of undergraduate deferment appear to rely on the data in Table 3. Men aged twenty-seven through thirty-four in 1964 were at prime military liability ages in the Korean War, however, and the comparatively small size of the manpower pool in relation to manpower requirements resulted in a high proportion of service for all strata. College students served at almost the average rates for the entire male population during that period; only graduate students were able to avoid military service. More recent data, applicable to the growing manpower pool and decreasing manpower requirements of the late 1950's and early 1960's, are available from Selective Service itself, and are presented in Table 4. These data show that by 1964 men aged twenty-six who had been to college were much less likely to have served in the armed forces.[14] The difference in the two bodies of data with respect to service experience of college students is not due to the failure of the latter data to segregate graduate students. Only 6 percent of college graduates had student deferments, and even if all of these escaped service, the proportions of service experience on the part of college graduates as a group would still be distinctly

---

[14] The data in Table 4 are probably conservative, since the military service category includes both active service and reserve service. Professor Walter Oi has separated active-duty veterans from the reservists and in an analysis reported in his paper "The Costs and Implications of an All Volunteer Force" shows that in the cohort of men born in 1938 "Over three fourths of qualified high school graduates served in the active duty forces, while less than one-third of college graduates discharged their draft liabilities in this way." See *Hearings before the Committee on Armed Services*, U.S. Senate, 90th Cong., 1st sess., on S. 1432, "Amending and Extending the Draft Law and Related Authorities," p. 455.

TABLE 4
MILITARY SERVICE OF 26-YEAR-OLD MEN IN 1964, BY EDUCATIONAL LEVEL

	Less than High School	High School	Some College	College Degree	Total
Entered military service	50%	57%	60%	40%	52%
No military service (total)	50	43	40	60	48
	100%	100%	100%	100%	100%
The "no military service" group can be broken down as follows:					
Available for service (I-A)	1%	1%	1%	3%	1%
Married (service unlikely)	. . .	. . .	. . .	2	. . .
Unmarried (service probable)	1	1	1	1	1
Not available for service	50	42	40	56	47
Unacceptable (I-Y, IV-F)	25	12	14	12	18
Student deferments	. . .	. . .	2	6	1
Occupational deferments (II-A, II-C)	. . .	. . .	1	11	2
Dependency deferments	23	29	23	25	25
Other deferred and exempt groups	1	1	1	3	2

SOURCE: Selective Service sample inventory of registrants, reported in *Hearings*, p. 10011. Figures may not add to 100 percent in all instances due to rounding.

lower than at all other educational levels. It is clear that under the manpower surplus conditions of the 1950's and early 1960's, college students as well as graduate students experienced military service at distinctly lower proportions than any other group (except for the lowest levels of education) in the population.[15]

The national data just reviewed say nothing about the impact of the draft at different economic levels. But data from the 1960 census show clearly that college attendance is related to income. According to the census data, only 19 percent of persons from sixteen through twenty-four from families with incomes under $5,000 per year reported some college attendance, while 33 percent of persons in the $5,000–$7,500-per-year range and 49 percent of those in the $7,500–$10,000 bracket reported college attendance. The implication of these figures is that men from higher income families are less likely to see service than men from lower income families.

---

[15] It should be noted that the advantages conferred by the student deferment are not limited to increased chances of complete avoidance of military service. The availability of this deferment also permits those financially and otherwise able to go to college in effect to choose their time of service, possibly avoiding those years when military service would involve maximum danger. The increase in the II-S classification (Table 5) demonstrates that this may have occurred between 1965 and 1966.

TABLE 5
PERCENTAGE OF ELIGIBLE-AGE REGISTRANTS IN MAJOR
SELECTIVE SERVICE CLASSIFICATIONS, WISCONSIN, 1966

Classification	Description of Classification	Percentage of Eligible-Age Group in Each Classification: State Medians of 80 Boards		Range of Variation between Highest and Lowest Boards, 1966 (in Percent)	
		Fiscal 1965	Fiscal 1966	Lowest	Highest
I-A	Available for service	9.2%	5.8%	4.4%	8.3%
I-C	Now in service	10.8	11.8	8.6	18.1
I-Y	Available in emergency	4.4	6.7	2.4	11.5
I-D	In reserves	3.8	4.8	1.7	8.8
II-A	Occupationally deferred	1.3	1.5	0.3	3.9
II-C	Agriculturally deferred	0.9	1.0	. . .	5.7
II-S	Student deferments	6.6	9.2	1.9	19.7
III-A	Hardship and dependency deferments	17.4	18.8	12.5	25.2
IV-A	Completed service	18.5	17.1	12.3	23.7
IV-F	Unfit for service	14.4	13.1	9.3	30.7
	Enlistments	2.1	3.3	. . .	. . .
	Inductions	0.7	2.0	. . .	. . .

This conclusion is supported by data quite different from those so far examined. To examine the impact of the draft further, we analyzed Selective Service classification data on a month-by-month, board-by-board basis for the eighty local boards of Wisconsin.[16] These records included no educational data, nor did they reveal any other socioeconomic characteristics of individual registrants. Therefore, we were able to relate Census Bureau data describing the socioeconomic characteristics of local board jurisdictions only to the classification performances of those boards; however approximate the use of such aggregate data may be, the absence of any other data has led us to make some cautious appraisals on this basis. We should add that our analysis relies on 1965 and 1966 data. The 1967 renewal of Selective Service legislation altered the terms of deferment somewhat (details are discussed in a later

---

[16] The inquiry was begun in December 1965 and has continuously enjoyed the full cooperation of the Wisconsin State Selective Service System. State Director Bentley Courtenay, with the permission of General Hershey, made the nonconfidential records of his state headquarters available and aided in securing questionnaire responses from 81 percent of all local board members in the state, plus interviews with forty local board members and thirty members of the state selective service personnel at various levels. We wish to express our appreciation for his assistance and that of his officers. Without their rigorous and detailed review and criticism of our work we might have made factual errors; our judgments are our own, of course, and needless to say, members of the Wisconsin State Selective Service System neither share them nor bear any responsibility for them.

TABLE 6
STUDENT DEFERMENTS BY MEDIAN INCOME OF BOARD JURISDICTIONS, WISCONSIN, 1966

| | Median Income of Families | |
| | Boards in Low-Income Areas (below $5,000) (N = 46) | Boards in High-Income Areas (above $5,000) (N = 34) |
Fiscal 1966 II-S Levels		
More than 1% above state median	11%	56%
Within 1% of state median	44	35
More than 1% below state median	45	9
	100%	100%

section), but in our opinion the status quo was altered so slightly that the analysis that follows is still relevant.

Table 5 shows the state medians in proportions of eligible-age registrants (total registrants less classification V-A, overage) in each of the major classifications during 1965 and 1966, as well as the range between the highest and lowest local boards in 1966. The deferment categories with the most men are dependency/hardship (III-A), unfit for service (IV-F), and student deferment (II-S); the latter increased substantially (by 39 percent) between 1965 and 1966. The table shows that the highest board has ten times as many registrants in II-S and five times as many in I-D (reserves) as the lowest board, and there are sharp differences also in occupational-deferment and unfit-for-service classifications. Clearly, the impact of the draft is not the same in every draft-board jurisdiction. Extensive analysis convinces us that this variation is rooted in the socioeconomic differences between these jurisdictions rather than in any systematic pattern of local-board behavior; within this single state we found almost no evidence of systematic variation which could be attributed to local-board idiosyncrasies or localized norms.[17]

Table 5 indicates that nearly 20 percent of the eligible-age group in some boards had student deferments. Table 6 compares proportions of student deferments by income of board jurisdictions. Because many boards in this state cluster about the state median, we have segregated them by the relatively narrow margin of 1 percent of the eligible-age group above and below the median; the sharply contrasting distribution of boards in these two directions correlates closely with income differentials and leads us to conclude, not surprisingly, that educational deferments are more likely to go to men from higher income families.

We can come closer to a specification of this relationship, and of possible

---

[17] This analysis appears in James W. Davis and Kenneth M. Dolbeare, *Little Groups of Neighbors: The Selective Service System* (Chicago: Markham Publishing Company, 1968), chap. 6.

exceptions to it, by means of the scatter diagram in Figure 1. In this case, we used proportions of families with incomes under $3,000 per year in the jurisdictions of the boards as the correlate of student deferment for purposes of greater precision, and the general distribution again shows deferment by income level. Some special features make for individualized variability, of course, such as the proximity of colleges and universities or the varying proportions of relatively wealthy persons in each board jurisdiction. We may note also that the greatest range in student-deferment proportions, with relatively little range in income, is found in urban areas, suggesting the relevance of special factors in those areas, such as a proportion of nonwhites within the population.

So far, our data have indicated that many registrants in this state, probably the sons of upper income families, hold educational deferments. The more interesting question is whether those men who obtain student deferments serve in the armed forces after their graduation. Certainly some will, but several pieces of evidence suggest that they will see service at distinctly lower rates than any other group. Our detailed analysis of Wisconsin experience suggests strongly that registrants from higher income areas undergo military service at lower rates than registrants from lower income areas. Table 7 relates total proportions of military-service experience (current service *and* completed service) to the income levels of the board jurisdictions. The overall incidence of military service is lowest in the higher income area and highest in the lower income areas; the proportion of boards that are above the median decreases sharply as one moves from the lowest to the highest income areas, with only 11 percent of the boards with over-$6,000-income jurisdictions being more than 1 percent above the median.

TABLE 7
SERVICE IN ARMED FORCES* BY INCOME OF BOARD JURISDICTIONS, WISCONSIN, 1966

| | Median Family Income of Board Jurisdictions† | | |
	$3,000–$4,000 (N = 19)	$4,000–$6,000 (N = 42)	Over $6,000 (N = 19)
More than 1% above state median	53%	36%	11%
Within 1% of state median	11	33	37
More than 1% below state median	37	31	53
	101%‡	100%	101%‡

* Includes classifications I-C (in service) and IV-A (completed service).
† Median family income data based on U.S. Census, 1960. In the case of boards comprising less than an entire county (eleven boards), census tracts were allocated geographically to construct socioeconomic profiles of each board jurisdiction.
‡ Figures add to more than 100 percen because of rounding.

FIGURE 1
II-S DEFERMENTS BY INCOME LEVELS

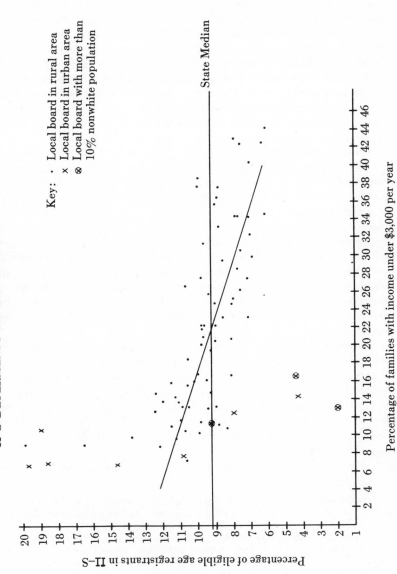

Key: · Local board in rural area
     × Local board in urban area
     ⊗ Local board with more than
        10% nonwhite population

State Median

Percentage of eligible age registrants in II–S

Percentage of families with income under $3,000 per year

The close correlation between student deferment and income levels previously noted appears to have carried over to the point of establishing an income-related overall pattern of service experience. But if student deferment has the closest correlations with income, it is not the only factor involved in this relationship. Occupational deferment combines with student deferment to give higher income men a better chance of avoiding military service. Table 4 showed that 11 percent of twenty-six-year-old college graduates held an occupational deferment in July 1964, as compared with 1 percent of all other twenty-six-year-old men. (Military service after age twenty-six was rare then, and is unlikely now; for all practical purposes, such men will never see service.) And among Wisconsin local boards occupational deferments were most numerous in higher income areas.

We have not included men in classification I-D (reserves) in our computations of men who have seen military service, because we have defined military service as active duty. While some I-D men are former service personnel, most are six-months or no-prior-service men. As of May 1968, few organized reserve units had been called up, and only a small proportion of those men who have had no training at all have been activated during the Vietnam period. Under these conditions, and despite the extended liability of reservists, it appears to be an advantageous classification—and it is available primarily to the higher income, better educated registrants. Among Wisconsin local boards, only the lowest income boards had less than 4 percent of their eligible-age group in class I-D; the higher income boards were all above this figure.

Defense Department comparisons of the educational attainment of men entering the reserves with men entering the services via induction reveal sharp disparities[18] consistent with our contention that service in the reserves is another income-related advantage. The rise in Wisconsin reserves proportions between 1965 and 1966 shown in Table 5 occurred chiefly in the higher income areas. Local-board members concur in the view that deferment policy provides a means for the more fortunate registrant to avoid active service in a time of maximum danger.[19]

The advantage of higher income registrants can be illustrated in another

---

[18] *Hearings*, p. 10012, and unpublished Defense Department statistics that show that, in 1964, 15.7 percent of the men joining the reserves had college degrees while only 5.7 percent of the men inducted into active service had degrees.

[19] In a mail questionnaire sent to Wisconsin local board members in September 1966, we asked respondents (among other questions) to indicate their agreement or disagreement with the statement "The reserves and the National Guard are frequently a means whereby registrants successfully avoid the draft," with the following results (from 314 respondents):

Agree strongly	31%.
Agree	43
Don't know, depends	11
Disagree	10
Disagree strongly	3
No response	2
	100%

way. To test our hypothesis that the risk of military service for qualified men in low-income areas was higher than the risk for qualified men in higher income areas, we subtracted the "fit only in emergency" (I-Y) and "unfit" (IV-F) classifications from the totals of eligible-age registrants in each board, and then computed the registrants' actual service liability by finding the ratio of the two service categories (I-C and IV-A) to the total. The resulting service liability ratios ranged from 1 to 3.2 in the wealthier urban boards to 1 to 2.5 in the relatively low-income, most heavily Negro board, and 1 to 2.3 in a very low-income rural board. This means that actual military service was experienced by 1 in every 2.3 physically and mentally qualified men in the low-income rural board, but by almost 50 percent less, or 1 in every 3.2 men, in the wealthier urban boards. Here, as elsewhere, we have clear evidence that the income-related advantages in present deferment policies (chiefly the student deferment) are sufficiently great to overcome the countervailing effects of higher proportions of unfitness in the lower income areas and establish the income-based pattern of military service.

So far, we have been working with data that include all men currently or previously in service, without regard to their avenue of entry. This leaves open the possibility that the lower income registrants may have enlisted in disproportionate numbers, thus in effect voluntarily creating the pattern we have discerned. In order to test this possibility, we have to distinguish enlistments from inductions and compare both with the income levels of board jurisdictions. The results of such an analysis are presented in Table 8.

TABLE 8

ENLISTMENTS AND INDUCTIONS, BY INCOME LEVEL OF BOARD JURISDICTIONS, WISCONSIN, 1966

	Boards in Low-Income Areas* (N = 39)	Boards in High-Income Areas† (N = 41)
Enlistment rate‡		
Low	36%	22%
Medium	51	49
High	13	29
	100%	100%
Induction rate§		
Low	33%	49%
Medium	28	36
High	39	15
	100%	100%

* More than 20 percent of families earning less than $3,000 per year.
† Less than 20 percent of families earning less than $3,000 per year.
‡ Based on percentage of eligible-age group enlisting during fiscal 1966. (Low, less than 3 percent; medium, 3–3.99 percent; high, over 4 percent.)
§ Based on percentage of eligible-age group inducted during fiscal 1966. (Low, less than 2 percent; medium, 2–2.49 percent; high, over 2.5 percent.)

These proportions are not drastically different, and a shift in a small number of boards would restructure them; but the table is most instructive for its negation of the assumption that the poor enlist. The enlistment rate tends to be *lower* in the lower income jurisdictions and relatively *higher* in the high-income jurisdictions. Conversely, the induction rate is higher in the low-income areas and lower in the high-income areas. This suggests, in response to our original inquiry, that the higher service experience of the low-income boards is *not* due to enlistments, but, quite the opposite, is due to the heavy weight of inductions there. The high-income areas, with their apparently higher enlistment rates, would, in accordance with the formulas for allocating induction calls, receive lower calls for induction from the state headquarters; induction calls would be proportionately higher in those areas that did not provide men through enlistment. This seems to be the case here, with perhaps some additional impact on the lower income areas deriving from the availability of men there.

National data permit a somewhat broader perspective on patterns of enlistment. The question of who enlists is related to the level of induction calls: men with higher levels of educational attainment and higher scores on service aptitude tests tend to enlist because of draft pressure, while under conditions of low induction calls, enlistments come proportionately more from lower socioeconomic and aptitude levels.[20] The net results create the patterns shown in Table 9. While the data in the first part of the table reflect the experience of the Korean War and the immediate postwar years, current (though less complete) data regarding enlistments in the last two years are entirely consistent; together they reinforce our point that high-income, high-status men are more likely to enlist and less likely to be drafted than low-income, low-status men. The proportionately higher rates of service which we have found in lower income areas, in short, are not the product of enlistments; they are caused by inductions from those areas. The data in the second part of the table confirm our point that income-related opportunities shape the pattern of service experience. Of those Negroes who see military service, more than half do so via induction; exactly one-third of whites have been inducted while the rest have served via officer programs, reserves, or enlistment. Lower proportions of Negroes experience military service, of course, but the reason lies entirely with the difference in the "unfit for service" category.[21] Indeed, for the physically and mentally acceptable Negro, service prospects are higher than for whites. The National Advisory Commission reported that "proportionately more (30 percent) Negroes of the group qualified for service are drafted than whites (18 percent)—primarily

---

[20] Morris, *Hearings*, p. 9938.

[21] Slight changes in Defense Department minimum standards, such as that made in 1966 for the purpose of bringing in 100,000 men otherwise classifiable as I-Y, can have substantial impact on Negro service proportions. For example, 43 percent of Negroes given preinduction examinations in fiscal 1966 were accepted in contrast to 29 percent in 1965; the effect of the change on whites was less than half as great, from 60 percent to 65 percent (UPI wire story from Army report, May 25, 1967).

TABLE 9

(A) ENLISTMENT AND INDUCTION, BY SOCIOECONOMIC STATUS AND RACE

Race and SES*	Age in 1964			
	27–30		31–34	
	Inducted	Enlisted	Inducted	Enlisted
White	16%	84%	34%	66%
Negro	25	75	51	49
White high SES	11	89	27	73
White low SES	20	80	40	60

* Based on father's occupation and education. See Albert D. Klassen, *Military Service in American Life since World War II: An Overview* (Chicago: National Opinion Research Center, 1966), pp. 37–45, for the bases of the index.
SOURCE: Klassen, *Military Service*, Table A–VI.5d, p. 253 (part of the Defense Department draft study).

(B) FORM OF MILITARY SERVICE, BY RACE, OCTOBER 1964

	White		Nonwhite	
Entered military service	66%		49%	
Inducted		22%		25.0%
Enlisted		30		22.0
Officer programs		4		0.4
Reserve programs		10		1.7
Never entered service	34		51	
Unfit for service		21		42.0
Other deferred and exempt groups		13		8.0
	100%		100%	

SOURCE: National Advisory Commission on Selective Service, *In Pursuit of Equity: Who Serves When Not All Serve?* (Washington: U.S. Government Printing Office, 1967), Table 5.8, p. 158 (based on Census Bureau survey of civilian men aged 16–34 years and Defense Department surveys of active-duty personnel, October 1964).

because fewer Negroes are admitted into Reserve or officer training programs."[22]

We may assess the differences in the draft's impact on the two racial groupings in greater detail through comparison of the classification proportions of two adjoining local boards in Milwaukee, one with high-income white residents and the other with a relatively low-income population, almost 50 percent Negro, which is presented as Figure 2. Conspicuous differences between the two boards appear in the student-deferment, occupational-defer-

[22] *President's Commission Report*, p. 9.

FIGURE 2
COMPARISON OF PROPORTIONS OF REGISTRANTS IN
SELECTED CLASSIFICATIONS, TWO BOARDS

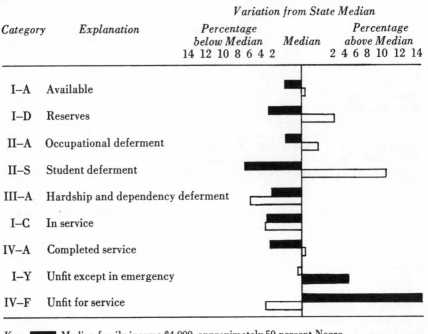

Category	Explanation	Variation from State Median		
		Percentage below Median 14 12 10 8 6 4 2	*Median*	*Percentage above Median* 2 4 6 8 10 12 14
I–A	Available			
I–D	Reserves			
II–A	Occupational deferment			
II–S	Student deferment			
III–A	Hardship and dependency deferment			
I–C	In service			
IV–A	Completed service			
I–Y	Unfit except in emergency			
IV–F	Unfit for service			

Key: ▬▬ Median family income $4,900, approximately 50 percent Negro.

☐ Median family income $8,500, approximately 1 percent Negro.

ment, reserves, and "unfit for service" classifications, all of which conform to our interpretations. It is clear that residents of the two areas have radically different opportunities to claim such deferments; under the circumstances, it is remarkable that service experience is so similar. With a much smaller pool of acceptable men, the Negro board provides nearly the same percentage of men to the armed forces, again indicating that, for those registrants in the Negro board who *are* physically qualified, liability for military service is high indeed.

To conclude the study of the income-related impact of national deferment policies, we examined the record of thirty-seven boards, all in rural areas, where more than 20 percent of families had incomes under $3,000 per year and less than 10 percent of families had incomes over $10,000 per year. Their classification patterns are the same as those previously described, but now in exaggerated form (Table 10). These lowest income areas are dramatically low in II-S deferments, distinctly high in mental and physical unfitness, and high in hardship and dependency deferments. The combined effect of the presence of all these factors is a rate of service experience above the state median,

TABLE 10
CLASSIFICATION AND ENLISTMENT CHARACTERISTICS OF LOW-INCOME BOARDS, WISCONSIN, 1966*

	Completed Service and In Service (I-C, IV-A)	Student Deferments (II-S)	Hardship and Dependency Deferments (III-A)	Mental and Physical Unfitness (I-Y, IV-F)	Enlistments
More than 1% above state median	43%	0%	51%	38%	5%
Within 1% of state median	27	49	38	46	92
More than 1% below state median	30	51	11	16	3
	100%	100%	100%	100%	100%

* The 37 boards with jurisdictions in which more than 20 percent of families had incomes under $3,000 *and* less than 10 percent had incomes over $10,000.

which is not due to high enlistments. We conclude that the absence of the student deferment has overcome the countervailing factors and has exposed these registrants to greater liability. National deferment policies as applied through the mid-1960's (and, so far as we can tell, continuing into the present) have the effect of making the incidence of military service closely related to income levels: men with the advantages of income and education do not experience service at the same rates as their less advantaged contemporaries.

III. SOME FURTHER CONSEQUENCES OF PRESENT POLICIES

We think the data in the preceding section show that increasing manpower surplus, accompanied by extensive granting of deferments, has precluded realization of the value of equity under present policies. Instead, substantial inequities—discrimination along income-based lines, or by residence or race —have developed. What has happened to the value of efficiency under these conditions? To answer this question, we must examine the means employed to implement conscription as well as the findings already reviewed.

For efficiency to be achieved, four criteria would have to be met. Our evidence suggests that, in the 1960's, none of them has been. First, there would have to be a carefully considered and reasonably appropriate definition of what the national interest requires in the way of manpower. We would argue that such a definition should rest in part on projections of available manpower on a long-term basis, together with projections of both foreign and domestic social and other policy problems on an equally long-term basis, in order that relative priorities could be established. Not only defense-related needs, but also pressing domestic social, educational, and technical requirements should be considered. Priorities defined in Selective Service materials, however, are generalized, short-term, and chiefly scientific and military in character.

Second, the definition of the national interest in manpower usage would have to be communicated to local boards with enough specificity to make possible reasonably close adherence by local boards across the country. National headquarters so far has done no such thing; it has instead stated deferment policies in the broadest terms, and has reminded local boards that such guidelines are "advisory only." No effort has been made to encourage conformity with national policies, and variations that have resulted have been defined as desirable. Some state headquarters have added supplementary interpretations for the benefit of their local boards, and the result is a wide number of conflicting instructions for the nation's local boards. The President's Commission reports one classic example in which the states divided sharply over instructions to local boards regarding what course load would qualify a registrant as a "full-time student." Some said twelve credit hours, some fifteen; some told their boards to adhere to whatever the college considered a full-time student; and some said nothing and permitted their boards to make their own definitions.[23] Illustrations could be multiplied, but the point is made: no clear or consistent view of the nation's interests is communicated to local boards. Indeed, it is possible to identify instances where national or state interpretations reflect the requests of trade associations, particular corporations, or unions for quite specific deferment practices. In dairying Wisconsin, for example, cheesemakers or drivers of milk tank trucks are granted occupational deferment by some boards, but not by others.

Third, the performance of local boards would have to be consistent with the transmitted definition of the national interest, *or* the accumulated body of decisions by the 4,087 local boards of the country would have to be taken as representing the national interest even in the absence of guidance based on broad national consideration of what that interest was. The former seems impossible in the light of the absence of a definition and of any single clear specification of standards; the latter seems impossible unless we are to convert the body of local-board decisions into a version of the national interest by definition or as an act of faith.

The inconsistent performances of different elements of the Selective Service System demonstrate that no single definition of national interest has been transmitted; rather each local board, appeal board, and state system is left to do its own defining. Although our analysis in Wisconsin indicated, and the research of the President's Commission confirmed, that Wisconsin is a state with low variability between boards in jurisdictions with similar socio-economic characteristics, this is not the case in all states. The research con-

---

[23] *President's Commission Report*, p. 27.

ducted by the President's Commission revealed substantial variation between boards in similar areas in many states,[24] and this is compounded by the varying instructions issued to local boards by the fifty-six state headquarters of the system. It is compounded further by varying performances by appeal boards in different states, whose decisions normally reflect the interpretations neither of the national nor of the state headquarters, but of the five members of the ninety-five appeal boards. Participant observation in nine urban local boards over a six-month period of 1966 showed that little or no attention was paid to the guidelines from national headquarters, particularly the critical-skills list,[25] and that board members reached their decisions on a wide variety of personalized value premises, experiences, and prejudices. Very little decision-making, interestingly, was based on knowledge of either registrant or the needs of the community, because board members almost never knew registrants and frequently lived outside the particular jurisdiction, and, we may add, their jurisdictions probably had little socioeconomic integrity in any event. The President's Commission evaluated (among other things) occupational deferment classification performance on the part of a sample of 199 local boards, and found that "about half [of the registrants] reclassified into II-A were in neither a critical occupation nor an essential industry as defined by the Department of Labor."[26]

By any measures adopted, we have convincing evidence of dissimilarities in the treatment of similarly situated men. Nonuniformity in classification is a hallmark of the system. The only way in which this performance record can be interpreted as serving the national interest through efficient utilization of manpower resources is by defining the national interest as the sum of the shifting views of 4,087 local boards.

We would have asked as our fourth point that there be some evidence of the effects of the "channeling" accomplished by the system through these deferment policies. We know of no evidence on this, however, except for some scattered indications that some registrants, probably the better educated men, take alternative courses of action in contemplation of the draft. Our sample surveys of the general public and of registrants in Wisconsin indicate that a relatively small number of men have changed their courses of study or their vocational plans principally because of the draft. Some of our respondents were convinced that *others* had acted so as to qualify for deferment, such as by having children or going to school. We do know also that the marriage rate among the immediately affected age groups, and those age groups only, rose by 10 percent during the nine months immediately after President Kennedy declared such men last in the order of call in 1963.[27] But the Selective Service System has never sought to support its argument that men have been chan-

[24] *President's Commission Report*, Appendix, sec. 2, p. 83.
[25] See Gary L. Wamsley, "Local Board Behavior," in the forthcoming volume on Selective Service edited by Roger D. Little (New York: Russell Sage Foundation, 1968).
[26] *President's Commission Report*, p. 27.
[27] *Hearings*, p. 10015.

neled into socially productive occupations because of national deferment policies, and, given the premises on which such channeling would have to be based, it is perhaps just as well.

We do not believe that this situation can be characterized as efficient use of manpower resources in the national interest. Recalling the manipulation of deferment criteria for the principal purpose of controlling the size of the manpower pool, and noting that the President's Commission found the performance of some appeal boards to amount to economic protectionism (some boards never reversed an appeal from an out-of-state local board, while others did so as much as 88 percent of the time),[28] we are confident that we have only begun to detail the factors that prevent such an interpretation.

It might be argued that efficiency is served under the present system in the very gross sense that the lower income, less skilled (and most unemployed) segments of the population are drawn into military service while those with other capabilities are deferred. But the lack of any kind of "fit" between unemployability and lack of skills on the one hand and induction on the other—brought about chiefly but not exclusively by high physical and educational standards of acceptability for service—militates against this possibility. So do the arbitrary and idiosyncratic performance of local boards and the demonstrated variability among state boards and appeal boards. If such an argument were not foreclosed by these factors, it would probably raise serious additional value questions and equity-efficiency conflict under our present manpower-surplus conditions.

In any summary evaluation of present policies, we must not lose sight of the fact that the Selective Service System has for more than two decades filled all calls for induction, as well as motivated countless other enlistments, without provoking significant resistance from the society. This is an important benefit, the more important because it appears to be the only benefit. Ranged against it on the cost side are the several dimensions of inequity already fully described; the social dislocations that are the product of the kind of "channeling" which passes for efficient use of manpower in the national interest; and the uncertainties related to induction at a relatively advanced age.

It has been argued that these are by-products of a decentralization that is fundamental to popular acquiescence in conscription, but our sample surveys suggest that the reverse is the case: decentralization and conscription by local men is perceived as one of the *bad* things about the system. Let us digress for a moment to establish this point. Table 11 shows the responses of the adult population of Wisconsin to our inquiries concerning knowledge about and attitudes toward the conduct of the draft by local draft boards in the state. (A total of 52 percent of respondents knew that the draft was conducted by local boards. All respondents were advised of this fact before being asked the preference question reflected in the table; those who knew of the existence of local boards were more favorable to the idea than those who had not pre-

---

[28] *President's Commission Report*, p. 108.

TABLE 11
APPROVAL OF LOCAL BOARD CONCEPT BY ATTITUDE TOWARD FAIRNESS OF THE DRAFT

Attitude toward Local Boards†	Attitude toward Draft*				
	Fair (41%) (N = 248)	Depends (7%) (N = 40)	Not Fair (35%) (N = 212)	Don't Know, No Answer (17%) (N = 107)	Total (100%) (N = 607)
Good idea	44%	40%	28%	33%	36%
Depends	5	10	10	4	7
Not good idea	44	45	58	31	47
Don't know	7	5	4	32	10
	100%	100%	100%	100%	100%

* Q.1: With regard to your knowledge of the draft here in Wisconsin, would you say it is working in a manner that is fair to all, or not?
† Q.2: What do you think about having local people involved in drafting men? Is this a good idea or not?
SOURCE: Wisconsin Survey Research Laboratory, clustered area probability sample, September 1966.

viously been aware that local boards did the drafting, but still split 45 percent to 43 percent against the idea.) The most significant finding from this inquiry is the fact that the local-board concept is not nearly so popular as the Selective Service System and its supporters argue. Not even those who think the draft itself is fair support the local-board concept more than they oppose it; in the state as a whole, 47 percent say local boards are *not* a good idea, while only 36 percent say that they are, and at a time when the draft itself is evaluated as not unfair. We asked those who said that local boards were not a good idea why they felt that way, and almost every respondent answered with some form of allegation of bias or prejudice on the part of boards. The only strata within the state which contained more respondents who favored local boards than opposed them were the higher levels of education and occupation, a finding that is part of a body of evidence, reported elsewhere, which leads us to the conclusion that the draft gains support from the more advantaged and more politically influential elements of the population partially because of their reduced liability combined with their local management of the system. National data indicate that these findings are not unique to the state of Wisconsin; perceptions of the draft as fair correlate with the capacity to qualify for alternatives to military service in the NORC report of their work for the Defense Department Draft Study of 1964.[29]

[29] Oppenheim, *Attitudes*, p. 20. Those men who had heavy investments in education or other civilian-related skills were more likely to think the draft unfair than "light investors"; but in every investment level, those men who would not enter military service,

The evidence reviewed in the course of this brief digression leads us to the conclusion that the consequences we have identified cannot be justified as necessary though perhaps undesirable by-products of an absolutely essential form of organization. Decentralization and local participation are *not* essential to popular acquiescence in conscription; they may be functional in one sense as a means of drawing off resentment and focusing it on the local board rather than on the principle of conscription itself, but in other respects they seem to be dispensable.

Our analysis thus leads us to the conclusion that the present system is producing unnecessarily high costs in exchange for the single essential benefit it returns. Attempts to serve both equity and efficiency in the employment of manpower resources in this way lead to the attainment of neither, and the prospect for the future, with its increasing manpower surplus, is for greater and greater inequities—higher and higher costs—if the present practices are continued. What are the alternatives? We shall consider several briefly, before taking up our own proposals.

IV. ALTERNATIVES TO PRESENT POLICIES

Several alternatives to the present form of conscription have been suggested in recent years, though none has as yet been adopted. In the paragraphs below we comment on several of the proposals that have received the most attention, and offer speculations where applicable upon their consequences.

NATIONAL SERVICE

Several plans for national service have been put forward, the gist of the major ones being to provide opportunities for service, either military or social, to all the nation's youth, male and female.[30] Some advocates of national service would have it compulsory and others not, but all include as a goal the rehabilitation of disadvantaged youth. Because about eight million persons might be participating at any one time, there are staggering problems of effective employment of such people: what sorts of jobs, where, with what impact on the labor market, at how much cost? There are constitutional issues of the power of the Congress to compel nonmilitary service, practical questions about who would end up in the military, value questions concerning the intrusion on people's lives, and so many other issues that national service seems to us to be beyond the realm of probability if not possibility.

---

either because they qualified for deferment or because of physical disqualification, were most likely to consider the draft fair, and those who remained draft-eligible tended to think it unfair.

[30] The goal of national service is advocated in publications emanating from the National Service Secretariat, Donald Eberly, Executive Director, 522 Fifth Avenue, New York, N.Y. For a representative statement, see *A Plan for National Service* (November 1966).

UNIVERSAL MILITARY SERVICE OR UNIVERSAL MILITARY TRAINING

Another solution to the problem of inequities in military liability is to take every able-bodied male into the service, and some see advantages as well from administering military training to the entire male population, either for personal improvement or for the nation's benefit. The chief objections here are practical, although there are some who reject the idea of universality in military service as inconsistent with democratic values. The practical problems arise from the size of the manpower pool, the costs of absorbing such huge numbers of men in the services, and the incapacity of training facilities to cope with such an influx unless they were radically expanded. The estimates of the future manpower pool are as follows:

Year	Men Reaching 18th Birthday
1966	1,920,000
1968	1,860,000
1970	1,930,000
1972	2,050,000
1974	2,120,000

SOURCE: Defense Department estimates, reported in *Hearings*, p. 10003.

These estimates compare with a total of 1,170,000 in 1950, and their growing numbers will create a total available pool (ages nineteen through twenty-five) nearly 60 percent larger than in 1950. It will be recalled that universal training and service were rejected in 1951, partly for cost reasons and partly for value reasons; it seems even less likely that these approaches will be acceptable as solutions in the future.

A VOLUNTARY ARMY

The abolition of conscription carries an attraction that unites left and right, but it also encounters both philosophical and practical opposition.[31] Some of the former is based on the belief that in a democracy military service should be widely shared by the citizens. Yet it seems clear that the men most likely to enlist and re-enlist in a voluntary army would be from the less advantaged (though not poverty-level) sectors of the population. Some oppo-

---

[31] The strongest argument is contained in Bruce Chapman, *Wrong Man in Uniform* (New York: Trident Press, 1967). Examples of scholarly analysis may be found in Stuart Altman and Alan E. Fechter, "The Supply of Military Personnel" (paper presented at the meetings of the American Economic Association, December 1966) (con), and Walter Y. Oi, unpublished paper read at the Chicago Conference on the Draft, December 1966 (pro). Milton Friedman, another advocate of a voluntary army, has defended his position in the *New York Times Magazine* (May 14, 1967, p. 23). His case was rebutted in a letter from Stuart Altman which was printed in the June 4 issue, p. 12.

nents of a voluntary army argue also that a mercenary army would pose a threat to the society. In addition to these value-based arguments, there are several practical problems presented by a voluntary army.

1. How high would military salaries have to be raised to make service competitive in the labor market, and what total costs would be involved? The Defense Department study of 1964 sought to ascertain whether men would enlist if there were no draft, and to estimate the size of the armed forces that could be sustained solely from volunteers at various pay and unemployment levels. There are so many factors in this equation (including the occurrence of shooting wars) that there is room for wide disagreement over feasibility, but we may cite some basic statistics. Table 12 shows the responses of various groups of men who had enlisted in service to nearly identical variants of the question "Would you have enlisted if there had been no draft?" asked by the Defense Department in October and November of 1964. In all probability, the proportions would be much higher now, but these are sufficient to show the scope of the problem: not only does the draft provide substantial proportions of new accessions by induction, but a good share of the enlistments are draft-motivated as well.

TABLE 12
PROPORTIONS OF MEN WHO HAD ENLISTED IN MILITARY SERVICE WHOSE SERVICE WAS DRAFT-MOTIVATED,* 1964

Officers	% Draft-Motivated	Enlisted Men	% Draft-Motivated	Reserves	% Draft-Motivated
	41%		38%		71%
Breakdown by source:		Breakdown by age:		Breakdown by age:	
ROTC	45	17–19	31	17–19	40
OCS	51	20–25	58	20–21	77
Direct appointment	58			22 and over	89
		Breakdown by education:		Breakdown by education:	
		Non–high school graduate	23	Non–high school graduate	31
		High school graduate	40	High school graduate	59
		Some college or college graduate	58	Some college	71
				College graduate	90

* Based on the responses "No, definitely" or "No, probably" to the question "Would you have enlisted if there had been no draft?"
SOURCE: Defense Department surveys of men in the armed forces, October and November 1964, reported in *Hearings*, pp. 10038, 10039.

Proponents of the voluntary army argue that this situation would be drastically changed by paying members of the armed forces the wages their services would be worth in the open market, or by raising wages to the point necessary to fill the armed forces to the levels required. The proponents have a sound point when they argue that current military-service wage rates in effect impose a tax on those who serve,[32] and that both justice and the national economy would be served by paying military personnel wages equivalent to the value of their services in the open labor market. If this were the basis from which increases in wages needed to constitute and maintain a voluntary army were computed, the costs involved would not appear so high. These estimates range all the way from $4 billion to $17 billion to maintain a 2.7-million force level under various possible conditions, with the Defense Department's best estimate of net costs with a 4 percent unemployment rate being $8 billion.[33]

We should emphasize that the feasibility of a voluntary army depends heavily on the force level that is to be maintained. The cost estimates reviewed above are based on a force level of 2.7 million, but in mid-1967 there were 3.45 million men under arms. Not even the strongest advocate of a voluntary army considers it feasible until it is possible to reduce force levels.

The Defense Department's research sought to ascertain the effects of higher pay on enlistments if there were no draft, with some disquieting results for the cause of a voluntary army. Men aged sixteen to twenty-five years were asked, "If there were no draft now, and you had no military obligation at all, which condition would be most likely to get you to volunteer?" Table 13 presents responses by age and educational status. It seems apparent that pay scales comparable to those of the open labor market would not be sufficient, and that substantially greater salaries or other inducements would be necessary. Faced with the characteristics of motivations and potential costs which are intimated in the research reports from the Draft Study of 1964, the Defense Department has understandably been less optimistic about the feasibility of a voluntary army than have the proponents of the cause.

2. A second and to us even more serious problem in the voluntary-army proposals is the problem of flexibility. The present combined compulsory and "voluntary" procurement system has succeeded in meeting rapidly fluctuating demands for manpower, and it does not seem likely that mere manipulation of wage rates could achieve the same results. Experience has shown that it is sometimes necessary to draw in a million men the year after taking in less than half that number; would it be possible to raise wages sufficiently (and publicize the fact sufficiently) to induce such numbers to enlist within the time period in which their services were required? Presumably such wage increases would have to be extended to all those already in service, with potentially ballooned costs across the board. Could such wages, if raised in

[32] W. Lee Hansen and Burton A. Weisbrod, "Economics of the Military Draft" (unpublished paper, University of Wisconsin, 1966).

[33] *Hearings*, p. 10043.

TABLE 13
MOST IMPORTANT INDUCEMENT TO VOLUNTEER, BY AGE
AND EDUCATIONAL STATUS

| | Not in School | | In School | |
| | 16–19 | 20–25 | 16–19 | 20–25 |
Conditions	Years	Years	Years	Years
Military pay the same as civilian life	4%	5%	2%	3%
Military pay considerably higher than in civilian life	21	25	16	23
If given a $1,000 enlistment bonus	6	3	3	0
If guaranteed training in job or skill useful in civilian life	29	23	20	9
If sent to civilian school at government expense before or during service	18	19	31	30
If given opportunity for civilian school or college after service	8	8	12	12
Other miscellaneous conditions	7	10	6	9
If officer training available	7	7	11	14
	100%	100%	101%*	100%*

* Figures do not add to 100 because of rounding.
SOURCE: U.S. Census Bureau Survey of civilian men, October 1964, reported in *Hearings*, p. 10051.

the manner described, be reduced again when the need slackened? The cost issues are secondary to the problem of adding sufficient strength to the military in time of national need, and the voluntary-army advocates have not (perhaps cannot) lay to rest doubts on this score. One route taken is to suggest that some form of the draft be retained as support for the program in the event of such an emergency, but this seems to us to carry with it other problems, such as maintaining an organization without a regular function to perform.

In addition to lacking numbers flexibility, a voluntary army might also lack skills flexibility. At present the enlistment of men from higher educational levels is frequently draft-motivated, and of course some men from the higher educational levels are drafted. It is these men who can be readily trained in languages, intelligence analysis, electronic repair, and other skills necessary for the modern army. Even if the voluntary army could attract the required numbers, it is by no means clear that it could attract men with the necessary attitudes and skills.

The alternatives presented above were rejected, largely because of the problems we have outlined, by the official participants in the 1966–67 draft debate. But the National Advisory Commission on Selective Service, the Civilian Advisory Panel on Military Manpower Procurement, and President Johnson all suggested changes in the system in existence until June 30, 1967.

We summarize below their recommendations, together with the major provisions of the Military Selective Service Act of 1967.

NATIONAL ADVISORY COMMISSION PROPOSALS

The Commission considered and rejected the alternatives already mentioned and concentrated on altering the existing system more or less incrementally. The Commission's report, *In Pursuit of Equity: Who Should Serve When Not All Serve?* presented data similar to those we have presented and emphasized the inequity of the present system due to economic discrimination and variability among local boards, appeal boards, and the states. The chief recommendations made by the Commission to the President were as follows:

(a) Selective Service should be continued.

(b) The System should be reorganized to reduce the number of local boards to 300–500, with professional classifiers acting in accordance with nationally uniform classification standards and under a centralized arrangement with eight to ten regional offices. There would be local boards that would hear appeals from the actions of the initial classifier. Data processing equipment and methods should be used to maintain current and uniform handling of all registrants.

(c) Student deferments should be eliminated except for officer training programs.

(d) With the exception of hardship deferments, all deferments should be eliminated.

(e) Men should be inducted on a youngest-first basis at age nineteen.

(f) Men should be inducted by a random selection system in which their vulnerability would be limited to the year in which they were age nineteen.

(g) Non-prior-service men should not be allowed to enlist in the reserves or National Guard after being classified I-A. If reserve units cannot otherwise maintain their strength, they should be staffed by induction under the random selection system.

The President's Reaction. The President's message to Congress dealing with the draft asked for only two of the Commission recommendations; many of the recommendations were already within his existing authority under the Universal Military Training and Service Act of 1951. Primarily he asked Congress to extend the Selective Service System's authority to induct men who had not previously been deferred, and in addition he asked for standby authority to induct men into the reserves. He announced that he was referring the matter of Selective Service System reorganization to an interagency task force for study and review. He declared his intention of instituting a youngest-first call and said that he was instructing the Director of Selective Service to develop a random selection system in conjunction with the Secretary of Defense. He proposed to defer action on ending undergraduate student deferments for one year pending discussion in the Congress and by the public. but declared his intention to end graduate-student deferments.

THE CIVILIAN ADVISORY PANEL RECOMMENDATIONS

This panel, appointed by the chairman of the House Armed Services Committee to aid the Committee in its deliberations and also (apparently) to counterbalance the National (President's) Commission, made recommendations (not, however, based on research) which differed substantially from those of the National Commission. Among their many recommendations were the following:

(a) Induction authority should be extended.

(b) Care should be taken to ensure that any effort to establish greater uniformity in local board actions avoids diminishing the discretionary authority of local draft boards.

(c) Deferment should be granted for bona fide students of institutions of higher education who request and qualify for such deferment, and this deferment should remain in effect until the student terminates his student status, receives his undergraduate degree, or reaches the age of twenty-four.

(d) Occupational deferments should be continued.

(e) The "Modified Young Age Class System" should be adopted.

(f) A lottery should not be adopted to perform any of the functions of the Selective Service System and a data processing system centralized in Washington should not be adopted at this time.

Congressional Action and the Military Selective Service Act of 1967. Congress virtually ignored the recommendations of the National Advisory Commission and enacted changes that followed closely the recommendations of the Civilian Advisory Panel. Undergraduate student deferment was made a matter of right and occupational deferments were continued. Random selection was prohibited without further legislation by the Congress, but a youngest-first order of call was left within Presidential discretion. And men were given the right to enlist in the reserves or National Guard up until the date scheduled for their actual induction. Thus, every problem that is documented in our analysis, and particularly inequity in induction patterns and variability among local boards, seems likely to become more pronounced in the next four years under the act as extended.

V. POLICY ANALYSIS AND POLICY RECOMMENDATION: THE PROBLEM OF SELECTING AMONG ALTERNATIVES

Our analysis of the probable consequences of alternative military manpower procurement policies has clarified the implications of each, and perhaps it has (at least for practical purposes) simplified the problem of choice. But it does not, and probably cannot under most circumstances, fully solve the problem of choice. The critical question therefore is: Can we, acting as professional political scientists, recommend one alternative over others? There is no doubt that we could do so in our capacity as citizens, of course, but do the training expertise, and other professional skills that we or others may possess *as political scientists* enable us to make recommendations? We believe that the answer depends upon the state of knowledge in the particular policy area, the character of the analysis conducted, and the objectivity with which data and interpretations are presented. Not all subject areas will admit of professionally responsible recommendation, but some aspects of some areas will; in other words, the issue of professionalism hinges not upon the *fact* of recommendation, but upon the manner and circumstances in which the recommendations are made. Let us examine the process of choosing among alternatives in the military manpower procurement field.

In one sense, the content of public policy reflects the distribution of power resources and relative skills in wielding such resources among actors in the political process. But it also reflects a balance struck among *assumptions* accepted, *conditions* perceived, *goals* established, *value priorities* asserted, *means* available, and *effects and by-products* considered tolerable. Policies undeniably have, as one of several elements, a value component. But this need not in and of itself prevent the political scientist from making recommendations. The pressing character of public problems and the exigencies of governmental needs mandate employment of the social scientist's research skills and concepts, and those who develop superior knowledge will be asked to recommend solutions. In any given case, and whether or not the data and circumstances are sufficient to enable the researcher to act within the bounds of his professional expertise, it may be necessary for him to recommend measures to cope with public problems. In such cases, the social scientist will—and should —do the best he can with the data at his disposal. But some problem contexts may permit more. In three of the six elements just defined as making up the ingredients of the substance of policy, research may produce knowledge that will support recommendation as a professional act. These are the areas of relevant conditions, means available, and effects and by-products produced. Herein lies the strength of the social scientist: through sophisticated use of the current techniques of empirical research, he may be able to identify causes and effects with sufficient precision to be able to advise and recommend. The less we know, the more that remains for mere speculation, and the more we fall back on value preferences; conversely, the more we know, the more it is at least theoretically possible to reduce speculation and both reduce the number of and focus the issues for value choices.

For the social scientist faced with a request to employ his knowledge and respond to the existence of pressing public problems with recommendations for their solution, there are at least three general ways to choose among alternatives. First, he might frankly declare what values he considers appropriate, and seek to defend their propriety in some way. This might be through evidence of their widespread acceptance within the polity, or through evidence of their relevance in the past or under similar circumstances elsewhere, or through justification that sought to demonstrate their propriety by other criteria, such as their harmony with ideals of justice or democracy. Second, he might assume various possible values alternatively, in effect leaving the final choice to others. Among the alternative values considered, the stated goals of the present policy structure could be posited and means prescribed for their fuller attainment. Third, he might so assiduously develop data and refine interpretations of causes and effects in the areas of his peculiar strength (conditions, means, by-products) that the range of value choices would be drastically narrowed and so sharply focused that recommendation would involve a minimum of value preference. These broad categories of alternative-selecting approaches are arbitrary constructs, of course; rather than being really separable or mutually exclusive, they overlap, and any real situation will involve aspects of each. But situations will vary in the proportions in which each is applicable, with some problems of alternative selection favoring one approach more than others. The element of value choice is inescapable. We cannot avoid it, and it is better that we recognize it and confront it fully than consciously or unconsciously to conceal value preferences in the design or presentation of our research. There are, however, varying proportions of value choices involved in different acts of recommendation, and those in which there is a narrow area for value assertion (because of a well-developed set of data and interpretations) are professionally distinguishable.

Recommendation in the area of military manpower procurement, we believe, partakes sufficiently of the third category above that we can choose an alternative as political scientists. Very briefly, let us summarize the extent to which our data fill the requisites about conditions, means, and by-products, and structure the choice to be made. Before doing so, it is imperative that we make clear the parameters within which we operate. This may be done through the vehicle of the other three elements in the policy balance—assumptions, goals, and value priorities. Our assumptions, partly dictated by space exigencies of this paper, are that the United States will continue to have at least the present level of international commitments for the next five to ten years, that the maintenance of an armed force will be necessary, and that this force will at least for the next five years be composed of more than 2.7 million men. These assumptions in company with the data developed eliminate the alternatives of token armed forces and a voluntary army. The shift to a noncoercive procurement policy is an attractive proposal meriting full inquiry, but not even its strongest advocates believe it possible at force levels of nearly 3 million men. We assume also that the demonstrable financial and other costs of national service and universal military training will continue to foreclose their serious consideration. This brings our question down to one of the form of conscription policy. (We do not mean to define away all hard value choices in the course of this illustration; a glance at the range and intensity of the polemics in the draft-law debate of 1966–67 confirms that there is adequate value conflict remaining over the question of what form conscription policy should take to sustain its use for our purposes.)

We understand the goals of present policy to be the staffing of the armed forces on a flexible basis with minimum dislocation to the society and economy, and with maintenance of a level of public support and acquiescence sufficient to permit the accomplishment of the primary task. The major values with which the present policies have been designed are those of efficiency in use of manpower resources, and then equity in liability for military service. For the moment, we take these two as givens, and return to our data and interpretations.

We have seen that the *conditions* that are most significant for military manpower procurement purposes are those of steadily increasing manpower surplus over the armed forces' needs. Sharp increases in the incidence of college attendance have also occurred in the last two decades. The *means* now employed—decentralized local boards with decision-making power held by civilian volunteers—give rise to variability both within and between states. In part, this variability is based on differential impact of deferment policies on areas of different socioeconomic character, exacerbated by the allocation of quotas and calls to small jurisdictions, but an important share of it is traceable to the discretionary actions of boards themselves. The principal *by-products* identified were inefficiency in utilization of manpower resources, inequities in service liability following income and college-attendance lines, and widespread antipathy to the local-board concept. Close interrelationships exist among these factors: rising manpower surpluses give rise to the need to grant deferments freely, which precludes equity and inhibits efficiency; the use of local boards precludes efficiency and promotes antipathies among many members of the general public.

We think the following conclusions have been established: Present conscription policies have delivered the necessary numbers of men to the armed forces in a flexible manner, no small attainment. But the goals of minimum dislocation have not been met as well as the evidence suggests that they could be, and there is even the indication that public acquiescence in one aspect of conscription is weak. The values of efficiency and equity have not been served, except in symbolic or rhetorical terms; indeed, the inequities revealed by the evidence are a major indictment of present policies, if the stated values of the policies are taken at face value. We think that the evidence suggests that improvements can be made which will enable conscription policy to continue to provide men flexibly, but with fuller realization of some of its other stated goals and reduced dislocations and antipathies.

The conditions of manpower surplus are fixed, short of total mobilization, and college-attendance proportions are probably only slightly less so. Efficiency in the use of manpower resources under such conditions seems so unlikely as to be almost impossible. The local-board system could be eliminated, of course, and replaced by a nationally uniform system of classification based on carefully established criteria of national needs, but this would not assure efficiency; there would also have to be means of checking the continuity of men's employment in jobs that were known to meet the criteria of serving the national interest, perhaps for a period of up to fifteen years per man. The extent of surveillance and controls over the careers of young men requisite to attaining efficiency seems inconsistent with the usually accepted values of this society. We may be in error, of course, but we think this is a predictable and unprovocative value choice which we reasonably can expect to be shared broadly.

If efficiency is unattainable except under circumstances of radically altered means and atypical value choices of controls over personal lives, what are the prospects for achieving greater equity? Here we think the evidence leads in another direction. With a manpower surplus and mass college attendance, it is still possible to achieve equity without undermining flexibility of delivery of men or such efficiency as can be expected under any system. Not surprisingly, our recommendations resemble those of the National Advisory Commission on Selective Service, which we served as consultants. Essentially, we suggest elimination of all but the most essential deferments, induction at an early age (between eighteen and nineteen), and selection in sequence from a randomized order of call established nationally by mechanized randomizing processes.

Those deferments that are equally available to all, and which are necessary to the maintenance of an armed force, can remain unchanged. We have no quarrel with the setting of physical or mental requirements, though we are not confident that the present ones reflect minimum standards for all military tasks, and we suspect that standards are in part a reflection of the Army's need for men. We do challenge almost every other deferment as it is presently applied.

The student deferment is in our eyes the most discriminatory and the most vulnerable. We would eliminate it entirely, rather than attempt to limit its duration or prohibit its eventuation into other forms of deferment; under either of these alternatives, the deferment is still available to the higher income registrant, permitting him alone to choose his time of service and avoid the years of maximum danger. Because the services obtain many of their officers from ROTC programs,[34] we would defer ROTC students, as well as medical and dental students, who would be subject to a postdegree draft, just as they are now.

The elimination of fatherhood, occupational, and reserve deferments is not as drastic as may at first appear, when it is realized that we advocate earlier service. Not many men will have claims for such deferment between ages eighteen and nineteen, but we oppose them for those who might. The act of becoming a father should not bring deferment from service, and no injustice would result if the rule is clear in advance and not retroactively applied. The increased cost to the government in the form of dependency allowances seems a small price to pay to close this path of escape from military service. Some hardship cases would probably still have to be granted

---

[34] According to the *Report of the National Advisory Commission*, p. 43: "The military services get almost 80 percent of their new officers from college sources. The most substantial component of these are university ROTC students (about 40 percent of the new officer population) who receive special (class I-D) deferments. The other 40 percent of new officers are college and professional school graduates who receive general II-S student deferments while in college. This includes doctors and dentists, who make up about 17 percent of the new officer group each year."

deferment, although we would want them scrutinized objectively and without regard to the relative costs to the government. Occupational deferments should not be numerous, for few men can be truly irreplaceable in a critical occupation at age eighteen. We propose to use Selective Service to provide men for the reserves on a free and open basis. We will be charged with jeopardizing the integrity of the reserves, but this course will eliminate the economic biases, as well as potential favoritism and, in some states, racial discrimination, which exist in the present reserve selection procedures. The reserves and the National Guard should be freed of their attributes of a private associaton, and we see no way to accomplish this other than by requiring them to obtain their no-prior-service personnel through conscription processes.

The second part of our three-step proposal is induction between ages eighteen and nineteen. We think this desirable because it involves the least interference with careers and education, and provides the greatest certainty for individuals, educational institutions, and employers. Once a registrant has passed his year of liability, he would no longer be subject to service except in time of great national emergency. With reduced numbers of deferments, the manpower pool of eighteen-year-olds should be large enough to meet service requirements each year. When men emerge from service they could receive some form of government educational assistance if they wanted it. After the first two years of transition to such a system, therefore, the colleges should be able to count on a steady flow of probably greater numbers of students than under the present system. During the transition period, the colleges will suffer the absence of about one in every six male students who would otherwise have been in attendance.

The larger pool of men and the earlier age of service enhance the general desirability of instituting equitable selection procedures. Our third step, therefore, calls for a random selection to be made at age eighteen. This would involve randomized, possibly computerized, ordering of all eligible men to establish an order of call for the year. Registrants would know in advance whether they were likely to be inducted or not, a probability dependent chiefly on world conditions. If their situations changed during the year in such a way as to raise a claim for one of the few possible deferments, they would have recourse to appeals. Students deferred from one round of randomized selection because of their ROTC status could, in the event of failure to maintain good standing, or at their own option, enter the next subsequent selection group for a year of liability.

These three proposals, as a package, would go a long way toward eliminating present faults in the system, yet the advantages of the present system would be retained. Though each man's burden would not be the same (some would have to serve and some would not), at least the risk (or opportunity) of service would be the same for all registrants. Until his year of eligibility was over, no man could be sure he would not have to serve, but at least the period of uncertainty would be shortened. This system would interfere with the lives of individuals no more than the present system, and substantially less than any of the universal proposals. Clearly it has an element of compulsion not in the voluntary system, but it is also more flexible and more surely capable of producing the required numbers of men.

Such a system might be implemented by an organization quite different from the one now in existence. With few deferments and random selection there would be no need for local boards to classify and select men for induction. A much more centralized and professionalized organization could be used to administer the provisions we propose, but we have dealt elsewhere with the matter of organization change.[35] It is sufficient to point out that the kinds of changes we suggest in deferment and selection practices may (and probably would) have implications for the design of the implementing organization.

The foregoing recommendations are somewhat stark, principally because of space limitations. We have not, for example, given any consideration to such factors as the political costs of change in policies. Our focus in this section has been exclusively on the problem of political scientists' capacity to provide various forms of guidance for policy-makers as to the substance of policy and the merits of various possible problem-solving programs. We are aware that the substantively "best" policy may not be practical under given circumstances, and that there are many entirely defensible reasons why policies should not be changed even when "better" ways are acknowledged to be available. Nor have we considered many issues in the detail that their importance and complexity warrant. These too have been sacrificed for the purpose of presenting an illustration of one version of a policy-oriented approach to the study of politics.

Among the several potential payoffs that we think inhere in such an approach, recommendation is only one. And we are more than perfunctorily tentative in our argument that some forms of recommendation are under some circumstances within the range of the professional responsibilities of the political scientist who is inclined to make them. Recommendation was possible here because the areas for speculation were greatly reduced, and the evidence sharply narrowed the range of values that were attainable. This felicitous set of circumstances might not obtain in other subject areas, and perhaps some will feel that they did not exist even here.[36] In either case, the discipline

---

[35] Davis and Dolbeare, *Little Groups of Neighbors.*

[36] Since efficiency is unattainable without an organization and policies that would in all probability be anathema to Americans, and equity seems to be within the reach of possible policy adjustments, manpower procurement policy may seem to be uniquely subject to recommendation. But other areas may be, upon examination, equally susceptible to professional recommendation by political scientists.

If this much be granted, the question may arise as to whether those political scientists who are so inclined have any special discipline-based expertise to bring to the general area of policy recommendation, or whether they would be interchangeable with, say, competent economists or sociologists. We think that the training and scholarly interest of political science as a discipline create a strong though not exclusive entitlement and responsibility in this area. While the interests and methods of social science disciplines overlap substantially, each discipline also has its own distinctive questions,

should develop standards that will facilitate the identification of those recommendations that can carry the imprimatur of professional respectability. But even if we should arrive at the point where we sanitize political science entirely against the making of all recommendations except in the capacity of citizens, two vital implications will survive: empirical techniques will increasingly be employed by increasingly sophisticated social scientists to enable governments to respond more adequately to the multitude of pressing public problems in their environments, and we can add much to our understanding of the nature of political life by the study of public policy as an independent variable, its impact and effects, feedback and support processes, and so on, without ever reaching the boundaries of recommendation or immediate relevance to government action.

---

problems, and areas of expertise. If the policies may be undertaken in part or entirely by governmental institutions; if the impact of these policies must be assessed in comprehensive terms, including the political consequences; if alternative administrative feasibility is relevant; if the alternative values to be maximized must be justified in terms of their demonstrable and probable consequences (past, present, and future) ; and if an understanding of the contemporary political process and its strengths, weaknesses, and supports is requisite, then political scientists should be included in such endeavors. In short, we see competent political scientists as synthesizing the research products of many disciplines in professional and objective ways, interpreting these findings in terms of target goals and probable consequences within the policy, and formulating recommendations that will serve the nation's needs effectively. Continuously guided by the developing research techniques and findings of the pure empiricist and employing open and assessable evaluative standards in a professionally competent manner, the interested political scientist can add important dimensions to policy recommendation. Not only is he able to make such contributions, but he brings an additional and desirable increment of professional expertise to the task.

6

Water Resource Development: Some Problems in Economic and Political Analysis of Public Policy*

VINCENT OSTROM

I. THE WATER PROBLEM

There are quite tangible physical reasons, unrelated to the wiles of politicians, for problems of water resource development to become deeply involved in the political process. *The* water problem is, in fact, a multitude of problems, but most are problems of fluidity. Wherever water behaves as a liquid, it has the characteristics of (1) a common-pool flow resource, involving (2) a complex bundle of potential goods and bads, which sustain (3) a high level of interaction or interdependence among the various joint and alternative uses. The interrelationships among all three of these characteristics simply compound the difficulties of settling upon stable, long-term institutional arrangements for the economic development of water resources.

THE COMMON-POOL FLOW-RESOURCE PROBLEM

A simple case of a common-pool flow-resource problem can be illustrated by the development of a groundwater supply from an isolated basin overlaid with a property ownership pattern where numerous individual owners have equal and independent rights to tap the water beneath their land. The decision

* I wish to acknowledge the helpful comments of the participants at the Cape Newagen conference, and also those made by Robert Bish, Philip Gregg, Ronald Oakerson, Allan Schmid, Mark Sproul-Jones, and Louis Weschler on an earlier draft of this paper. I am also indebted to the Water Resources Research Center at Indiana University for its support of my current research efforts and to Resources for the Future, Inc., for the support of earlier research that contributed toward this paper.

rules of private-property law require an owner's willing consent to take action involving the use or control of his property. Without political interference each proprietor would be free to exploit the water underlying his land for his own benefit. The most aggressive proprietor can attempt to capture the lion's share by pumping as much as possible from under his land. Each other proprietor has an incentive to follow a similar strategy and maximize his individual return. Each will be led by the structure of the common-pool situation to make excessive expenditures, to overproduce in the short run, and to waste the physical resource potential in the long run.

Since the net return to each overlying proprietor would be greater if all agreed to act collectively in arranging the optimum development of the resource, the rational solution would involve collective action by all overlying proprietors. However, the decision rule for collective action by private proprietors acting individually would require unanimous consent. No one would be willing to agree to restrict his independence in decision-making unless all others would agree to restrict their independence of decision-making and could be forced to comply with the terms of such an agreement. If all others should restrict their production and leave one person free to pursue his own independent course of action, that person would be free to capture the lion's share. The development of a common-pool flow resource is apt to lead toward a dog-in-the-manger attitude: each proprietor pursues his advantage and ignores the consequences of his action upon the welfare of the other proprietors.

The common-pool problem is the classical case of a situation where the rational self-interests of all individuals would suggest a collective solution, but where the prospect of collective action on the basis of the decision rule requiring the willing consent of each proprietor is negligible. Someone would usually find it expedient to hold out for the lion's share, and only one holdout would effectively veto any collective arrangement. A rational solution requires that the rule of willing consent be relaxed and that collective action be authorized on the basis of some alternative decision rule requiring less than the willing consent of each and every proprietor. Such action requires recourse to the decision-making facilities provided by governmental institutions, which are facilities for making and enforcing decisions where willing consent cannot be required of all affected persons for each specific decision.[1]

THE COMPLEX BUNDLE OF POTENTIAL GOODS AND BADS

Any major river system is a potential source of a complex bundle of goods and bads for the people who can draw upon and utilize its potentials. Water is essential to all life processes and to all productive enterprises, and

---

[1] William J. Baumol, *Welfare Economics and the Theory of the State* (Cambridge: Harvard University Press, 1952); James Buchanan and Gordon Tullock, *The Calculus of Consent* (Ann Arbor: University of Michigan Press, 1962); and Mancur Olson, Jr., *The Logic of Collective Action* (Cambridge: Harvard University Press, 1965), provide the basic theoretical formulation pertinent to these conclusions.

offers a variety of opportunities of substantial importance to human welfare. In a consideration of the goods or services that can be derived from a river system, a distinction can initially be made between land uses and channel uses. Land uses include the provision of water for domestic consumption, stock watering, municipal and industrial purposes, irrigation, and the discharge of waste products. These uses tend to be related to volume of water, and water can be metered by volume and marketed by the volume used. Channel uses emphasize utilities to be derived from the flow characteristics of a stream, such as navigation, recreation, fish and wildlife, flood control, pollution abatement, and power production.

Land uses require special works to divert water from its source and to transport water to the location of use upon the land. Water for such uses is typically confined in a distribution system and can be treated as a marketable commodity. But even in the case of a municipal water supply system, common-pool flow-resource characteristics manifest themselves in a number of ways. A distribution system capable of handling large demands requires a continuous flow, uninterrupted by the happenstance of intervening property ownership. Again the structure of incentives inherent in the common-pool problem arises. If each proprietor whose property is traversed by a pipeline were free to hold out for as much as he could get, the costs of acquiring right of way for a water distribution system would become extraordinarily high, to the long-run disadvantage of the aggregate community of water users. As a result, the extraordinary powers of eminent domain (i.e., the power to compel the sale of an easement or right of way for "just compensation") is usually made available to any enterprise offering water services for sale to the public. A water distribution system can thus be constructed on a least-cost basis, with compensation being required only for the opportunities forgone by intervening landowners by virtue of the fact that their land is occupied by an adverse easement.

In turn, the high capital costs of constructing a distribution system capable of sustaining a continuous flow imply that the first proprietor will preempt a marketing service area and a second or third proprietor can be effectively precluded from entry. In short, continuous-flow distribution systems give rise to natural monopolies. The implied political *quid pro quo* for the power to traverse the property of unwilling landowners creates a liability on the part of profitable water distribution enterprises to public regulation of their pricing and service policies.[2]

Other common-pool flow characteristics show up in the design, construction, and operation of municipal water distribution systems. An important use of water is for fire suppression, and such a use depends in part upon the flow characteristics of a water distribution system. These "fire-flow" characteristics of a municipal water supply system, in turn, enter into calculations for determining fire insurance rates on insurable property. Similarly, water quality standards in relation to public health requirements are an incidental

---

[2] See, e.g., *Fallbrook Irrigation District* v. *Bradley*, 164 U.S. 112, 158–59.

common-pool attribute of water supplied by a distribution system. Grievances associated with the "lack of water" for fire-control purposes and with epidemics of water-borne diseases have been important factors associated with the shift from private to public ownership of municipal water distribution systems during the course of the past century.

Finally, an additional facet of the flow-resource problem associated with the distribution of water for various land uses arises from the return flow of water which is residual to any particular pattern of use. Water is rarely consumed *in toto*. In municipal supply systems, the residual supply is often used to perform the added function of disposing of wastes through sewers before the water is again discharged into a watercourse to intermingle as a part of the flow-resource system. Residual waters discharged after their cycle of land uses may be so heavily polluted as to be toxic and injurious for subsequent uses, and thus constitute a "bad" for other downstream users. In irrigation systems, on the other hand, the return flow residual to prior uses may have substantial economic value in replenishing groundwater supplies or for subsequent diversion by other irrigators at downstream locations. The use and reuse of residual waters, which flow into and become a part of the aggregate resource pool, create many of the most sensitive political problems in management of water resource systems and in the interrelationships among enterprises involved in water resource development.

Channel uses of a water resource system pose even more difficult problems of management and allocation than those involved in the management and allocation of water supplies for land use. Where a common-pool flow resource is subject to use in its natural state for the ultimate enjoyment of a consuming population, a common-pool resource meets all the criteria associated with a purely public good.[3] A private proprietor might be able to deny access to a particular site along a stream, but private proprietors cannot effectively deny access to a river system for boating, swimming, fishing, or other such recreational uses. All who can gain access to a stream are free to use it. Within very broad tolerances, use by one does not preclude or interfere with use by others. Only a public monopoly can exercise control over such a resource where access is either denied to everyone except under the terms and conditions regulating the public use of such a resource or extended to everyone under the terms and conditions of public use.

The physical conditions bearing upon various channel uses give rise to different opportunities for constituting appropriate organizational arrangements to develop and manage such services. The provision of flood-control facilities and the regulation of a stream for flood-control purposes provide a benefit to the affected property owners which is available to all in like circumstances. None can be technically excluded from enjoying the benefit. A charge for flood-control service cannot be instituted except as a compulsory

---

[3] An extensive literature on the theory of public goods has been developed by Paul A. Samuelson, Richard A. Musgrave, Albert Breton, Julius Margolis, James Buchanan, Mancur Olson, Jr., Gordon Tullock, and many others.

tax levy. The task of devising a tax that would function as an efficient service charge proportional to the benefit received would be extraordinarily difficult. Landowners at each different contour of a flood plain would enjoy a different level of benefit.

On the other hand, the use of water for sports fishing can be subject to exclusion by prohibiting all without a license from fishing. A license fee can be conceptualized as the equivalent of a price charged by a legal monopoly. But fish and game departments cannot exercise effective monopoly control over anadromous salmonoid fisheries in the open ocean. The common-pool problems involving anadromous fisheries are thus of fundamentally different spatial proportions than the common-pool problems involving flood control and the discharge of floodwaters.

The use of a river for navigational purposes is somewhat analogous to its use for fishing purposes. Improvements to enhance navigation might be financed by a service fee charged those using a stream for navigational purposes. While exclusion is technically feasible and service fees might be established to place the burden for the cost of the improvement upon the beneficiaries, a problem may arise over the economic feasibility of establishing such marketing arrangements. If the cost of collecting service charges exceeds the revenues produced, then a system of service charges would not be warranted on economic grounds.

The use of the hydraulic gradient of a stream for the production of hydroelectric energy is relatively easy to conceptualize in marketing terms. At the production level the use of a stream for the generation of power is part and parcel of the common-pool flow-resource situation. However, electrical power can be metered and sold under circumstances that are crudely analogous to, but simpler than, the distribution and sale of water for land uses. Electrical energy as a product derived from a common-pool source can be marketed to the ultimate consumer.

Thus the complex bundle of economic goods and services that comprise the potential yield of a water resource system ranges in a spectrum from those that can be subject to provision in a market economy to those that can be provided only as public goods or services. At one extreme would be the marginal case of the production and distribution of bottled water, and at the other extreme would be the provision of flood-control services. Between is a range of services subject to provision under imperfect market conditions or subject to an unequal provision as a public service. The provision of most water services involves special problems of a systemic character which are not amenable to simple solution by provision in a competitive market economy.

INTERDEPENDENCE AMONG JOINT AND ALTERNATIVE USES

The final element of complexity associated with the water problem is the high degree of interdependence or interaction among the joint and alternative uses that can be made of a water resource system as a common-pool flow resource. Patterns of interaction may, under certain circumstances, be complementary or facilitative, so that the use of water for one purpose enhances its use for another purpose. Or the patterns of interaction may be competitive or exclusive, so that a use or an increase in use for one purpose precludes the use or diminishes the potential supply for another purpose.

Under conditions of extreme variation between peak flood flows and low flows that coincide with peak demands, any measure to increase the low flow for land use by storing floodwater could have a joint payoff in reduced flood damages as well as increased supply of water for subsequent diversion. However, increasing diversions for consumptive land uses during the low-flow season without commensurate increases in supply from storage may impair the diverse channel uses of a river system. Flood control, power production, and diversion of water for land uses often have substantial complementarities. When such situations occur, other problems arise regarding assignments of costs and benefits. Who pays for what, and who gets what benefit?

Each pattern of use has relatively specific parameters, and substantial variations beyond those parameters begin to have significant influence on the uses to which water can be put. Perhaps the most sensitive channel use of a stream is as a fishery. The maintenance of a fishery may be relatively sensitive to conditions of water temperature, sedimentation, pollution, oxygen content of the water, and the maintenance of an unobstructed flow. Unless these values are taken into account in the construction of dams, in the screening of diversion works, in regulation of the quality of return flow, and in maintenance of a live stream flow, the utilization of a river system for these other uses is apt to impair or even preclude the use of that stream as a fishery. Is a fishery simply a resource to be destroyed by default through the failure of the individual calculus to take such costs into account in the exploitation of a common-pool resource system? Or, if they are to be taken into account, how is the accounting to be made in the context of specific institutional arrangements?

Peripheral changes in the economy, changes in water technology, and changes in consumer preferences may significantly affect the equilibrium of supply and demand for different uses of a water resource system at different points in time. Before the development of the railroad and the automobile, for example, a high priority was given to the use of water for transportation purposes. Large expenditures were made for canals and other navigational facilities. The use of water for navigational purposes during much of this century is proportionally much smaller than it was during the first half of the nineteenth century because of peripheral changes in the economics of land-based transportation facilities. Our contemporary era of affluence, with increased leisure time and abundant automobile transportation, may see substantial growth in demand for the use and enjoyment of flowing water for recreational purposes in its natural environs. The development of electricity and the invention of the deep-well turbine pump at the turn of the century significantly expanded the potential water supply available from groundwater sources. Desalinization of ocean water and weather modification may again alter supply conditions in the future.

The basic task in the management and development of water resource systems is the devising of institutional arrangements that will properly proportion the supply of water to each joint and alternative use and reallocate the supply among those joint and alternative uses to meet changing conditions of demand and supply. I turn next to the problems of water resource development and allocation viewed from the perspective of economic analysis, and then to an examination of the terms and conditions for political action involved in water resource development.

II. RESOURCE ALLOCATION, INVESTMENT, AND PRICING POLICIES

The solution to a problem of resource allocation in economic theory requires that a resource be allocated to its various uses until the marginal unit of the resource allocated to each use is equal in value to the marginal unit allocated to every other use. The value reflected by that point of equilibrium represents the economic price that at any given point in time will efficiently allocate the available supply to all of the competing demands. If patterns of demands change, a new price equilibrium should be reestablished, so that, though the quantities supplied to various uses may have changed, the marginal value for each use will be the same. A resource would thus be continuously allocated and reallocated to maintain an equilibrium among all uses so that value of the marginal unit is equal in each and every use.

Investment in development is justified when the potential supply of a resource can be devoted to a potential use for which benefits exceed costs. For a packageable good, revenue should be sufficient at a marginal price equilibrium to cover the cost of producing the marginal unit of supply over an appropriate time horizon which will take account of the opportunities forgone in alternative forms of investment. The flow of anticipated benefits discounted at an appropriate rate of interest to reflect the opportunity cost of capital should at least equal the anticipated costs of any incremental development before that development is economically justified.

The economic solution is theoretically attainable in a perfectly competitive market dealing with homogeneous packageable goods that can be freely (in a legal and political sense) exchanged for a price under market conditions. When economic analysis is applied to the conditions of allocating and developing water resources, some rather paradoxical problems arise; the optimal solution for the single entrepreneur often deviates significantly from the socially optimal solution.

This disjunction between the optimum for a single entrepreneur and the social optimum derives from two circumstances. The first is the discrepancy that may arise between the calculation of costs and benefits by the individual proprietor using a common-pool resource as against the aggregate calculation of costs and benefits for all users. The second circumstance arises when the cost of developing each incremental source of supply is significantly higher than that of each previous source of supply. I shall examine these two situations in turn.

DISCREPANCIES BETWEEN INDIVIDUAL AND SOCIAL CONSIDERATIONS IN CALCULATING DEVELOPMENT PROGRAMS

Common-pool flow resources, which yield a complex bundle of goods and bads and which are subject to a high degree of interdependence among different joint and alternative uses, are apt to manifest a high degree of divergence between individual benefit-cost calculations and social benefit-cost calculations. The short-run economic interest of the individual is to maximize his personal advantage and to disregard the calculation of opportunities that he causes others to forgo. The optimal solution for the individual entrepreneur is likely not to be optimal for the aggregate of all users in relation to their total pattern of use.

This disequilibrium between the individual and the social calculus can theoretically be resolved by constituting the structure of economic relationships in such a way that both positive and negative spillover effects will be taken into account and an appropriate transfer of payments be made among the people affected. Such solutions require recourse to the political process in order to assign costs and secure payments without regard to the willing consent of each person to make them. Public expenditures must complement individual expenditures if investment policies are to take account of external effects as well as the separable benefits enjoyed by individual proprietors. Water resource development thus requires a mix of both public and private investments if an optimal result is to be achieved.

The literature in economic analysis has dealt extensively with the common-pool problem and the divergence between economic costs and benefits realized by individual entrepreneurs and social costs and benefits. Extensive recognition has been given to the problem of calculating spillover effects and "externalities," and to the problem of constituting enterprises so as to "internalize" the externalities. The essential function of public enterprises in internalizing the externalities of water resource development has gained increasing recognition in this literature.[4]

PROBLEMS OF WATER PRICING POLICIES

The development of any flow resource may also give rise to serious difficulties deriving from alternative pricing policies. In the interest of an economic solution, water users can rationally be expected to develop the cheapest source of water first. When the limits of that source of supply are reached, alternative supplies from more distant sources will be sought out and developed. In an area experiencing a high rate of growth over a period of

---

[4] Contributors to this literature include John V. Krutilla, Otto Eckstein, Allen V. Kneese, Irving Fox, Roland N. McKean, A. Allan Schmid, and J. W. Milliman.

time, several sources of supply may be added from progressively more distant sources and at an increasing cost for the average unit of water from each marginal addition.

Economists usually argue that the marginal cost of the last added unit should establish the price for all units of production. Such a pricing policy would assure that water users take account of the increasing marginal value of water in their decisions as water users. They would accordingly learn to use water more economically, cease to use it for uneconomic uses (i.e., where costs would exceed benefits), and reallocate the supply to more valued uses.

If we have the case of a sharply rising long-run marginal-cost curve for the incremental addition of increasingly costly sources of water supply, the least-cost solution for the consumers of such an enterprise would be to average out the aggregate costs over the total amount supplied and follow an average-cost pricing policy. Such a price might be substantially less than the average cost of the last marginal unit;[5] and so, average-cost pricing would not create the appropriate incentive for users to allocate water to their economic use, given the marginal value of water. The corollary of this condition is that a water production agency operating under conditions of a marginal-pricing policy with a sharply rising marginal-cost curve will realize a substantial "producer surplus," "economic rent," or profit.

A typical plotting of alternative pricing policies with a sharply ascending marginal-cost curve, as reflected in Figure 1, is indicative of the broad discretion inherent in a monopoly situation.[6] The rectangle OEFI represents the gross revenue derived from a profit-maximizing pricing policy in which costs are represented by the space below line AL, and the balance is producer surplus, economic rent, or profit. A marginal-cost pricing policy would generate revenues represented by rectangle ODGJ, and line BM would distinguish producer surplus or profit from costs. In an average-cost pricing policy, rectangle OCHK would represent gross revenues where gross revenue would equal cost. Producer surplus or profits varies radically from profit maximization to marginal-cost pricing to average-cost pricing.

If the firm functioning as a monopolist were a "nonprofit" public enterprise controlled by voters who were also its exclusive customers, we would be presented with the somewhat paradoxical result that economists would advise voters to charge themselves at marginal cost, which would return a very substantial profit to their publicly owned water supply system. Where marginal-cost pricing significantly diverges from average-cost pricing,

---

[5] I use the *average cost* of the marginal blocks added to total supply because water systems are built in increments that involve large blocks of added capacity. If any other cost unit is used, decisions to build added capacity would be based on one set of assumptions and decisions to use would be based upon other sets of assumptions with radically varying consequences for price structures.

[6] See Jack Hirschleifer, James C. De Haven, and Jerome W. Milliman, *Water Supply* (Chicago: University of Chicago Press, 1960), p. 57, for a similar formulation. Compute their data on water-production costs for the city of Los Angeles, p. 305, to note the radical divergence of different pricing policies.

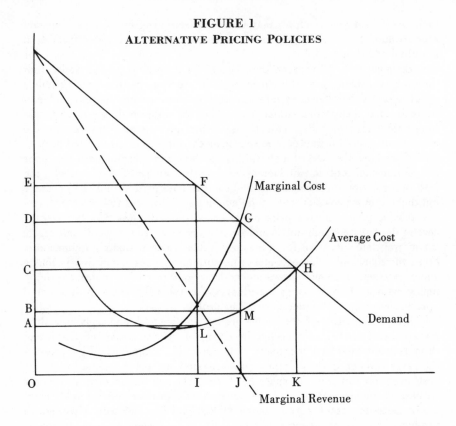

FIGURE 1
ALTERNATIVE PRICING POLICIES

the interests of producers will significantly diverge from the interests of consumers. Economists have traditionally assumed such a divergence. Yet an increasing marginal-cost curve is also typical of many publicly provided services. Political scientists might do well to reexamine assumptions that the interests of consumers and producers tend to converge in the public sector.

Assuming that the voters in a locally controlled public enterprise forgo their least-cost solution as consumers and approve of marginal-cost pricing, we are then confronted with the problem of rationalizing the economic conduct of water producers who appreciate the potentials for profit in this fortuitous circumstance. Very large margins in rate of return give rise to a wide range of strategic entrepreneurial opportunities. If the producer were a nonprofit government agency serving a local community of water users, substantial incentive would exist for those functioning as water producers to preempt as large blocks of water supply as they could feasibly undertake within the limits of available financial resources. One might anticipate a rather aggressive rivalry among such enterprises in attempts to preempt the potential sources of supply on behalf of different communities competing for limited water resources. Marginal-cost pricing would not seriously dampen producer incentives to preempt development opportunities, even though it would be expected to lead consumers to lower their level of demand. Behavior analogous to economic imperialism by local government agencies would be the expected pattern.[7]

Public entrepreneurs under such circumstances might also find substantial incentive to take advantage of any potential opportunities to develop complementary joint uses where revenues would justify the marginal expenditure. As a result, a public water supply system might use water flowing through aqueducts from high in the mountains to generate electrical energy and further increase the profitability of the enterprise. The prospects of large margins of return might even create incentives to exploit opportunities entailing short-term losses in order to enhance long-term opportunities.

Nonreimbursable public expenditures to assure an appropriate level of development for a nonmarketable service such as flood control would simply magnify the entrepreneurial opportunities inherent in multiple-purpose water resource development. If payments are not required to compensate for the opportunities forgone in alternative channel uses of water for fish and wildlife, recreation, or the like, problems of misallocation will inevitably follow.

While average-cost pricing of the total supply produced by each enterprise would tend to dampen independent entrepreneurial initiative somewhat, it would also tend to create an increased voter incentive to sustain a high level of investment to generate opportunities for economic development where a favorable rate of return could be procured by added increments of water supply. People living in a desert region with a high economic potential except for the scarcity of water may have every incentive as voters to support an aggressive pattern of water resource development. The structure of incentives in such situations inevitably leads to overdevelopment and misallocation. If demands at average-cost pricing exceed the supply available at that price, alternative rationing mechanisms will have to be used to allocate the available supply in the absence of a significant increase in price.

If such enterprises were privately owned and profits were dispersed as dividends, the structure of incentives would not be significantly altered. The equity would be capitalized at a proportionately higher level. Gross expenditures for investment would be reduced but a similar scramble to preempt resources and gain control over the profit-producing potentials of such resources could be anticipated. The force of public regulation over the service charges of such enterprises has the cumulative effect of establishing a regulated price that approximates average-cost pricing by limiting profits to a "fair" rate of return on the aggregate investment.

Contrarily, "economic" development (i.e., development based upon the

---

[7] Mason Gaffney, "Diseconomies Inherent in Western Water Law," *Economic Analysis of Multiple Use* (proceedings of the Western Agricultural Economics Research Council, Tucson, Arizona, January 23, 1961), pp. 55–81.

prescriptions of economic theory in relation to marginal-cost pricing) might generate substantial resentment on the part of the community of water users about the "unfairness" and "unreasonableness" of their "plight" as against the "windfall profits" enjoyed by water purveyors. The political terms of trade in the United States tend to preclude such "economic" solutions, and most utility pricing for water services is based on an average aggregate cost of production plus a "fair" rate of return to profitable enterprises. The "proper" settlement, if any, of this type of paradoxical, contradictory, and conflict-laden situation is not conclusive if the political costs of the "economic" solution are considered.

III. THE TERMS AND CONDITIONS OF
POLITICAL ACTION

Since the short-term economic calculus does not in these circumstances pro-duce satisfactory results, what then is the nature of the political calculus that might enable these problems to be remedied? Rational economic behavior, in the view of most economists, should be controlled exclusively by economic, not political, calculations. Somehow there should be political arrangements external to the economic process which could issue the appropriate commands and require the self-interested, law-abiding, economic man to pursue those courses of action which are consistent with maximizing the aggregate social welfare of the community.

Logically, if there were an omniscient Ethical Observer or Benevolent Despot who could (1) observe all potential discrepancies between individual and aggregate welfare calculations, (2) pronounce appropriate changes in the rules to rectify such discrepancies, and (3) function as a referee in enforcing the modified calculus, then individuals would be free to function as economic men in pursuit of their own short-term economic advantage in harmony with the aggregate social-welfare functions specified by the Ethical Observer. As a theoretical device the Ethical Observer is essentially external to the problem of equilibrium analysis in economic theory. No great violence is done to market theory by positing an Ethical Observer to function as an omniscient and omnipotent political referee at zero cost. However, the postulation of omniscient, omnipotent, no-cost political capabilities can do substantial vio-lence to applied economic analysis whenever political terms and conditions begin to assume a significant influence on economic conduct in a segment of the economy composed predominantly of public enterprises. These enterprises are governed more by reference to the political process than by reference to market competition. *Political action is not a zero-cost process.*

The use of the Ethical Observer as a theoretical device also leads toward the analytical bias of assuming all economic behavior to be *lawful* and concerned only with an exchange of *goods*. The strategic possibility of using threats in bargaining and of considering the economics of "bads" has only recently been developed in economics literature concerned with the dynamics of conflict and threat systems.[8] The input-output ratios in producing "bads" are of fundamentally different magnitudes—as anyone who has contemplated the "economics" of Molotov cocktails appreciates—than the input-output ratios involved in the usual benefit-cost analysis of "economic" undertakings. The task of resolving conflict and maintaining a social system at a point of political equilibrium where a population finds it agreeable to sustain productive pursuits rather than violent and destructive activities is a difficult problem, and can never be empirically analyzed as a zero-cost function.

Political analysis relevant to decision-making in a democratic society cannot begin by using the analytical device of an Ethical Observer as an underlying philosophical assumption. Instead, we must begin with the much more difficult and radical assumption that individual men in a democratic society must assume responsibility for reconciling the conflicts that derive from circumstances where short-term individual and group interests deviate significantly from long-term aggregate social welfare. The terms and conditions for making such calculations are established through the political process.

A CONCEPT OF POLITICAL PRICE

A useful distinction between the calculations inherent in an economic situation and those implicit in a political situation can be derived from the concept of price. Wicksteed has defined price as "the terms on which alternatives are offered to us."[9] Since we do not always confront "offers," Wicksteed's definition can be modified to read, "the terms on which alternatives are *available* to us." As Wicksteed indicated, "Price . . . in the narrow sense of 'the money for which a material thing, a service, or a privilege can be obtained' is simply a special case of price in the wider sense."[10] Price in this narrower sense is the *economic* price. The "political" terms on which alternatives are available to us is another special case of price, i.e., the *political* price. Thus the economic price and the political price need to be totaled to establish an aggregate price. A price in the wider sense reflects both an economic and a political component among "the terms on which alternatives are available to us."

With such a conception of price we would assume that a rational self-interested individual, seeking to maximize his aggregate net welfare or income position, would have to make a mixed calculation of both the economic and political price of the alternatives available to him. He would make his decisions on the basis of the aggregate economic and political terms that

---

[8] Kenneth E. Boulding, "Towards a Pure Theory of Threat Systems," *American Economic Review*, 53 (May 1963) : 424–34.

[9] Philip H. Wicksteed, *The Common Sense of Political Economy*, ed. Lionel Robbins (London: Routledge & Kegan Paul, Ltd., 1957), p. 28.

[10] *Ibid.*

leave him in the most favorable net position. The economic price, by definition, would be more easily calculated in money terms. The political price cannot be quantified in any precise sense, but represents conditional opportunities and exposure.[11] The price of any good or service, in the wider sense, may theoretically have radically varying ratios between the economic and the political component. Social relationships that we normally characterize as "economic" involve those situations where the ratio in an aggregate price is predominantly composed of the market price expressed in monetary terms; and those social relationships that we normally label "political" involve the obverse, where the political price expressed as conditional opportunities and exposures becomes proportionately larger in the aggregate price.

A POLITICAL PRICE IMPLIED IN ALL LEGAL RELATIONSHIPS

The structure of all legal relationships implies a paradigm of political terms and conditions which can be expressed as a correlative assignment of capabilities (rights, powers, privileges, and immunities) and limitations (duties, liabilities, exposures, and disabilities) in relation to all social conduct.[12] The capability for action inherent in any claim to a right involves a commensurate set of limitations inherent in the legal positions of others. These assignments of capabilities and limitations establish the political price inherent in all transactions.

In private economic transactions the legal position of an individual might be formulated in the following way: An individual is free (i.e., has the legally assigned opportunity or capability) to act independently in the pursuit of his individual economic interest subject to the limitation (i.e., the legally assigned exposure) that he does not cause harm or injury to others. Any person who considers himself to be harmed or injured by the actions of

---

[11] The out-of-pocket cost of litigation, for example, can be very high. If one were prepared to go all the way in litigation involving a controversial point of law, I would guess that the minimum expected cost would be $50,000 to $100,000. Litigation spanning a period of more than two decades and involving costs of several million dollars is not unusual in western water controversies. The costs of political decision-making and the problems of financing those costs deserve careful examination by political scientists.

[12] This paradigm of the structure of legal relationships is drawn from the works of W. N. Hohfeld and John R. Commons. Commons, in *Legal Foundations of Capitalism*, reprint ed. (Madison: University of Wisconsin Press, 1959), modified Hohfeld's paradigm and applied it to a general discussion of the institutional structure of economic relationships. Commons' presentation is excellent except for some relatively superficial discussion of "physical power" or "violence" as the basis of political association. Contemporary anthropologists have drawn heavily upon this work, but, as far as I have been able to determine, economists and political scientists have made little use of it. The sociologically oriented political scientist might wish to consider whether roles derive from the strategic opportunities inherent in the rules ordering the games of life or whether rules derive from roles. If the former is true, a sociology based upon role theory has more to learn from political science than political science has to learn from such a sociology, if we are to understand "regularities" in social behavior.

another is entitled (i.e., has the legally assigned opportunity or capability) to seek an appropriate remedy through the political process subject to the calculated risk or limitation that his claim may not be sustained. Not all injuries are subject to remedies as liabilities.[13]

Thus, every transaction and every social relationship has an implied political price. For the bulk of transactions and social relationships that people sustain with one another, the political price can be minimized by relying upon the decision rule of willing consent or voluntary agreement of each and every person involved.

Those conditions that are conducive to the maintenance of an effective, workable competition in a market economy, are also conducive to individual decision-making on the basis of willing consent. A good that is easily confined or packaged, amenable to exclusive control by individual action, and not the source of consequences that adversely impinge upon others, can readily be treated as a personal property subject to individual ownership with minimal necessity for public regulation.

Since most social relationships in a democratic society are governed by the decision rule of willing consent or voluntary agreement, I prefer to consider this the base rule in the constitution of a democratic society.[14] It is a most useful rule for facilitating agreeable arrangements at minimum costs, but an insufficient rule for dealing with conflict and other disagreeable situations. Thus, all legal relationships imply a second order of decision-making where the rule of willing consent can be relaxed so that decisions may be reached in the absence of willing consent. Governmental institutions are created for the purpose of making decisions and sustaining performance in the absence of voluntary agreement and willing consent.

The political price associated with any potential value can be expected to climb sharply when recourse is sought to this second order of decision-making requiring use of governmental decision-making arrangements. Yet recourse to governmental decision-making arrangements theoretically affords opportunities to proceed at a lesser cost than acting individually. Otherwise, there would be no incentive to use such facilities, and the state would indeed wither away!

Cost Functions Comprising a Political Price

Buchanan and Tullock have taken an initial step in developing a theoretical basis for analyzing the cost functions involved in the price of political action.[15] They describe two cost functions applicable to all collective decision-

---

[13] E.g., "acts of God" are not compensable as legal liabilities except where covered by liability insurance. Losses caused by economic competition are usually not subject to liability. Presumably the right to do business carries the commensurate liability of being exposed to the competitive behavior of other entrepreneurs.

[14] The majority-vote rule is only one of several rules, albeit an important one, for reaching decisions in the absence of willing consent.

[15] Buchanan and Tullock, *Calculus of Consent.*

making problems. One, illustrated in Figure 2, describes the potential costs, harms, or deprivations that can be expected to flow from assigning decision-making responsibility to a subset of the individuals comprising a collectivity. This cost function, which they call "expected external costs," is a declining cost curve that descends rapidly from a point representing reliance upon only one decision-maker to a point of zero cost, where the total population is included among the decision-makers.[16] From the perspective of the population subject to such decision rules, the curve describes their anticipated cost of potential deprivations. From the perspective of those exercising the decision-making capabilities, this same curve would describe their opportunity for potential indulgences.

Buchanan and Tullock describe another cost curve that has a contrary trend. This curve, illustrated in Figure 3, they characterize as "expected decision costs," represented by the expected expenditure of time and effort involved in decision-making.[17] If the decision-cost curve represents only out-of-pocket costs, there would be little reason to anticipate symmetry in the two cost curves. However, if time-and-effort costs are conceptualized to include opportunity costs, the strategic bargaining power inherent in the ultimate veto position in a common-pool situation would be as great as the power inherent in the assignment of full authority to one decision-maker. The expected-decision-cost curve would thus tend to be symmetrical, at least at the end point, with the expected-external-cost curve.

When these two cost functions are combined, as illustrated in Figure 4, they describe a single total political-cost curve with a U-shaped characteristic.[18] The least-cost point is somewhere in the midrange with expectations of sharply ascending costs as power is concentrated with either a single person holding full authority or a single person exercising an ultimate veto.

The Buchanan and Tullock analysis deviates radically from the Ethical Observer solution. The Ethical Observer solution would yield zero cost in potential deprivations, in forgone opportunities, and in actual expenditures on decision-making. This is a no-cost solution. Buchanan and Tullock deny the possibility of no-cost decision rules. All decisions involve political cost. Even the market is not a cost-free decision-making mechanism.[19] Buchanan and

---

[16] *Ibid.*, p. 65.

[17] *Ibid.*, p. 70. Herbert J. Kiesling, in a paper entitled "A Criticism of the Potential Costs of Alternative Decision-Making Rules as Constructed by Buchanan and Tullock in Their Book, *The Calculus of Consent*," found it desirable to give greater emphasis to a "strategic bargaining" component apart from the "time and effort" component in expected decision costs as a means of recognizing the potential veto position occupied by the *n*th person or a small set of *n*th persons in a collectivity relying on a rule of unanimity. Strategic bargaining costs can also be conceptualized as opportunity costs inherent in time-and-effort costs as reflected by the opportunities forgone by not making a decision or by making a decision only under the terms agreeable to a holdout. As a result, I have chosen to think of time-and-effort costs as including opportunity costs associated with the time and effort expended.

[18] *Ibid.*, p. 71.

[19] See R. H. Coase, "The Nature of the Firm," *Economica*, 4 (November 1937): 386–405.

COST FUNCTIONS IN POLITICAL PRICING
FIGURE 2   FIGURE 3

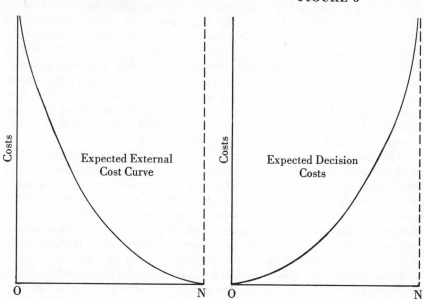

FIGURE 4

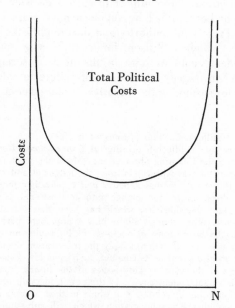

Based on James Buchanan and Gordon Tullock, *The Calculus of Consent* (Ann Arbor: University of Michigan Press, 1962), pp. 60–70.

Tullock imply that a least-cost rule can be conceived for each kind of decision-making situation depending upon the nature of the circumstances involved. The least-cost position in their formulation is at the low point on the political-cost curve. If the least-cost position is at a point below the level of benefits that can be derived from collective action, then a rational group of men should be willing to relax the requirement of the rule of willing consent and to substitute a decision rule that would approximate the least-cost solution.[20] Thus, collective decisions can be reached on the basis of an individual political calculus allowing for collective action if the requirement of willing consent is relaxed and some alternative decision rule is substituted.

If we as political scientists can begin to assess the costs of political action in light of the terms on which alternative decision-making arangements are available to people within a political system, we may be in a position to make an increasingly significant contribution to the analysis of public policy. At the same time, such a method of analysis should contribute to a better understanding of the operational dynamics both of particular decision structures and of a relatively open political system composed of a multiplicity of different decision-making structures that offer a large number of alternative political remedies for diverse problems. If, for example, the potential costs of opportunities forgone as a consequence of a political stalemate may be very high, a decision rule authorizing decisions by a single person could be relied upon. Of course, one would expect the potential opportunities for self-indulgence by such a decision-maker to be very great and the anticipated cost of potential deprivations for those subject to such a decision to be very high. This calculus might be modified by supplementary rules to condition and constrain such an exercise of authority and thus modify the anticipated costs of political action. Woodrow Wilson, for example, was much aware of the initiative a President could exercise in the area of foreign policy.[21] But Wilson's life ended in tragedy because of his failure to calculate accurately the political price for sustaining the initiative he had taken as President of the United States.

---

[20] Buchanan and Tullock, *Calculus of Consent*, p. 83.

[21] A new preface to the fifteenth printing of *Congressional Government*, dated 15 August 1900, contained the following observation: "Much the most important change to be noted is the result of the war with Spain upon the lodgment and exercise of power in our federal system: the *greatly increased power and opportunity for constructive statesmanship* given the President by the plunge into international politics and into the administration of distant dependencies, which has been that war's most striking and momentous consequence. When foreign affairs play a prominent part in the politics and policy of a nation, its Executive must of necessity be its guide; must utter every initial judgment, take every first step of action, supply the information upon which it is to act, suggest and in large measure control its conduct. . . . Upon his choice, his character, his experience hang some of the most weighty issues of the future. . . . Interesting things may come out of this singular change. . . . [T]he new leadership of the Executive . . . will have a very far-reaching effect upon our whole method of government. . . . It may bring about, as a consequence, an integration which will substitute statesmanship for government by mass meeting. It may put this whole volume hopelessly out of date" (New York: Meridian Books, 1956, pp. 22–23; emphasis added).

In considering the dispersion of authority in a federal system of government with two sets of governmental institutions, each composed of diverse, relatively autonomous decision structures, one might again advance a hypothetical formulation based upon Buchanan and Tullock's two cost fuctions. Reliance upon a single-sovereign solution, with full and final authority vested in a single unit, would probably result in great opportunities to impose potential deprivations upon others and to derive substantial indulgences for those who functioned in such a decision-making structure. As the. number of alternative units increases, the anticipated costs of potential deprivations would be expected to diminish. In turn, the long-run strategic decision-making costs would tend to increase as those who were dissatisfied with a particular decision would seek alternative political remedies from different decision structures.[22]

Rational individuals, when confronted with such a cost calculus, would attempt to reach a workable solution that would constitute an agreeable settlement to everyone concerned rather than expose themselves to sharply increasing long-term strategic decision costs and increasing opportunity costs associated with continued conflict. They would follow a mixed strategy; they would use governmental decision-making facilities where these were appropriate, but they would complement such action with ancillary efforts to reach a negotiated settlement outside the formal arena provided by any particular decision-making structure.[23]

Presumably the least-cost position for each person, with reference both to political costs and to the benefits of collective actions, would vary. It would not be unreasonable to expect politicians to distort the political dialogue by an overemphasis on the opportunity costs inherent in delay.[24] As political entrepreneurs, politicians must sustain a level of support sufficient to assure reelection by facilitating the solution of political problems and performing public services on behalf of their constituencies. In general, one might anticipate that in a political system composed of a number of units with a large variety of relatively independent public enterprises, some politicians would voice persistent demands for action at the same time that they were employing delaying tactics until countervailing interests could be convinced of the advantage of the actions they propose. Political "crises" need not always be viewed as crises, in fact, but as a normal characteristic of political discourse in a political system that offers a variety of political remedies. Our modes of analysis should permit us to penetrate beneath the surface rather than take the protestations and harangues of political discourse at face value.

---

[22] Gordon Tullock has conceptualized a similar formulation in a paper on the theory of federalism not yet published.

[23] I have discussed the problem of mixed strategy in a "polycentric" political system much more fully in an unpublished paper on "Operational Federalism."

[24] James M. Buchanan, *Public Finance in Democratic Processes* (Chapel Hill: University of North Carolina Press, 1967). See especially chap. 10, on "The Fiscal Illusion."

IV. WATER INSTITUTIONS AS POLITICAL ARTIFACTS

The types of organizational arrangements and policies used to form and govern enterprises to provide water services reflect the terms and conditions for political action inherent in the decision-making arrangements of the political process. For any enterprise to become an effective organization, the conditions of political feasibility established by the political process must be met. Only those arrangements that can sustain affirmative decisions over the long run will become stable increments in the development of longstanding institutional arrangements for organizing human activity. The course of institutional development is one of decision-making, of reaching agreement about the constitution of social relationships in all human endeavors.

An examination of the history of a particular political community should enable us to draw some inferences about the nature of the political process from the type of solutions that are evoked in undertaking collective action. I shall examine efforts in the state of California to reach such solutions in the development of that state's water resources.

CALIFORNIA'S FAILURE TO DEVELOP A DEFINITIVE LAW OF WATER RIGHTS

A century of controversy has gone into various efforts to formulate a definitive law of water rights in California. The result is a tangled jungle of contradictions and ambiguity filled with enough loopholes to baffle and confuse any knowledgeable expert who tries to conceptualize the California law of water rights as a logically coherent system of rules.

A new system of water law was first fashioned among the early California gold miners to determine the allocation of water rights on the basis of prior appropriation (i.e., first in time, first in right). The state supreme court, however, sustained the common-law doctrine of riparian rights granting all proprietors of land adjoining a stream equal access to it for reasonable use of its water upon riparian lands only. The state legislature, in turn, subsequently sought to convert all riparian rights to appropriations based upon historical use and to permit all subsequent development of surface waters to occur only by appropriation. The courts held this action void insofar as it circumscribed the inchoate rights of riparian proprietors and thus deprived persons of property without due process of law. The courts, in turn, recognized all appropriations that met the statutory requirement of continued adverse use over a period of five years as establishing a prescriptive right against all riparian owners whose rights had been impaired. Substantial portions of the statute permitting the exercise of administrative discretion in the licensing of appropriations and in the adjudication of water rights were adjudged to be beyond the competence of the state legislature, and consequently to be an unconstitutional infringement of judicial authority.

Instead of relying upon the common-law doctrine in establishing ground-water rights, the courts formulated a new correlative-rights doctrine allowing all landowners to exercise a right to the reasonable use of groundwater supplies subject to the correlative right of all other proprietors to make reasonable use of such supplies without reference to the place of use. An effort was made in 1928 to reconcile some of the contradictions in the California law of water rights by the adoption of an amendment to the state constitution requiring the state courts to modify previous decisions by which new appropriators had frequently been enjoined from diverting water when such diversion would impair the prior rights of riparians to the full natural flow of the stream. This pattern of confusion in the California law of water rights is currently being compounded by a line of federal court decisions defining the special prerogatives of federal agencies and their degree of immunity from and liability to the provisions of state law.

In general, one can conclude that the California law of water rights has become so complicated that no entrepreneur can know precisely what he owns when he claims a water right. The present director of the California Department of Water Resources, W. R. Gianelli, had clearly reached such a conclusion when he observed:

> Without agreement any of the parties could find enough loopholes in California water law to tie up the other parties indefinitely in litigation with the end result that nothing gets built and the parties are subject to long delays and considerable expense.[25]

Gianelli's observation clearly implies that California's system of government has failed in its essential political function of formulating a clearly understandable set of legal prescriptions that would permit economic men to pursue their economic opportunities of water resource development within the limits of lawful conduct without further necessity to function as political men. Gianelli suggests that the burden of political action to devise agreeable arrangements for undertaking any new program of water resource development falls primarily upon the water developer or entrepreneur. In effect, the shortcomings of the law create both an obligation and an opportunity. The economic entrepreneur must also be a political entrepreneur.

The definition of equitable interests through litigation rarely settles conflicts over water rights, but serves only to determine the respective bargaining positions of the various parties in formulating a solution to their mutual problems and in assigning the burdens or costs associated with that solution. The correlative-rights doctrine manifest in several species of California water rights usually implies an obligation on the part of each claimant to assume a burden proportionate to his benefits. Thus it is not possible for one person to be assured of a constant supply while someone else must assume the primary burden or obligation for any shortages. Assigning proportionate burdens to all water users creates an incentive for each to search out a

---

[25] Memorandum by W. R. Gianelli to Harvey O. Banks (formerly Director, Department of Water Resources) on "Conflicts in the Development of Recent Major Water Development Projects," dittoed (September 18, 1959), p. 7.

mutually satisfactory solution rather than attempt to shift the burden to the few highly exposed or disadvantaged individuals.

THE PUBLIC-ENTERPRISE SOLUTION

Instead of pressing for a general solution by reformulating and rationalizing the law of water rights, water users in California have devised particularistic solutions to undertake collective action by organizing some form of public enterprise. Political elements of such solutions are often expressed in the form of a charter, constitution, or organic legislation creating a new form of public enterprise. The basic political decisions are made in the course of negotiating the terms and conditions for the charter of such an enterprise. Substantial unanimity is essential if the necessary legislative, judicial, and electoral approval is to be assured.

Such political solutions are usually the complement of an engineering plan to undertake and operate the physical works in a specific program of development. The organization of a public enterprise usually permits collective action through a self-governing public corporation, and thus precludes anyone from exercising the strategic bargaining power inherent in a holdout position. Such public enterprises are usually organized to include the aggregate community of people benefiting from the development of the resource potential, with collective decision-making arrangements to provide for political representation of the local community of water users in all decisions affecting water resource development for the community.

The institutional substructure of the California water industry is today comprised of many hundreds of public water districts and municipal utility systems organized as public enterprises. Such enterprises have been tiered one upon another to perform diverse and complementary functions. An enterprise producing a supplementary supply of water may thus come to function as a producer and/or wholesaler serving a variety of other public enterprises functioning as water distributors. The general configuration of institutions providing water services in California reflects substantial vertical differentiation with an institutional base formed by individual water users who are either consumers of predominantly public enterprises or "independent" water producers supplying their own consumptive requirements from a "natural" source of supply managed by public enterprises. The large-scale operations involving statewide and federal interests are organized through agencies of the state and federal governments functioning as the principal large-scale water production and management agencies.

The system of public enterprises that form the institutional complex of the California water industry also manifests characteristics of substantial horizontal differentiation. Water distribution systems for rural areas are usually organized independently of those serving urban areas, and the size of the individual distribution systems varies significantly throughout the state. Sewer systems are usually organized independently through other public enterprises, with separate facilities for sanitation sewers, storm drains, and agricultural drains. Agencies concerned with the management of channel uses of a resource system are also substantially independent, specializing in fish and wildlife, recreation facilities, flood control and navigation, hydroelectric power generation, or storage of water for diversion purposes and for the regulation of stream flow. Still other agencies may be concerned with the conservation and management of groundwater supplies.

INCREMENTAL DECISION-MAKING IN A POLYCENTRIC POLITICAL SYSTEM

The structure of authority defining the political terms and conditions available to the people of California gives access to different levels of government with substantial capabilities for independent political action at each level. In addition to the legislative authority normally assigned to political instrumentalities of the state and national governments in the American constitutional system, authority is reserved by the people of California to legislate directly through initiative petition and referenda in regard to statutory enactments and constitutional revision. A strong constitutional commitment to home rule gives municipalities quite independent sets of political alternatives for organizing enterprises to provide water services with minimal reference to state authorities. A variety of public proprietary services can also be provided to local "unincorporated" communities as a result of a strong county home-rule tradition permitting county authorities to act on behalf of local residents within the general latitudes of state law. A significant measure of autonomous rule-making authority is also exercised by judges in state courts acting under equity jurisprudence. Much of California water law is a product of judicial "legislation" formulated as equitable solutions to cases involving water rights.

Efforts to devise general solutions to water problems have been destined to failure because of the relatively easy access to a large number of governmental decision-making structures and the great diversity of conditions affecting the supply of and demand for water resources in different parts of California. Substantial disagreement simply means that those who win one round in a political struggle are confronted with the task of sustaining their position for another round in a different political arena. Even the weight of federal authority may not be enough to preclude an alternate arrangement: a new state Department of Water Resources was organized to supply water at a more agreeable political price than is available from federal agencies.[26]

---

[26] This alludes, in part, to controversy over the 160-acre limitation, subsidies to agricultural water users, and other federal policies. Urban water users have little (i.e., some but not much) incentive for paying to subsidize water for agricultural purposes; and some agricultural users would prefer to pay a higher price for water and not be subject to an acreage limitation. While no one has explicitly announced that the purpose of the Department of Water Resources is to function as a rival large-scale water producer offering different terms and conditions (including a higher dollar price for irrigation water) than the large-scale federal water producers, the implication is obvious. While federal law prevails in the service policies of federal agencies, the state need not

Instead of seeking general solutions, Californians have demonstrated a clear preference for the political strategy of seeking particular solutions to specific problems in the development of their water institutions. If substantial consensus among those directly involved can be reached on some particular solution to a specific problem, that agreement can usually be sustained and confirmed through the decision-making facilities afforded by the general political system.

Given the very large number of interdependent relationships inherent in the variety of common-pool flow-resource situations that manifest themselves in water resource developments for a large, diversified state like California, it would be impossible to cover every contingency by the constitution of a new independent public enterprise to deal with each and every set of interdependent relationships. Once a basic structure of complementary public enterprises is established, problems can then be solved incrementally by (1) negotiated agreement among enterprises, (2) incremental change in the structure for governing internal agency relationships, (3) change in statutory public policies affecting agency relationships, or (4) a combination of all three.

Since the costs of political action can be significantly reduced if a general agreement can be reached, a substantial incentive exists to find agreeable solutions.[27] Thus the negotiation of an agreeable solution to common interests is the basic method of decision-making among public enterprises operating in the California water industry. The availability of alternative governmental decision-making facilities assures that no one can occupy an ultimate holdout position, and each has an incentive to seek a settlement in light of the comparative costs of different political alternatives.

The process of negotiation is, in effect, the hidden hand in government functioning to give due consideration to common values among diverse interests in much the same way that competition functions in the market to give due consideration to the exchange value (i.e., common value) of separ-

---

accept the absolute priority of agricultural use inherent in federal reclamation law as controlling the allocations of water supplied by state or local agencies not contracting for services with the Bureau of Reclamation. Some of those who see state and local governments as archaic strongholds of a rural-based political power structure might do well to analyze the way federal policies are used to impose outdated priorities plus subsidies on behalf of agricultural developments in areas being overwhelmed by urbanization.

[27] By "general agreement" I mean a circumstance where *an effort is made* to secure a decision or agreements acceptable to all parties but with due recognition that this may not be possible. If a substantial majority of those participating can find an agreeable solution, and if others are willing to settle while withholding formal assent, then a general agreement has been attained. Concepts of justice and equity are based upon systems of reasoning about the institutional order of social life; and about the reasonableness of solutions in righting wrongs or in making decisions regarding individual welfare functions and aggregate social welfare functions. It is possible to agree to a rule as reasonable even though its application means greater deprivations than benefits for particular individuals or aggregates of individuals. Willing consent to voluntary agreements may not be forthcoming in such a situation, even though there might be gracious acceptance of a social obligation. This is the fundamental ground upon which concepts of authority and legitimacy must depend if they are to have any psychological or political validity.

able goods. For negotiations to open the way to a solution in the political process, each negotiator must know the political price inherent in the available alternatives. An opportunity is then created to reach a settlement by negotiations on the basis of a lesser-cost solution, given the political price established by alternative methods of decision-making. Errors will be made in assessing and calculating strategic opportunities. We cannot anticipate that all decisions will be reached under optimal political terms and conditions. A relatively high political price will have to be paid when parties to an action miscalculate the alternative terms and conditions available to them and fail to settle for a lesser-cost solution. All social structures are subject to error. Incentives can be created to avoid errors, to reduce the future costs of past errors, and to reduce the prospects of repeating errors; but no arrangement is errorproof.

V. RESOLVING PROBLEMS OF MISALLOCATION AND OVERDEVELOPMENT THROUGH THE POLITICAL PROCESS

Where goods involving interdependent utility functions can be provided by a highly differentiated system of public enterprises, problems of misallocation can be alleviated by adjusting the terms of trade between different sets of such enterprises and consequently among different sets of users. When one set of users realizes a benefit from a common-pool flow resource to the disadvantage of another set, the other users are paying a cost in forgone opportunities in proportion to the special benefit or misallocation being enjoyed by the privileged beneficiaries. If the aggregate price to the specially privileged beneficiaries is increased so as to eliminate the opportunity costs imposed upon others, a reasonable equilibrium among diverse uses of a common-pool flow resource should be reestablished.

The economic dictum that a resource should be allocated to its various uses until its value for each use is equivalent to its value for every other use serves as a reasonable criterion, but it can be applied only imperfectly in practice. The criterion is properly applied only to an aggregate social price or an aggregate social value. A price measured in monetary terms most closely reflects full social value when it is applied to marketable commodities having insignificant social costs and benefits or minimal spillover effects. As social values not expressible in monetary terms increase in significance, a market price becomes an increasingly poor measure for the aggregate value of a good. If nonmonetary values are to be recognized in a pricing system including user taxes for publicly provided goods or services, then one would anticipate the necessity of establishing a weighted and segregated pricing structure. If public provision of a good or service is justified, one would expect a public pricing and/or taxing system to be "administered" rather than left to the control of the free play of market forces.

Rather than rely exclusively upon the marginal value of water for its "highest" use in analyzing misallocational problems, we must compare the value of water for its "higher" uses with the value of water for opportunities that are being forgone. If the values being forgone are significant, and if those values are the result, in part, of adverse preemption by the "higher" users, then a political incentive will exist to modify the terms of trade between the two sets of users and reduce extremes in misallocation. In the absence of market mechanisms to adjust the supply and demand of water for dissimilar but interdependent types of use, those who are injured or are paying the costs of forgone opportunities will have to seek remedies through the political process. And this they have done repeatedly in California.

Given the political calculations inherent in the previous discussion, it is reasonable to anticipate that as the value of water devoted to fisheries increases and as the costs of forgone fishery opportunities increase by the adverse preemption of water for other purposes, then fishery agencies and organizations of fishermen will press for the inclusion of any such opportunity costs in the "price" of water appropriated for other purposes. The price of water at its source should at least be equal to the value of forgone opportunities. The political costs of establishing such a policy need not be high in light of an increasing demand for water in outdoor recreation. The corollary of such a policy is the establishment of a pricing policy among public agencies conducting outdoor recreation programs to include the provision of sports fisheries to pay the incremental costs for such programs without requiring other water users or general taxpayers to assume the added incremental burden.[28]

Problems of misallocation will only be exacerbated if tax money collected without reference to benefits from water resource development is used to sustain developmental programs of benefit to a discrete and disparate set of users and without general benefit to the taxpaying population as a whole. If the terms and conditions inherent in political action create an incentive to raid the public treasury in order to avoid the economic costs inherent in allocating common-pool water supplies to their respective uses, the political process does not provide an appropriate calculus in the short run to bring individual incentives into harmony with the aggregate social welfare, but may instead serve to magnify or distort the allocational problem.

The possibility of compounding misallocation upon misallocation in

---

[28] If a municipal water supply system opens its reservoirs for recreational use and the costs of processing water are increased as a consequence, the costs should be borne by those enjoying the recreational benefits. If the two communities of users are identical, then no difficulty need arise, but if they represent disparate populations, it is difficult to argue that one should go to an expense to produce a benefit for the other. I have excluded welfare considerations bearing upon redistribution of income from these discussions. I doubt that this purpose can be effectively served by water resource allocational policies. Too frequently discussion of income redistribution effects are no more than political illusions; when, for example, the poor are dispossessed in the name of "urban renewal" to improve the welfare position of the well-to-do, when wage earners are required to pay a disproportionately large share of the costs of free medical care to the aged, or when free public recreational facilities are provided only at distant locations requiring high transportation costs to gain access.

public decision-making is an inherent part of the calculus implicit in any political system organized upon the basis of a diversity of decision rules. As I have indicated earlier, we can anticipate very great costs in potential deprivations if authority to act is vested in one person and all other persons in a collectivity are compelled to pay the costs associated with such decisions. Money paid to the treasury for such purposes may represent a compounded deprivation (i.e., paying a price for having something costly done to oneself). Money in a public treasury thus may have a very low order of value (i.e., a much lower value than money in a personal bank account), and under certain circumstances persons may rationally attempt to find ways to commit funds in the public treasury to "noneconomic" uses within the scope of their political influence, but uses that represent a higher order of social return to them than having such funds used to deprive themselves still further. The lesser-cost solutions for individuals in such a situation would emphatically not be to commit all areas of decision-making to one-man rule, but rather to limit their exposure to one-man rule to circumstances where the opportunity costs of a contrary rule might be even greater. But the costs in potential deprivations produced by a mixed structure of decision rules may cause highly divergent and seemingly irrational calculations to be made as people seek to take best advantage of the aggregate opportunities available to them.

I shall not undertake the task of comparing the opportunity costs of attempting to maintain law and order in Vietnam with domestic opportunities for water resource development in order to sustain a conclusion that "uneconomic" investment of federal funds for water resource development may be the more "economic" use of those funds. Action based upon such a process of reasoning may lead to very high costs in potential deprivation among the Vietnamese, the American forces, and the American taxpayers, *and* to increased costs in forgone opportunities for those who have their sources of water supply preempted at no cost by those able to raid the treasury and effect a transfer of water to their "higher" economic benefit. Unless the political process can be used to facilitate agreeable arrangements for sustaining all human endeavors, the social costs inherent in imposing solutions upon unwilling people can quickly escalate as one conflict triggers other conflicts.

As the requirement of willing consent is relaxed, the political process is apt to create an intoxicating illusion of affording opportunities to get something for nothing, or of being able to impose a "rational" order upon a "chaotic" situation. Both the spoilsman and the radical reformer are apt to make short-term political calculations of winning on the assumption that the essential structure of the political process is a win-lose contest based upon capabilities for securing a minimum winning coalition. Such contests do exist, and such strategies are possible. The strategy of the holdout is possible. A political system must therefore provide remedies for dealing with the spoilsman and the radical reformer, just as it provides remedies for dealing with the holdout, who by ignoring the consequences of his behavior imposes costs upon others.

If one looks not to the short-term gain to be derived from a preemptive win, but to the long-term problem of resource management, short-term wins can give rise both to high costs in inefficient resource allocation and to high long-run strategic decision-making costs in unresolved controversy. Public entrepreneurs concerned with sustaining the operation of a resource development agency in the long run must be prepared to sustain the viability of their enterprises without regard for who "wins" or "loses" particular political contests in the short run. In their political calculations, public entrepreneurs cannot afford to lose; and the only way to preclude a political defeat or a veto is to sustain decisions on the basis of an economic strategy to attempt to maximize the aggregate social welfare. The political counterpart of this economic strategy is the attempt to secure a negotiated settlement by willing agreement with due recognition that such a solution is not feasible without potential recourse to decision-making structures that permit decisions to be made in the absence of willing consent. Occasional decisions can be made by a minimum winning coalition, but they are risky and can have a very high political cost, as people are free to pursue political opportunities in other decision structures and return to engage in the contest over and over again.

The political process does not afford both the necessary and the sufficient conditions to assure efficient and harmonious results. It can provide the necessary conditions to enable people to secure optimal results. It can never provide the sufficient conditions, independent of human choice. A perfectly competitive market economy would assure the necessary and sufficient conditions for the efficient allocation of some goods in economic theory only so long as law and order are postulated. The sufficiency of economic theory dissolves when the law-and-order postulate is relaxed. The provision of law and order is a costly process. As we come to know the political process in the form of a political calculus elucidating the terms on which alternatives for decision-making are available, perhaps we can begin to evaluate the political price of policy alternatives.

The misallocational problem in the California water industry can perhaps best be solved by seeking means to adjust differences so that the price of water at its source covers the cost of opportunities being forgone in alternative uses for that water supply. Water production from groundwater basins in southern California is now being taxed to cover the costs of groundwater-basin replenishment and conservation programs. A water-yield tax to cover forgone opportunities inherent in excluded alternative uses of surface waters would tend to correct problems of misallocation and to adjust water prices to include the cost of excluded alternative uses.

If these misallocational problems can be kept within reasonable limits, and if public funds do not come to have an unreasonably low value in opportunity costs, the aggregate overdevelopment of water resources in California should not assume disturbing proportions. In a world plagued by problems of underdevelopment, a mild case of overdevelopment provoked by an aggressive public entrepreneurship may be a benign disease. Others may wish to learn more about the political terms and conditions for producing such a benign affliction in order to remedy still more serious problems of public policy.

7

The Analysis of Public Policy:
A Search for Theories and Roles

ROBERT H. SALISBURY

This paper attempts several tasks. I shall begin by examining what political scientists mean when they employ the concept of public policy. I hope to persuade the reader that there is substantial agreement about the general boundaries of that notion and that this is not, therefore, a question to be lingered over. Next I shall argue that political scientists have traditionally been greatly preoccupied with policy analysis but that they have largely confined their attentions to a particular category of policy, what I call constitutional policy. In this preoccupation descriptive and prescriptive analysis have been very often combined, but a number of reasonably explicit criteria for analytic measurement and evaluation have been employed. I shall turn then to a consideration of substantive policy. I intend to join in the typologizing and modeling games, partly to help organize the existing literature and partly to suggest what I believe to be the crucial role that policy content must be assigned as a component variable in the analysis of any political system. Finally, I shall raise briefly the question of the way in which political scientists may employ their credentials as professional analysts of political systems and processes to affect policy outcomes.

This last task is, of course, an especially dense political thicket, but the rest of the undertaking already requires such hardiness of spirit that I am emboldened to undertake the encounter. Throughout I have tried to keep the focus on the analysis of policy outcomes and have incorporated other variables only when, and to the extent that, they may reasonably be linked with policies in explanatory statements. But my conception of what properly constitutes a policy focus is so catholic that remarkably little of what political scientists have done needs to be omitted. The problem therefore has been to select appropriate illustrative cases from a much larger pool and to aggregate them within a framework that seems to me to be promising. In the process, however, I have doubtless trampled on nuances of meaning and done injustice to the contextual richness of particular studies. Moreover, I have left out much that could be included. I can defend myself only with whatever virtue my efforts at synthesis may have for comprehending where we are and suggesting where we might go next.

I. WHAT WE MEAN BY POLICY

It is commonplace to lament the absence of clear understanding concerning the basic terms of political analysis, but it appears that the range of disagreement concerning the notion of "policy" is not so very great. One may distinguish three major positions on the question, sometimes taken separately and sometimes in combination. The most common usage of the term "policy," surely, is derived from some version of David Easton's definition of the proper object of political analysis: "the authoritative allocation of values for the whole society."[1] Public policy consists in authoritative or sanctioned decisions by governmental actors. It refers to the "substance" of what government does and is to be distinguished from the processes by which decisions are made. Policy here means the outcomes or outputs of governmental processes.[2]

A second view of policy would confine the usage to "broad" or general questions, and use another term for detailed choices made within the framework of "policy." Thus policy consists of a general frame of authoritative rules, and, while the precise boundary between policy and nonpolicy is nearly always debatable in the particular situation, the distinction crops up over and over. Dichotomies like "discretionary versus ministerial acts," "political versus nonpolitical," "controversial versus routine," and, of course, "policy versus administration" suggest the manifold permutations on the theme and remind us of the wide currency of the usage.[3]

A third way of talking about policy is rooted in the assumption that political behavior is goal-oriented or purposive. Policy here means those actions calculated to achieve the goal or purpose. Thus one may speak of "policy orientations," or "the policy of the AFL-CIO." Lasswell and Kaplan define policy as "a projected program of goal values and practices."[4] Closely

---

[1] David Easton, *The Political System* (New York: Alfred A. Knopf, Inc., 1953), pp. 129ff.

[2] In a more recent statement Easton defines policy as "decision rules adopted by authorities as a guide to behavior . . . In this sense, policies would be just a term for a kind of authoritative verbal output" (*A Systems Analysis of Political Life* [New York: John Wiley & Sons, 1965], p. 358). See also pp. 6–9 and 27–29, above.

[3] Thus Easton: "But the term [policy] is used in a second and broader sense to describe the more general intentions of the authorities of which any specific binding output might be a partial expression" (*ibid.*). From the days of Frank Goodnow on the distinction is a familiar one.

[4] Harold D. Lasswell and Abraham Kaplan, *Power and Society* (New Haven: Yale University Press, 1950), p. 71.

related would be the Bentleyan conception that political behavior is always to be understood in terms of its interest or purposive orientation. According to this view, all political activity should be viewed as policy-oriented, and one must logically encompass the policy substance if one is to comprehend the behavior directed toward that set of goals.

These conceptions of policy are combined in Friedrich's definition:

> a proposed course of action of a person, group or government within a given environment providing obstacles and opportunities which the policy was proposed to utilize and overcome in an effort to reach a goal or realize an objective or a purpose. . . . It is essential for the policy concept that there be a goal, objective or purpose.[5]

Friedrich and most other writers agree that there is a difference between specific decisions or actions and a program or course of action, and that it is the latter to which the term "policy" refers.[6] Policy is necessarily an abstraction, therefore, to be approached through aggregative or summarizing analytic procedures. It is *patterns* of behavior rather than separate, discrete acts which constitute policy. The concept of policy is thus anti–case study in its implications for research strategy and encourages controlling for idiosyncratic variables.

Unless one wishes to contend that policy refers only to broad decisional rules and that implementation or other subsequent behavior is to be examined in terms of some other focus, it follows from these conceptions that political science can hardly avoid being policy-centered. That is, if authoritative outputs of the political system, actions aimed at affecting those outputs, and the goals or purposes or interests at stake in authoritative decisions are what we mean by policy, we cannot logically escape dealing with it.

The apparent paradox is, of course, that so much political science inquiry has escaped this logical necessity, or at least seemed to do so. I believe the answer lies in two directions at once. One is revealed in the recent literature suggesting that variations in political processes, with which political scientists have undoubtedly been concerned, may have relatively little explanatory value in accounting for variations in policy outputs. We shall examine these findings later, but, insofar as they are valid, it follows that we may have spent so much time investigating process factors of relatively minor importance that it has been easy to ignore the substance of public policy, for which our research has little relevance.

A second part of the explanation, however, is that in fact political scientists have long been concerned, and vitally so, with policy analysis, but

---

[5] Carl J. Friedrich, *Man and His Government* (New York: McGraw-Hill Book Co., 1963), p. 79.

[6] Reitzel, Kaplan, and Coblentz suggest rather the reverse, however: that policy refers to specific actions designed to achieve objectives or realize interests (*United States Foreign Policy, 1945–1955* [Washington: Brookings Institution, 1956], p. 473).

only of a particular kind of policy, namely, *constitutional policy*. That is, we have spent much labor analyzing authoritative decisions that prescribe the rules and specify the structural characteristics of the authoritative decisional system, i.e., government. That these questions are policy issues is obvious, and that political scientists have invested heavily in their analysis is even more so. Whether the investment has turned an explanatory profit may be debated, but in consequence of this work I think we are richer in what Froman calls "policy theory"[7] than we may realize.

Later I shall explore the matter of constitutional policy in more detail, but first it may be well to consider two general problems that plague research in this, or any, area: how may we observe and measure policy data, and how may we classify and categorize these data for purposes of building empirical theory?

II. THE FORMS OF DATA FOR POLICY ANALYSIS

A good many of the uncertainties of policy-centered studies, I think, stem from doubts about how to order the data of policy decisions. Often they are not directly amenable to quantification. The terms in which they may be compared, cross-sectionally or longitudinally, are unclear. And therefore, unless one is willing to settle for the insights of a case-study narrative, it has been difficult to see how empirical theory of any breadth could emerge from such a focus. Let us consider these problems.

Several possibilities for the treatment of policy variables are present. The simplest, and one that has been used in the study of such policies as urban renewal adoption, fluoridation, and several issues in the realm of constitutional policy, is a straight dichotomy between adoption and nonadoption. Policies are passed or they are not. There are all the virtues of simplicity in such a treatment, but two considerations make it less than satisfactory, even when the data permit it. For one thing, many if not most policies that may appear as dichotomous variables will do so only if one takes a rather narrow cross section for one's observations. Thus, while at a given point in time one group of communities may have adopted urban renewal and another group may not, at a later point some portion of the latter is likely to have undertaken the policy. If one adds a time dimension to the observations, one then looks at such things as speed and facility of adoption, continuous variables, rather than a simple yes or no.[8] Secondly, the policy may be adopted in one set of

---

[7] Lewis A. Froman, Jr., "An Analysis of Public Policies in Cities," *Journal of Politics*, 29 (February 1967) : 95.

[8] Thus, though these studies differ on many other dimensions too, one may contrast the findings of Maurice Pinard, to the effect that communities with certain demographic characteristics that presumably indicated high alienation are likely to refuse fluoridation of water, with those of Robert Crain and Donald Rosenthal, who argue that the *process* by which the fluoridation issue is diffused in the community makes a critical difference to the question of adoption. Pinard uses a simple dichotomy of yes-no on the issue ("Structural

subsystems, rejected in another, and never proposed at all in a third. To lump groups two and three in the same category may lead to spurious results. Again it would seem incumbent upon policy analysts to search for ways of representing the policy data in more continuous form.

This recognition has led a large number of students of policy outcomes to concentrate their attention on expenditures. The data are always expressed in quantities that, so long as accounting conventions are stable, can be neatly arrayed for comparative analysis both longitudinally and cross-sectionally. Spending data have given us much the most systematic policy analyses we have, and their characteristics surely provide guideposts for research on other forms of policy data. That is to say, if we are to engage in systematic inquiry that adequately represents the relevant dimensions of policy types and variations, we must devise ways of specifying what is "more" and what is "less," and so we must learn to count.

How are we to count the dimensions of policy which are not originally expressed in quantitative units? We need not shy away from the recognition that the problem is often difficult, but there are certainly technical strategies for attacking it which have as yet been inadequately exploited. Thus one can imagine devising measures that represent the intensity and direction of communications flows respecting policies,[9] measures of intensity of conflict over policies, or measures of complexity of themes or subjects contained in policies. Measurement is never sufficient for analysis, but it is surely necessary.

Equally necessary, and far more dependent on conceptual than on technical imagination, is the development of appropriate typologies for categorizing and thereby ordering for theoretical purposes the nearly infinite array of authoritative decisional behaviors which we refer to as policies and which we are seeking to understand. As we noted earlier, the very notion of policy itself implies some degree of aggregation of specific decisions, either over time or among different decisional units or both. But this realization only helps to name the problem; it does not answer it.

The literature contains a considerable shopping list of typologies specifically designed for categorizing the content of policy outputs.[10] The least ambiguous and most often employed is a straightforward nominalist typology. That is, one accepts as theoretically meaningful the categories employed by the participants in the decisional systems. Many of these categories—for example, agriculture or education—are based on differentials in client groups pressing for or affected by the policies. Some may be based on distinctions in

---

Attachments and Political Support in Urban Politics: The Case of Fluoridation Referendums," *American Journal of Sociolgy*, 68 [March 1963]: 513–26). Crain and Rosenthal use more continuous variables and get a richer result ("The Fluoridation Decision: Community Structure and Innovations," unpublished manuscript, 1965).

[9] See the imaginative efforts along this line of James A. Robinson in *Congress and Foreign Policy Making*, rev. ed. (Homewood, Ill.: Dorsey Press, 1967).

[10] Froman, "Analysis of Public Policies," summarizes much of the list. See also Chapter 3 above.

the structure of the decisions; e.g., self-executing versus non-self-executing, constitutional versus substantive, or appropriation versus authorization. Still others are derived from differences in the decisional units involved: federal, state, local; executive, legislative, judicial; subcommittee, committee, floor; etc. And more may come to mind. Regardless of which nominal categories one uses, the theoretical potentialities are restricted to the extent of the uniformities in use of the categories. They are taken as they are found in the real world, and the real world is often uncomfortably slippery and devious.[11]

In order to move theory to higher levels of generality, more abstract typologies must be invented with the capacity to order a more inclusive range of data, and they must be theoretically meaningful without regard to the names the real world assigns to its activities. At the same time, however, there are cogent reasons for continuing to invest in the analysis of policy cast within nominal categories. For one thing, the object of analysis may not always be the building of more general theory. We are not so rich in lower level descriptive statements that we can afford to stop seeking them, even if we were agreed, as we are not, that we are never to be interested in explaining, let us say, variations in educational policy because we are interested in educational policy. Moreover, even if we were to agree that the sole object of our inquiry should be to build general theory, it is not clear that we always advance the cause by abandoning the nominal categories in favor of more abstract formulations. As an example, Froman's effort to aggregate community policies into categories of areal and segmental appears to me to founder on an inadequate understanding of the substance of the particular or nominal policies he is attempting to aggregate. Thus there is much reason to dispute his classification of employment in educational services as an areal policy— one that affects "all the families within a school system . . . simultaneously."[12] Depending on the *kind* of urban renewal project, it may or may not be segmental, as he classifies it. And clearly, if city manager adoptions are areal in impact, so also are mayor-council retentions. It is not simply captious criticism to suggest that theoretically suggestive typologies may sometimes do such violence to the complexity of the data as to render the theory irrelevant. The prudent strategy will surely be one of critical pluralism, with many scholars exploiting a variety of approaches at different levels of generality while critically and continuously reviewing and refining the work of other participants in the enterprise.

In that portion of the enterprise which operates at a more abstract level there are several typological possibilities, most of which have been only essayed rather than fully utilized, but they provide at the least a useful

---

[11] Thus comparative state policy analysis has proceeded faster than its counterpart at the urban level in part because of the much readier comparability of state expenditure categories. On the difficulties of comparative urban studies, see the essay by James Q. Wilson, "Problems in the Study of Urban Politics," in *Essays in Political Science*, ed. Edward Beuhrig (Bloomington: Indiana University Press, 1966).

[12] Froman, "Analysis of Public Policies," p. 104.

starting point. I shall not review them all in detail, but I shall attempt to identify their similarities and differences and see what might be done with them.

Policy typologies may be based on data that are composed of perceptions of the actors. Thus whether a particular policy is classified as zero sum or non–zero sum may depend on how the relevant actors perceive it, and similarly with the distinction between symbolic and material policies. Lowi, in a different approach, attempts to classify policies as distributive, redistributive, or regulatory in part according to their "impact on the society."[13] Or one might classify according to the internal structure of the decisions, using such criteria as amount, complexity, or self-execution. Froman's areal-versus-segmental distinction appears to involve some combination of internal characteristics of the policies with their impact on the system. In evaluating the utility of the alternatives we must go immediately to the operational problem, and this appreciably narrows the real research alternatives. "Impact on the society" appears to me beyond our present capacity to measure in any way that goes beyond the plausible hunch. If this is so, then the criterion itself is really a special case of the criterion of actor's perceptions, with observers replacing decision-makers as the active parties. We know, at least in principle, how to approach the data of perception, and if we recognize the accessible data as largely of this kind, we may enhance our abilities even more. From this point of view, whether a policy is classified as distributive or redistributive depends on how it is seen by the actors, and I suggest that any hypotheses we might advance relating process variables to policy types would, in fact, assume that policy types were so derived. It would be odd, I think, if actors very often behaved in systematically variable ways without perceiving some parallel variations in the substance of their actions.

This still leaves an option in the form of internal decision structures as the classification criterion. Where observers can agree on variations in decision form—as they obviously can when using nominal categories, and also probably by using distinctions in amount or complexity of policy—this criterion is especially valuable because it shortcuts the necessity of interviewing the actors.[14] But there are many potentially interesting questions that are not yet amenable to such shortcuts and which do take advantage of unambigu-

---

[13] Theodore J. Lowi, "American Business, Public Policy, Case-Studies, and Political Theory," *World Politics*, 16 (July 1964) : 677–715. Lowi actually seems to go both ways; he conceptualizes policies in "terms of their impact or expected impact on the society" (p. 689), but in discussing redistributive policy he says, "Expectations about what it *can* be . . . are determinative" (p. 691).

[14] It would seem to me appropriate to subject, for example, agricultural policy decisions and bills of the past thirty years to content analysis. My hypothesis would be that over time the structure of policy has grown increasingly complex, especially in its treatment of commodities. This change would, I think, be more or less systematically related to the "commodityization" of agricultural production. See John P. Heinz, "The Political Impasse in Farm Support Legislation," *Yale Law Journal*, 71 (April 1962) : 952–78.

ous features of the public record. Moreover, as Froman's effort has illustrated, categories invented by the observer may create as many problems as they solve.

From the array of extant possibilities, I propose to employ a typology that is adapted from Lowi's formulation and uses data derived from actor perceptions.[15] The typology differentiates four possible main types: distributive, redistributive, regulatory, and self-regulatory. Distributive policies are those perceived to confer direct benefits upon one or more groups. Typically such policies are determined with little or no conflict over the passage of the legislation, but only over the size and specific distribution of the shares. Redistributive policies likewise confer benefits, but also are perceived to take benefits away from other groups. They therefore involve more intense conflict over passage itself, over the legitimacy of the action as well as the specific content. Regulatory policies impose constraints on subsequent behavior of particular groups and thus indirectly deny or confirm potentially beneficial options in the future. Conflict over regulatory policy is likely to be ambiguous and shifting, since the specific content and direction of benefits and costs is not known; only, so to speak, the "guidelines."[16]

Self-regulatory policies also impose constraints upon a group, but are perceived only to increase, not decrease, the beneficial options to the group. The relevant perceptions in each case are those of the active participants in the policy-making process. This would include all those making explicit demands on the decisional system, as well as those taking an active part in it. In the self-regulatory policy situation, only a small group, such as lawyers or oil companies, makes demands, and typically there is little or no opposition.[17]

A question that immediately arises is how this formulation fits the distinction between zero-sum and non-zero-sum policies. The argument may be advanced that none of the four types necessarily implies zero-sum conditions. Distributive and self-regulatory policies are, one would suppose, invariably non-zero sum, since there is comparatively little implication of conflict or even of overt self-perceived losers in such situations. Redistributive and regulatory policies, on the other hand, may approach zero-sum conditions.

---

[15] I propose to beg the question, important though it be, of how to get at the appropriate perceptual data. I suspect much of it can be taken and ordered from the public record, but much would depend too on sophisticated interviewing instruments whose shape is beyond the scope of this paper.

[16] This is why the conversion of a dispute over substance to one over procedure may be expected to reduce the intensity of the conflict. I should also note that what Lowi means by regulation may be somewhat different. He stresses the "sector" level at which regulatory policy operates, an indicator that would be compatible with my argument. Beyond that, however, either he or I remain unclear as to the precise meaning of his usage.

[17] Good examples of self-regulation policy include not only professional licensing (see V. O. Key, *Politics, Parties and Pressure Groups*, 5th ed. [New York: Thomas Y. Crowell Co., 1964], pp. 122–23), but the successful quest of the National Association of Retail Druggists for fair-trade legislation (see Joseph Palamountain, *The Politics of Distribution* [Cambridge: Harvard University Press, 1955], chap. 8).

But if side payments are permitted, these conditions are mitigated, and I shall argue that in American politics even redistributive policies are generally decided in distinctly positive-sum games.[18]

A special case of regulatory policy is what I have termed constitutional policy. The making of this equation has some theoretical implications I shall consider later, but political scientists have traditionally been so preoccupied with this set of policy issues that I think it requires special attention. This attention will also give me the opportunity to raise another range of considerations; namely, evaluative criteria, which are more readily discussed apart from the typology and analytic model I shall employ to discuss substantive policy.

III. CONSTITUTIONAL POLICY AND EVALUATIVE CRITERIA

The question of what sets of decisions are to be included within the meaning of constitutional policy is not a simple one. The category is probably both broader and narrower than traditional inquiries might imply. Thus I would think that many issues of political participation, whether structural-legal or behavioral, are properly thought of as aspects of the decisional system and its rules. So perhaps with the norms of decision-maker behavior which Matthews calls "legislative folkways." On the other hand, although many constitutional policy questions are decided by judges, not all judicial policy-making deals with constitutional policy. The line is often a hazy one, but I would suppose that a distinction may be maintained, if only in relative emphasis, between decisional rules by which subsequent policy actions are to be determined and decisions that directly confer material or expressive benefits upon one or another contending group. Thus many of the decisions regarding equal protection or the First Amendment or criminal procedure seem to me to confer quite immediate and specific benefits (or costs) upon particular

---

[18] Another typology I think especially suggestive is one that differentiates between incremental and innovative outcomes. There is thus far little reported research that explores this distinction, and I shall not attempt to explore it here. Nevertheless, it seems reasonably clear that there are innovative policy breakthroughs from time to time which do not, as incremental choices may, reflect comparable shifts in system resources or, in any easily observable way, major changes in the structure of political demands. Once made, in the area of state spending policy, for example, they often establish new and lasting levels from which incremental adjustments may depart. But how and why they are made, especially if they are made in the absence of system crisis of some kind, remains mysterious, to me at least. William Buchanan has called my attention to the major increase in Virginia's state spending which has occurred since the death of Harry Byrd, Sr., despite the continued presence in authoritative positions of former Byrd protégés. A comparable jump shift took place in Kentucky some years ago without any obvious political explanation. For an effort to explore the incremental character of the federal budgetary process, see Otto A. Davis, M. A. H. Dempster, and Aaron Wildavsky, "A Theory of the Budgetary Process," *American Political Science Review*, 60 (September 1966) : 529–48.

groups, while the issue of apportionment, no matter who decides it, is one primarily specifying rules that help to shape subsequent decisions over substantive concerns.

The analysis of constitutional policy, as of other kinds, may place the policy variable either as dependent or independent. There is a rather substantial body of literature which in a general sort of way attempts to relate constitutional policies to one of two other broad types of data. One portion of this literature explores the connections between constitutional policies and the pattern of demands of politically relevant groups in the polity.[19] Of particular interest, perhaps, has been the long-standing inquiry into the interaction between a pluralistic society and a fragmented constitutional or decisional system.[20] A major issue in these efforts has always been, of course, to determine in which direction the predominant influence runs, i.e., whether constitutional policy is dependent or independent. A variation on this broad theme is represented by the recent literature dealing with the relationship between community characteristics and forms of local government.[21] This literature, I think, is reasonably unambiguous in its assumption that the constitutional policy in question, e.g., the incidence of city-manager government, is best understood as a dependent variable, with region, size, and homogeneity of population looming large as the decisive independent factors.[22] Whether from a Madisonian or Bentleyan or Marxian perspective, I suspect that this is the generally prevailing mood concerning the form of the constitutional policy-demand pattern interaction: that the policies are best viewed primarily as the consequence of group activities or whatever, rather than as their cause.[23]

On the other hand, if one looks at the literature analyzing the relationship between constitutional policies and what one might term system resources or systemic conditions, the analysis tends often to run the other way.

---

[19] For a recent attempt, see Froman, "Some Effects of Interest Group Strength in State Politics," *American Political Science Review*, 60 (December 1966): 952–63. At different levels of complexity and contextual richness are Forrest McDonald, *We the People* (Chicago: University of Chicago Press, 1958); Robert S. Friedman, *The Michigan Constitutional Convention and Administrative Organization: A Case Study in the Politics of Constitution-Making* (Ann Arbor: Institute of Public Administration, University of Michigan, 1963); and Robert H. Salisbury, "The Dynamics of Reform: Charter Politics in St. Louis," *Midwest Journal of Political Science*, 5 (August 1961): 260–75.

[20] See especially Robert A. Dahl, *A Preface to Democratic Theory* (Chicago: University of Chicago Press, 1956) and *Pluralist Democracy in the United States* (Chicago: Rand McNally & Co., 1966).

[21] See, for example, John H. Kessel, "Governmental Structure and Political Environment," *American Political Science Review*, 56 (September 1962): 615–20; Raymond E. Wolfinger and John Osgood Field, "Political Ethos and the Structure of City Government,"*American Political Science Review*, 60 (June 1966): 306–26; Edward C. Banfield and James Q. Wilson, *City Politics* (Cambridge: Harvard University Press, 1963); and a large number of others.

[22] See the summary of this literature in Froman, "Analysis of Public Policies."

[23] The proportional-representation debate may still be sufficiently alive to call this conclusion into question.

There is a considerable body of argumentation and a lesser amount of analysis suggesting that decisional rules and structures of authority have some meaningful, causal effect on such broad features of the system as its consensus or its integration or its capacity for problem-solving.[24]

I shall explore further the analysis of policy taken as a dependent variable at a later point. Here let me concentrate on the impact of policy as an independent variable by considering what seems to me to be the criterion of overriding significance in the literature respecting constitutional policy, namely, the degree of integration or fragmentation of the decisional system. For illustrative purposes, and to see what can be said regarding policy-centered analysis, I shall suggest a number of other criteria by which to order the examination of the dependent variables, either system resources or demand patterns. Much of what is said here is relevant also to the later discussion of substantive policy. There, however, I shall employ only one or two major ordering criteria, and the reader may transfer the argument at his leisure.

There would appear to be at least three criteria for examining the effect of constitutional policy on demand patterns: *group benefits, equity,* and *integration.* Thus one may inquire into the differential advantages conferred upon various groups or putative groups by alternative decisional rules. A familiar hypothesis, for example, is that fragmented structures of authority tend to benefit status quo interests.[25] The criterion of equity is closely related in that it too calls for an assessment of relative potentials for access and advantage among contending groups. It differs in the greater likelihood that it will be employed for normative purposes than the more neutral criterion of group benefits. But also the equity criterion impels the analyst to consider longer and broader spans of time and issues in order to assess the evenhandedness with which the decisional system operates. Thus a Beardian may reach rather different conclusions about the U.S. constitution using a group-benefit criterion than a Madisonian, who, using in part an equity criterion, might conclude that many groups would enjoy roughly equivalent access under the constitutional policies adopted at Philadelphia.

The integration of demand patterns has been invoked as a criterion to evaluate constitutional policy in two important areas of concern. One relates to the matter of consensus, especially regarding the rules of the game. It is often argued, for example, that in a heterogeneous society fragmented decisional systems play a part in facilitating such consensus, since if the system is to work at all, some agreement is essential on the rules of play.[26] The other

---

[24] I take this to be the thrust of James McGregor Burns's argument in his *Deadlock of Democracy: Four-Party Government in America* (Englewood Cliffs, N.J.: Prentice-Hall, Inc., 1963).

[25] See, generally, David Truman, *The Governmental Process* (New York: Alfred A. Knopf, Inc., 1951), and Grant McConnell, *Private Power and American Democracy* (New York: Alfred A. Knopf, Inc., 1966).

[26] A recent discussion of the relationship between pluralism and consensus is Dan Nimmo and Thomas Ungs, *American Political Patterns* (Boston: Little, Brown & Co., 1967).

prominent argument holds that a fragmented decisional system reduces integration on substantive demands by making it more difficult for effective aggregation mechanisms, such as cohesive parties, to develop.[27]

It could certainly be argued that a criterion of *stability* referred to consensus underlying the demand patterns of a political system, but discussions that employ this criterion seem to me generally to treat it as a more abstract characteristic of the system, evidenced by other indicators such as literacy, radios, or riots rather than by explicit politically relevant demands as such.[28] Other criteria concerned with the impact of constitutional policy upon system resources would certainly include *development, efficiency,* and *rationality.* Again, for purposes of illustrating the classic nature of the questions, we may adduce the following hypotheses:

(1) Fragmentation of the decisional system encourages consensus on rules, which enhances system stability.[29]

(2) Fragmentation, with its multiple and competing subsystems, encourages innovation, leading to development.[30]

(3) Given complex and uncertain demand patterns, fragmentation leads to efficient resource allocation.[31]

(4) But, given clear and transitively ordered preferences, fragmentation leads to inefficient resource allocation.[32]

(5) Fragmentation makes individual rationality of choice more difficult.

(6) But, given an aggregate array of complex and intransitively ordered preferences, fragmentation may enhance system rationality.

(7) Fragmentation makes problem cognition more difficult and major systemic change more expensive, and may therefore reduce system stability under conditions of great stress.

It should be apparent that the partially contradictory nature of these hypotheses suggests the paramount need of systematic inquiry into the questions. It should be apparent too that these criteria may be employed both for normative purposes and for purposes of empirical theory. It is also clear, I think, that if one is to be concerned with constitutional policy, one cannot escape involvement, implicit or explicit, in the analysis of system resources

---

[27] See Stephen K. Bailey, *The Condition of Our National Political Parties* (Santa Barbara, Calif.: The Fund for the Republic, 1959), or E. E. Schattschneider, *Party Government* (New York: Farrar & Rinehart, 1942).

[28] Ivo K. Feierabend and Rosalind L. Feierabend, "Aggressive Behavior within Polities, 1948–1962: A Cross-National Study," *Journal of Conflict Resolution* (September 1966).

[29] See Truman's discussion to the effect that pluralism, at least when combined with overlapping memberships, leads to consensus on the rules of the game (*Governmental Process, passim,* and especially pp. 503ff.).

[30] See, for example, C. E. Lindblom, *The Intelligence of Democracy* (New York: Free Press, 1965).

[31] Aaron Wildavsky's *Dixon-Yates* (New Haven: Yale University Press, 1962) is an impressive study of this kind of case.

[32] William Riker's *Democracy in the United States* (New York: Macmillan Co., 1953) is one of the clearest among the many statements of this general position.

and demand patterns as well. The converse, however, is not so evident. That is, it does not necessarily follow that in order to understand the level of wealth and economic development or the pattern of group activity in a society one needs to understand very much about the formal decisional system. Indeed, there is considerable evidence to support the contrary position. Unless, therefore, we are to content ourselves by saying with Dye that constitutional policy may be important primarily for its own sake, that we value the "way we do things" even though it makes no substantive difference to what we do,[33] we must concern ourselves with a larger problem, namely, whether the decisional system can be regarded as a significant independent variable at all. The examination of this question leads us into a broad consideration of substantive policy analysis, and we turn now to that task.

IV. SUBSTANTIVE POLICY: AN ANALYTIC MODEL

The profound implications for political scientists of the pioneering study by Dawson and Robinson have not altogether been realized.[34] What they showed, and what Hofferbert, Dye, and others have subsequently confirmed and elaborated, is that the principal variables with which we have traditionally been concerned, e.g., demand patterns reflected in party competition, do not "explain" variations in the authoritative outputs of a polity.[35] With Easton many political scientists have accepted outputs as the ultimate dependent variable to be accounted for. But now it appears that not only party competition and interest-group demand patterns, but such decisional-system characteristics as apportionment made little difference to output. What do matter are system resources. Wealth, urbanization, perhaps settlement patterns, and other such factors account for both political-system characteristics *and* decisional outputs.[36] No doubt the political system constitutes a kind of "black

---

[33] Thomas R. Dye, *Politics, Economics, and the Public: Policy Outcomes in the American States* (Chicago: Rand McNally & Co., 1966), p. 300.

[34] Richard E. Dawson and James A. Robinson, "Inter-Party Competition, Economic Variables, and Welfare Policies in the American States," *Journal of Politics*, 25 (May 1963) : 265–89.

[35] Richard I. Hofferbert, "Ecological Development and Policy Change in the American States," *Midwest Journal of Political Science*, 10 (November 1966) : 464–85, and "The Relation between Public Policy and Some Structural and Environmental Variables in the American States," *American Political Science Review*, 60 (March 1966) : 73–82; Dye, *Politics;* and Phillips Cutright, "Political Structure, Economic Development, and National Social Security Programs," *American Journal of Sociology*, 70 (March 1965) : 537–50.

[36] For an application of this argument in explaining differences in state political systems taken as wholes, see John Fenton, *Midwest Politics* (New York: Holt, Rinehart & Winston, 1966), and Daniel Elazar, *American Federalism: A View from the States* (New York: Thomas Y. Crowell Co., 1966). Fenton has elsewhere attempted to rehabilitate party competition as a significant variable by distinguishing between issue-centered and job-centered or traditional party competition. The argument has appeal, but his evidence is not persuasive. See *People and Parties in Politics* (Chicago: Scott, Foresman & Co., 1965).

box" through which system resources are processed in order to result in policy decisions. But the implication of these studies is that, except for its own sake, analysis of the black box will yield little of interest respecting outputs or policies.

This, I submit, is a devastating set of findings and cannot be dismissed as not meaning what it plainly says—that analysis of political systems will not explain policy decisions made by those systems. Moreover, there is another, quite different kind of argument which leads to much the same conclusion. This is the argument of incrementalism: that nearly all the time policy will vary only marginally from what it has been. Accordingly, the best predictor of future expenditure may be past expenditures, which seem to account for some 90 percent of the variance.[37] And if this is so, there is little room for any other variables except for the odd case of significant or innovative departures from the norm. To be sure, the innovative cases are likely to be the most exciting to study, but in the United States they are pretty largely exceptions. Incrementalism as an empirical theory of organizational behavior surely requires drastic changes in the focus of political science research, and it implies that at least in stable political systems there are at best very narrow parameters within which "political" variables can function.

Both kinds of studies, those stressing system resources and those taking the incremental approach, conceive of policies mainly in terms of expenditures and employ nominal categories for classifying them. Does the contention hold when we conceive of policies along other lines? Much of the argument that follows is to the effect that (1) under an alternative conceptualization of policy outcomes, political-system variables again become of critical importance, though the continuing strength of the relationship between system-resource variation and the *amount* of policy output is conceded, and (2) it is absolutely essential, if we are to justify the relevance of examining political-system characteristics, to incorporate substantive policy as an explicit part of our analytic model.

The adaptation of Lowi's formulation described earlier presents formidable problems of observation and measurement, but as against other abstract types derived from "policy theory," I doubt they are more severe. In any event, I wish to argue that each of the four policy types defined—distributive, redistributive, regulatory, and self-regulative—may plausibly be linked theoretically with different interactions between political demand patterns and decisional-system patterns. Let us consider the diagram in Figure 1.

I have already alluded to most of the terms represented in the figure, and I do not want to define them more than is absolutely necessary. The model resembles other political-system models in contemporary vogue, differing

---

[37] I am indebted to Ira Sharkansky for an advance look at his *Spending in the American States* (Chicago: Rand McNally & Co., 1968), which demonstrates this relationship. Also *cf.* Lindblom, *Intelligence of Democracy*, and Davis, Dempster, and Wildavsky, "Theory of the Budgetary Process."

FIGURE 1

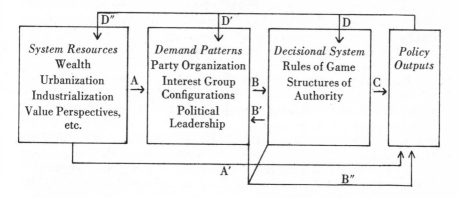

chiefly I think in the distinction made—and it is crucial for the argument that follows—between demand patterns and the decisional system. What we have termed constitutional policy is represented by linkage D in the model, and the hypotheses we suggested relating constitutional policy to demand patterns and system resources are represented by linkages D′ and D″.

Now the argument of Dawson and Robinson and the others is essentially to the effect that linkage A′ is primary for explaining policy output variation. Implicit in that argument is that demand patterns and decisional systems vary mainly as functions of system-resource variation, and that, rather than exerting any important independent effect on the *amount* of policy outputs, they function essentially as neutral transmission mechanisms. My argument is that the interactions of demand patterns and the decisional system (linkages B and B′) are systematically associated with differentiated *types* of policy, though probably not with amounts. That is, while system resources may account for the amount of money that is spent, the active political system continues to be decisive in determining the kind of policy, including the groups that benefit or suffer, the extent of conflict, the ability to innovate or adapt, and other questions discussed earlier under the heading of evaluative criteria. Let me explain.

Demand patterns refer to the patterns of groups and individuals—interest groups, parties, and other political entrepreneurs—articulating demands and pressing them upon the decisional system. Employing a venerable analytic dimension, we may consider the extent to which demand patterns are integrated or fragmented. The ultimate in an integrated demand pattern might be reached in a secure authoritarian regime where one class or group, homogeneous in its own values, is the only effective actor in the play. The ultimate fragmentation would be an extremely heterogeneous, disaggregated array of interests, each pressing its claim for an authoritative decision on the same issue independently of all the others.

We are not here speaking of the range of values in a community, but of the range of those values expressed in the form of demands for governmental action. Such demands may be cast in the form of a "claim upon other groups," but so far as the perceptions of political actors are concerned, it need not be so. Only in a logical, holistic view must one demand for subsidy necessarily be at the expense of some other group. Moreover, we must assess demand integration separately on each issue and allow for the genuine possibility that it will vary from one issue to the next.[38]

Within the continuum of demand integration-fragmentation many configurations are possible. A strong one-party system whose leaders effectively aggregate and control demand (Byrd's Virginia?) is highly integrated. A weak one-party system is not.[39] An effective "lib-lab" coalition of interest groups may be relatively integrated,[40] but an alliance of disparate farm groups attempting to facilitate mutual cooperation among the groups would be less so.[41] Integration is measured by the range, diversity, and compatibility of substantive demands made as well as by the unity or disunity of activity among groups making them.

Now we lack any very good general theories about the conditions under which various types of demand patterns are likely to emerge. Nevertheless, there are some fragments of theory which speak to the American case, at least, and they will give us a starting point.[42]

The American polity began with a highly heterogeneous pattern of demands, and this heterogeneity has continued until quite recently to dominate much of the policy content of political decisions. But urbanization and industrialization operate to aggregate putative class interests with the result that over time, and especially during the New Deal and after, the demand patterns have been increasingly aggregated, partly in the form of large organized interest groups allied with one another according to shared ideological perspectives, and partly in the form of moderately strong political parties. Further and contrariwise, however, technological innovations have the effect of facilitating specialization of function, and hence of interest, and hence of demand. A technological society is one in which interests proliferate, and one thus finds the paradox of urbanized industrial society with increasing aggregation of demands unjoined with technology-induced proliferation of interests. Yet both tendencies seem to me observable facts about contemporary American politics with significant implications for policy analysis.

Before we encounter further complexity, however, let us consider the

---

[38] *Cf.* Dahl, *Who Governs?* (New Haven: Yale University Press, 1961).

[39] V. O. Key's classic contribution in *Southern Politics* (New York: Alfred A. Knopf, Inc., 1949) and his contention that *political*, as distinguished from party, competition has an important bearing on policy outputs have not yet been shown to be invalid, since the more recent studies employ interparty competition as the measure. In any event, as Key shows, demand patterns can be observed, and they vary profoundly from state to state.

[40] Stephen K. Bailey, *Congress Makes a Law* (New York: Columbia University Press, 1950).

[41] See Heinz, "Political Impasse."

[42] Illustrative references for the points that follow can be cited at length but, I think, without improving the persuasiveness of the argument. Hence I have omitted them.

probable content of policy demands made under varying conditions of demand pattern. That is, are the demands stemming from integrated groups different in kind from those in a fragmented situation? Consider a homogeneous class in an authoritarian system. Pretty clearly its demands are largely redistributive in the sense that the class seeks to take from one group and give to another. Similarly, the rhetoric of class-struggle ideologies, on both sides, has stressed the redistributive effects of their policy demands once the desired coordination of effort and self-consciousness of interest, i.e., integration of demand, is achieved.

Conversely, fragmented demand patterns are commonly thought of in association with distributive policies. Many diverse groups seeking governmental distribution to themselves of public lands, or pensions, or river and harbor improvements, or income subsidies, or other kinds of assistance—these have been characteristic of much traditional American politics. And even today, despite the undoubted increase in redistributive rhetoric, much policy continues to be viewed as primarily distributive, even as American society continues to manifest substantial pluralism in demand patterns.

Thus far we have said that integrated demand patterns are associated with redistributive policies, fragmented demand patterns are associated with distributive policies. Yet there are other possibilities. For example, when a professional or quasi-professional group presents a policy claim to a legislature, the total relevant demand is typically highly integrated in the sense that members of the group are cohesive and no one else pays any attention to the issue. The result is likely to be a licensing law that delegates the control over entry into the profession to the members of the profession.[43] This is an example of self-regulation policy, and it can be shown, I think, that a considerable portion of the policy demands of economic groups in America has been of this type.[44] The active interests are integrated but they seek self-regulation, not redistribution. Why? Part of the answer, surely, is that groups seeking self-regulation are likely to be small relative to the total polity and do not believe they could win a redistributive game. But this, in turn, is related to the decisional system from which they seek support. An important factor in persuading a group to seek self-regulation rather than redistribution is their perception that other groups who would be adversely affected by redistributive policy could with relative ease enter the decisional arena and frustrate the demand.[45] The first group cannot indefinitely control the decisional system against competing groups, though it can secure a delegation of authority to itself. And the reason for this is that the decisional system itself is fragmented. That is, there are multiple nodes or points of power within the system which opposing groups activated by redistributive policy demands

---

[43] The literature on teacher certification, much of it polemical, makes this point. See, for example, James Koerner, *The Miseducation of American Teachers* (Boston: Houghton-Mifflin Co., 1960).

[44] See Palamountain, *Politics of Distribution.*

[45] This seems to me the essence of Samuel Gompers' classic position regarding the feasibility of labor's entry into politics.

might capture and thereby block the demands. And so the group seeks self-regulation.

In short, the type of policy which is demanded is a function of the degree of integration in both the demand pattern and the decisional system. If the decisional system is fragmented, as American legislatures have characteristically been, an integrated demand pattern will be manifested in a quest for self-regulative policies. If the decisional system is integrated, on the other hand, as in a system dominated by a strong executive, one may expect integrated demand groups to seek more redistributive policies. More on this later.

It remains to describe the fourth policy type in our original formulation, regulative policy. Perhaps the best illustration of regulative policy characteristically is associated with the judiciary. The courts are highly integrated decisional systems, hierarchical in structure, with powerful norms constraining the lower courts to conform to the decisions of higher courts. And in many policy areas, though certainly not all, that pattern of demands upon the judiciary is diverse and fragmented. It may be so regarding many issues of criminal law, for example, or with regard to First Amendment freedoms. The resultant policy output is constraining upon subsequent actions of the interested parties and an unknown array of future parties, specifying that at least some of them will not be permitted to engage in certain kinds of activities. When the pattern of demand upon the courts is also integrated, however, as in the business-dominated era of the courts in the late nineteenth and early twentieth centuries, or in the recent period of civil-rights litigation, the policy results are best understood as redistributive.

It was mentioned earlier that constitutional policy is a special case of regulatory policy. Such policy is normally made by integrated decisional systems. By this I mean decisional units with unambiguous authority over subordinates or subjects, unchallenged by competing units. A court, a constitutional convention, or a referendum vote are typical examples. Now if the demand pattern were also integrated, I think it plausible to argue that the conflict would not result in a constitutional decision, but in a redistributive showdown. Historically, it has been precisely because demand was fragmented that the United States and some other systems have been genuinely, not just *pro forma*, concerned with constitutional issues. The fragmentation of demands leads participants to seek agreement on rules of the game.

Our paradigm is summarized in Figure 2. Let us now consider some of the dynamics of the model. It seems a reasonable reading of American political history that demand patterns have become somewhat more integrated over time, and that, in broad outline at least, so have decisional systems. Thus we do not doubt that executive leadership of the decisional systems has increased, and this is clearly integrative. We would predict, therefore, that American public policy would become increasingly redistributive. To what extent is this prediction borne out by reality?

Had this paper been written in the 1930's, or even perhaps during the heyday of the Fair Deal, one would not have hesitated much over the *general* conclusion that redistribution was more and more the hallmark of public

FIGURE 2

Decisional System	
Self-Regulation	Redistribution
Distribution	Regulation

Demand Pattern

Fragmented   Integrated

policy. Now it seems a more complex process, and I think there are at least two classes of reasons. One is that redistributive policies are rendered less redistributive in the perceptions of those who contend over them by the introduction of distributive features. That is, if an initially redistributive game is perceived to have a positive sum result, its conflict potentialities are reduced as the extra benefits are distributed. Thus a poverty program taxes the rich to give to the poor, but it is perceived as providing advantages to the nonpoor also in the form of reduced unrest, expanded markets, and greater social equity. Progressive taxation is defended not simply on its redistributive merits, but also because it generates social capital for public-sector investment, which benefits many groups, including the wealthy. In the United States the demand patterns have, despite the rhetoric of the NAM, been subject to renewed *dis*aggregation as distributive possibilities for all sorts of groups continue to appear. In one sense, this is a way of describing the continued vitality of American pluralism. In another, it identifies the sharing of middle-class values, which are preeminently distributive, by all, or nearly all, sectors of the society. In still another sense, the continued salience of distributive aspects of public policy reflects the prosperity of an affluent society in which zero-sum redistribution has not been a necessary means to reallocate either material or symbolic goods. And, recalling the point made earlier, technological specialization has in any case operated to bring about a proliferation of substantive policy demands.

The other group of factors militating against a growth of redistributive policies relates to changes in the decisional system. One major consequence of the redistributive policies associated with the notion of the welfare state has been the creation of larger and more complex bureaucratic agencies to administer the programs. Some of these began as regulative agencies, some as agencies for redistribution of benefits. All, however, to one degree or another introduced fragmenting influences into the executive branch and reduced thereby the effect of increased executive integration regarding policy initiation.[46] Moreover, it has been characteristic of many of these agencies to develop a symbiotic relationship with the interests to be regulated, so that regulation turns into a variety of self-regulation.[47] In other cases, the initial impetus toward redistribution may be mitigated by the incorporation of the groups expecting to be hurt in the actual administration of the program. Thus, as Eckstein tells us for the British case,[48] doctors may denounce Medicare as injuriously redistributive, but they end up running the program.[49]

If demand patterns become disaggregated in the face of continuing integration of the decisional systems, we would expect policies that had begun as redistributive to become increasingly regulative. One might argue that labor-management relations have, in part, followed such a course since 1935. If demand patterns remain integrated and the decisional system becomes fragmented, as it might with administrative decentralization, we would expect self-regulation to supersede redistribution. Probably the most characteristic pattern, however, is for some fragmentation to occur in both the demand and the decisional system. In any case, there is a kind of redefinitional process constantly at work to shift policies out of the redistributive quadrant, often back into the distributive portion of the matrix (see Figure 3).

Another point of importance should be apparent from this analysis. Groups make demands not only about substantive policy, but also about constitutional policy. That is, they advocate more or less integration in the decisional system, and it follows from our analysis that, let us say, business groups might well be expected to prefer a fragmented decisional system in order to secure self-regulation when the given demand pattern there will be a preferred type of decisional system and hence a preferred constitutional policy.[50]

---

[46] See the discussion of Agriculture Department agency proliferation in Charles Hardin, *The Politics of Agriculture* (Glencoe, Ill.: Free Press, 1952), and in Grant McConnell, *The Decline of Agrarian Democracy* (Berkeley: University of California Press, 1953).

[47] See Marver Bernstein, *Regulating Business by Independent Commission* (Princeton, N.J.: Princeton University Press, 1955), and Samuel Huntington, "The Marasmus of the ICC," *Yale Law Journal*, 60 (April 1952) : 467–509.

[48] See Harry Eckstein, *Pressure Group Politics* (London: Allen & Unwin, 1960). Eckstein concludes his analysis by arguing that to understand pressure groups in a system one must incorporate the system's policies, governmental structures, and political culture. Thus he says very nearly what I argue here, though I think without fully developing the theory that links these components together.

[49] It should perhaps be added that a decisional system that, as in Congress, employs as a primary unit the geographically defined district or state must think of demands and encourage others to think of themselves in largely distributive terms. Rather than thinking of labor, farmers, businessmen, or the poor in general, such a system disaggregates them into particular geographically specialized unions, commodity groups, firms and industries, and neighborhoods.

[50] See, for example, James Burnham's outspokenly conservative defense of congressional fragmentation, *Congress and the American Tradition* (Chicago: Henry Regnery Co., 1959), and James McGregor Burns' outspokenly liberal defense of Presidential integration, *Deadlock of Democracy*.

FIGURE 3

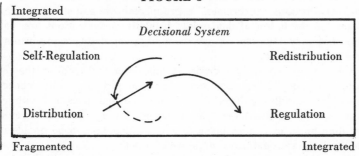

We have spoken thus far of general system interactions and tendencies, but it seems apparent that at a given point in time there will be wide variations in the operative demand patterns and relevant decisional systems for particular substantive policies. That is, tariff policy or farm policy may be more regulative (integrated decisional system, fragmented demand), while education policy or housing policy may be more distributive (fragmented decisional system, fragmented demand) and policy regarding entry into the professions or television broadcasting may be self-regulative (integrated demand, fragmented decisional system). Variability notwithstanding, are there any tendencies that may be generalized concerning the behavior of the variables we have identified as crucial to the type of policy which emerges? We have already noted some tendency toward a kind of oscillation in the two variables, increased integration followed by increased fragmentation, with a resultant tendency for policy outputs of a system to follow a looping pattern back and away from the redistributive quadrant of the matrix.

Is there any general tendency toward an equilibrium point in the matrix, and if so, where will it be located? Lowi argues, following Truman, that in industrial societies the number of tangent relations among groups is increased, and with the increase comes a correlative increase in the necessity of regulation.[51] This is certainly a classical argument and one we should not discard lightly. It is surely plausible to interpret the growth of such regulative (and integrative) mechanisms as the executive budget process as possessing continuing effect not altogether overcome by the reassertion of bureaucratic autonomy.[52] Nor is executive leadership entirely negated by the stubborn presence of legislative recalcitrance. By the same token, the autonomous interests of diverse unions or business trade associations or farm commodity groups or whatever do not always destroy the aggregative effect of peak associations or party coalitions. A general statement might be that secular changes in the location of policy modes in a system tend toward the regula-

---

[51] Lowi, "American Business."

[52] See Richard Neustadt, "Presidency and Legislation: The Growth of Central Clearance," *American Political Science Review*, 48 (September 1954): 641–71, and "Presidency and Legislation: Planning the President's Program," *American Political Science Review*, 49 (December 1955): 980–1021.

tory quadrant of the matrix and that equilibrium is reached to the extent that formal organizations, government or group, stabilize and structure the expression and/or resolution of demands.[53] In short, organizations are stabilizing factors and may facilitate achievement of a regulatory equilibrium in the system's policy output.

Whether the above hypothesis, or any other that employs the conceptualization of policy types suggested here, is empirically valid depends upon whether the variables adduced can be observed and measured with sufficient reliability to make this more than a literary theory. Bad measures may be worse than none, of course, but it is not an advantage to be unable to make the analysis operational. How might we proceed?

The analysis of American states and cities has proceeded somewhat farther in this matter and may offer some clues. For example, Zeigler has suggested that the judgments of expert informants about the "strength" of the interest-group system may yield useful data that can then be related to other characteristics of the polity.[54] In various ways, scholars have long been assessing the "strength" and centralization of control (integration) of the party system. Schlesinger has attempted to specify components of gubernatorial strength[55] which might be adapted to measures of decisional system integration, especially if taken in combination with comparable readings on executive-legislative relations.

Let us suppose that we were to examine the states systematically regarding a range of substantive policies on which all made decisions. If we observed the number and variety of groups making demands concerning each set of policies, we should be able to say that there were many diverse groups expressing demands on each, or one or a few groups on each, or one or a few groups on all. The range of content of the demands might also vary from little to much. We might construct for each state a matrix similar to that in Figure 4. The upper left case would bespeak an integrated demand pattern of limited scope which we would expect, *ceteris paribus*, to be associated with self-regulative policy concerns. The lower left case, on the other hand, suggests integrated demand on a broad range of issues leading toward redistributive policy. The upper right case shows fragmented demand of limited scope; the lower right shows fragmented demand of broad scope. Comparisons of demand patterns among states, issues, and groups would be illuminating by itself, and ought to have theory-building consequences too.

The third task, and perhaps the most difficult, is to reclassify policies that in the real world are necessarily nominal in type into the conceptual types we

---

[53] American farm policy and politics during the past several decades presents, I believe, a persuasive case study illustrating this general argument, and with Professor John Heinz of the Northwestern University School of Law I hope to complete this study in the near future.

[54] See Harmon Zeigler, "Interest Groups in the States," in *Politics in the American States*, ed. Herbert Jacob and Kenneth N. Vines (Boston: Little, Brown & Co., 1965), chap. 4.

[55] Joseph A. Schlesinger, "The Politics of the Executive," in *ibid.*, chap. 6.

FIGURE 4

Number of Issues	Number of Groups					
	1	2	3	4	5	6
1	XXXX	XXX	X	X	XX	XXXX
2	XXX	XX		X	XX	XX
3	X	X	X	XX		X
4	X	XX	X		X	XX
5	XXX	XXX		X	XX	XXX
6	XXXXX	XX	X	X	XX	XXX

have set forth. To do this we might begin by agreeing that appropriations are mainly distributive policies[56] and that taxation questions are typically redistributive. An issue in these two sets is the extent to which the taxation issues are mitigated by expectations of favorable appropriations or related program benefits. The less conflict generated by taxation issues, the more distributive the policy output. And, hypothetically, the more fragmented the demand pattern, the less heat would be generated over taxation. To take another area, home rule for local governments would be self-regulative policy at the state level.[57] So also would occupational licensing legislation.

If I interpret Gilbert Steiner's fine study correctly, national welfare policies tend to fall somewhere near the distributive–self-regulative line. He observes a relative lack of integration in the decisional system and low salience of demand, but it is not entirely clear whether such demand as exists is fragmented among categorical client groups or more integrated in social-work organizations. To the extent that the latter is true, one would expect policy to be self-regulative, with social workers defining the standards and levels of support, while the total moneys available would reflect a distributive pattern resulting from competition with other claimant groups. Steiner uses the term "automated" to describe the process, which would seem to suggest what we have here termed self-regulation.[58] At the local level the extent of spot

---

[56] Richard Fenno's brilliant analysis of the appropriations process in Congress shows, however, that as the House Appropriations Committee has achieved a high degree of integration for itself, it is able to convert appropriations policy into an effective means of regulation (*The Power of the Purse* [Boston: Little, Brown & Co., 1966]).

[57] See my discussion of the local unity norm of the Missouri legislature, whereby demand integration is required as a condition of granting local self-regulation authority: "Schools and Politics in the Big City," *Harvard Educational Review*, 37 (Summer 1967): 408–24.

[58] Gilbert Steiner, *Social Insecurity: The Politics of Welfare* (Chicago: Rand McNally & Co., 1966), especially pp. 239ff.

zoning as against comprehensive zoning might indicate something of the extent of distributive as against regulative policy in a city, and so might a comparison between the number of stop signs and the extent of synchronized traffic lights. The point here is not to categorize every conceivable kind of policy, but to suggest that categorization is possible. The possibility probably requires, however, that there be some comparative data. That is, policy *A* is more readily classed as distributive when there are policies *B, C,* and *D* available with which to compare it. And clearly comparison of political systems is essential if any reliable observations are to be made concerning demand patterns and decisional systems.

I do not intend these efforts at rehabilitating political variables to suggest that they supersede system-resource variables in explanatory power. Rather I mean to suggest that they are relevant to changes in the type of policy outputs in a polity at any given level of amount of those outputs. We are always, no doubt, interested in explaining the political system for its own sake (and ours), but, within the limits that the recent literature alluded to forces us to acknowledge, we may still find work to do which is relevant to the explanation of policy outputs also.

V. A NORMATIVE CONCLUSION

In conclusion, let me consider briefly the role of the political scientist whose concern with policy analysis is not simply with building improved empirical theory, but with playing an active role, though still as a professional political scientist, in the policy-making process.[59] I specify these conditions since obviously anyone who chooses may play the active part as a private citizen. I would argue, moreover, that no political scientist plays a legitimate professional role of any kind if he does not do his conscientious best to make his actions congruent with the best available empirical theory relevant to his behavior.

Within these constraints, several possibilities remain. There is the role of technician, wherein one says that if *A,* then *B.* This is as useful as the predictive values one can derive from one's professional understandings, but it is probably not the interesting question. Rather, that question is: When nobody asks—when no other source specifies the content of the 'if' clause—what is a political scientist entitled to say about policy questions? I would suggest that, based on what I have said above, there are at least two points that legitimately and relevantly can be made.

The rhetoric of redistributive policy is generally misleading and seldom predictive of the subsequent implementation of policy so couched. I think a

---

[59] For an impressive recent presentation of arguments respecting this question, see *The Use of Social Research in Federal Domestic Programs;* Part III, "The Relation of Private Social Scientists to Federal Programs on National Social Problems" (Committee on Government Operations, House of Representatives, April 1967).

political scientist may properly point out that at least in the United States there are powerful reasons for expecting positive-sum results with significant distributive or regulative or self-regulative components to even the most strongly argued redistributive dispute. If a political scientist says this, and he is persuasive, he may change the perception of the participants so as to give a self-fulfilling quality to his prophecy. But the reduction of the actual policy conflict is in a sense a by-product of a prediction grounded in a more general theoretical perspective that political scientists may possess to a more refined degree than other social observers.[60]

The second point returns us to our classic preoccupation with constitutional policy or perhaps generally with regulative policy. I mentioned earlier a variety of criteria by which such policies might be evaluated, and to engage in this task and to convey the findings to whatever publics may be relevant seem to me legitimate and sometimes inescapable functions of the political scientist. If variations in the decisional system are largely matters of taste without substantive impact, we must say so. If they do make a difference, we must report that in any arenas that matter. But, above all, we must have the basis in theory and research which enables us to tell what makes a difference and for whom.

---

[60] A classic statement of this kind is Pendleton Herring's *The Politics of Democracy* (New York: W. W. Norton Co., 1940, 1965).

Part Three

STUDIES OF FOREIGN POLICIES

8

The Political Scientist
and Foreign Policy

LINCOLN P. BLOOMFIELD

The last time a certified, card-carrying political scientist stood at the apex of the American policy-making pyramid was half a century ago. Today, the President, much of the Cabinet, and most of the Congress would doubtless argue that what they are practicing is by definition "political science." And so it is. But again by definition, as well as by training and inclination, the practicing politician is more that than scientist, and the academic political scientist, however skillful or aware he may be as a politician, is clearly expected to be more of a scientist.

These, then, are the two extremes: the President or ward politician, the diplomat or combined command chief, whose political "science" is at best unstructured and pragmatic; and the independent academic scholar who makes explicit his premises, orders his data in self-conscious intellectual systems, and bases his conclusions on empirically derived evidence. Between the two extremes are a host of others, practicing more or less politics and more or less science. They range from the tame, in-house political scientist on a government research or policy-planning staff, to the independent scholar who practices politics instead of scholarship, however isolated his campus, however ivory his tower.

The material on which all of these operate is "foreign policy." But the differences among their operating styles and roles are major. The complexity of the differences is illuminated by parsing out the essential components of foreign policy and strategy in descending order of abstraction:

Values
Goals (often defined as meaning valid for fifteen years or more)
Objectives (under fifteen years)
Doctrines (bodies of value combined with goals and objectives)

179

Strategies (overall programs of action, both military and diplomatic)

Policies (individual sectors of programmatic action)

Tactics (the means, in a specific time and place, to implement policies)

Unhappily for precision, these are all, on one occasion or another, used interchangeably to mean "policy." Consider some common conversational remarks about "policy": "What is our policy toward China?"; "U.S. policy favors the Mexican resolution on credentials"; "Our NATO policy is graduated and flexible response"; "It is U.S. policy to support democracy and freedom anywhere in the world"; "What *is* U.S. foreign policy, anyway?"

Indeed, all of the hierarchical levels represent forms of governmental or intergovernmental "policy," diplomatic or military. But only some represent *action.* Some of them depend on others of them, if they are to be rational. For instance, tactics have no business being discussed until policies are formulated. Policy in turn can rest logically only on agreed national strategies designed to achieve objectives. Objectives must by definition conform to national values, and so on. Clearly, some very different levels of meaning exist within this hierarchy.

When the central components of the policy and action processes are listed, it should be added that the scholar perhaps most often finds himself involved, inside or outside the government, in areas that stand somewhat apart from this hierarchy. His most frequent contribution is to adjuncts of the decision-making process: instruments, agencies, and forums (UN, NATO, diplomacy, conferences, etc.); propaganda about policy; planning (about which more below); research and analysis; and data-collecting.

It can be seen that the range of possible roles for the political scientist runs along a fairly well-identified continuum. But in the middle of this continuum there is, to complicate the metaphor, a Rubicon. On one side lies the world of policy. On the other is the world of thought. The man in the policy apparatus may be full of thought, but his output takes the form of *action* or it means nothing. The scholar may be on a weekly jet to and from Washington or the UN or wherever, but what he does as an academic political scientist turns at root on abstract, didactic, heuristic thought. The policy man's reputation will be made on the quality of his judgments for purposes of action. The scholar's reputation in the academic world will depend on the quality of his scholarship. Inescapably, and after all the qualifications are cited, that is the nature of his primary role, whatever secondary roles, avocations, hobbies, or consulting jobs he may have.

Thus when we ask "What does (or can) the independent political scientist contribute to policy that is distinctive?" we clearly mean "distinctive from what other people, political scientists or not, do in the action-oriented world of the policy apparatus." It already becomes evident that the distinction is not really between those who are interested in *policy* and those who are not. Both practitioner and scholar often are interested. The distinction lies in the man's genuine *responsibility for action.* Action, at the national or intergovernmental level, is the unique product of government. The nature of the system, even the laws preclude anyone else from taking diplomatic or military action in the name of the people of the United States.

We are, then, justified in distinguishing the policy realm from the realm of scholarship according to the criterion of *responsible action*. The question before us can then be rephrased: "What does (or can) the independent political scientist contribute to (policy) action that is distinctive?"

There are a number of ways in which to attack that question. One useful typology has been suggested by Austin Ranney,[1] in identifying five kinds of positions commonly taken concerning what the role *ought* to be: (1) the political scientist should confront values and deal with them head-on with a view to prescribing actions; (2) he should act as the decision-maker's Merlin, so to speak, predicting consequences of alternative courses of action; (3) he should stick to process and leave policy content to subject experts (but what if he is one himself?); (4) he should develop objective criteria for measurement, comparative analysis, and cost-benefit decision-making; (5) he should rigorously limit himself to value-free descriptions of the "how," leaving norms to others.

Embedded in this range of roles are of course some of the most acute tensions of contemporary political science, particularly in its more self-conscious, navel-contemplating moments. Should a scholar study policy, or should he help—in his role of scholar—to formulate it? Should he, that is to say, restrict himself to the mechanics of politics, like a kind of permanent member of the black gang, loyally toiling in the engineroom; or should he involve himself in the content of policy up on the bridge, where the action is? Alongside this is the more venerable issue: should the political scientist as scholar commit himself in his scholarship to values and norms, or should he deliberately eschew them? Should he climb to the top of Plato's ladder of values in order to find and proclaim the "Good"? Or should he modestly stop at rung 2, limiting his concern to epistemology, i.e., "knowledge of the Good"?

My own approach to these issues, and to the more operational questions regarding role and contribution, will be circuitous, in part because I am unsure how I would formulate my own stand in the abstract, and in part because the editor has asked me to draw to the maximum extent on my own professional experience, such as it is. What follows is thus partial, impressionistic, even anecdotal (where anecdotes seem to serve the purpose). It makes no pretense at being comprehensive, although I would argue that some of my conclusions, both about process and about content, might have some general applicability.

I have organized my thoughts under five headings, representing the range of political analysis from a priori, abstract theorizing all the way to the "usability" in current operations of this or that scholarly product. Along the way are the sectors of advance planning and its illegitimate offspring, justifi-

---

[1] See Chapter 1 above.

cation after the fact, and the area where reexamination of first premises is or is not acceptable political analysis.

I. THE THEORETICAL BASE

If he is to be faithful to his label, the political scientist will want to approach any given problem by constructing an appropriate intellectual edifice of reasoning, evidence, and system from which logical conclusions can legitimately be drawn. In doing this he may employ methods of data gathering and manipulation ranging from survey research through model building and factor analysis to simulation. If his game is research, such conclusions as he draws (and he may draw none) will be styled "findings." If he is concerned with policy, he must draw conclusions that may or may not take the form of prescriptions for action. In neither case will he be content to base his end judgments merely on intuition, personal memory of history, or just plain fiat. (If he is a policy-maker, he may of course do all these save the last with impunity unless he is the President.)

This logical edifice of the political scientist is, in effect, a body of theory. If the subject matter is foreign policy or military strategy, his theoretical underpinnings usually take the form of a structured view of the national or international systems or subsystems. He typically perceives these as composed of identifiable constant factors plus independent and dependent variables, interacting in a dynamic process through which inputs eventually become translated into outputs. He may color this picture with a personal philosophy that ascribes Hobbesian vices to uncontrolled elements of the system, or, alternatively, Lockeian or Rousseauian virtues. If he is a good scientist, he will make his personal bias explicit.

In the study of foreign policy, two broad avenues of approach seem to underlie attempts to be systematic and logical (i.e., "scientific").

The first seeks to derive specific policies by means of the "vertical" logic to be found in a value hierarchy of the sort I described at the outset. At the summit of this hierarchy one finds the quintessential values held by the society or system (Plato's Good). In descending order are the increasingly operationalized levels of "policy," ending in action in the form of tactics.

In the study of international politics and strategy, the beginning of a contemporary effort to be scientific came several decades ago when pleas began to be entered for just such a hierarchical approach aimed at restoring reason and order to the logical policy network that once was explicit in the hands of Hamilton, Madison, and John Quincy Adams, John Calhoun and Henry Clay. Policies, we were told in my professional youth, needed to be better anchored to goals, and tactics to strategies. Walter Lippmann thus asked during World War II for a better connection, as a start, between "ends and means."[2] There began a new self-consciousness about U.S. policy goals

---

[2] Walter Lippmann, *U.S. Foreign Policy—Shield of the Republic* (Boston: Little, Brown & Co., 1943).

and objectives that continues, in increasingly routinized form, to this day.

A more specific criterion was supplied a decade later when Hans Morgenthau proposed "the national interest" as the touchstone for policy. The extraordinary popularity of that suggestion, given its fairly general and even obvious nature (however well Morgenthau said it—and he said it uncommonly well), was due both to the fertile intellectual soil on which it fell and to the elegant theoretical platform from which Morgenthau was able to argue.[3]

In a culmination to this sense of malaise, the United States during the 1950's underwent a national identity crisis, characterized by a veritable spasm of national soul-searching about the meaning of this country's role in the world, hopefully to be followed by a rational ordering of policy actions. The several efforts of the time were interesting chiefly in illustrating how difficult in fact it is to make up a theory of foreign policy—in effect a theory of reality —as one goes along. But one enduring result was to build into the U.S. policy structure the notion that an orderly, explicitly articulated intellectual framework is required as a base on which to erect concrete policy actions.

The military establishment had some special advantages as well as incentives in exploiting this development. Soldiers work with far more tangible materials than their diplomatic brethren. And then, military officers have been increasingly exposed to the disorderly, relatively formless, often unquantifiable material of politics and society. The hierarchical approach to foreign policy is one way to order this material. In addition, it uniquely satisfies the military professional's penchant for authoritative sources of directive and rank-ordered echelons of commands. One classic example is found today in the U.S. Air Force's Basic Directive on Doctrine, Objectives, and Strategies, commonly—and revealingly—called simply "The Plan."

But it is common knowledge that the diplomatic and civil sides of policy-making have been far less infected with the urge for theory. They have been far less penetrated even by the rather simpleminded deductive process by which policies are inferred from a descending order of explicitly articulated values, goals, and strategies. Experience, intuitively felt, is generally believed by both diplomats and politicians to be the needful ingredient of sound judgment, and sound judgment is deemed the key ingredient of decision-making. There is enough truth in this for one to distrust excessively abstract or rigid formulations of goals in the face of complex cases and imperfect information about them. But the tendency to chuck the intellectual baby out with the pedantic bath water results, *inter alia*, in excluding the things political scientists, at their most scholarly, do and say.

The major exception is the State Department's Policy Planning Council (formerly Staff). There, a succession of basic national policy directives, policy books, think pieces, and the like have been produced. Numbers of foreign policy innovations over recent years originated with S/P, and in general one shudders to contemplate the foreign policy establishment without

---

[3] Hans Morgenthau, *In Defense of the National Interest* (New York: Alfred A. Knopf, Inc., 1951).

this gadfly and its men who are paid to look over the horizon. Given the nature of priority agendas, government policy planners have not always been able to get very far ahead of the process. They have sometimes seemed to be describing the anatomy of the policy structure as it could be retroactively discovered, rather than supplying new foundations on which to erect innovative policies. The exceptions that have come to public light (e.g., NSC 68) are noted for their institutional novelty.

But even where innovations, theory, and self-conscious analysis are all welcomed and performed, the "political scientist" in the government just does not play the same role as the one outside. There is a major difference between official efforts to adopt "doctrine" and the effort by the free scholar to formulate a theoretical structure that can lead him, through its own inner logic and pattern, to results he cannot foresee at the outset.

For government officials, definitions of values, goals, and strategies acquire a fixed quality that in time takes on the stature of revelation. And when theory becomes the party line, it automatically loses one of its prime qualities as science. There is nothing insidious in this so long as policy does not ossify. But any institutional commitment to a major program creates monumental inertia and a profound disinclination continually to reexamine basic elements in policy. It will be recalled that one of the most egregious things John Foster Dulles could think of to say in 1954 toward Europeans lukewarm about the proposed European Defense Community was that the United States might have to undergo an agonizing reappraisal of its basic policy—a threat obviously intended massively to deter those displeasing us at the time.

In this sense, the Secretary of State resembled the working farmer for whom the ultimate threat would be to pull the crops up by the roots in order to see how they were doing. But for the agronomist, the hybridizer, or the ecologist, nothing could be more natural, for otherwise how could anything ever be learned about roots? Or, for that matter, about plants? Just so, for the scholar, unless he is a fanatic or becomes self-deluded, the theoretical structure is always a first approximation, open to revision, emendation, and reformulation. For the policy-maker, theory is a "black box" that may be useful only to the extent it generates action recommendations. But for the scholar, interest is often centered as much on the black box as on its product. Here is one of the central points of difference that will always differentiate the scholar's role from that of the practitioner: an abiding *curiosity* about the system, what makes it tick, and the general rules it illustrates. For the action man, it is always enough that it works.

We have been considering the first of two kinds of intellectual approaches to more systematized thinking in the foreign policy field. The second, to continue the classic figure, is not Platonic, but, broadly speaking, neo-Aristotelian. Here reality is captured by simulating it in the form of a dynamic "system" that moves. The aim is to describe the system rather than to deduce correct policies from normative values.

Systems approaches have profoundly influenced policy-making in the

Pentagon and, in the form of systematic program planning and budgeting, are spreading throughout government via the Bureau of the Budget. In political science a method also called "systems analysis" has been used to reproduce what its authors believe to be the essential process at work. Important examples are to be found in the work of Ernst Haas and Leon Lindberg (using David Easton's model) on the processes of international integration. By formally modeling the dynamics of the system, the scholar, it is asserted, can more rigorously examine empirical evidence about general processes of integration—or disintegration. The search for units in the political universe which can be counted, correlated, and interpreted reflects in turn a theory of political behavior a central feature of which is the creation of formal mathematical (or other) models as simulacra of reality. Voting behavior has come to be, for some behaviorally focused American political scientists, what calculations of strategic deterrence have become for the strategist. The trouble with international relations models is of course that the significant numbers are often two or three, at the most a dozen or so representing the membership of an alliance. Regional organizations bring the numbers up to twenty or thirty. But the UN is one of the few phenomena in the field involving numbers that exceed, say, fifteen (NATO), twenty-one (OAS), thirteen (Arab League), and so forth. Quantitative analysis of voting in the UN, complete with orthogonally rotated factor matrices, represents one effort by political science to bring science to this range of problems.

Here the gulf between scholarship and policy is great. The State Department recently announced with pride the use of computers to calculate the potential effects of various weighted voting schemes in the UN (all potentially unfavorable to this country). But beyond that there is little empathy between the two points on the continuum represented by the scholarly analyst of UN voting behavior and the U.S. government's top experts on UN policy. The latter's indifference to orthogonally rotated matrices represents in part a gulf in idiom, in part a lack of leisure, in part a contempt of scholasticism—and in part the fact that some of the early findings generated by these studies bore little resemblance to manifest reality.

II. ANTICIPATING CONSEQUENCES

Max Weber once wrote that the mature man is aware of a responsibility for the consequences of his conduct. Men of judgment in policy-making capacities should possess this quality in strength. Some of them do. The problem is to proliferate individual insight and intuition to a multitude of situations that might come to the wise man's attention too late, or arrive in the "in" baskets of others, or never be dealt with at all until it is too late for imaginative staffwork. It is of great importance to know how political science can contribute to an improvement in general powers of political prediction. For prediction constitutes a major desideratum for U.S. policy-making. In an age when failure to judge properly the consequences of a fateful course of action could be calamitous, national survival calls for better advance planning. This means systematically anticipating contingencies, analyzing alternative courses of action, and making reasonable predictions about the future.

Once more, the military establishment, for a variety of reasons, historically does better at contingency planning than the civil sector. War games are a classic device for anticipating situations that armies and navies might encounter. The so-called "free" war game encourages the devising of strategies to cope with unexpected situations, and the building of the results into policy doctrine. In practical terms, contingency planning harmonizes with the permanent need of the military services to be able adequately in advance to procure and produce supplies and equipment, recruit and train personnel, deploy forces, pre-position matériel, etc. This unavoidable lead time is built into the military situation. Decision-makers are only too painfully aware of the futility and frustrations generated by last-minute improvisations. Diplomacy can act at the eleventh hour, but for many military operations it takes weeks or even months to bring the required forces to bear.

This matter of lead time can thus be a serious problem when it comes to backing diplomacy with power. Scholars in the 1950's borrowed the gaming simulation technique from the military as an experimental approach to diplomatic contingency planning. My adaptation at M.I.T. in 1957–58 of the RAND political game arose out of an acute sense that we needed better contingency planning on crises involving the UN than we had been using in Washington. The improved political-military exercise format, to whose design Thomas C. Schelling made a most helpful contribution, made of our 1960 "POLEX II" game a model for the Pentagon's "cold-war games."[4]

The action-science spectrum is sharply illuminated by contrasting this form of policy-type, crisis-scenario man game with some other contemporary experiments in simulation. Political scientists during the same period were experimenting with a more structured and abstract form of simulation of diplomatic and strategic interaction. Its aim was not so much improved contingency planning, as enhanced comprehension of the systemic processes of international relations, with a view to improved theory. Harold Guetzkow's work at Northwestern University on "Inter-Nation Simulation" represented a highly innovative strain of "gaming" which was far more explicitly scientific and theory building than the so-called RAND-M.I.T. approach.

In recent times both sides have tried to offset their particular deficiencies, Guetzkow and his associates by moving closer to policy utility, I and others by seeking to build a more explicit theoretical base for the so-called policy-type game. My own games have so far been tied to current operational requirements. As a result of this constraint, many relevant questions remain unanswered and even unexplored in the policy games. These include: better understanding of the variables to be accounted for in simulations; the relations between individual and collective behavior, and between small-group

---

[4] See L. P. Bloomfield and Barton Whaley, "The Political-Military Exercise—A Progress Report," *Orbis* (Winter 1965).

theory and national decision-making; the cultural inadequacies of nonnationals simulating foreigners; the significance of numbers in decision-making; communication problems such as misperceptions under stress; and more.

Political scientists working on gaming *ought* to be as interested in these questions as in whether *A* got into a hypothetical thermonuclear war with *B*, and what policy tracks led in what direction. The Joint War Games Agency probably cannot devote significant resources to such questions. Some gamers have, including those using Guetzkow's INS, and others such as Robert North, Charles Hermann, and David Schwartz. We at M.I.T. propose to become more self-conscious about these matters in the next round of policy games.

The other half of the issue of better anticipation of consequences has to do with prediction itself. With the aid of tools of mathematics, economics, and operations research, the military establishment seems more confident than the political and social sectors in forecasting future trends. But in both the foreign policy and strategic realms one of the inherent weaknesses of governmental forecasting is that it too is infected with the reactive nature of policy. One typical recent example was a study sponsored by one of the military services involving a twenty-year projection of its strategic requirements. It is generally consistent with the style of U.S. planning that in this study the actions of other governments are taken as the prime basis for developing U.S. strategy, for forecasting U.S. requirements, and, in general, for making U.S. policy. A standard device employed in such exercises is a dead giveaway to their chronically defective and reactive character. This is the practice of starting with something labeled "Definition of the Threat." Certainly it is essential to define "the threat," if that is the problem. The trouble is that by itself it merely reinforces the assumption that, even in "imaginative" predictive exericses, U.S. policy is responsive rather than innovative. Perhaps that is as it should be for a status quo power. But as political scientists increasingly come to play a role in such planning exercises, perhaps the unarticulated major premises of this static and even self-fulfilling approach to international interaction will be at least made explicit.

III. EX POST FACTO RESEARCH AND ANALYSIS

U.S. foreign policy, so we are told, is frequently "made on the cables." Crucial decisions, that is, are forced by the need to respond to external events elsewhere. As a matter of fact, perhaps even more often, major decisions about policy are brought to a head and given shape through the medium of high-level public speeches. The President or a high Cabinet official will often accept a pending invitation for a public address from a stockpile of deferred acceptances because there is something he wishes to say and he needs a platform from which to say it. In a lesser sense, it is also true that *because* he sometimes has to appear on a commencement platform or at an American Legion convention or whatever, something must be said that at least sounds innovative.

Depending on the lead time, the sophistication of the great man or his ghosts, the audience, and the felt need for some new synthesis of policy, the speech can be the canvas on which he can paint with as broad a brush as he chooses. It may stimulate a staff process that extrudes a shaped and coherent policy product. If he is a genuine statesman it can carry official rhetoric all the way to the top of the policy hierarchy where national values are seriously redefined. More commonly, current policy may on such occasions be intellectually and verbally relocated in a larger structure of strategy and doctrine. At worst, the occasion will be used to utter noble-sounding pronouncements at the level of values, goals, or strategies which bear little or no resemblance to what the government is in fact doing.

This feature of the policy process is not necessarily bad. At a minimum it informs the democratic constituency about the current state of affairs regarding this nation's role in the world. At its best it will reveal inconsistencies or gaps in the doctrinal foundations of policy that piecemeal tactical moves successfully conceal. This awareness can, in turn, generate a new synthesis from which more rational lines of future policy may be deduced. By demonstrating the paucity or superficiality of an accepted policy approach, this kind of forced occasion for policy-making may find the potential speechmaker demanding of his staff some "new initiatives." When an administration is split within itself, the new pronouncement can provide some assurance of internal conformity to the President's will.

It should be clear that in this sense the midnight speech sessions may accomplish, retroactively and with *post factum* logic, that which the political scientist as planner should better have done in advance of the policy (and perhaps did, but no one at high levels read his erudite product). The difference is between the ideal of taking logical thought in *advance*, with all the aids to analysis and reason that modern social science should be able to provide, and backing into it after the hunch players have in effect already formulated policy. If political analysts ever feel prostituted, it is when they are required to do their "research" after decisions are made which rationally should depend on the evidence thus gathered. Here is another point where the difference is acute between the role of in-house political scientist and that of his brother in the ivory tower.

Decision-forcing deadlines lie in the instrumentalities and institutions through which foreign policy often operates. Here too planning, research, and analysis all too often follow the basic judgments forced by inexorable schedules.

The classic example is the need to justify and explain policy before the Congress in order to secure enabling legislation and appropriate funds. As PPBS and other program-planning systems come to be superimposed on the life cycles of foreign affairs, there will perhaps be far more serious official attempts to analyze policy "hierarchically," systematically, and in advance. Already portions of the foreign policy-making community have had to agonize over efforts to quantify transactions traditionally regarded by their official custodians as ineffable, evanescent, and above all nonquantifiable. One can understand why the State Department experiences trouble in persuading top scholars to undertake the translation of Hitchcraft into the idiom of Foggy Bottom.

Quadrennial elections in the United States are commonly believed by foreigners to inspire all kinds of aberrational policies. The fact is of course quite the opposite: policy-making sometimes grinds to a virtual halt some months prior to the election, in the belief that until one knows the will of the electorate, short of great emergencies no new directions are possible. Even here, in the sense that relative inaction is a form of policy, as well as in the sense of opposition-party initiatives, the quadrennial deadline sometimes forces out a species of rethinking (along with large quantities of nonthinking).

The NATO Foreign and Defense Ministers' annual meetings build in a requirement for reviewing programs and policies. Some have been seminal; but most in recent years do not seem to have succeeded in generating the kind of substantial rethinking of the European and Atlantic problems that many have felt to be called for by the times.

The UN General Assembly has for over two decades called forth urgent analytical efforts of one sort or another, ranging from the trivial to the profound. One constant feature has been an annual urge, particularly on the part of the U.S. representative in residence in New York, to have some new things to say, new proposals to put forward, new uses to find for the organization, and new images of U.S. policy to reflect.

On more than one occasion over the years the top levels of government have appeared to wish genuinely for something closer to the fundamental than the superficial end of the spectrum. In 1955, to take one personal recollection, the U.S. Secretary of State was correctly concerned over the implications of the influx of new states into the UN. That development coincided with other indications that a decade-old U.S. stance required basic reexamination, given the deterioration in the tactical position of the once all-influential United States, along with signs of shifts in the Soviet posture.

As the Department's policy planner on UN matters, I was assigned on the basis of the Secretary's wishes to a six-month fundamental reappraisal of the U.S. problem in the UN—the first (and possibly last) such comprehensive official overview. Our staff analysis sought to go behind superficialities to underlying concepts, deriving in the process some fresh conclusions concerning goals and strategies, and from these specific policies deducing tactics. There was Department-wide participation in the analytical process, and the product was one of which it was possible to feel proud as an example of decent in-house political science. When it was presented to the Secretary a month or two before the General Assembly session in the fall, his impatient reaction was "No, no, what I want are some gimmicks to go into my opening speech—a close enough paraphrase."

All in all, then, policy made on the cables, in speeches, and for international conference deadlines inevitably eclipses more leisurely structural efforts. It is thus often only after policy is made that the planners and the scholars are invited to create sound, empirically validated theory on which to found recommended strategy and tactics. This can have the positive result of inspiring retroactive research and analysis in an effort to reconstruct the foundations of ongoing policy. At its best it can pull together into generalized doctrine the results of successful or unsuccessful responses in particular cases, and even lay the groundwork for new initiatives. But the political scientist, when he is acting as scholar or scientist, must above all beware of becoming a propagandist; given the frequency of that role inside government, one can only conclude that there is basically no place for scholars as such on the inside—only scholars playing the role of bureaucrats.

IV. "AGONIZING REAPPRAISALS"

When a political scientist analyzes foundations of policy, his aim is to be entirely objective. Naturally, this may not always be perfectly achievable. But ideally, "pure" research and analysis should take the form of a let-the-chips-fall-where-they-may quest for the unvarnished truth, however painful or revolutionary it may turn out to be. Even more to the point of this essay, those who may be sponsoring, supporting, or requesting such an analysis by an objective scholar ought, in an ideal world, to share his passion for the truth. Is the Emperor really stark naked? Say so! Is the United States unconsciously acting in a paranoid or obsessive fashion? Spell it out! Is a policy turn of 180 degrees called for? Just tell us in which direction!

I do not personally know of any such formal invitation to political scientists by the diplomatic component of the U.S. government, although it is far from uncommon in scientific and engineering areas, even sometimes in economic and defense planning. Policy-makers are unlikely to feel that their approach is *fundamentally* deficient—and in truth it rarely is. Another constraint on radical change in U.S. foreign policy is that, in a consensus-based policy apparatus such as ours, alterations are necessarily modest and incremental. Revolutionary root-and-branch assaults (to continue Charles E. Lindblom's figure of speech) are unlikely to be tolerable, short of profound upheaval.

But it is not unheard of for government to sponsor more than just incremental inquiries into foreign policy or strategic problems. Typically these are likely to be done in-house and classified. But on occasion an outside political scientist may be invited through a grant, research contract, or consulting capacity to be thoroughly objective even as to some major premises ("Don't hesitate to say where you think we're wrong"). Of course, even here there are realistic ultimate limits. The hard-pressed bureaucrat or political leader usually has a rather clear idea of the bounds of political or diplomatic reality. The turn to be contemplated for European or NATO policy, or U.S. intervention strategy, or the peacekeeping role of the UN, or inspection requirements for disarmament agreements, would be at maximum 45 degrees, and even that would be fairly unsettling.

It may thus happen (and this is the suspicion of those critical of external "policy research") that the government is most likely to choose relatively "safe" researchers—men who are known to accept the basic premises of ongoing policy and be generally in tune with the Establishment's view of the world. The private scholar is encouraged to range freely through alternatives —but the sponsoring agency believes it will not be betrayed. Even if the latter is receptive to more than just a new and more elegant justification of the current policy line, it trusts that fresh ideas will uproot accepted doctrine only marginally.

Of course, the government sponsor may innocently urge what he calls "fundamental rethinking" without believing that the political scientist might wind up undermining the very moorings of official doctrine. If he does so, it may come as a nasty surprise, and his report will doubtless be found unacceptable. The researcher may even be put on a kind of blacklist for future contracts. New contract provisions may be drafted by the agency's general counsel to tighten up the permitted boundaries of freedom of inquiry (although the Freedom of Information Act corrects for this).

One example that illustrates possibilities—and limits—is the reappraisal of United States strategy and policies with respect to the United Nations done at M.I.T. from 1957 to 1960 with government financial support. This was undertaken as the sort of comprehensive scholarly reexamination of U.S. policy that one never had the time—or the basic encouragement—to do in the State Department. In order to provide the necessary moorings and touchstones for this particular policy sector, it proved necessary to develop a new and detailed formulation of the hierarchical structure of values, goals, objectives, strategies, etc., for U.S. policy as a whole.[5] Nevertheless, I would surmise that this fell into the "safe research" category. The fact that the analysis was found "usable" both by incumbent policy planners and also by the opposition candidate in the 1960 election obviously implies that the research, whatever its innovative conclusions (and they were modest), rested on theoretical and systemic foundations generally consistent with the policy community's strategic view of the world.

As social-science-type research is increasingly government sponsored, it may be thought that scholarly independence will be weakened. But there is no inherent reason why the scholar cannot reexamine fundamental premises of policy, suggest hitherto invisible theoretical underpinnings, and conclude with policy directions that were hitherto unacceptable. Even the political scientist performing so-called mission-oriented research can achieve a satisfactory and even moral compromise between the demands of policy and scholarship. There is no *intrinsic* reason why he cannot do research of direct concern to government while insisting on accompanying it both with innovative conclusions and with elements of "basic research" that will contribute to the corpus of scientific and theoretical knowledge. This mix is far from unattainable, even though it requires adopting a position that has to be argued out with the

---

[5] The study was subsequently published as *The United Nations and U.S. Foreign Policy* (Boston: Little, Brown & Co., 1960; rev. ed., 1967), by Lincoln P. Bloomfield.

sponsor. The chief constraint may in fact be the scholar's own limitations of time and energy, rather than any necessary immiscibility, so to speak, between policy relevance and the purity of political science scholarship.

I can testify to instances where political scientists (sometimes in collaboration with natural scientists or hardware specialists) rejected the government's research questions as *mal posées* and reframed them, in the process reexamining premises that no one asked them to reexamine, suggesting approaches that would normally be heretical, and recommending policies that would be, at a minimum, difficult for government to adopt. Rather than always being "punished," they have sometimes been thanked. And in some instances they have been officially asked to pursue further the inconsistencies and dilemmas of U.S. policy which they brought to the surface in the course of analysis.

This last happens to have been my recent experience in a series of contract relationships with the U.S. Arms Control and Disarmament Agency. The task there was to open up an examination of the problem of security and arms control for the developing regions of the world, which required an across-the-board analysis—theory and all—of the broader problem of local conflict, its control, and the U.S. role therein. This latter research required reappraisal of the postulates of U.S. intervention, bringing to the surface some sharp issues fairly painful for U.S. policy to face. The distance between pragmatic decision-making and scholarly theory building suddenly looked considerably less, given broad-gauged people in government who felt the need for reexamination in the face of thin patches on the policy surface, and unalienated but independent political scientists on the outside whose sense of the fastidious did not prevent them from accepting *as a starting place* the official formulation of the problem.[6]

Sometimes, of course, this bridging process verges on the ludicrous. After much debate internal, the U.S. government through Secretary of State Herter made its response to the Soviet 1959 call for general and complete disarmament. In the Herter speech of February 1960 the U.S. reply was essentially "Yes, but . . ." One of the "buts" was the need for an "international military force" that would grow in strength through the disarming process to the point where eventually no state or group of states could effectively challenge it (a formulation subsequently modified).

I recall being asked by a high State Department official shortly afterward to "Tell us what we mean by 'international military forces.'" It did not require much independent analysis to conclude that the United States government was, in effect, calling for world government, but without calling it that, or fully accepting what its proposal entailed. Strategic analysis also suggested that such a force would require nuclear weapons. Neither insight was popular in government circles. But in fact there followed some major governmental and scholarly activity on the subject involving studies by State and Defense

---

[6] See Lincoln P. Bloomfield and Amelia C. Leiss, *Controlling Small Wars: A Strategy for the 1970's* (New York: Alfred A. Knopf, Inc., 1969).

(and on my own part the running of some related political-military games on the subject, as well as some privately financed travel and writing).[7] Again, research and analysis, fundamental appraisals, and in the end modified policies *all followed* an initial policy assertion that could not by any stretch of the imagination be described as having been thought through in advance.

A final example completes this necessarily personalized catalogue of instances. In a summer study sponsored in 1962 by ACDA (and managed by IDA) a group of natural and social scientists was asked to reexamine and hopefully break through obstacles in the realms of inspection and enforcement of disarmament agreements. In the course of this study several participants realized that they had always been uneasy about the official criteria for identifying what arms could be controlled at what stage of the disarming process. The problem was looked at again against a rather different basic criterion: the conviction that measures that depended on substantial penetration and intrusion into the vital centers of societies, notably, but not exclusively, Soviet, were doomed to failure. If one wished to make progress of any sort, the degree of intrusion needed to be minimal unless it could be automated.

From this hypothesis came a new theoretical and methodological basis for analyzing weapons systems at all stages of production and deployment, keyed to a detailed scale of intrusiveness. We rated the data according to degrees of technical confidence with which specific measures could be verified. The analysis produced what amounted to a substantially revised suggested first-stage package of arms control and disarmament steps.

These findings ran into several levels of official sensitivity, notably the semantic issue of "intrusion" (which some officials rejected as improper to speak of, despite the fact that it was clearly the central issue). The ending was happy from a standpoint of scholarship, as some years later permission was secured to publish a version of that analysis along with other selected papers from the study.[8] Moreover, "minimum intrusion" has become officialese.

The task of the independent political scientist in these episodes could be summed up as supplying a brand of what might be called "scholarly staff-work" at the level of strategic analysis. Ideally such analysis should in each case have preceded initial decision-making. In all these cases it came somewhat after the fact. In some cases there was a fairly open invitation to do one's stuff as a political scientist, i.e., reexamine premises, develop a theoretical base, synthesize it into a systemic view, gather data, evaluate it, infer

[7] For the first, see the *Report of Four Political-Military Exercises* (sponsored by Institute for Defense Analyses under contract to Office of Assistant Secretary of Defense for International Security Affairs [Cambridge, Mass.: Center for International Studies, M.I.T., 1964]); for the latter, see Bloomfield *et al.*, *International Military Forces: The Problem of Peacekeeping in an Armed and Disarming World* (Boston: Little, Brown & Co., 1964).

[8] Lincoln P. Bloomfield and Louis Henkin, "Inspection and the Problem of Access," in *Security and Disarmament*, ed. Richard J. Barnet and Richard A. Falk (Princeton, N.J.: Princeton University Press, 1965).

consequences, identify alternatives, and recommend action. In other cases, the more fundamental the level of reexamination, the more horrified the sponsor —in one case at the top level, in others at the working level.

I suggested at the outset that policy planning at times resembles the *métier* of the political scientist at work. But given the inescapable constraints on the official policy planner, perhaps there is still a role for the independent political scientist to perform, bounded only by the broad limits of the overall official formulations of the problem and his own capacity to communicate his findings in policy-relevant ways. Few ideas are totally new, and he may merely help tip the scales in an internal policy argument. But that too can be of high value.

V. THE "USABILITY" OF SCHOLARSHIP

One is all too familiar with first-class political science output that is untimely —too soon, too late, or not visibly relevant. But there are cases at the other extreme. Political science analysis is sometimes seized upon by policy-makers because the time is ripe for change supported by sound theory. The easy recent examples are chiefly in the military-strategic field. Rapid developments in technology finally made it impossible for even the most antediluvian conventional warrior or battleship admiral (who, incidentally, both turn out to be partially right) to stem the tides of change. William Kaufmann's work on limited war in the early 1950's, Henry Kissinger's study for the Council on Foreign Relations on limited nuclear war (which he subsequently amended), and RAND analyses of strategic deterrence problems were all seminal in their impact. The arms-control field, as a kind of analogue of strategic analysis, has experienced some of the same responses. Some influential analyses have been purely theoretical, cast in terms that would normally deter a busy desk officer from trying to dredge up the usable meat. But where the need is great enough, the material is struggled through.

However, in foreign policy and diplomacy generally, my unresearched impression is that unless they are extraordinarily timely, new scholarly syntheses are not usually welcomed, grasped, or even read. The obvious exception is the work of the area specialist. Vernon McKay on Africa or Alan Whiting on China, Edwin Reischauer on Japan or Philip Mosely on Russia— these all look more like a kind of professional brotherhood that embraces both desk officers and political scientists grappling with a common problem, as governmental and private scientists have classically done.[9] That ideal is far from achievement in the more general field of international relations.

In my own limited research experience, the UN analysis mentioned earlier coincided with a felt need for a new look. Our current research on the control of local conflict happened at its outset to coincide with intensification

---

[9] As originally described by Don K. Price in *Government and Science* (New York: Oxford University Press, 1962).

of the Vietnam involvement, and at its mid-point with the 1967 Middle East war. These sobering events helped this particular study to feed into a broader official concern about intervention. But it needs saying once more that both of these sponsored "new looks"—the one at the U.S. role in the UN, the other at U.S. involvement in local conflicts—would ideally have been of maximum value sometime *before* the research was done, rather than at some later time.

This brings us at last to the physical availability of the results of political science scholarship in the international field. It is no secret that some government agencies suffer embarrassment in the face of the mounting stockpiles of externally commissioned research, some of it remaining unread, the pile rapidly growing, the nuggets fast disappearing in mountains of bound reports. This is no worse, however, than the far older problem of the agency into whose files disappear forever the work of its own planners whose recommendations were not timely. (How often has one heard the heartfelt cry, "But I wrote a paper on that only two years ago!") And both of these problems are not too different from the epidemic disease of libraries caused by excessive production of printed matter. Automated data coding, storage, and retrieval methods will hopefully restore memories to policy-makers who still believe they must invent anew every solution required by every new problem.

But more fundamental is the problem of availability, not of documents, but of the ideas the documents contain. This is particularly the case when it comes to experimental theory building, or methodology that is most unlikely to look action-relevant. We must assume for the sake of argument that even here there are nuggets worth the policy-maker's effort to mine. How then does political science at its most pure—or scientific—reach the man with practical problems, limited time, and chronic contempt for the academic scribblers and theorists who cannot come up with usable answers right off the bat?

Strangely enough, some in high places read an astonishing amount of scholarly output, whether because they are at heart scholars, desperate for ideas, or hungry for more erudition, or because they are simply compulsive readers. One way to communicate with these policy-makers from the ivory tower is to mail them reprints of articles. A more basic solution is to trade roles, at least temporarily. Assignment of a desk officer to a war college or university invariably makes him more conversant with and generally more tolerant of "pure" political science, just as temporary or periodic government service is invaluable for exposing the scholar to the actual pressures and constraints on the action officer. It should be added, however, that when they change places they sometimes adopt the new role and play it with a convert's zeal.

There is, in the end, a profound natural gulf between the two ends of the spectrum. The pure scholar loses his purity when the price of influencing the policy-maker is loss of precision in his language, complexity in his theory, and adequate space to lay out his ideas. If he is uncompromising, he will not communicate at all with the rushed cable-reader impatient of anything outside his immediate compass. There may be no real need for the action man to be acquainted with the theory and method of political science, so long as he recognizes the worth of viable or interesting conclusions. But the truth may be that he cannot really afford to miss any bets, however esoteric they may seem. As President Kennedy once put it, "Domestic policy can only defeat us; foreign policy can kill us."

9

Moral Fervor, Systematic Analysis, and Scientific Consciousness in Foreign Policy Research*

JAMES N. ROSENAU

[The best route to enhanced credibility in the Soviet-American relationship,] if one may speak most directly, is to stop lying, faking, and posturing.[1]

[In the modern era] the scope for wrong-doing in foreign policy has greatly expanded; and of its expansion governments have not been reluctant to take advantage. In their dealings with other governments, and with other peoples, their behavior is characteristically bad. It is deceitful. It is treacherous. It is cruel.[2]

These are not the exhortations of office-seekers or the exclamations of aroused citizens. They are the observations of two distinguished scholars who have earned a reputation for careful and detached inquiry and who wrote these lines as parts of serious attempts to apply their expertise to problems of foreign policy. The discrepancy between the bewildered simplicity and moral

* The preparation of this paper was facilitated by the Center of International Studies of Princeton University and its support is gratefully acknowledged. I am also indebted to my wife, Norah, for her many clarifying reactions to the earliest version of the paper.
[1] Milton J. Rosenberg, "Attitude Change and Foreign Policy in the Cold War Era," in *Domestic Sources of Foreign Policy*, ed. James N. Rosenau (New York: Free Press, 1967), p. 135.
[2] James Eayrs, *Right and Wrong in Foreign Policy* (Toronto: University of Toronto Press, 1966), p. 32.

fervor of these excerpts and the complex qualifications and cautious conclusions that usually mark their research is, I would contend, typical of what happens when scholars turn their attention to foreign policy phenomena.[3] Such phenomena seem to invite the abandonment of scholarly inclinations.[4] Ask almost any scholar what is possible and desirable with respect to urban redevelopment and he is likely to avoid a direct answer, responding that the problem is complicated, that a host of variables are operative, and that the causal connections are difficult to trace. Ask almost any scholar what is possible and desirable with respect to Vietnam or the Middle East and he is likely to give an unqualified answer—one that derives from moral judgment, assumes motivation, and simplifies causation. Consciousness of scientific method, so evident elsewhere in the study of human behavior today, has yet to become predominant in the analysis of foreign policy.

Much the same can be said of those political scientists whose professional concern with foreign policy phenomena leads them in analytic rather than normative directions. Although the work of specialists in the field may not be pervaded with moral fervor, neither is it characterized by scientific consciousness. Rare is the inquiry that specifies the independent and dependent variables that are being investigated, that sets forth explicit hypotheses in which the relationship of the variables is posited, and that then generates data designed to test the hypotheses. Hardly less rare than testable propositions are propositions that can be rendered testable, that identify discrete units of action which can be observed with sufficient frequency to allow variations in their structure and in the sources and consequences of their behavior to become evident.

Stated differently, most inquiries into foreign policy phenomena do not contain variables that vary, that increase or decrease under different conditions. To be sure, specified causes and effects may be recognized as capable of operating in other ways and thus are often called "variables." However, the nature of these other ways and the range across which the variation can occur —what shall be called here, for purposes of emphasis, the "variance" of variables—is conspicuously absent from most inquiries. Instead variables are usually analyzed exclusively in terms of the way they operate in the particular situation being examined. Consequently, they are rarely seen to vary—to slacken or intensify, widen or narrow, rise or fall, grow or diminish, strengthen or weaken. The words "more" and "less" do not pervade the literature of the field. Foreign policy actors are not conceived in terms of

---

[3] For a number of other examples of this discrepancy, see my "Behavioral Science, Behavioral Scientists, and the Study of International Phenomena," *Journal of Conflict Resolution*, 9 (December 1965) : 509–20.

[4] Even historians are apparently capable of responding favorably to the invitation. For a cogent discussion along these lines, see Francis L. Loewenheim, "A Legacy of Hope and a Legacy of Doubt: Reflections on the Role of History and Historians in American Foreign Policy since the Eighteenth Century," in *The Historian and the Diplomat: The Role of History and Historians in American Foreign Policy*, ed. Loewenheim (New York: Harper & Row, 1967), pp. 1–71.

behavior that would be more in one direction and less in another if more of a particular circumstance prevailed and less of another. Rather most of the research into foreign policy phenomena is problem-oriented and consists of data and conclusions derived either from descriptive case histories or from broader assessments in which the variance of the variables is limited to the problem being considered.

I. SYSTEMATIC VERSUS SCIENTIFIC INQUIRY

More often than not, to be sure, both the cases and the broad assessments are systematic. The cases systematically analyze the evolution of conflicts and the actions taken to resolve them. The broader accounts systematically cluster together a number of situations with which a nation has coped in the past or must cope in the present and then systematically generalize about the factors and goals that seem to be relevant to the nation's behavior in all the situations. To be systematic, however, is not in itself to be scientific, a point that is succinctly illustrated by the old analogy to the telephone book, which is surely one of the most systematic documents ever produced, and also one of the least scientific. For all their systematic reconstruction of decision and action through time, most case histories neither test nor yield propositions that are applicable beyond the specific situation considered. When the events subjected to systematic examination run their course, the case is treated as complete, and even if the analyst draws "some lessons for the future" from it, these are virtually never cast in the form of hypotheses that are testable when comparable problems subsequently arise.

Likewise, for all their systematic treatment of the factors underlying a nation's foreign policy, the broader assessments are not usually compiled through a process of hypothesis testing, but rather are derived from an informed and careful piecing together of a generalized pattern out of those events and trends that strike the analyst as relevant. Having thus identified the pattern, the analyst has no reason to speculate about how it might be differently structured if different events and trends had unfolded. Hence he has no need to cast his conclusions as to the pattern's importance and consequences in hypothetical terms, or even to indicate a range within which the main variables that comprise it are likely to vary. Like the case histories, therefore, the broad assessments do not in themselves provide a basis for further inquiry. They are concerned with a specific problem and, having examined the sources and solutions of it, they simply come to an end.

Several consequences follow from the disjunction of systematic analysis and scientific consciousness in the study of foreign policy. The most crucial of these is that knowledge about foreign policy behavior does not cumulate. Since the case histories and the broad assessments neither test nor yield hypotheses, their conclusions cannot be placed in a larger context. Thus no "established" findings or propositions can be gleaned from the vast literature on foreign policy that would be comparable to the twenty-nine major propositions and their many corollaries uncovered in the research on domestic political institutions.[5] At any moment in time there is considerable knowledge available about the prevailing international scene, but virtually all of it becomes obsolete when conditions change. At that point the case writer may write a new case and the generalizer may develop new generalizations, but while monographs may thereby cumulate, knowledge does not. Not having allowed for variations within a larger context, the cases and the broad assessments are time- and problem-bound.

A second consequence of the lack of scientific consciousness, and one that is closely related to the noncumulative nature of foreign policy knowledge, is the paucity of rewards for self-sustained inquiry. The inclination to cast problems in the form of hypotheses practically guarantees that the researcher will be confronted with an endless series of intriguing questions. Human behavior being as complex as it is, hypotheses are rarely confirmed in their entirety. Even when a hypothesis approaches full confirmation, questions arise as to the scope of its application, pressing the researcher to carry his tests of its validity to the point where eventually the hypothesis is disproved and new ones are framed to account for the discrepant behavior. In the case of the systematic but nonscientific modes of research, however, the incentives to probe further are not so intense. Even as the case histories and broad assessments satisfy one's curiosity about the particular foreign policy episode or problem investigated, so do they tend to dampen one's imagination with respect to the dynamics of foreign policy. There are no questions left over. All the relevant circumstances have been described, assessed, and put into place. There is no built-in predisposition to ask what would happen if variables were differently structured. Hence, having grasped the particular moments in history recounted by the cases or having comprehended the particular dimensions of the problem explored by the broad assessments, the mind tends to come to rest.

And since foreign policy analysts do not set out to test explicit hypotheses, they can never be wrong. Their analyses might be inappropriate, superficial, or out of date, but they cannot be wrong. A researcher might fail to anticipate a major event such as the ouster of Khrushchev or the sudden collapse of the Arab armies and thus be embarrassed by the conclusions reached in his assessment, but such embarrassment need not last long. Not having started with a hypothesis that the unanticipated event reveals to be unsound, the researcher need not concede or even recognize that his reasoning was ill founded and that a new formulation is in order.[6] The analyst with a

---

[5] Bernard Berelson and Cary A. Steiner, *Human Behavior: An Inventory of Scientific Findings* (New York: Harcourt, Brace & World, 1964), pp. 417–36.

[6] If need be, he can always resort to humor in the form of an antiscience quip to alleviate the embarrassment. As Zbigniew K. Brzezinski is reported to have observed when events in October of 1964 negated his published expectation that Khrushchev would have a long tenure in office, "If Khrushchev couldn't predict his downfall, how would you expect *me* to do it?" See William H. Honan, "They Live in the Year 2000," *New York Times Magazine*, April 9, 1967, p. 64.

scientific consciousness, on the other hand, cannot ignore his errors. By casting his expectations in if-then terms, he has made explicit the conditions under which he would be shown to be wrong. Either his hypotheses are confirmed or they are not. The latter outcome points to flaws in his comprehension of the subject, provokes thought as to where his reasoning went astray, and thus challenges his scientific consciousness even further.

It might be argued that the deadening effect of case histories and broad assessments is not the fault of their authors, that the authors have fulfilled their responsibilities by carefully depicting a historic sequence of events or cogently analyzing the dynamics of a situation, and that it is up to others to exploit the cases or the assessments for any more general hypotheses they may contain. Such an argument, however, runs counter to experience. The fact is that case histories and broad assessments rarely generate further research. If a case writer does not test or derive explicit hypotheses from his materials, others are seldom provoked to apply and extend the comprehension gleaned from them. If the author of the broad assessment does not offer if-then propositions, others are disinclined to pursue the implications of his reasoning in more than a casual fashion. Hence, to repeat, nothing cumulates.

Elsewhere a colleague and the present writer have stressed that there is no inherent reason why this must be so. Both systematic and scientific analyses aspire to greater understanding, and while they do not use the same methods to realize their common goal, neither are their methods mutually exclusive. Theoretically, therefore, it is possible for the scientific researcher to glean relevant findings and insights from case histories and broad assessments and then cast them into hypotheses to be tested by new materials.[7] Self-evident as this may be, however, it does not accord with experience. Whatever the theoretical possibilities may be, researchers in the field simply do not get aroused to transform the findings of case histories and the insights of broad assessments into the bases for further inquiry. The reasons for this discontinuity are doubtless many and varied, but the lack of cumulation and the existence of the discontinuity seem incontestable.

The seven case histories summarized in the Appendix to this paper illustrate this point. None of the findings of any of the cases is cited by subsequent researchers. None of them has served as the basis for other inquiries into comparable phenomena. None has even stimulated other cases. No one has written a case history of the 1961 Berlin crisis or the 1964 foreign aid program, to mention two obvious situations to which case writers might reasonably have been expected to be attracted as a result of the existence of dramatic accounts of the 1948 blockade of Berlin and the 1957 effort to expand the foreign aid program.[8] Case histories, in short, are short-lived. As curiosity gets aroused by more recent episodes, a case passes into oblivion,

---

[7] Klaus Knorr and James N. Rosenau, eds., *Contending Approaches to International Politics* (Princeton, N.J.: Princeton University Press, forthcoming), chap. 1.

[8] See W. Phillips Davison, *The Berlin Blockade: A Study in Cold War Politics* (Princeton, N.J.: Princeton University Press, 1958), and H. Field Haviland, Jr., "Foreign Aid and the Policy Process: 1957," *American Political Science Review*, 52 (September 1958) : 689–724.

serving only the occasional historian who chances upon it and uses it to get a "feel" for the era he is studying.

The broad assessments are similarly fated. Most of those written in the 1950's, for example, now serve merely as background reading for historians. The literature on limited war fostered by the Korean conflict is not central to the research monographs generated by the Vietnam war. Nor does the arms-control literature of the 1960's appear to be rooted in the spate of serious inquiries into strategic problems that were published in the previous decade. To be sure, the more recent analyses are not oblivious of the work done in the earlier periods. Frequent references to the pioneering efforts of, say, Brodie, Bull, Kahn, Kissinger, Osgood, and Schelling can be found in the more recent writings on limited and arms control. More often than not, however, the earlier inquiries are cited by way of pointing out how circumstances have changed and how new interpretations are therefore necessary. Each researcher and each generation of foreign policy analysts, it would seem, starts afresh, interpreting the prevailing scene in terms of the problems it presents and thus offering nothing on which to build when the set is changed and the curtain goes up on new actors playing different roles.[9]

One other consequence of the nonscientific character of foreign policy research needs to be noted, namely, that it commands little respect among those in positions to apply its concepts and findings to the actual conduct of world affairs.[10] While the advice of foreign policy specialists is, as Bloomfield notes in Chapter 8 above, sought by and provided to the agencies and personnel of government, the resulting interaction would not seem to be a typical client-expert relationship. It derives less from the client's dependence on the expert's expertise than from the official's need to clarify and check out his thinking with detached and knowledgeable observers. Certainly it does not involve the kind of dependence on expertise that characterizes officialdom's relationships with many other types of specialists on human behavior. Plainly, neither officials nor nongovernmental leaders defer to the foreign policy

---

[9] There are, of course, exceptions. We are describing a central tendency and do not wish to imply that the literature is completely barren of enduring research. A few broad assessments (but hardly any case histories) stand out as sources on which new generations of researchers depend. Morton A. Kaplan's *System and Process in International Politics* (New York: John Wiley & Sons, 1957) comes readily to mind as a work that continues to be cited as a basis for inquiry even though it was published more than a decade ago. Such exceptions, however, support the point about the research-provoking nature of inquiries that are infused with a scientific consciousness. Almost invariably the exceptions are works that offer hypotheses, that cast political processes in terms of variance that is greater under certain conditions and less under others. Similarly, an important part of the research employing simulation techniques, especially the studies conducted or stimulated by Harold Guetzkow, can be fairly described as cumulative. But again the exception seems to prove the rule. Many of the simulation runs reported by Guetzkow and his colleagues are designed to test and extend the findings of previous runs. See Harold Guetzkow *et al.*, *Simulation in International Relations: Developments for Research and Training* (Englewood Cliffs, N.J.: Prentice-Hall, Inc., 1963), *passim*.

[10] See Louis Morton, "The Cold War and American Scholarship," in *Historian and Diplomat*, pp. 123–69.

expert's judgment on the adequacy of an international posture to the same extent that they do, say, to the economist's views on the soundness of a fiscal policy or the psychiatrist's assessment of the mental state of an accused murderer. Indeed, the assessments of the foreign policy scholar hardly even enjoy the respect of family and friends. Anyone who has ever done research on foreign affairs can testify that nonprofessional acquaintances never hesitate to dispute and reject offhandedly the conclusions derived from months of painstaking inquiry. Most people, officials and ordinary citizens alike, consider themselves to be as qualified or as unqualified as the next person in international affairs, and thus those who specialize in such matters are not viewed as experts. While there are no doubt many reasons for this, surely an important one is that such "experts" have no expertise. Lacking a scientific consciousness, they have not built up a body of rigorously tested knowledge or even a coherent set of testable propositions that specify what is likely to happen over a range of diverse circumstances. The economist offers elaborate theories and supporting data as to what happens to supply when demand increases, and the psychiatrist can refer to a vast storehouse of empirical material to support his diagnosis of what form of mental illness is likely to result in particular symptoms. The political scientist who specializes in foreign policy, however, can provide only illustrations from past experience and informed impressions of present practice. So why should anyone defer to him? The knowledge he offers can be acquired just as easily by reading a good newspaper or conversing with knowledgeable friends. He may bring to bear a richer variety of data and a more refined capacity for seeing interrelationships, but like the journalist and the intelligent citizen, he bases his foreign policy assessments and recommendations on untested impressions rather than on a rigorously substantiated body of knowledge.

To assert that foreign policy research is not cumulative, that, indeed, it tends to stifle questioning and thought, and that its gatherers hardly differ from journalists and informed citizens is a strong indictment that, in all fairness, needs to be documented. As it stands, the indictment is only an impression.[11] Although it is based on a long acquaintance with the literature of the field, it may well be skewed by a preference for the scientific mode. Certainly there are those who make quite the opposite indictment and contend that research in the field is too scientific.[12] Thus it is possible that a systematic

---

[11] Moreover, it is exclusively a comment on the literature of the field and is not intended to detract from the point made by Bloomfield elsewhere in this symposium that the contribution of foreign policy researchers has been an important one, even though their work has not been cumulative.

[12] For an expression of this viewpoint, see Kenneth W. Thompson, "Normative Theory in International Relations," *Journal of International Affairs*, 21 (1967): 289. On the other hand, there are those who would agree with the judgment made here. For example, although he did not classify it as an indictment, Henry Kissinger has recently noted that "American writing on foreign policy has generally tended to fall into three categories: analyses of specific cases or historical episodes, exhortations justifying or resisting greater participation in international affairs, and investigations of the legal bases of world order" (*New York Times*, February 12, 1967, sec. 7, p. 3).

content analysis of the literature would reveal more sensitivity to the variance of variables and a greater incidence of explicit hypotheses than it is claimed here exist. An inventory of research practices might show that the recent trends toward aggregate data analysis and simulation involve more than a small minority of the researchers in the field. However, in the absence of an elaborate inventory of the literature—and plainly one ought to be compiled— we can only proceed on the assumption that our indictment is essentially valid and that it is sufficient to present some sample evidence indicating that the forgoing is not simply a product of bias (see the Appendix).

Before we turn to the main purpose of this paper, however, one aspect of the indictment does need to be clarified. Lest it create false issues, conjuring up images of complex formulae, quantified data, and statistical manipulations, emphasis must be given to the fact that foreign policy researchers are not being indicted for failing to employ elaborate procedures and mathematical computations. It is the implications of the initial premise with which researchers approach foreign policy phenomena that are at issue, not the refinements of their methodology—the consciousness of scientific method, not its detailed application. Stated most succinctly, a scientific consciousness involves an automatic tendency to ask, "Of what larger pattern is this behavior an instance?" Analysts continuously motivated by this question cannot be content just to derive a conclusion from their observations. Their initial premise is that each conclusion must serve as the basis for new observations, that the function of data is not only to test prior expectations, but also to generate new ones. Because it treats every observation as an instance of a more general class of events, a scientific consciousness also impels speculation about the conditions under which the observed behavior would not have occurred or would have occurred in a different form. Such speculation in turn leads researchers, virtually without forethought, to infuse their variables with variance and to cast them in the form of hypotheses whose testing will either affirm or negate their conclusions about the more general class of events.

Systematic but nonscientific analysis, on the other hand, does not give rise to consideration of the ways in which changing conditions might foster varying behavior. Once the antecedents of the observed behavior have been thoroughly examined and other possible interpretations have been carefully considered, the conclusions that the behavior seems to suggest can be accepted. The search is not for a larger pattern, but for inherent meaning. The analyst asks, "What are the sources of this observed behavior and what are its consequences?" The issue for him is whether a sufficient number of factors have been examined to justify the answer to the question. Hence, although informed and systematically developed, this answer need not be relevant to other situations in the past, present, or future. Inevitably, therefore, the analyst must rely on his impressions of the interconnections among situations if he offers generalizations that span two or more of them. The generalizations may well stem from much thought and long experience in the study of foreign policy situations, but they will perforce be impressionistic. Since conclusions about each situation are not structured so that they can be verified in other situations, systematic but nonscientific analyses provide no cumulated body of confirmed findings that the researcher can fall back on when he registers observations about the similarities and differences among several situations. It is in this sense that the journalist or the knowledgeable friend have as much to offer as the foreign policy specialist if the latter does not have a consciousness of scientific method.

It follows that the crucial distinction between scientific inquiry and that which is systematic but not scientific lies in the manner in which data are used and not in the amount or even the kind of data gathered. If the initial premise that the researcher brings to his data is rooted in a scientific consciousness, it does not matter whether he has made a single observation or a multitude, since he will treat both the single event and the many events as part of a more general class of phenomena. The essence of scientific inquiry is thus not to be found in complex formulae or neatly arrayed tables of data. The case history can be a scientific document if its data are used as a basis for anticipating how other, as yet unexamined, data might be arrayed. Likewise, the broad assessment can be essentially scientific if the impressions it sets forth are cast in hypothetical terms that are susceptible to further exploration. Consider, for example, the proposition that "As societies enter the phase when integration tends to take precedence over development as a main problem, there is greater concern for international order and less interest in foreign adventures that might lead to war."[13] It appears in a broad historical analysis, and yet this particular work gives rise to an urge to engage in new research precisely because it is filled with conclusions cast in such a fashion.

On the other hand, a plethora of quantitative data depicting a nation's recurrent foreign policy behavior can be subjected to nonscientific techniques of analysis. The presence of tables of data is no guarantee that a scientific consciousness has been at work. Many a work can be found that contains a number of systematic tabulations but no hypotheses. In his investigation of the 1951 Japanese peace treaty, for example, Cohen presents twenty-nine elaborate tables, which range from presentations of press coverage to content analyses of John Foster Dulles' speeches and the central themes of Senate debate.[14] Yet, as indicated below in the Appendix, this case history does not employ its quantitative data for other than descriptive purposes and thus fails to manifest a scientific consciousness.

In short, the indictment of the foreign policy field set forth here does not amount to a call for all researchers to abandon their present modes of inquiry for new ones. There is no implication that every analyst should be required to undergo retooling in mathematics and training in statistics. Nor does it imply that a policy-oriented concern with current problems needs to be replaced by

---

[13] C. E. Black, *The Dynamics of Modernization: A Study in Comparative History* (New York: Harper & Row, 1966), p. 135.

[14] Bernard C. Cohen, *The Political Process and Foreign Policy: The Making of the Japanese Peace Settlement* (Princeton, N.J.: Princeton University Press, 1967).

an aspiration to construct general theory. Rather it calls on researchers to supplement their efforts, whatever the purposes of these may be and however many data they may encompass, with a sensitivity to the variance of any variables that are used and to the larger relevance of any conclusions that are reached. Such a sensitivity in no way hinders policy-oriented research and it does not require sophistication in quantitative procedures. It does hold forth the hope that a cumulative body of reliable findings on foreign policy may emerge and that the recommendations of policy-oriented researchers will then be held in greater esteem than is presently the case.

Assuming that it is essentially valid to conclude that foreign policy research is at present long on systematic analysis and short on scientific consciousness, the question arises as to why this should be so. What is it about foreign policy phenomena that renders them so conducive to nonscientific inquiry? And how might they be made more susceptible to the derivation and testing of explicit hypotheses?

II. THE PROBLEM OF URGENCY

Two of the reasons for the present state of foreign policy research are self-evident and require only brief comment. One of these is the vital importance of the problems posed by the subject. The growing destructive capacity of modern weapons and the ever present possibility of a nuclear holocaust add a dimension of urgency to foreign policy problems that leads many analysts to compromise their research standards and forgo the patience and detachment they normally bring to their work. The notion that foreign policy phenomena are simply data to be explained is for many students of the subject a betrayal of responsibility. "The problems have to be solved now," they seem to say. "If we take the time to treat a foreign policy event as an instance of a larger pattern, none of us will be around to discern that larger pattern!" Thus reinforced with moral and seemingly practical reasons for not being overly concerned about the cumulation of findings that extend beyond particular situations, many researchers feel no impulse to allow for the variance of their variables and to cast their conclusions in terms of hypotheses that can be subjected to further exploration.[15]

The trouble with such reasoning is that it posits a false dichotomy between scientific inquiry and policy-oriented solutions. The fact that specific

---

[15] It must be noted, however, that moral fervor and fear that the arms race may eventuate in nuclear holocaust do not necessarily lead to a curbing of scientific consciousness. Curiously, some of those who feel most strongly about such matters, i.e., those who call themselves "peace researchers," can often be found among the small minority of foreign policy analysts who are sensitive to the variance of variables and the derivation of testable hypotheses. A perusal of the recently founded *Journal of Peace Research* and the annual volumes of the Peace Research Society (International) will reveal a much greater scientific consciousness than a comparable survey of such older and more established journals as *Foreign Affairs, Orbis, World Politics*, and *International Affairs*.

policy recommendations emerge from an investigation does not preclude the derivation of hypotheses from the materials examined. As has already been indicated, the maintenance of a scientific consciousness requires a perspective and not a procedure with respect to the processing of data. If the researcher is unable to await the outcome of quantitative tests of complex propositions, he can still place the results of his inquiry in a larger context without undermining their immediate applicability. Nothing is lost, except perhaps some succinctness, if in urging a certain course of action upon the policy-maker the researcher indicates the more general class of behavior from which his recommendations are drawn. If, for example, he is urging American policy-makers to take a firm stand in the face of China's emerging nuclear capabilities, little would be sacrificed if he made it clear why he thinks firm stands are more likely to induce international actors to accept arms-control measures than accommodative stands.[16] If it is true that at present his recommendations are necessarily rooted in impressions and have no more reliability than those of a thoughtful journalist or an informed citizen, the question arises whether he can afford *not* to supplement his specific conclusions with disciplined speculation about the larger patterns into which they fit.

III. THE PROBLEM OF COMPLEXITY

Another obvious deterrent to scientific consciousness in foreign policy research is the complexity of the subject. The number of variables that may underlie the impact and success of a policy is so astronomical that many researchers regard foreign policy phenomena as inherently not susceptible to scientific treatment. As two distinguished analysts have put it, "When it comes to studying foreign policy in its various manifestations . . . the social scientist is . . . asked to explain and predict attitudes whose complexity makes a mockery of the few 'scientific' tools we have. . . . To attempt generalizations and construction of models that will give us a rigorous scientific understanding and prediction of foreign policy is a hopeless task."[17] Without in the least denying the complexity of foreign policy phenomena, it must be emphasized that this line of reasoning is profoundly fallacious and a major obstacle to cumulative research in the field. It is based on an erroneous conception of science. As has already been indicated, science implies only a certain method of handling data and nothing about their particular nature. If the relevance of science were limited only to simple phenomena, the great

---

[16] For an illustration of the fact that it is possible not to place recommendations on this subject in a larger context, see Morton H. Halperin, *China and the Bomb* (New York: Frederick A. Praeger, Inc., 1965), the last three chapters of which contain no such hypotheses, although they present thirteen recommendations of what the United States "must" do and sixty-four courses of action that it "should" follow.

[17] Kenneth W. Thompson and Roy C. Macridis, "The Comparative Study of Foreign Policy," in *Foreign Policy in World Politics*, ed. Macridis, 2nd ed. (Englewood Cliffs, N.J.: Prentice-Hall, Inc., 1962), pp. 26–27.

explosion of knowledge that marks the twentieth century would not have occurred. Physics, chemistry, economics, psychology, and the many other areas of inquiry that have advanced so rapidly in recent decades would still be intuitive enterprises if those who investigated such matters held the attitude quoted above. Indeed, it is reasonable to argue that these advances occurred precisely because researchers did not stand in awe of their subject matter and turned to the scientific method in order to untangle its complexity.

However, to reject the argument that foreign policy phenomena are too complex to be analyzed scientifically is not to deny their extraordinary multitude and variability. On the contrary, in view of the analytic innovations suggested below, it is extremely important that their complexity be fully recognized. In order to ensure this recognition and facilitate the subsequent analysis, an example of the scale of complexity with which foreign policy researchers must contend can usefully be outlined. Consider Latin America and the number and variety of specific policy situations that comprise the foreign policy of any nation toward that region. Figured conservatively, what is summarily called a nation's "Latin-American policy" involves attention to 89,100 continuing situations and several hundred thousand items of data. These figures were derived by positing "Latin America" as consisting of five basic types of units, each of which possesses three basic characteristics. Three of the units are to be found in nations, namely, their publics, their nongovernmental elites, and their officials. The other two units are of an international kind, one consisting of international organizations in which formalized interaction between nations takes place and the other of the unformalized interaction that comprises international relationships. The three characteristics of each unit are its attitudes, its behavior patterns, and its structure; attitudes refer to tendencies to act in a certain way, behavior patterns to the way attitudes are expressed in the form of concrete action, and structure to the patterns of interaction among the component parts of a unit or between one unit and other units in its environment.

If we now combine the units and their characteristics into a three-by-five matrix (see Figure 1), we can identify fifteen basic types of situations toward which policy-makers outside Latin America may have to act in attempting either to preserve prevailing attitudinal, behavioral, and structural patterns or

FIGURE 1

	Publics	Elites	Officials	International Relationships	International Organizations
Attitudes					
Behavior					
Structure					

to promote desired changes in them. Obviously, however, these fifteen types are only the beginning of an adequate classification. If we make the simplifying assumption that the public of each nation consists of four elements—the active modernist, the passive modernist, the active traditionalist, and the passive traditionalist—then the first column of the matrix must be treated as four columns, giving rise to twelve types of situations involving publics. Assuming that each nation has four elite groups, the business, labor, religious, and military elites, each of which in turn is composed of traditionalists and modernists, then the second column of the matrix emerges as actually eight columns, which, when combined with the three rows, result in twenty-four types of situations involving elites. Assuming further that it is meaningful to distinguish between the executive and the legislative officials of each nation, then we end up with six types of situations involving officials. If it is also presumed that as a minimum the activities of three individuals within each elite group and each segment of officialdom are particularly crucial to the course of events, then ninety "individual" situations must be included in the total.

If account is then taken of the fact that the 12 public situations, the 24 elite situations, the 6 official situations, and the 90 individual situations are to be found in 20 countries, it turns out that 2,640 national situations have constantly to be monitored by those who formulate and conduct a nation's policies toward Latin America. And to these 2,640 national situations must be added a wide variety of international ones. For illustrative purposes let us say that 10 international organizations, such as the Organization of American States, the World Bank, and the Alliance for Progress, are active in the region, and that each of the 20 nations has a discernible and significant unformalized relationship with 5 other nations in the hemisphere, thus giving rise to 100 international relationships in the region. In turn the 10 organizations and 100 relationships must be seen as having attitudinal, behavioral, and structural dimensions, so that 330 international situations must be added to the 2,640 national situations in order to get a more complete picture of the specific policy situations that are unfolding at any one time. Nor do these 2,970 situations tell the full story. At least one more simplifying assumption must be made—that all human affairs can be divided into 3 functional areas, the social, the economic, and the political—with the result that as a minimum "Latin America" consists of 8,910 basic situations that may be of concern to policy-makers abroad at any moment in time, and over which they must therefore attempt to exert influence.

Even the total of 8,910 situations, however, does not adequately describe the region as it appears to officials outside Latin America. For each of these situations tends to overlap with a number of others. A riot in Venezuela can precipitate protests in Colombia. An election result in Chile can have consequences for Bolivia. Public unrest in Argentina can give rise to major changes in the foreign policies pursued by Argentine officialdom. A coup d'état in Peru can contribute to friction among the elites of Guatemala. Action against Cuba can drastically alter attitudes in the OAS. Inflation in Brazil can have structural implications for the Alliance for Progress. Indeed, if one makes the not unreasonable assumption that each of the 8,910 situations overlaps with at least 5 others, and if these overlapping situations are in themselves treated as situations, the total amounts to 44,550 situations.

And there is more. Whether or not officials outside Latin America regard their own actions as variables, certainly foreign policy analysts cannot ignore the feedback consequences of international behavior. Each situation at one moment in time has the potential of being altered at the next moment as a result of the foreign policy action directed toward it, so that if the analyst's concern extends across at least two moments in time, the 44,550 policy situations appear as 89,100 situations. Further complexity arises when it is recognized that three or four nations outside Latin America may seek to preserve or alter any of the situations within it, and that the degree of preservation or alteration can vary considerably depending upon whether political, economic, or military policies are directed at the situations. Consequently, from the perspective of the analyst examining the Latin-American policy of one of the three or four nations during, say, a major era of international life, the 89,100 situations may actually consist of several hundred thousand data to be taken into account.

But one need not be overwhelmed by so much complexity. For the analyst who possesses a scientific consciousness, such complexity becomes an opportunity, and the existence of hundreds or thousands of data serves as a source of motivation and not of despair. He assumes they rest on an underlying order and regards discernment of this order as an endless challenge. He does not see the many data as capricious and beyond comprehension. He starts with the faith that none of them occurred by chance, but that all of them were brought into being by events that are at least theoretically knowable.[18] He can thus proceed with his attempts to move to higher and higher levels of generalization, both supported and urged on by the firm belief that the multitude of reasons for the multitude of data can be subsumed under more encompassing explanations. In short, an analyst with a scientific orientation, far from being aghast at complexity such as that posed by the Latin-American example, views it as a chance to trace larger patterns and build cumulative knowledge.[19]

Yet there is no magic in science. Complexity does not automatically yield

---

[18] By allowing for events that are "theoretically knowable," the scientist avoids being bound by the technology for testing hypotheses that may be available at a given time. Like other technologies, those of observation and measurement are not stagnant. Propositions that are unverifiable today may well be testable tomorrow (as those who once made forecasts about the far side of the moon will now happily affirm). Thus the foreign policy analyst need not be paralyzed by the fact that so many of the events in which he is interested occur in places to which he presently does not have access. He needs only to be certain that the data he seeks to predict are theoretically capable of being observed, rather than being dependent on, say, divine revelation for confirmation.

[19] For an elaboration of the philosophical underpinnings of a scientific approach to foreign policy phenomena, see my "Games International Relations Scholars Play," *Journal of International Affairs*, 21 (1967) : 293–303.

to an analyst's scientific approach. Unlike those who are not interested in going beyond impressionistic and broad assessments of what all the data appear to add up to, the scientist is committed to adhering to rigorous rules of procedure that require him to break the complexity down into its component parts before proceeding step by step up the ladder of generalization. He starts by asking what a few data are instances of, hoping thus to cumulate answers that will eventually reveal the pattern of which all the data are instances. Hence the analyst who proceeds scientifically as well as systematically resists the temptation to explain a nation's "Latin-American policy." For him Latin America poses not one but many research problems, each of which must be solved before all-encompassing generalizations can be offered.

The development of a scientific consciousness and acceptance of its philosophical underpinnings are not simple steps and require more than an acknowledgment of the complexity of foreign policy phenomena. Obviously, this acknowledgment must be accompanied by confidence that the complexity is surmountable, and this in turn depends on the availability of the basic ingredients of a scientific approach, namely, independent and dependent variables that are clearly differentiated, that have specified forms of variance, and that are, when brought together in testable hypotheses, appropriate to the questions that sustain the curiosity of researchers. If these fundamentals are lacking, it is difficult for researchers to maintain a scientific consciousness even if they recognize that the scientific approach does not preclude a concern for urgent policy problems and accept the fact that their subject matter is extremely complex. For the absence of clarity at this basic level hinders the derivation and accumulation of reliable findings that foster confidence in the potentialities of scientific inquiry and that discourage a return to case histories and broad assessments. Hindrances of this sort, it would seem, are a major cause of the present state of foreign policy research. There is little clarity about the prime variables of the field, and thus it is to an elucidation of these more subtle obstacles to the development of scientific consciousness that we now turn.

IV. PROBLEMS OF THE DEPENDENT VARIABLE

The core of any hypothesis about human phenomena is the behavior that the researcher is seeking to comprehend and that is predicted to undergo change as conditions vary. This behavior constitutes the dependent variable of his hypotheses, and as such it not only must undergo changes that are capable of being observed and measured, but it must also be appropriate to the kind of knowledge being sought. If the behavior is too narrowly conceived, the observation and measurement of its variation under different conditions will yield findings that can never provide more than partial answers to the questions being asked. For example, the psychologist interested in social behavior is not likely to develop findings appropriate to his concerns if neurological reactions constitute the behavior he observes and measures. Such reactions may indeed vary in different individuals exposed to different social situations, but to increase comprehension of them is not to satisfy curiosity about interpersonal activity. Likewise, if the behavior is too broadly conceived, its observable variations will be so gross that the researcher will not be able to develop answers to his specific queries. The psychologist who casts all social behavior in terms of a cordial-hostile continuum is not likely to uncover many differentiated findings. Doubtless every social behavior could be located at some point along this continuum, but findings that depict how different people shift their location on it in response to various stimuli will also fail to alleviate the researcher's curiosity about the nuances of interpersonal activity.

The two prime dependent variables used in foreign policy research, decisions and policies, present problems of this order. The authoritative efforts of a national society to maintain control over its external environment through the preservation of desired situations abroad and the modification of undesired ones can be viewed as the central concern of foreign policy research,[20] and neither decisions nor policies appear to be appropriate forms of behavior in terms of which to develop knowledge about these authoritative efforts. Stated most succinctly, hypotheses that seek to predict decisional behavior are too narrow to provide more than partial comprehension of these efforts, and hypotheses that seek to predict policy behavior are too broad to provide incisive understanding of them. The limitations inherent in decisions as dependent variables can be readily grasped by noting that ordinarily a society must engage in a series of behaviors and not in a single behavior in order to preserve or alter a situation abroad. Other factors besides the society's efforts are at work in the situation, and many of these generate resistance to its efforts. Hence, not only must the behavior that initiated the effort be sustained through time, but new behaviors are needed in order to cope with the resistance it encounters as well as with other unexpected developments that occur as the situation evolves. The preservation or modification of situations abroad ordinarily does not depend on a single choice among alternative courses of action, but is a consequence of a series of decisions, each of which is in part a function of the outcomes of the previous decisions. However, as the concept of decision-making has developed in foreign policy research, it refers to activity at a particular moment in time and does not allow for the sequential nature of the behavior that initiates, sustains, and terminates foreign policy efforts. To be sure, decisions are not posited as instantaneous and allowance is made for the welter of activity and passage of time that precede choice, but once a decision is made, the dependent variable is presumed to have been observed and the analysis comes to an end. This is not to deny, of course, that the implementation of a decision will ordinarily produce effects requiring new decisions. Decision-making analysts

---

[20] For an extended formulation of this view of the nature of foreign policy, see my *Calculated Control as a Unifying Concept in the Study of International Politics and Foreign Policy*, Research Monograph No. 15 (Princeton, N.J.: Center of International Studies, 1963).

acknowledge the relevance of outcomes by including the expected consequences of decisions among the independent variables that shape the choices
made. But such a procedure is not the same as taking into account the ways in
which the actual consequences abroad feed back into the foreign policy effort
as it is unfolding. Usually these consequences are postponed for consideration
in relation to a subsequent decision. As has already been indicated, however,
the difficulty with such postponements is that researchers are seldom provoked
to investigate the subsequent decisions of a sequence. It is thus hardly
surprising that the cumulated findings generated by the decision-making
approach to foreign policy have never been very substantial.[21] Confined to a
single behavior and unconcerned with outcomes, findings based on decisions
as variables can provide only partial answers to the questions that perplex
foreign policy researchers.

Events in Vietnam since February 1965, when the United States decided
to alter the situation through the use of bombers, provide a vivid illustration
of the insufficiency of decisions as dependent variables. What is analytically
challenging about American behavior in that situation is not the bombing
decision and the unwillingness of the North Vietnamese to alter their attitudes
and behavior. The original bombing decision appears to have heightened this
unwillingness and thereby necessitated a series of new choices, each of which
further escalated the conflict and occasioned the necessity of another decision.
An analysis in which any one of these decisions constitutes the dependent
variable is thus ill designed to fulfill the aims of the foreign policy researcher.
He is interested in explaining the entire sequence of American behavior in the
situation and thus needs dependent variables that are appropriate to such a
concern.

Much the same can be said about the Latin-American example. Suppose
the researcher is interested in predicting the behavior of a nation that, for the
sake of its own security as well as for humanitarian reasons, aspires to the
construction of stable polities and economies in Latin America. Assuming that
the nation translates this aspiration into a decision to try to bring about such
conditions, plainly the researcher would not be encompassing the phenomena
of interest to him if he concentrated solely upon this decision. Nor would it be
sufficient if the nation sought to alter or preserve the 89,100 situations in
Latin America through one one-hundredth as many implementing decisions
and the researcher were able to gather complete information on all of these.
The cumulated findings derived from these 891 data would still be inappropriate to the hypotheses he wished to test. For again many of the implementing
decisions would have a significant impact on many of the situations in Latin
America and would thus create new conditions toward which new foreign
policy efforts would have to be directed. Tempting as it might be for the
researcher simply to project movement toward the original aspiration on the

---

[21] For an elaboration of this point, see my "The Premises and Promises of
Decision-Making Analysis," in *Contemporary Political Analysis*, ed. James C. Charlesworth (New York: Free Press, 1967), pp. 189–211.

basis of the 891 data he had accumulated, not very much time would elapse before he realized that the bases of his projections no longer obtained and that his dependent variable failed to yield data adequate to explain the full sequence of behavior that engaged his interest in the first place. To be sure, some of his data might prove relevant to the understanding of future decisions, but he could not be sure which of the original decisions reflected firm commitments that would be reiterated as new situations evolved and which would be revised as a consequence of their own impact.

Perhaps out of recognition of the inherent limitations of decisions as dependent variables, many foreign policy researchers focus on policies as the behavior central to their inquiry. Conceived narrowly as the goals that a national society sets for itself with respect to aspects of its external environment and the actions that it has taken or will take in order to realize or maintain these goals, policies have the advantage of subsuming both decisions that initiate behavior and those that implement it. In this narrow sense, moreover, a focus on policies does not preclude analysis of the feedback of decisional outcomes and does not confine attention to activity at a single moment in time. Unfortunately, however, these possibilities are often overlooked when policies are actually used as dependent variables and a much broader conception tends to dominate their usage in research. In this conception, a policy designates a variety of unrelated goals and, consequently, a wide range of unrelated action sequences. This broader construction prevails because researchers tend to organize their inquiry around the aspect of a nation's external environment that interests them rather than around a goal it seeks to realize or a situation it seeks to alter or preserve. In part they do so because many of the environmental aspects are constants in a rapidly changing world. Unlike the goals and behavior that underlie foreign policy efforts, at least the environmental aspects have a location in geographic space and often have finite boundaries in time. Hence they seem to offer parameters within which the researcher can organize his inquiry. In fact, of course, this constancy is misleading in that it predisposes researchers to treat any and all actions that may be or are directed at a particular environmental aspect in the same context and as thus reflecting essentially the same policy. If, for example, Venezuela is the aspect of the United States' external environment that interests a researcher, then no matter how many U.S. pronouncements about or involvements in Venezuelan affairs he has investigated, he is likely to presume that the conclusions derived therefrom govern American goals and behavior with respect to any situations that may arise in Venezuela and which the United States may wish to preserve or alter. The result is likely to be an article entitled "United States Foreign Policy toward Venezuela," which purports (at least implicitly) to encompass the totality of American relations with that country and tends to discount the variance in those relations. If the researcher's interests are continental in scope, then he presents his findings in a volume on "United States Foreign Policy toward Latin America," which moves even further from empirical phenomena and collapses unrelated goals and behavior sequences into an even more general totality. Nor does this exhaust the possibilities in the broad construction of the concept. A number of researchers have interests that are global in scope, and have filled many library shelves with treatises on, simply, "United States Foreign Policy," which offer relatively few examples in support of a broad discussion of the values and behavioral norms that guide American efforts toward any situation abroad that requires preservation or alteration.

In short, in their most common usage as dependent variables, policies have no fixed behavioral boundaries and are so variable, amorphous, and all-encompassing that the findings they yield obscure variance and defy cumulation. While it is at least logically (if not empirically) possible to identify decisions in terms of the activity that initiates, sustains, and terminates them, such is not the case with policies broadly conceived. The basic structure of the behavior they subsume cannot be inferred from findings descriptive of them. Indeed, behavior is not even a necessary component of policy variables. Often analysts refer to policies that consist not of concrete action, but of commitments or attitudes that might be translated into action if new situations arise abroad which warrant it. Clearly a scientific consciousness is difficult to develop if the phenomena one is inclined to predict have no empirical referents. If researchers are to acquire the habit of hypothesizing, they ought to have available dependent variables that have at least a theoretically observable structure, that are not as limiting as decisions and not as encompassing as policies, and that can cumulatively provide the kind of findings appropriate to the testing of hypotheses and to the questions that stimulate foreign policy researchers.

One obvious solution to the need for more appropriate dependent variables is to insist that hypotheses be founded upon the narrow conception of a policy. As previously noted, this narrow construction has a number of advantages and it does seem to be suitable to the interests of researchers. Such a solution, however, would quickly founder. The broad conception of policy is too deeply ingrained in the terminology and analytic habits of the field to be simply put aside. The distinction between the narrow and broad conception could thus not be maintained for long, and the present state of inquiry would soon be reestablished. Hence, while recognizing that analytic habit is not necessarily altered by terminological innovation, the last section of this paper offers the *undertaking* as a variable that meets the needs of foreign policy research.

V. PROBLEMS OF THE INDEPENDENT VARIABLE

If the behaviors through which national societies initiate, sustain, and terminate efforts to preserve or alter situations constitute the dependent variables of foreign policy research, the independent variables are all those factors that shape these behaviors and determine the variance. Elsewhere we have suggested that these can be usefully subdivided into five main types—idiosyncratic, role, governmental, societal, and systemic—and that an assessment of the relative potency or causal strength of each type is necessary to hypothesizing about the foreign policy behavior that is likely to occur under specific conditions.[22] The step from the identification of relevant types of independent variables to the specification of those within each type and the operationalization of their variance is not an easy one to take. A host of problems must be solved, and appropriateness and clarity are again impotant criteria. Variables must be appropriate in the sense that they account for enough of the foreign policy behavior to justify the researcher's efforts, and they must be marked by clarity in the sense that their variance is ranged along meaningful and observable dimensions. There is some evidence, for example, that foreign policy behavior is more likely to occur in the summer than at other times of the year,[23] but the relative potency of the seasonal variable is probably so low that further efforts to refine it would be inappropriate.[24] Similarly, the nature of a society's political structure is presumably highly relevant to its external behavior, but such a presumption must be translated into clear-cut degrees or kinds of relevance before political structure can be used as an independent variable in researchable hypotheses.

While the task of identifying and operationalizing the more "robust" of the independent variables is an urgent one, an effort to carry it forward requires more time than is available here.[25] Two problems that will probably prove especially difficult to solve, however, can usefully be flagged. One of them in particular seems so insurmountable that it is no doubt a major barrier to the development of a scientific consciousness in foreign policy research. This is what might be called the feedback problem. It stems from the fact that foreign policy research is concerned with independent variables that unfold through time and it arises most acutely in the case of societal and systemic variables. Both within and outside the society that initiates a foreign policy undertaking, events occur or situations emerge as it unfolds that are sufficiently potent to feed back into the undertaking as determinants of its future course. These feedback variables can be reactions to the under-

---

[22] Rosenau, "Pre-Theories and Theories of Foreign Policy," in *Approaches to Comparative and International Politics*, ed. R. Barry Farrell (Evanston, Ill.: Northwestern University Press, 1966), pp. 45–51.

[23] Johan Galtung, "Summit Meetings and International Relations," *Journal of Peace Research*, no. 1, 1964, pp. 36–54.

[24] The location of the cutoff between an appropriate and inappropriate variable could be derived on the basis of statistical criteria. Correlations over .30 or .40 are usually regarded as significant by those who employ statistical methods. Since correlations of this order account for roughly 10 or 12 percent of the variance, it is reasonable to view any variable that accounts for less than this amount of the observed foreign policy behavior as inappropriate. Surely seasonal variables do not exceed the cutoff point.

[25] I am presently associated in such an effort with nine colleagues, all of whom concur that, while the task poses extraordinarily difficult problems, it does seem to be manageable.

taking or they can occur quite independently of it. An undertaking may precipitate the fall of a cabinet abroad or stimulate the rise of an opposition party at home; or it may be in progress when a U-2 is downed, a Stalin dies, a Middle Eastern war erupts, a common market is formed, or a new president is elected. These are typical of the many types of developments that can operate as potent independent variables after the undertaking has been initiated. The goals of the undertaking remain essentially the same, but the path of action toward them may be altered as a consequence of feedback. In effect, therefore, the foreign policy researcher must look at independent variables that are operative during as well as prior to the behavior he seeks to explain. Stated in still another way, some of the independent and dependent variables are concurrent in time even though it is necessary for the researcher to treat them as analytically separable.[26]

Plainly feedback processes greatly complicate foreign policy research. They require that the analyst be able not only to predict how the national society of interest to him will respond to stimuli, but also to anticipate internal and external reactions to its behavior in order to know what feedback processes will be operative as independent variables. Stated in terms of the Latin-American example, the researcher must not only comprehend the decision-making dynamics of the society whose undertakings toward Latin America he seeks to explain and predict, but also have some knowledge about decision-making phenomena in the twenty national societies of that region in order to allow for new events or trends that will significantly deflect, slow, or otherwise affect the undertakings as they unfold.

Yet the complexity introduced by feedback variables is not as awesome as it might appear.[27] While there can be no doubt that the tasks of foreign policy research are made more difficult by the need to account for independent variables of this sort, there are several mitigating considerations. One is the aforementioned point that the researcher need be concerned only with robust variables. Many phenomena can therefore be ignored. To take on the task of tracing feedback is not to be required to account for every response that a foreign policy undertaking is likely to generate or for every development abroad or at home that may occur as it unfolds. Only those responses or events that may significantly affect the path of action followed by the undertaking need be the focus of concern. Presumably these will not be so

[26] For an extended discussion of the operation and analysis of feedback processes in political systems, see Karl W. Deutsch, *The Nerves of Government: Models of Political Communication and Control* (New York: Free Press of Glencoe, 1963), chap. 11.

[27] For an account of procedures that further reduce the awesomeness of tracing and assessing feedback processes in political research, see Herbert A. Simon, "Political Research: The Decision-Making Framework," in *Varieties of Political Theory*, ed. David Easton (Englewood Cliffs, N.J.: Prentice-Hall, Inc., 1966), pp. 22–23. For a rare work that demonstrates that feedback variables in foreign policy can be empirically analyzed, see Charles A. McClelland, "Decisional Opportunity and Political Controversy: The Quemoy Case," *Journal of Conflict Resolution*, 6 (September 1962) : 201–13.

great in number and variety as to make the problem unmanageable. Not every cabinet that falls abroad or every opposition party that arises at home can deflect, slow, or otherwise affect an undertaking. All twenty societies of Latin America may react to a particular aspect of an undertaking, but this does not mean that the analyst has to investigate all twenty situations. Conceivably none of the twenty reactions will be sufficient to have a major impact upon the undertaking. Or perhaps the reactions of only two or three of the larger Latin-American societies will serve as significant feedbacks.

Second, and relatedly, it must be remembered that much of the knowledge required to anticipate and account for feedback processes has to be acquired anyway. The very societal and systemic variables that are likely to be significant during an undertaking are also likely to be among those that would be deemed sufficiently robust to warrant investigation prior to its initiation. The stability of the governments in the region toward which an undertaking is directed, for example, is likely to be treated as a potent systemic variable under any circumstances, so the fact that one or more of them may fall as the undertaking unfolds does not introduce a new analytic dimension into the researcher's inquiry. He has already allowed for the processes represented by the cabinet collapse and thus is prepared to handle it as an independent variable at any stage of the undertaking. Similarly, public sentiments and political processes at home will undoubtedly be regarded as potent societal variables underlying the initiation of any foreign policy undertaking. Hence the emergence of an opposition party as a response to a particular undertaking ought not to introduce independent variables that the researcher is not equipped to analyze. In terms of the Latin-American example, if an undertaking designed to generate viable polities and economies in that region is significantly deflected and slowed because of the resistance to change of nongovernmental elites in all twenty countries, it is highly unlikely that the researcher will be caught unaware. Doubtless he will have already operationalized elite attitudes as a potent independent variable and ranged them along a resistant-receptive continuum. Consequently, if he has based his original hypotheses on essentially receptive attitudes, he does not need to develop new knowledge or conceptualize new variables to take the feedback into account. All that is required are revised hypotheses in which the resistant end of the elite attitude scale is accorded greater potency.

Nor need improbable developments—such as the downing of a U-2 or the death of a Stalin—which are entirely unrelated to undertakings, but which nevertheless operate as potent independent variables, be viewed as an unmanageable feedback problem. The death of a leader and the collapse of a spy mission may not be predictable in their precise historical form, but their consequences can be included in the range across which the researcher's dependent variables are conceived to be operative. Some leadership deaths and some exposed spy missions will profoundly affect the character of an undertaking, whereas others will have no impact upon its path and pace whatsoever. In order to ensure that these polar consequences of improbable events are included in the variance of the variables, the researcher can at least pose a kind of null hypothesis by asking, "Under what circumstances will an undertaking be substantially set back?" or, pressing nullity still further, "What unforeseen developments can lead to its abandonment?" and then take account of even the seemingly absurd answers in the framing of his variables.[28]

Another noteworthy problem of the independent variable, and one made especially acute by the analytic recognition given to feedback processes, concerns the phenomena that are often called "policy contents" and that seem more precisely designated as "issue-area" phenomena.[29] Stated most succinctly, these refer to the kind of values over which an issue is waged and toward which a policy is directed. Evidence is mounting that the values at stake in a conflict operate as sources of the behavior of the parties to it; that individuals, officials, and groups behave differently in different issue areas; and that therefore the dynamics of political processes and political systems vary from one issue area to another. In terms of both the nature and the outcome of the legislative process, for example, it would seem to matter whether civil-rights or foreign policy issues are before the U.S. Congress. For all practical purposes, there are two Congresses, and to comprehend the one that handles civil-rights issues is not necessarily to understand the one that copes with foreign policy questions.[30] In short, the contents of a policy, or, in the terminology used below, the goals of an undertaking, are in themselves independent variables, both as they stimulate initial behavior on the part of officials and publics and as they feed back into the ensuing actions.

Although much remains to be done by way of identifying and exploring the kinds of domestic policy issues that can be clustered together into empirically meaningful discrete areas, the task has not even been launched with respect to foreign policy issues. There is a widespread assumption that foreign policy questions evoke different forms and degrees of behavior than do domestic ones, but the common elements of the former type and the ways in which they might be fruitfully subdivided have been the subject of only the most impressionistic speculation.[31] Whereas elaborate typologies of the values

---

[28] To recur to an earlier example (see note 6 above), Khrushchev may not have known he was going to be ousted, but Brzezinski could have operationalized the variance of his variables in a way that allowed for such a development.

[29] For a general definition of the issue-area concept, see my "Pre-Theories," pp. 71–88. For a stimulating review of the problems of issue-area categorization, see Chapter 3 above, by Lewis A. Froman, Jr.

[30] Cf. Warren E. Miller and Donald E. Stokes, "Constituency Influence in Congress," American Political Science Review, 57 (March 1963): 45–56. Additional empirical evidence of issue-area phenomena can be found in Robert A. Dahl, Who Governs? Democracy and Power in an American City (New Haven: Yale University Press, 1961); V. O. Key, Jr., Public Opinion and American Democracy (New York: Alfred A. Knopf, Inc., 1961), chap. 9; and H. Douglas Price, "Are Southern Democrats Different? An Application of Scale Analysis to Senate Voting Patterns," in Politics and Social Life: An Introduction to Political Behavior, ed. Nelson W. Polsby, Robert A. Dentler, and Paul A. Smith (Boston: Houghton Mifflin Co., 1963), especially pp. 751–56.

[31] A recent example is my "Foreign Policy as an Issue-Area," in Domestic Sources of Foreign Policy, ed. Rosenau (New York: Free Press, 1967), pp. 11–50.

that may be at work in domestic situations are available,[32] no equivalent materials have been developed for the classification and analysis of foreign policy undertakings.[33] Not even such commonplace categories as left, center, and right, or radical and conservative, appear usable as an initial basis for thinking along these lines. Whereas the characterization of domestic policies in terms of these distinctions conveys at least a modicum of meaning, their application to foreign policies invariably is more confounding than clarifying, and it is a measure of both the neglect and the complexity of the problem that no better distinctions of this crude sort have been developed.

To be sure, researchers have not totally ignored the content dimension of foreign policy behavior. Classifications of policies do exist, but they usually consist of the means employed to satisfy values rather than the values themselves. Often, for example, distinctions are made among economic, military, and diplomatic means, and their utilization is presumed to connote the operation of similarly separable values. Indeed, it would seem that military policy has evolved into a separate field of research, with courses taught and texts written on the subject, but without any effort to test empirically the underlying assumption that all undertakings founded on the use or threat of military instruments have common characteristics that operate in similar and significant ways.[34] Such assumptions, however, are clearly premature. Values do attach to the means employed in foreign policy, and these may be sufficiently potent to have a significant impact on behavior, but there is no evidence that distinctions based on the instruments of policy subsume meaningful differences in international behavior. A nation can either fight for or negotiate over the same value, and the question is thus one of differentiating between the values that elicit fighting and those that foster negotiating behavior. Posing the problem more explicitly, do foreign policy undertakings directed at, say, disarmament matters have certain common dimensions that are not shared by undertakings concerned with recognition of geographic boundaries? Are the latter in turn differentiable from issues pertaining to the population explosion or to the building of viable political institutions? At what level or levels of generalization, in other words, should issues be clustered together and treated as independent variables?

Answers to questions such as these are urgently needed not only because issue areas seem likely to be robust independent variables. A greater compre-

---

[32] See, for example, Ernest A. T. Barth and Stuart D. Johnson, "Community Power and a Typology of Social Issues," *Social Forces*, 38 (October 1959): 29–32; Seymour Martin Lipset, "The Value Patterns of Democracy: A Case Study in Comparative Analysis," *American Sociological Review*, 28 (August 1963): 515–31; and Robin M. Williams, Jr., "Individual and Group Values," *Annals of the American Academy of Political and Social Science*, 371 (May 1967): 20–37.

[33] However, Harold Sprout is presently engaged in an attempt to classify "national goals in foreign policy and international politics," using a distinction between substantive (or core) and instrumental values as the point of departure.

[34] For a lonely exception, see Bernard C. Cohen, "The Military Policy Public," *Public Opinion Quarterly*, 30 (Summer 1966): 200–11.

hension of such matters also appears central to the development of scientific consciousness. At least it seems reasonable to assert that the lack of even the crudest categories for classifying foreign policy issues greatly inhibits the inclination to search for underlying patterns in international behavior. At present there is a tendency for researchers to think in terms of issues rather than issue areas, and to assume that each issue is different from every other issue, an assumption that negates the possibility of asking, "Of what is this an instance?" and that inevitably leads to the idiographic case study.

VI. THE CONCEPT OF THE UNDERTAKING

Let us conclude on an innovative note. We have criticized the present state of research for lacking hypotheses or even analytic tools that would foster a readiness to frame, test, and revise hypotheses. Yet identifying problems is not the same as solving them. To decry the shortage of conceptual equipment that permits foreign policy behavior to be treated as sequential through time and that allows for the operation of feedback processes is not to offer a constructive suggestion for developing such equipment. Most notably, it is not to offer a behavioral entity that has a temporal dimension, that subsumes independent feedback variables even as it also serves as an adequate dependent variable, and that recurs with sufficient frequency to be cumulated and yield (or fail to yield) patterns that confirm (or fail to confirm) hypotheses. In order to demonstrate that such tools of science can be fashioned and manipulated by the foreign policy researcher, therefore, the remainder of this paper outlines what appears to be an appropriate behavioral entity and indicates how it might be used.[35]

We shall refer to this basic entity as the *undertaking*, since this label connotes the serial, purposeful, and coordinative nature of foreign policy behavior. To anticipate the presentation that follows, undertakings are what foreign policy researchers observe, what they trace in case histories and mea-

---

[35] An initial hesitation about the wisdom of suggesting the addition of yet another concept to the field was overcome when it was learned that understanding, if not research, had been advanced by the introduction of similar concepts into another discipline that was —and still is—faced with problems comparable to those confronting foreign policy research. Indeed, although developed independently, the formulation presented here closely parallels the essays of two psychologists, Murray and Sears, who argued that the single action (or S-R) was an inappropriate entity for the study of social behavior, that it failed to account for the interactive and temporal dimensions of an individual's comportment, and that therefore new conceptual entities had to be developed. Murray called his entity the "interpersonal proceeding" and Sears referred to his as the "dyadic unit," and taken together their essays make a persuasive case for the procedure of using fresh terminology and concepts to rethink the stubborn and enduring problems of a field. See Henry A. Murray, "Toward a Classification of Interaction," and Robert R. Sears, "Social Behavior and Personality Development," in *Toward a General Theory of Action*, ed. Talcott Parsons and Edward A. Shils (Cambridge: Harvard University Press, 1952), pp. 434–78.

sure in quantitative studies, what they attempt to analyze and explain, what they represent in their models and predict in their hypotheses.

An undertaking is conceived to be a course of action that the duly constituted officials of a national society pursue in order to preserve or alter a situation in the international system in such a way that it is consistent with a goal or goals decided upon by them or their predecessors.[36] An undertaking begins when a situation arises abroad that officials seek to maintain or change. It is sustained as long as the resources of the society mobilized and directed by the officials continue to be applied to the situation. It terminates either when the situation comes to an end and obviates the need for further action or when officials conclude that their action cannot alter or preserve the situation and abandon their efforts. Undertakings thus can be small scale or large scale. They can require the negotiations of a single ambassador, the activities of a vast bureaucracy, or the endeavors of a mobile army. They can extend across months or years, countries or continents, crises or stalemates. They can be directed at individuals or groups, political parties or social structures, nations or regions, enemies or allies. They can be sustained through continued activity or intermittent involvement, through conflict or cooperation, through military threat or diplomatic overture.

In other words, undertakings, unlike policies and decisions, encompass goals *and* their implementation. Their distinctive quality is that they focus on what government does, not on how it decides to do it or on what it commits itself to do. Whereas it is possible for the student of policies to find the phenomena that interest him exclusively in a speech or statute, the single document can never suffice as evidence for the student of undertakings. The commitment to action reflected in the speech and the decision reflected in the statute may bear little resemblance to what in fact transpires as governments undertake to alter or preserve their external environments, and it is this analytic gap that a focus on undertakings seeks to bridge. In effect, by examining a bounded sequence of actions and reactions across a span of time and in a situational context, undertakings fuse commitments with their enactment, decisions with their outcomes, resources with their utilization.

Although undertakings involve varied types of activity, they have specifiable analytic boundaries. These are defined in terms of the behavior, decisional and implementive, associated with the pursuit of goals in concrete situations. The key to the operational identification of undertakings lies not in their goals, but in the situations they are designed to affect. The empirical referents of situations, conflicts over the prevailing structure of relationships, are readily recognizable. The actors who are parties to a situation, the time at

---

[36] Although cast in terms of foreign policy, obviously the concept is equally applicable to the analysis of domestic policy. Whether officials seek to preserve or alter situations abroad or at home, they engage in sequences of behavior that are here regarded as undertakings. Indeed, given the greater availability of data on domestic decisional and feedback processes, it could be argued that the concept is especially suitable to internal "policy" phenomena.

which the actors begin to dispute and seek change in the prevailing structure, the geographic space in which the structure is located, and the point at which action ends and the conflict ceases are all manifest phenomena and thus accessible to the researcher. Tracing the temporal, spatial, and functional boundaries of a war in Vietnam, a coup d'état in Peru, the establishment of new missile sites in Cuba, a worsening balance of payments, restlessness on the part of Jordanian refugees, a blockade in Berlin—to mention but a few obvious examples—is not an insurmountable problem even though the time, location, and behavior encompassed by the various situations differ considerably. Goals, on the other hand, pose an enormously complex challenge to the empiricist. Frequently they are cast in highly abstract terms. At other times they are not articulated by the actors and have to be inferred from behavior. Sometimes the articulated goals are not the true ones and are designed to mislead. Almost always, moreover, goals undergo modification as the situations toward which they are directed evolve. The overall commitment to preserving or altering a situation is not likely to change, but the dynamics of the situation will usually require acceptance of greater or lesser degrees of preservation or alteration than were anticipated. Thus it would seem that as long as undertakings are defined in terms of situational rather than goal referents, the danger that they will come to be used in the broad and amorphous way that marks the usage of the policy concept will be minimized.

To be sure, the danger is never eliminated. The empirical referents are not always mutually exclusive and unmistakable. Undertakings do overlap and situations are interdependent, so that to a certain extent the delineation of their boundaries is necessarily arbitrary. Hence there will always be the temptation to define situations and undertakings in such a general way that their temporal, spatial, and functional referents are obscure and ambiguous. From one perspective, for example, it might seem useful to regard the state of world order as a single situation and to treat all the diverse activities designed to preserve or promote peace as one grand undertaking. Plainly such a formulation renders the undertaking as unusable as the policy. A major purpose of adopting the undertaking as a unit of analysis is to facilitate the cumulation of numerous and discrete data, each consisting of meaningful and comparable sequences of behavior. To generate such data, therefore, the researcher must err in the direction of specificity rather than generality when exercising the arbitrariness that is inherent in the delineation of the boundaries of situations and undertakings. This means that he must maximize precision with respect to all three types of empirical referents—temporal, spatial, and functional. If, for example, he is precise only about the spatial referents, but ignores the temporal and functional ones, the danger of excessive generality looms large and the ability to differentiate dependent variables that can be subjected to hypothesis testing is correspondingly reduced. Viewed spatially, Latin America can be seen as one situation and efforts to promote its stability can constitute a single undertaking. Viewed functionally as well as spatially, it can approach 44,550 situations and, as noted, this figure can rise to 89,100 when the temporal dimension is introduced. Or take the example of postwar Berlin. Its spatial referent is unmistakable, but temporally it has been the scene of several international conflicts separated by many years during which a prevailing structure was accepted by the parties to the conflicts. Hence, to ignore the temporal dimension and treat postwar Berlin as one continuous situation is to obfuscate variability in foreign policy behavior. When the Soviet Union undertook to alter, and the United States to preserve, the arrangements of that beleaguered city in 1948–49, both societies framed goals, developed strategies, mobilized resources, applied pressures, and reacted to countermoves in ways that differed substantially from their behavior in the Berlin conflict of 1961–62. The latter constituted a new undertaking for both societies, in part because the 1948–49 episode added a historical precedent that had not existed in the earlier conflict. Similarly, opportunities to cumulate findings and observe variance will be missed if precision is maintained with respect to the temporal dimension but not with respect to the other two. If, for example, the "Camp David" period of Soviet-American relations, running from the Khrushchev-Eisenhower meeting of September 1959 to the U-2 incident of May 1960, is treated as a single situation, then a variety of functionally unrelated efforts to preserve or alter arrangements in diverse parts of the world that were undertaken during the eight-month period might be falsely subsumed under the larger effort to maintain a cordial relationship and thus overlooked as discrete data.

If we assume that the operational utility of undertakings can be maintained by the rule of erring on the side of specificity, the question arises of how they are to be used as dependent variables. What variance in undertakings, that is, is the student of foreign policy interested in? Suppose that the researcher had gathered data on a thousand foreign policy undertakings of each of sixteen national societies: what aspects of these data should his hypotheses seek to predict? Suppose further that the sixteen societies consisted of eight that were large and eight that were small, with four of each of the eight having open polities and four having closed polities, and with two of each of the clusters of four having developed economies and two having underdeveloped economies: what patterns within the thousand undertakings of each society would the researcher want to identify in order to make comparisons among the societies and thereby assess the role of such independent variables as physical size, political structure, and economic development? While an elaborate attempt to answer questions such as these cannot be essayed here, the need for a clear specification of dependent variables is so essential to the fostering of a scientific consciousness that it seems useful to suggest a few aspects of undertakings that may be worth pursuing as dependent variables.

Perhaps the most easily measured dependent variable is the *duration* of an undertaking. The time that elapses from the inception to the conclusion or abandonment of an effort to alter or preserve a situation abroad can be established without too much difficulty and readily lends itself to comparative analysis. To a certain extent, of course, duration is a function of the nature of the situation that officials undertake to affect. It took much less time to get missiles out of Cuba than it has taken to build political institutions in Vietnam, partly because the scope and dynamics of the situation were much less complex in Cuba than they are in Vietnam. Nevertheless, presumably variance in the duration of undertakings is also a function of some of the independent variables of interest to foreign policy researchers. In part, for example, it may be a reflection of capabilities, of the ability of a society to cope with its external environment. If one has data on a thousand undertakings in each of sixteen societies, it seems reasonable to assume that the impact of situational differences will be greatly reduced, thus allowing one to hypothesize that the average duration of undertakings will be appreciably less in large developed societies than in large underdeveloped societies, and that both types of large societies, being able to draw upon more resources, will be able to conclude their undertakings significantly more quickly than small underdeveloped societies. The duration of undertakings may also reflect political structure and political style. It might be hypothesized that closed polities have greater flexibility in foreign policy than open ones and can thus abandon their undertakings more swiftly, a proposition that is readily testable through the duration variable and our hypothesized data bank. Similarly, researchers who have notions about how certain societies differ in their style of statecraft might treat the duration variable as a measure of foreign policy skill and hypothesize that large developed societies with a cumbersome style will record a pattern of significantly longer undertakings than will similar societies with a polished style.

Another dependent variable that presents a minimum of measurement difficulties is what might be called the *undertaking potential:* the number of undertakings that a society is capable of launching and sustaining at any one time. It would be a simple matter, given the data on a thousand undertakings of sixteen societies, to calculate a rate of undertakings per month (UPM) for each society and thereby to test propositions about the potency of certain independent variables. A number of hypotheses along this line readily come to mind. Presumably, for example, geographic position affects the UPM; the more landlocked a national society is and the more neighbors it has, the greater its UPM. A small insular society would thus be hypothesized to have a significantly lower UPM than a small continental one. Even more provocative are the possibilities of using the UPM to measure, compare, and trace the changing position of societies in the international system, the basic hypothesis being that the more a society exercises leadership in the system, the more situations it will be inclined to become involved in, and thus the higher its UPM at any point in time and the greater the increase in its UPM through time. Still another use of the UPM might be to assess the potency of industrialization as an independent variable. It seems reasonable to hypothesize that the more industrialized a society is, the more complex will be its governmental bureaucracy and, consequently, the greater will be its capacity to sustain a high number of undertakings simultaneously. In operational terms, it appears reasonable to predict a very high correlation between the UPM and, say, the per capita income figures for the sixteen societies.

Although somewhat more difficult to operationalize, a third dependent variable that seems worthy of investigation is what might be called the *direction* of undertakings. Here we have in mind a dichotomous variable that distinguishes between those undertakings designed to preserve and those designed to alter existing situations abroad. If we assume that a satisfactory method could be devised to classify every undertaking as either essentially preservative or essentially promotive—an assumption that does not seem unwarranted—the directional variable could be used to probe the potency of societal factors as a source of foreign policy behavior. For example, it seems reasonable to hypothesize that dynamic societies—those undergoing rapid social change—are likely to engage in significantly more promotive undertakings than preservative ones, whereas exactly the opposite prediction could reasonably be made for static societies. Likewise, the relative strength of ideology and the "national interest" as independent variables might be explored through hypotheses that linked the former to promotive undertakings and the latter to preservative ones.

Other aspects of undertakings that might be pursued as dependent variables are their *scope* (are they directed at individuals, groups, nations, or regions?), their *stability* (do they exhibit constancy of purpose?), their *cost* (how extensive are the human and nonhuman resources they employ?), and their *contents* (are they concerned with the disposition of goods, territory, status, or welfare?). Variables such as these, of course, are based on less tangible phenomena. They would thus be considerably more difficult to operationalize, and the classification of undertakings in these terms would probably not result in as high a degree of intercoder reliability as would the use of the dependent variables outlined in the previous three paragraphs. But, at this stage, all that is needed is a satisfactory level of reliability—say, .75 or better —to provide confidence that the characteristics of phenomena rather than the quirks of coders are being measured. If such a level could be achieved in the case of these less tangible variables, many other stimulating hypotheses could be developed and tested.

Our task here, however, is not that of specifying and perfecting variables. Rather it is to show how their use might lead to the accumulation of knowledge about foreign policy that will satisfy both the curiosity of the researcher and the needs of the policy-maker. Hopefully the forgoing is sufficient to show that, if time and energy are invested in the development of appropriate variables, the predominance of a scientific consciousness can pay off as handsomely in foreign policy research as it has in other fields.

APPENDIX: AN ANALYSIS OF SEVEN CASE STUDIES

Although this paper does not test, with a systematic content analysis of the extant literature, the impressions it presents of the state of foreign policy research, in all fairness some evidence needs to be provided to support the charge that the available materials are not cumulative and are conspicuously lacking in a consciousness of scientific method. What follows is a brief analysis of seven case studies in the field. These may not constitute a representative sample, but each case is a thorough, recent, and widely read study. If a scientific consciousness is more prevalent than alleged here, presumably it should be apparent in these cases. Our procedure is to examine the concluding sections of each case to determine whether the described sequence of events was viewed as an instance of a more general class of phenomena and, if so, whether normative propositions, instrumental policy recommendations, and/or empirical hypotheses were derived from it. If our indictment is excessive, this procedure should yield at the very least a few empirical hypotheses.

Being lengthy and thorough, Van Dyke's account of the evolution of the United States space program serves as a good point of departure.[37] Stressing that neither the rational-comprehensive nor the successful limited-comparison method of decision-making[38] is depicted by his account, Van Dyke's final chapter suggests rather that the space program corresponds to those rare but important situations (such as Pearl Harbor or Korea) in which the end values are so crucial that they overwhelm and replace a rational or incremental approach to the choices that have to be made. Van Dyke posits three values, national security, national prestige, and national pride, as values that are powerful enough to govern behavior in this way and, in the final five pages of the book, addresses himself to the question of which of the three his case history is an instance. His answer, based mainly on his "reading of events" associated with the May 1961 decision greatly to enlarge the space program, is that the last of them was the crucial one: "As I reconstruct the situation, there was no call for rational-comprehensive analysis, and not much call for a comparison of possible ends or values. A few values of very great importance were at stake, pride above all."[39] Van Dyke does not moralize about the legitimacy of pride as a basis for a policy or make recommendations for the improvement of the space program. Neither does he speculate about the operation of pride as an independent variable in other situations or in relation to the other variables that he discounts as inadequate to explain the space program. The concluding chapter does not claim to have tested any explicit hypotheses and offers no new ones derived from the inquiry. It simply provides an overall assessment of why the behavior and events unfolded as they did. To be sure, having earlier noted that "a value provides motivation mainly when it is in jeopardy,"[40] in the very last paragraph of the book Van Dyke implicitly hypothesizes that the more national pride achieves satisfaction, the less potent will it be as a source of behavior. Explicitly, however, he only correlates the success of the space probes with diminution of enthusiasm

---

[37] Vernon Van Dyke, *Pride and Power: The Rationale of the Space Program* (Urbana: University of Illinois Press, 1964).

[38] As described in Charles E. Lindblom, "The Science of 'Muddling Through,'" *Public Administration Review*, 19 (Spring 1959) : 79–88.

[39] Van Dyke, *Pride and Power*, p. 272.

[40] *Ibid.*, p. 179.

for the program, a correlation that says nothing about the kind of situations in which pride is likely to be a governing value or the consequences that different degrees of jeopardy to it are likely to have for the decision-making process. In effect, although Van Dyke's scientific consciousness was sufficient to lead him to ask of what larger pattern the 1961 space decision was an instance—as a result making us more aware of values as a source of behavior and more appreciative of the possibility that pride can be a powerful variable —it was not enough to stimulate him to take the next step and make his findings testable in other situations and thus capable of being integrated into a larger research enterprise.

Since it focuses on matters that recur annually, any case history in which the U.S. appropriations process figures prominently should perhaps be especially conducive to the generation of hypotheses and the operation of a scientific consciousness. Hence let us now examine two cases with this characteristic—Schilling's extensive inquiry into the making of the 1950 defense budget[41] and Haviland's detailed account of the foreign aid program in 1957.[42] Certainly the former is not lacking in speculation. In a fifty-two-page concluding chapter Schilling undertakes to analyze and explain what he regards as the main finding revealed by his case history, namely, that the defense budget exercises a " 'gyroscopic' effect . . . on the content of foreign policy," since "Congress and Executive alike have tended to spin along at the same general level of expenditure year after year in spite of rather startling developments elsewhere in the nation's security position."[43] Two sets of independent variables are posited as the sources of the "gyroscopic tendencies" in 1950. One is "the structure of the policy process," with its "tendency . . . to be leaderless," and the resulting need for bargaining and consensus building. The other is the content of the ideas that comprised "the prevailing climate of opinion" with respect to defense budgeting. Although Schilling evidences some degree of scientific consciousness by devoting a number of pages to speculation about how changes in the structure of the policy process and in the four main ideas constituting the climate of opinion would have altered "the kind of choices made in the fiscal 1950 budget," he does not bring the analysis to a scientific conclusion with hypotheses that take advantage of his analysis and predict the outcome of budget-making in subsequent years. Rather the purpose of the inquiry turns out to be an evaluation of the adequacy of the policy-making process, and the only hypotheses to emerge are essentially normative propositions about the desirability of maximizing rationality and reducing the influence of the military over budgetary decisions. To be sure, by suggesting that both the structure of the policy-making process

---

[41] Warner R. Schilling, "The Politics of National Defense: Fiscal 1950," in Warner R. Schilling, Paul Y. Hammond, and Glenn H. Snyder, *Strategy, Politics, and Defense Budgets* (New York: Columbia University Press, 1962), pp. 1–266.

[42] H. Field Haviland, Jr., "Foreign Aid and the Policy Process: 1957," *American Political Science Review*, 52 (September 1958) : 689–724.

[43] Schilling, "Politics of National Defense," p. 220.

and the climate of opinion in which it unfolds are essentially resistant to change, Schilling's interpretation contains the empirical prediction that it is "unrealistic to expect" subsequent defense budgets to be any more responsive to the requirements of foreign policy than was the case in 1950.[44] Such a prediction, however, does not constitute a fruitful scientific hypothesis inasmuch as it treats the variables as constants. Having concluded that the determinants of the gyroscopic effect are resistant to change, Schilling does not allow for variance in their potencies and thus does not speculate about the extent to which differential budgetary responses would result from structural or opinion changes within the policy-making process or from profound shifts in the structure of the international system. Hence, while his case history raises a number of interesting questions and provides insightful glimpses into the dynamics of foreign policy, it offers little guidance for interpreting or anticipating, say, the budgetary episodes of the 1960's, by which time a substantial streamlining of the structure of the National Security Council and the Department of Defense had been accomplished, a thoroughgoing revision in attitudes toward budget-making and most of the other major foci of the climate of opinion had taken place, and a wholesale alteration of conditions abroad, including the balance of nuclear weapons and the coherence of the two great alliance systems, had occurred. Even in terms of its own purpose of assessing the adequacy of the policy-making process, in other words, Schilling's case is now obsolete. It is good, even superior, history and as such serves to heighten one's sense of the problems that arise in a political system marked by a wide dispersion of responsibility, but instrumentally and scientifically it can only be regarded as obsolete—not because it deals with events that occurred long ago or because the world has changed since 1950, but because in interpreting the events it did not place them in the larger context of a range of possibilities that could take the changes since 1950 into account.

Although explicitly inclined to treat his case as an instance of a larger pattern and to assess the consistency of his findings with those uncovered by other researchers, Haviland's inquiry into the 1957 foreign aid debate also lacks the essentials of an analytic approach that is scientific as well as systematic. He recognizes that "the annually recurring debate over foreign aid" permits the holding of "a stethoscope . . . to the heart of the United States foreign policy process," and accordingly indicates that his purpose in recounting what happened in 1957 includes shedding "some light . . . on the foreign policy process in general."[45] Carrying through on this commitment, Haviland devotes most of his concluding section to systematically comparing the 1957 episode "with the results of other analyses."[46] In particular, three findings are posited as confirming "conclusions reached in other studies." One finding concerns the role of the public. Haviland views the events he describes as affirming again "that the great majority of the public are not very

---

[44] *Ibid.*, p. 239.
[45] Haviland, "Foreign Aid," p. 689.
[46] *Ibid.*, p. 716.

well informed about foreign affairs, that their interest in the subject is likely to follow the fever chart of world crises in the news, and that it is a small educated minority who keep themselves the best informed and are the most internationally minded."[47] A second finding derived from the 1957 foreign aid experience deals with the role of party loyalty in legislative voting, which Haviland found to be consistent with the general conclusion of some other researchers "that the parts have a collective interest in the welfare of the whole party and that what happens to the whole affects all of the parts, some more than others."[48] Thirdly, with respect to bipartisanship Haviland notes that "On the whole, this study confirms the conclusion that the development of consultation, confidence, and cooperation between the leadership of the two parties is a necessary means of surmounting serious conflicts within each of the parties in order to mobilize a broad base of consensus to support major foreign policy positions."[49] Yet, notwithstanding the larger context of substantive process and research in which Haviland locates the events he recounts, from a scientific perspective his case has little utility. Once again the key variables are treated as constants. None of the three findings is presented as reflecting a factor in the policy-making process which, depending on how it is constituted in a particular year, can have different consequences for the structure and success of the foreign aid program at that moment in time. To what extent, for example, would the amount of funds appropriated for the program be likely to increase (or decrease) if the proportion of the public uninformed about foreign affairs declined (or rose) and the small educated minority that is internationally minded grew (or shrank)? To what extent does a larger (or smaller) legislative majority conduce to greater (or lesser) party support for (or opposition to) foreign aid appropriations? If the degree of consultation, confidence, and cooperation between the leadership of the two parties rises (or falls) substantially, somewhat, or minimally, is the foreign aid consensus likely to expand (or contract) substantially, somewhat, or minimally? Questions such as these are neither discussed by Haviland nor posed in the form of hypotheses to be tested in subsequent foreign aid debates. Consequently, his account offers little guidance for interpreting and anticipating the outcome of foreign aid controversies in which the proposed expenditures and the efforts to promote them are considerably more (or less) than was the case in 1957. In this instance, moreover, the lack of a scientific consciousness has had practical political consequences. In the years subsequent to 1957 a wide variety of techniques, from White House–sponsored conferences to prestigeful commissions to new legislative strategies, have been employed by supporters of the foreign aid program to obtain higher appropriations,[50] and each year advocates of the program are mystified by the outcome of their efforts and increasingly dissatisfied with findings such as

---

[47] *Ibid.*, p. 717.

[48] *Ibid.*, p. 719.

[49] *Ibid.*, p. 721

[50] *Cf.* Rosenau, *National Leadership and Foreign Policy: A Case Study in the Mobilization of Public Support* (Princeton, N.J.: Princeton University Press, 1963), chap. 1.

Haviland's. One wonders whether knowledge of the subject would not be much more extensive if these findings had been cast in the form of testable hypotheses that could be revised and expanded as each year's foreign aid episode was completed.

Perhaps no case study of foreign policy formulation in the United States is more thorough and self-conscious than Cohen's elaborate account of the international negotiations and national politics that culminated in the 1951 peace settlement with Japan.[51] Unlike the other cases noted above, Cohen's account eschews concentration on a particular aspect or agency of the policy-making process, and instead covers "all the major elements that might help to shape policy," including the public, the press, interest groups, the chief negotiators, and the executive-legislative relationship. Furthermore, Cohen's study has the advantage of being highly sensitive to the idea that "it is a far from simple task . . . to build up a useful body of relevant knowledge about over-all processes."[52] More than most case writers, Cohen is thus concerned about the larger relevance of his inquiry and expresses hope that it will generate other case histories that, taken together, will "ultimately . . . turn up a large body of related and comparable data on the various processes of [foreign] policy development."[53] Indeed, he argues that "it does not seem beyond the bounds of reason that there may be a time when enough will be known about the various types of foreign policy-making processes as a result of studies of this kind so that the probable processes awaiting new policy issues can be predicted from a brief analysis of only a few of the attendant factors and their relationships and of some of the other variables involved."[54] In the end, however, Cohen backs away from the implications of this commitment to comparability and prediction. After twelve chapters and 280 pages of detailed analysis he refuses to advance hypotheses that assess the relative potency of key variables and to predict the likely outcome when different potencies attach to them in other types of policy-making situations:

> It is . . . premature, on the basis of just one study of this type, to attach orders of importance to the many variables in the process of policy-making. It would seem, by way of example, that the nature of the policy issue itself has an important effect on the character of the political process that attends it; but it is too early to say if it is a controlling effect, or in what circumstances it may be a controlling effect, or even to make definite statements about the range of types of issues that have any effects at all.[55]

Evaluated in terms of a scientific consciousness, the response to such a quotation can only be that it is never too early to make statements about what

[51] Bernard C. Cohen, *The Political Process and Foreign Policy: The Making of the Japanese Peace Settlement* (Princeton, N.J.: Princeton University Press, 1957).
[52] *Ibid.*, pp. 5–6.
[53] *Ibid.*, p. 287.
[54] *Ibid.*, p. 8.
[55] *Ibid.*, p. 281.

affects what under specified conditions. As long as such statements are derived from past experience (i.e., at least one case study) and can be tested in a future one, the more definite they are, the better. Their definiteness will undoubtedly have to be qualified after other cases are examined, but how else can comprehension be refined and nuance be developed? Certainly not by waiting for an unspecified number of comparable cases to accumulate and then hoping that somehow their recurrent features will be self-evident. Patterns do not present themselves. They must be generated, and this cannot happen unless researchers are willing to hypothesize on the basis of their findings.

Curiously, while Cohen's concluding chapter is consistent with his disinclination to assess the potency of variables and to assert definite propositions, the rhetoric of the chapter suggests scientific predispositions. Arguing that his case history "has been productive of hypotheses that have some bearing not on the case alone but also on the larger study of the political process,"[56] Cohen devotes the chapter to a consideration of several of the "more important of these." The first to be considered started as "a useful assumption in organizing this study [and] emerges from it with the somewhat higher status of an unrefined hypothesis: that the climate of public opinion in the body politic, organized and unorganized political interest groups, and the media of mass communication are integral and important parts of the political processes of foreign policy-making."[57] Again we have a formulation lacking variables that vary. It is more of an assertion than a hypothesis. It asserts that the variables are "integral and important," but gives no hint of how different climates of opinion, different degrees of interest-group activity, and different emphases by the mass media might alter the character and products of the policy-making process. The "second major proposition—or set of propositions, to be more exact"—to emerge from Cohen's case history is even less scientifically adequate. For all practical purposes it contains no variables and merely asserts that the foreign policy-making process "is one in which there is a constant meshing of interests and attitudes, actions and reactions, of different, frequently competing groups in a more or less orderly fashion."[58] If, as seems reasonable, a proposition is considered to be a statement in which the structure, characteristics, or behavior of identifiable factors are alleged to vary in specific ways as a consequence of interacting with each other, plainly this is not a proposition. At best it is a summary and at worst it is a tautology that does no more than "reflect," as Cohen himself notes, "the inordinate complexity of the patterns of influence" that comprise the policy-making process.[59]

Nor can it be said that it is American policy-making processes in particular that are especially conducive to unscientific, even if systematic,

---

[56] *Ibid.*, pp. 281–82.
[57] *Ibid.*, p. 282.
[58] *Ibid.*, p. 285.
[59] *Ibid.*

analysis. Case histories of foreign policy processes in other societies are similarly devoid of explicit hypotheses in which the key variables are specified and their range of variation indicated. Epstein's impressive account of Britain's participation in the Suez crisis of 1956 is a good illustration.[60] Epstein concedes that "the difficulties in the way of suggesting generalizations from a case study seem so great that one might be tempted to forgo the effort altogether and simply tell the story of what happened in Britain during the Suez crisis." Yet his scientific consciousness is sufficient to lead him to assert at the outset that such a procedure "would not be enough to satisfy a political scientist," that the latter "is ambitious to understand how a political system works in more than a given situation." Indeed, noting that the political scientist's "purpose must always be comparative," Epstein extends his aspirations for his case study to other systems as well as other situations: ". . . the objective is not just to learn, from the Suez crisis, something about *Britian's* Parliament and parties, but hopefully also something about types of parliamentary and party systems."[61] However, eight chapters and some two hundred pages later, after he has recounted what various British cabinet officials, parliamentary groups, constituency organizations, the press, interest groups, and the general public thought and did before, during, and after the climactic events of early November 1956, Epstein's scientific consciousness has faded and the commitments set forth at the outset are hardly discernible in his concluding chapter. The latter consists largely of summary estimates of the various institutions and processes described, and while as a result it does offer some generalizations about the functioning of the British political system, none of these are presented in the form of testable hypotheses or even in such a way that testable hypotheses can be derived from them. Party cohesion, party competition, executive stability, and parliamentary debate are among the variables assessed, but Epstein's assessments do not include any indication of the range within which each of these can or might vary under different conditions. There is no attempt to differentiate between high and low party cohesion, between intense and weak party competition, between more and less executive stability, and between wide and narrow parliamentary debate. The reader is thus perplexed as to what to do with the generalizations. In the absence of variability, he can apply them only to circumstances similar to the Suez crisis, and since the latter is more of an extreme than a typical event in British political life, the generalizations are for all practical purposes useless.

Epstein's scientific consciousness deserts him even more fully with regard to his commitment to comparison. To be sure, his concluding chapter contains a few sentences in which the capacity of the British Prime Minister to engage in foreign policy undertakings without legislative consultation or approval is compared with that of the American President (and there is one brief reference to this capacity in the Third and Fourth Republics of France), but

---

[60] Leon D. Epstein, *British Politics in the Suez Crisis* (Urbana: University of Illinois Press, 1964).

[61] *Ibid.*, p. 3.

these are all offered in passing and do not, as they easily might have, consist of propositions that other researchers can verify with respect to U.S. behavior in foreign policy crises. Presidential initiatives undertaken without legislative approval in the Vietnam situation offer obvious parallels to the Suez crisis. Unfortunately, however, Epstein's concluding chapter provides virtually no observations that might be transformed into propositions applicable to Vietnam. Conceivably one might hypothesize about the Vietnam situation on the basis of his conclusion that the Suez episode does not "prove that overwhelming popular support, perhaps determined in advance, is essential for the successful prosecution of a foreign policy involving a military commitment,"[62] but this is about the only link that can be established between Epstein's general conclusions and subsequent research into other political systems. For the most part the few comparisons that he draws are so all-encompassing that they defy application to other systems. His final observation is illustrative of this defiance: "At the end, then, of this case study, it can be fairly concluded that Britain's Suez experience displayed a rigidly partisan political mold that appears to be a response of the parliamentary system to problems facing a major democratic nation in the first half of the twentieth century."[63] Epstein hoped at the outset that his readers might learn "something about other types of parliamentary and party systems," but it seems fair to say that he did not take advantage of the opportunity to fulfill this aspiration that his data made possible.

Let us turn now to a case history in which the dependent variables include the outcome of foreign policy behavior abroad. Despite its broader scope, however, the particular case under review, Davison's lengthy account of the Soviet Union's 1948 attempt to seal off Berlin by cutting its overland communications to West Germany,[64] does not reflect a scientific consciousness any more than do those in which the sequence of events is limited to the outcome of the policy-making process at home. Indeed, Davison's concluding chapter makes no effort whatsoever to treat the Berlin blockade as an instance of a larger pattern; rather it is devoted to emphasizing the importance of the last of the "four major factors" that enabled Berlin to overcome the blockade. The decision of the Western powers to defend their position in the city, the strong democratic leadership of the city, and the effective instruments of leadership available to the city's elite comprise the first three factors, but all of these are posited as having been highly dependent on the fourth factor, the resistance morale of the West Berliners. The sources and dynamics of this morale are compellingly explored by Davison, and the reader completes the case history fully in agreement with his conclusion that the breaking of the blockade was a triumph of heroic proportions. Yet no generalizations emerge from the analysis. Four main variables are specified and the interaction

---

[62] *Ibid.*, p. 203.

[63] *Ibid.*, p. 209.

[64] W. Phillips Davison, *The Berlin Blockade: A Study of Cold War Politics* (Princeton, N.J.: Princeton University Press, 1958).

among them is stressed, but how they might vary and interact in subsequent Berlin crises is not a subject of speculation on Davison's part. In effect, his analysis comes to end with the lifting of the blockade on May 12, 1949. To be sure, as a result of acquaintance with Davison's account any estimates one makes about other Berlin crises are likely to be much more sensitive to the significance of public opinion and political structure in that beleaguered city, but in disciplining this sensitivity the reader gets no help from Davison. He only notes that the variables were crucial in 1948–49, and since his analysis of them is so completely time-bound, their subsequent relevance in an era of nuclear stalemate cannot be hypothetically deduced from the case itself.

Finally, let us examine a case that recounts the events in 1953 that led to the selection of a new U.S. ambassador to the Soviet Union.[65] It is neither as complex nor as lengthy a case as the others, but it does deal with an important aspect of foreign policy and its inclusion here helps to demonstrate that the development of a commitment to a scientific consciousness need not start early in a professional career; for the absence of a readiness to move to higher levels of generalization is even more conspicuous in this case than in any of the others. Indeed, the case does not even state a general purpose at the outset. It merely begins with the advent of the vacancy in the ambassadorship and describes the problem this situation posed for the incoming Eisenhower administration. Furthermore, not only does the case fail to derive any hypotheses from the sequence of events; it does not even offer any conclusions. After describing the posture toward the ambassador-designate taken by the relevant executive and legislative officials and then recounting the clash that followed from the conflicting postures, the case simply comes to an end with a tally of the Senate vote on the nomination.

The case concludes with a very brief section of "Afterthoughts" in which some questions about the immediate implications of the nomination are raised, but no effort is made to suggest possible answers to them, much less to query the general meaning of the episode. A central theme of the case, for example, concerns the dilemma faced by Republican senators who had long complained about the "betrayal" of U.S. interests at Yalta, and who now were asked by a Republican President to approve the nomination of the man who had been Franklin D. Roosevelt's translator at that wartime conference with the Russians. Yet no attempt was made to apply the way in which the senators resolved this attitudinal conflict to other types of foreign policy actors, much less to other foreign policy situations in which senatorial behavior is relevant. What might have served as an ideal opportunity to formulate propositions about the relative potency of idiosyncratic and role variables was treated as nothing more than a dramatic moment of personal truth for several persons who happened to be members of the Senate in 1953. As such, to be sure, the case reconstructs a climactic episode in American politics, and, through lengthy excerpts from official documents, does so in a compelling fashion.

---

[65] Rosenau, *The Nomination of "Chip" Bohlen* (New York: Henry Holt & Co., 1958).

Looking back over the case a decade later, however, what stands out is not its dramatic content, but its lack of significance. Not having identified and assessed any general implications, the case now seems somewhat trivial.

In sum, all seven of these case histories of foreign policy behavior are long on systematic analysis and short on scientific consciousness. None of them yielded a single hypothesis about what foreign policy behavior would be likely to occur under a specified set of conditions. Our indictment of the state of research in the field may be exaggerated, but the forgoing evidence provides no basis for revising it.[66]

---

[66] Happily, however, a reason to revise the indictment slightly has arisen since the completion of this paper. In early 1968 a lengthy case history of an important foreign policy episode was published that so fully reflects a scientific consciousness that a fifty-page concluding chapter is devoted to the discussion of forty-nine general propositions derived from the preceding narrative. See Glenn D. Paige, *The Korean Decision: June 24–30, 1950* (New York: The Free Press, 1968), chap. 11.

Part Four

PITFALLS AND POSSIBILITIES

10

Description, Analysis, and Sensitivity to Change

LUCIAN W. PYE

There is always something rather dreary about attempts to appraise the state of the art in political science. This is strange because in much of life the posture of introspection is usually filled with adequate tension to provide the stuff of drama. It would be a bit unkind, if not downright masochistic, to suggest that in our field the drama is all on the surface and what lies at the inner core is almost static, and thus the state of our art is not progressing at a speed appropriate to the sensations we have of experiencing revolutionary changes. There are critics who would tell us that our sensations of change stem entirely from our pains at having constantly to learn new vocabularies as the invention of jargons races ahead of the pace of new ideas. But as a discipline we are certainly mature enough to be able to shrug off such criticism with an ambiguous smile, while still acknowledging to ourselves that we are often banal if not tedious in our discussions about the state of our learning.

Yet ever since Mary Baker Eddy it should be mandatory for any group or profession that identifies itself with that most elastic of words, "science," to pause periodically and reflect on the idiosyncratic meaning it may be giving to that prestigious but also wonderfully vague term. What dimensions of science have we held up as our professional ideals as we seek to become better social and political "scientists," and how have our peculiar notions about what it is to be "scientific" influenced the development of our discipline?

In the pages that follow I shall argue that in political science we have been in danger of worshiping a strangely distorted graven image of science. Our particular biases have somehow left us with a feeling for science which is almost devoid of that dynamic and forward-thinking quality which C. P. Snow so graphically identified as the distinctive attribute of science, and even though we have energetically proclaimed our revolt against our humanistic heritage, we seem ever to end up with the static and in that sense timeless views that Snow associates with the humanities. I shall argue further that our biased view of science, which has impeded our capacities for analyzing change, has also restricted our potential for either studying the dynamic processes of policy output or contributing effectively to policy-making. Just as we have tended to look to the past rather than to the future, so we have been more interested in analyzing sources and causes than in studying consequences and outcomes.

I. SOME BLINDERS IN CONTEMPORARY POLITICAL SCIENCE

LEANING TO ONE SIDE IN SCIENCE

The problem is usually, is it not, that we take such discussions to mean that we should dwell on methodological matters, and how we can become more scientific? This in turn generally causes us to take too seriously a rather warped social science view of science, a view that stresses rigor in logic and precision in measurement—necessary but far from sufficient elements of science—but one that discounts the creative idea, the scientific imagination, which is the very essence of all true scientific endeavors.

It is a mystery why the social sciences have been so peculiarly prone to underestimate the importance of bold speculation and creative imagination in characterizing science, and why we have tended to emphasize its humdrum aspects. Ask the physical scientist what is the state of his art and he will generally bring up the boldest, the most provocative, and the most jarringly original ideas that are just gaining currency in his field; he will almost never think to mention anything relating to either measurement or precision, except insofar as it contributes to the verification of a specific and significant hypothesis.[1] In contrast, in the social sciences we tend to think that we are advancing ourselves as scientists when we improve the precision of our measurements, a task that in the physical sciences is left to the engineers and the technicians.[2]

These first remarks may seem unduly provocative, irreverent, and possi-

---

[1] It is, I believe, significant that most scientists are uncomfortable with Thomas Kuhn's thesis that much of science consists of experiments to confirm the expected and that there are only periodic "revolutions" in science when new "paradigms" or ways of seeing reality are introduced: Thomas S. Kuhn, *Structure of Scientific Revolutions* (Chicago: Chicago University Press, 1962). Most scientists seem to find it easy to convince themselves that they are always about to engage in the thrill of discovery. It is possibly noteworthy that physical scientists do seem to enjoy accounts of the emotional reactions to research and discovery, while in the social sciences we have almost no counterpart to this form of autobiographical literature.

[2] There have, of course, been many significant advances in science which have depended upon improved methods of measurement—for example, the work of Robert Millikan and Max Planck—but the point was that precision in such cases was critical because the results of the measurement did have profound theoretical significance. The process of improving precision simply in order to increase routine accuracy can be left to technicians in the physical sciences.

bly completely irresponsible, but I have judged them necessary in order to jar us into a concern for what I feel is a most serious problem in the social sciences: our uncertainty and ambivalence about speculation and imagination. Our uncomfortableness about the place of speculation in science and our anxiety for the discipline of the routine or repeatable act helps in part to explain why in the study of the political system we have almost instinctively focused on the input side and have had so little to say about the scientific study of policy outputs.

Maybe the beginning of our difficulties came when, in turning our backs on the sterility of speculative philosophy as it became rigidified in the nineteenth century, we felt it necessary to treat seriously only that which we could measure and test. Later we have consistently sought to discipline our thinking to the confining limits set by our admittedly primitive and crude techniques of measurement. Our imaginations have had to be constrained to the dimensions of our crude technologies.[3]

At present I would judge that there is considerable tension within the social sciences, and especially between the generations, over precisely what should be the acceptable scope of hypothesizing. There are those who steadfastly insist that we must carefully discipline ourselves to keep our hypotheses at the level at which we have methods for testing them. In this manner we can accumulate discrete bits of knowledge which taken by themselves can often border on the trivial, but which if systematically put together can become the building blocks of significant structures of "hard" knowledge.[4] Others feel that theory building should always move ahead of our capacity to test and measure so as to ensure that we never lose sight of significance.[5]

At the risk of antagonizing both groups I would venture to suggest that the issue has less to do with formal methodology than with personal styles and idiosyncracies in thinking.[6] Some people are much more comfortable when

---

[3] For vigorous statements about the emptiness of speculative thinking and the need for thinking in terms of testable hypotheses, see William J. Goode and Paul K. Hatt, *Methods in Social Research* (New York: McGraw-Hill Book Co., 1952), chap. 6. As all charitable students of the philosophy of science will recognize, what I have in mind here are the arguments of the more extreme school of logical positivists who are hypersensitive to the possibility that a statement may be "meaningless" because it cannot be tested against "reality."

[4] *Cf.* A. J. Ayer, *Language, Truth and Logic* (London: Smith, Peter, 1946) ; C. A. Hempel, "Fundamentals of Concept Formation in Empirical Science," in *International Encyclopedia of Unified Science*, vol. 2 (Chicago: University of Chicago, 1952) ; A. M. Rose, *Theory and Method in the Social Sciences* (Minneapolis: University of Minnesota, 1954).

[5] I do not have in mind here the work of the linguistic philosophers who may in their way have been countering the "dead end" of the logical positivists, but whose works I feel I must not be understanding.

[6] For a very refreshing and open-minded view about the "myth of methodology," see Abraham Kaplan, *The Concept of Inquiry* (San Francisco: Chandler Publishing Co., 1964). But it should be noted that even after his vigorous attacks on the "myth" and his quoting of P. W. Bridgman's remark that the "scientist has no other method than doing his damnedest," Kaplan still found it necessary to subtitle his book: "Methodology for Behavioral Science."

dealing with limited and discrete concepts, while others are more clever when they are dealing with broader generalizations. That is to say, this may be a highly personal matter similar to the fact that some people are naturally skilled at establishing inclusive categories, others tend to think most readily in terms of equations, others are most facile when defining and manipulating words, and still others show their greatest strengths when exploring all the dimensions of single concepts. These are all differences in cognitive styles and not in the nature of the scientific method.[7] Ultimately cognitive styles are an individual matter, but it is true that through the accident of historical development in the various disciplines there often is a crude match between the assumed intellectual discipline of a field and a particular cognitive style.[8]

In the social sciences the problem of the relationship between the size of ideas and the capacity for testing does, however, have a more general significance because our biased concept of science is so strongly on the side of measurement as against imagination. The strength of this bias is to be seen in our reactions to the absence of one or the other of these basic characteristics of science: Everyone would agree that the opposite of precision in measurement—that is, sloppiness—is completely unacceptable to science, but somehow when banalities replace imagination we do not feel that science has been violated. Similarly, in the training of social scientists we spend a great deal of time and energy in teaching students the techniques for measuring and testing the validity of hypotheses, but we do not spend as much effort in warning them that being unimaginative is a violation of the most elementary canon of science. In our concept of science we do lean to one side, and it is the side that upholds caution and does little to sensitize us to the prospects of change.

THE DIGNITY OF BEING HALF A STEP BEHIND

There are, of course, a variety of other reasons why the social sciences are cautious and generally do not display the dynamic, forward-looking

---

[7] We may note here that although in the abstract the subject of methodology in the social sciences can be tiresome, discussions among practicing social scientists about methodology can often be peculiarly emotional and intense, for such discussions often represent ways in which intellectuals make "public" and "attack" what are in fact quite "private" and intimate matters. Most discussions about methodology stand two or three steps removed from any actual processes of thought, but at times debates on the subject move very close to the tender areas that intellectuals must protect as the most vital part of their identities. After all, what makes an intellectual an intellectual is a presumed ability to think clearly and effectively, and what is methodology but such a capability?

[8] There are numerous ways of categorizing cognitive styles, and there has even been some attempt at comparing differences in various fields of science. See, for example, Anne Roe, *The Making of a Scientist* (New York: Dodd, Mead & Co., 1952), chap. 11. Roe notes that in comparison with biologists, experimental physicists, and theoretical physicists, social scientists tend to be far less concrete, less prone to use diagrams and symbols, and much more inclined toward verbal imagery, verbal formulae; and, above all, social scientists are uniquely given to "kinesthetic" processes—that is, feelings of muscular tension when trying to think. Why we should be physically as well as intellectually muscle-bound is unclear to all save those who are patently hostile to the social sciences.

quality that is usually associated with science.[9] Our orientation is still profoundly historical, and even political scientists dealing with the contemporary scene feel more compelled to examine the origins of the situation than to analyze the probable future outcomes. We hope that by looking backward into the past we will be able better to face the future, but this is manifestly only a hope, not a systematic exercise.

It should not be necessary here to document the degree to which social scientists tend to examine problems only after they have emerged as realities in the real world of public affairs. During World War II social scientists did herald the end of empires, but our foresight was limited to the sensation that a glorious day might be coming. Only after public programs of aid and assistance to the new states had been initiated did we begin to appreciate the significance of this era of development, and only after disappointing experiences of a decade or more have we begun to understand the true complexities of economic, social, and political development. And in other fields ranging from urban affairs to the proliferation of nuclear weapons, our teaching and research tend to remain just half a step behind the emergence of new developments.[10]

In situation after situation we have taken it as our assignment to examine problems in depth and detail only after they have clearly begun to plague our society. And time after time we have been able to point out that if certain measures had been taken in advance, the problem might not have been so acute. To a strange degree we seem to be impervious to the possibility that all we are doing is crying over spilt milk. Others cannot be quite sure what we are doing because we do it with such dignity and thoroughness.

One of the reasons we are more comfortable riding slightly behind rather than ahead of the wave of the future is that we further tend to distort our self-concept as scientists by excessively valuing the capacity for judgment, something we do out of deference to our humanistic traditions. To be both a scientist and a man of judgment may in fact be a contradiction in terms. For

---

[9] In all the controversy that has followed upon C. P. Snow's characterization of the "two cultures" there has been some discussion about the existence of a "third culture," the social sciences, which might be a bridge between the other two. But there has been no suggestion that the social sciences might capture the "forward thinking" quality that Snow attributes to science. It is equally striking that in all the literature on the character of science in the social sciences there has been almost no reference to this presumed quality of science. Harold Lasswell, in calling for a more forward-looking political science, suggested that this could best be achieved by learning more about developments in the physical sciences rather than by expecting the social sciences to develop their own internal mechanism for encouraging forward thinking: Harold D. Lasswell, "The Political Science of Science," *American Political Science Review*, 50 (December 1956) : 961–79.

[10] This time lag in the social sciences is in part, of course, a function of the fact that academic research is supposed to be free of the artificial constraints of time; findings need never be reported until all the evidence is in. In practice, however, a great deal of social science research does have to operate in terms of deadlines as demanding as those of the decision-makers in public affairs. The tragedy of the social scientist is that he often gets himself under the discipline of deadlines, but on subjects that are tied to yesterday's headlines.

the scientific imagination demands that the scientist take high and even reckless risks in hypothesizing all manner of ideas. The creative scientist must treat seriously the outlandish notion and be willing to be wrong time after time.

On this score the political scientist tends to take for his standards those of the statesman rather than those of the scientist. For the statesman the risks of being wrong are unbearable, for one wrong judgment can be his complete undoing. The political scientist tends also to feel that a wrong prediction can be not only acutely embarrassing, but a direct challenge to his professional worth. The scientist, on the other hand, is constantly interested in his hunches, anxious always to explore them, and hopeful that some of them may prove correct. Above all, he does not feel threatened simply because some, indeed many, of his ideas may prove to be wrong.

In a strange manner the internal contradictions and dilemmas of the political scientist seem to leave him more often than not with the worst of all possible worlds, rather than the best of any. While cautious like the statesman about forecasting developments, he also avoids the statesman's concern with policy outputs, and instead likes at this point to revert to his identity as a scientist and relax in his consequent freedom to eschew any responsibility for policy, except as a private matter. Unfortunately, the statesman's caution without the statesman's responsibility for policy is for the common citizen a workable definition of a bore.

This concern of the social scientist about being wrong, and more importantly, his difficulties in admitting to being wrong, encourage us to make only the vaguest predictions, to keep our spirit of precision focused mainly on the handling of historic data, and to stress the sure thing. Our point is, however, more profound than just the propensity for the academic to use a cloudy prose to which he can always return after the fact to point to intimations of all the things that have come about. The logic of our situation compels us to a high degree to concentrate not only on the historical, but more importantly on the theme of continuity.

CONFUSING THE TRIVIAL WITH THE UNIVERSAL

To a striking extent the social scientist is far more sensitive to continuity than to change. It is not just in the field of history that we teach our students to prize their ability to spot the old in the new. With age and sophistication is supposed to come the wisdom of knowing that there is really nothing new under the sun, and hence one must develop a stubborn insensitivity even to recognizing novel developments. In the social sciences he who actually sights the first robin of spring is nothing more than a shallow enthusiast, for deeper minds know that spring will always arrive in its good time.

This tendency to emphasize continuity is also possibly related to another peculiar notion about science which bulks large in the social sciences. This is that science should be the search for universal laws that are unaffected by time or place, and this in turn produces the innocent view that wherever we find the elements of historical continuity we must be touching on the universals of human behavior. Instinctively we almost feel that things that come and go and which seem to be related to change cannot be of the essence, and that scientific, that is universal, laws should be of the essence. Change and all that surrounds change are seen as being either mere appearance, essentially idiosyncratic, or in other ways superficial. In short, change is related to trivia and not to the substantial, which is at the heart of universal laws.

In practice this outlook has often resulted, paradoxically, in undue attention to precisely the trivial, for it is often only the trivial that is a part of historical continuity. It is not our purpose here to argue as to how much change or continuity there actually is in history: our point is only that an excessive concern for noting continuity can readily result in finding similarities that have little meaning.[11] This is particularly likely, I would contend, when the analyst is somewhat insensitive to the importance of change.

THE PAROCHIAL CONCEPT OF UNIVERSAL THEORY

There is another way in which the universal and the trivial tend to get confused in the social sciences so as to encourage, paradoxically, a parochial outlook. The claim that since wherever we look we are looking for universal laws does seem at times to be taken to mean that we don't have to look everywhere. With respect to the dimensions of time, this has meant that students have felt justified in focusing only on the past, for if they are successful in uncovering "universal laws" they will have discharged their responsibilities to the future, without risking the dangers of forecasting the future.

Similarly students of the European or American scene have felt that as long as they cast their findings in a generalized form, they will be dealing in universal theory, and hence they can feel reassured that it does not matter that they have ignored the experience of all the rest of mankind. This striving for universal theory has thus given a great deal of dignity to the parochialism of Western area studies. Practices of Western man or the observations about behavior at a particular moment in Western history become the substance of universal propositions in a general theory.

Seen from the broader perspective of an awareness of world history and of cultural diversity, many such claims of universal theory seem both parochial and trivial. Indeed, as long as the search has been for unqualified laws, the results could only be trivial. Only when the approach takes a probabilistic

---

[11] The phenomena of communism in the Soviet Union and China has raised for students of both societies many questions about continuity and change, but it is significant that no important book on either system has been written around this theme. The theme is always provocative, as in the valuable symposium edited by Cyril E. Black, *The Transformation of Russian Society* (Cambridge: Harvard University Press, 1960). The problem is that we don't know quite what to make of continuity when we do discover it; yet unless we can identify the causes for either continuity or change, we are in danger of attributing magical powers to something called history.

turn and there is explicit appreciation of cultural diversity is it possible to get beyond the empirically simplistic and essentially definitional form of political theory. Political man in the abstract is a rather shallow figure when compared with British, French, Japanese, or American political man.

IN PRAISE OF DESCRIPTION

In continuing our examination of the ways in which the social sciences' peculiar concept of science has possibly reduced our sensitivity to change, we would note that in our profession there is a strong tendency to discount the art of description as being unscientific. It is commonplace for people to hold that descriptive studies are supposedly of a lower intellectual level of work than are analytical studies. Just as the generalist is presumed to outrank the area specialist, so the man who follows an analytical approach is seen to have risen above those who engage in "mere description."

It would be tempting at this point to look into the intellectual bases of the conflict between the generalist and the area specialist, but unfortunately this is not a matter that can be treated moderately, for it is too often a battle of extremes between the arrogant self-assurance of the theorist, who is concerned only with universal matters, and the cocky knowledgeability of the data specialist, who can demonstrate that there is nothing that is universal. At this point our concern, however, is with a stange paradox: as social scientists we have a vivid appreciation for the difference between analysis and description, we value the former as more scientific, yet at the same time we believe that precision and measurement are the hallmarks of science, and therefore we seem oblivious of the fact that in the physical sciences the value of precision and measurement is that they will yield more exact and rigorous *descriptions*. Logically it would seem that advocates of rigor and precision should be happy to join forces with the practitioners of descriptive studies, for both share a common interest in accuracy. Yet within the brotherhood of social scientists it is manifestly clear that neither is too comfortable with the other.

The reason for this is probably in part the fact that most descriptive studies tend to be "big picture" studies, and this means that they must employ hypotheses of a broader sweep than we are as yet capable of testing. Thus again we have the clash between those who want to keep our ideas within the bounds of our ability to test and measure and those who feel comfortable speculating at a level beyond the scope of systematic measurement. In short, those descriptive studies that are essentially big-picture analyses usually deal with implicit or explicit assertions of untestable causality.

As an aside we would note here that the literal-minded who are blind to implicit communication and who acknowledge only explicit generalizations are not necessarily acting in the spirit of science. To believe that authors know what they are doing only when they say what they are up to is a form of innocence that unfortunately is lacking in any charm. Those who happily engage in descriptive studies know that among wise men a great deal can be left unsaid while it may be the work of the fool to give words to the obvious. On the other hand, self-conscious champions of analysis often can leave out nothing; therefore, they feel compelled to leave in place all the scaffolding they have had to erect—to the point at times that the reader finds it hard to discern the building that is supposedly the object of the endeavor, and is left wondering whether, in the spirit of the Emperor's clothes, he should suggest that there might in fact be nothing at all behind the pretentious scaffolds.

Returning to the larger problem of causality in descriptive studies, we must admit that there is truth in the complaint that such studies usually deal with multiple causalities without giving any indication of their relative importance. In most descriptive studies the writer must usually either implicitly or explicitly single out the various factors that he believes to have been important in causing the change of events he is studying, and usually it is adequate that he has a catalogue of such causes. In the end, however, he remains in a weak position in trying to attach differing degrees of significance to the variables.

Granting this criticism, we would, however, return to the praise of descriptive analysis. First, just in passing, we would observe that the "mere" descriptive study that "only" tells us how a particular institution or process actually operates has accomplished a great deal indeed at this or any conceivable state of the social sciences. To ask for more is to reveal a lack of interest in the dynamics of the real world.

Secondly, descriptive studies of the big-picture variety usually deserve high scores because they tend to be sensitive to the themes of change. He who is trying to tell a story must be interested in dynamic developments and the evolution of the situation. It is change and the possibilities for change that provide the drama of events. The fact that descriptive studies often overreach themselves and try to explain more than they can is a minor objection in comparison to the worthwhile contribution they do make in sensitizing us all to the patterns of change. The evidence for placing such a high value on descriptive studies can be seen from the number of historians who have worked well in policy positions.

These observations about the intellectual value of underintellectualized descriptive studies represent nothing new, since in informal communications among political scientists it is customary to speak of precisely such works when citing a "fascinating" book that one has just read. What is novel is to suggest that it is time in our training of students to declare that such valuable endeavors are in no sense less "scientific" or less worthy than more explicitly analytical works.

THE FRUSTRATIONS OF A STATIC APPROACH TO CHANGE

In turning now to the central problem of analytical approaches in the social sciences and the problem of change, we must begin by making the commonplace but fundamental observation that the rapid advances in the social sciences have been almost entirely in the development of static rather than dynamic theories. There are numerous reasons why the social sciences in modern times have emphasized static analysis, and these go well beyond the fact that in theory such analysis should be easier. One consideration is the strong reaction of political scientists against our earlier normative and idealistic traditions, which has produced a great concern with simply understanding how things actually are. This stress on realism, which began in the 1930's in both political science and sociology, produced a cast of mind which distrusted utopian speculation and any easy view of the possibilities of reform, and hence of change. It became the mark of nonscholarly innocence to believe that dramatic improvement could be expected in society, for change could at best be only incremental. This mood was reinforced by such powerful concepts as equilibrium, the balancing of power, and countervailing forces. Wise men knew that the real need was to understand existing realities, because either they were going to be around for a long time or, if change was to come, it would have to be the modest consequence of the interplay of existing forces.

This mood of the social sciences which placed stress on the role of interest groups rather than on the leader—even during the years of Roosevelt, Hitler, Stalin, and Churchill—was finally shaken by the problem of understanding the prospects for social, political, and economic development in the new states that emerged in the wake of the colonial era. It would be hard to overstate the effects that the problem of development has had on the social sciences. Intellectually the dominant trend in the preceding years had been in a contrary direction, since scholars no longer found it fashionable to believe in either progress or evolution, and had generally accepted the viewpoint of cultural relativism and the assumption that every society should be accepted on its own terms.

The social scientists were suddenly compelled to recognize how far behind the times they had fallen when the leaders of the new states proclaimed that they wanted development, progress, and a rejection of old traditions, and when the economist, who was presumably the most advanced of the social scientists because he knew more mathematics, unashamedly began to talk about two categories of economies, the static and stagnant ones and those with self-sustaining growth. A concept of progress had been revived by the most sophisticated of social sciences, and now it was both necessary and respectable to talk about "developed" and "underdeveloped" societies. The other social science disciplines had to fall in step with the economist's theories of change. When leaders in the new states anxiously wanted to know the prospects for change in their societies, it would have revealed a form of intellectual bankruptcy to preach against progress.

The problem was not just that the social sciences lacked the theories that might have helped guide efforts at nation-building; they could not even suggest how much change could be expected in the new states. Approaches to the developing areas have thus been highly vulnerable to moods, first of undue optimism and then of possibly excessive cynicism.

In seeking to understand the prospects of change in the transitional societies of the Afro-Asian world, political science did turn to the social theorists and to the contributions of Émile Durkheim, Sir Henry Maine, and Ferdinand Toennies, and most importantly Max Weber and Talcott Parsons. These were the scholars who had historically sought to explain the social changes that came to Europe with the industrial revolution. Essentially they tried to categorize the key features of traditional societies on the one hand and industrial ones on the other.

There is no need for us here to spell out the well-known features of traditional and modern societies which this approach has emphasized. We would only note that further research has led to much more complicated views of each, so that we no longer see traditional societies as being quite so static as we used to think, and we recognize that in the most "modern" societies there must remain a great deal of what was once thought of as essentially traditional modes of behavior. Also the dichotomous scheme has in many studies given way to a threefold classification with the addition of a "transitional" category.

This categorization of the differences between traditional, transitional, and modern societies was of great value in sensitizing us to critical differences that could provide the basis for classificatory schemes. The approach encouraged social scientists to think in terms of typologies and to raise questions as to how systems would have to change so as to move from one category to another. The difficulty, however, has been that this approach really rests upon a series of separate static studies; it is as though we had taken snapshots of societies at different periods of time and then noted the changes from picture to picture. The snapshots can reveal a great deal about the characteristics of the society at any particular moment, but they unfortunately can tell us very little about what actually governs the dynamics of change. No matter how frequent the intervals between the pictures and how slight the change from picture to picture, there is nothing in the pictures themselves that can tell us what makes for change; they can only tell us what change looks like.

To use another analogy, we can say that this classificatory approach which we gained from the social theorists has greatly enhanced our skills in "judging" societies in the same manner as skilled judges can appraise prize cattle, but it has taught us little about the kind of science necessary for the controlled breeding of cattle. And there is quite a difference between the art of judging cattle and the science of breeding them; a difference comparable to that between static and dynamic analysis.

In practice the effort to build typologies of political systems has thus given us a greater sense of the diversity of politics, but not of the patterns of change. Indeed, the detail of our contemporary studies has at times given a quality of permanence to what was supposed to be in flux, and in many cases the category of transitional has in fact become quite as stable as either the traditional or the modern. For example, as I understand his analysis, Fred Riggs's "prismatic" societies are not necessarily in any greater state of disequilibrium than either the modern or the traditional.[12] Once again, our bias for static analysis has reduced our sensitivity to change and given us a greater tendency than ever to regard what is as being what has to be.

The frustration of trying to use a typological approach to the problem of change does create strain, which scholars seem often to resolve by the device of forgetting about change and extolling the legitimacy of present realities. The very uncertainties of Africa have compelled some students of that continent to justify and give respectability to such matters of the moment as the prevalence of one-party systems—but just at a time when such systems were about to give way to army rule. The effort to explain what is does seem to make us less sensitive to what is about to be.[13]

IN SEARCH OF THE DYNAMIC ELEMENT

Needless to say, not all work on the developing areas involves the classifying of types of systems, and there are countless attempts to take what is usually considered to be a more pragmatic and less "scientific" approach to change. This usually takes the form of trying to discover and isolate those who are going to be the next agents of change. This approach is most common among researchers in government, who are anxious to locate the next generation of rulers, presumably, if they can identify them early enough, so that something can be done about shaping their views before they come to power, and if they are too late for that, then at least they can protect other officials from being surprised. For among statesmen, to be surprised is only a step away from being wrong.

The search for the dynamic element in society can take the form of looking either for the next generation or for the particular institutions that may be rising in significance. Will it be the army, the parochial politicians, the national administration, or the Westernized intellectuals who will be shortly shaping developments?[14] The questions are certainly worth asking, but

---

[12] Fred Riggs, *Administration in Developing Countries—The Theory of Prismatic Society* (Boston: Houghton Mifflin Co., 1964).

[13] One's sympathies must really go out to the scholars working on Africa, for theirs has been a thankless assignment. But one can still properly ask whether they have done as good a job as they should in forward thinking and in preparing the consumers of their studies for the turn of events in Africa. Before the epidemics of military coups there were only a couple of significant reviews of the role of the military in Africa—and the most significant of these was done only so that Africa would not be left out of a general symposium on the military in the developing areas. Also under-studied was the degree of corruption and political skulduggery that eroded regime after regime, the significance of which appears to have been appreciated earlier and more fully by lay observers and journalists than by scholars.

[14] It should be noted that the fads and fashions in scholarly research, particularly as related to area work, are usually influenced by trends in public affairs, but scholarship at times does have a dynamic of its own. Thus it is at times difficult to judge whether an emerging new focus of scholarly interest signals a significant new trend in historical developments or whether it represents only a new area of discovery for scholars. For example, in the last few years the attention of American scholars working on India has

they are profoundly difficult to answer. And more importantly, is there anything in social science which can make us better able to answer such questions than the lay political observer and the journalist?

The problem is first that it is usually not a class or generation or institution, but rather the individual that becomes the critical ruler. And to forecast the fortunes of individuals is clearly not the province of social science. But aside from this rather fundamental difficulty, there is still the inescapable fact that we just do not have any theories that might guide us in our search for what is likely to be the next dynamic element in any particular society. What is called for with such an approach is the deep knowledge and understanding of the specialist on the particular country. This is a case where knowledge of the facts is all-important.

For our purposes it is not necessary to review any further the record of recent attempts at locating the dynamic element in the processes of political change and modernization, for it is now obvious that the problem of understanding change really is a part of the larger and classic problem of the relationship between generalized and particularized knowledge, between general theory and factual information. This is especially the case because change and development can take place only in a historical context, and each historical situation has its unique as well as universal dimensions. "Traditional" and "modern" only to a limited degree are useful abstract concepts; they must also have their particularistic elements.

Again we arrive at a point where it seems necessary to deal with the basic clash between generalist and specialist. But as we have noted above, the emotional feelings on both sides are such as to preclude any hope for objectivity, another requirement of science which gives social science a great deal of difficulty. It might be appropriate to avoid the problem entirely by observing that the good social scientist who would deal with change and the output side of the political system should in his own work realize a happy combination of both skills. This, however, would inevitably lead us to a discussion of how we should go about training new scholars with such an ideal blend of skills; but I refuse to do this because as dreary as discussions of the state of political science are, talk about graduate curricula is even more dreary. It is, therefore, a search for relief and not just a sense of timidity that leads me to pursue further this discussion of the relationship of knowledge (which is presumably scientific) to understanding change by examining how another group of intellectuals, who were patently not social scientists, made out in their attempts to comprehend the problems of social and historical change.

In turning now to such an unlikely source as the attempts of Chinese intellectuals to understand the relationship of tradition to modernity, we are

---

noticeably shifted to the level of state politics, but it is not clear whether in reality there has been a proportionate increase in the significance of state politics for Indian development or only a case of foreign scholars catching up on an area of enduring significance which was neglected in the past.

in part seeking the perspective and the heuristic advantages of an Aesopean world. Therefore, before noting these advantages, I must first make clear that my purpose remains that of bringing clarity to the muddle of the social scientist who wants to be both a scientist and a student of change, and hence I should in advance apologize for ribbing the Chinese—but then, this is not the political time to be caught apologizing to the Chinese.[15]

II. LEARNING FROM THE FLOUNDERING OF THE CHINESE

First, three quick reasons why we might profit from looking at the intellectual agonies that the sons of Han went through in trying to figure out what modernization was all about. The Chinese intellectuals from the middle of the nineteenth through the first two decades of the twentieth century were probably the most sophisticated group of men to deal explicitly with the issues of social change and modernization while being members of a society reeling under the impact of the modern West. They used words and concepts to explain the plight of their country which we can fully understand, and therefore we often find it quite easy to go along with their arguments.

I don't mean to suggest that other transitional societies don't have their intellectuals of worth, but for our purposes the second advantage of the Chinese example is that their intellectuals were not so Westernized as to be using no more than Western terms and concepts in trying to explain their dilemma. Some of the intellectuals in the currently transitional societies have learned all about the problems of the old and the new through Western sources, while possibly studying about underdeveloped areas at London, Chicago, or Cambridge, and thus we often find in their writings only a mirroring of our own notions. It is also helpful that the Chinese intellectuals grappled with their problem in the pre-Freudian era, so they were not given to excruciating soul-searching and endless rumination about their "rootless" condition, their violated "psyches," and their fractured "personalities." The Chinese intellectuals tried at least to deal with the problem at a level most political scientists find congenial.

Finally, the Chinese case should be of interest because, in spite of the first two points, they came very close to using concepts analogous to those we know in modern social science, but they also failed to find valid answers.

---

[15] Although the times may not be right for apologizing to the Chinese, I do feel it necessary to apologize to all students of Chinese intellectual history for what will be my rather cavalier treatment of a subject on which they have expended tremendous amounts of energy and infinite patience. For many of the interpretations that follow I am indebted to Joseph R. Levenson, and the only way I can discharge this debt and make amends for the scandalous way I am treating a subject dear to his heart is to press upon you all the wonderful pleasures of reading his truly witty and profoundly enlightening study, *Confucian China and Its Modern Fate: The Problems of Intellectual Continuity* (Berkeley: University of California Press, 1958). I know of no book that exposes with greater clarity and wisdom some of the basic dilemmas of modernization in traditional societies.

Therefore, maybe by going over their reasoning we can escape the same pitfalls. To put all in a slogan in the manner of Mao Tse-tung, a latter-day Chinese intellectual of modernization: "Let us build strength from the errors of others as we construct a better social science."

THE LI-CH'I ISSUE, AND THE DIFFICULTIES OF SCHOLARS' BECOMING USEFUL

To do justice to Chinese efforts to comprehend intellectually the problem of social change and modernization we ought to start with some understanding of the intellectual traditions of Chinese thought. But clearly this is no place even to outline in the grossest terms the burden of Chinese intellectual history. There is only one feature of this tradition which calls for our urgent attention, and this is the fantastic muddle the Chinese got themselves into over the issue of *li-ch'i*. It was this issue in Chinese thought which made the Chinese at one moment appear to be veering toward a scientific approach, and at the next moment end up with a mere play on words—a problem not unknown to social scientists.

As you are probably aware, the Chinese historically were incorrigible dichotomizers; they could always make everything into pairs, or into fours: four winds, four points of the compass. (In the profound bit of reasoning which set off an interminable discussion about the proper organization or structure of government, it was argued that an emperor needed only four chief ministers "because there are only four directions.") In neo-Confucianism one of the most fundamental pairs was that of *li* and *ch'i* (pronounced "chee"). All things in the universe, according to these Chinese sages, were a complex of *li* and *ch'i*, and much of man's failure in dealing with things came from a confusion of the two.

Li stands for the ideal form that exists only in the minds of men. It is the universal, the regulative principle, which gives order and form to our knowledge of all things.

Ch'i stands for mutable matter, for concrete things, for the particular.

Once the Chinese had made this division between the universal and the particular, the abstract and the concrete, the ideal and the real, they had a terrible time with the relationship between the two. In general they recognized that those who dealt skillfully with the values of the *li* were noble beings, the worthies of the empire, for they were clearly the intellectuals, who were never prisoners of mere common sense or any of the other senses. On the other hand, those who thought only in terms of *ch'i* were manifestly shallow people, the unreflecting part of the common herd. Only a cultural snob would insist that there was any significant difference between these Chinese sentiments and the feelings about the superiority of theorists over empiricists in much of contemporary social science. Yet even among Chinese thinking men there were differences in cognitive styles, and in particular there was a division between those who were more extreme in their inclination toward the *li* and those who still saw some value in thinking about the *ch'i*.

Now those who were strongly pro-*li* were indeed powerful thinkers who were breathtakingly clever in their handling of all arguments. They would begin by saying that things as they stand are nothing at all, for it is only the mind of man that gives order and significance to the physical world. This meant that those who were fully at home in the domain of the *li* showed great virtuosity in describing categories and elaborating concepts. (It would be dead wrong, however, to say they engaged in logical formulations, because these Chinese men of *li* looked down upon logical rigor as being a bit unnecessarily binding and something only for compulsive foreigners or "barbarians.") As might be supposed, every now and then one of those who still worried about the place of *ch'i* in metaphysics would bring up an unpleasant fact, and this could raise embarrassing questions about the significance of the categories and concepts. However, when the men of *li* were confronted with this problem, they generally responded with remarkable vigor by forthrightly denouncing all the senses as being the sources of human confusion. They even came to agree explicitly with Buddha that the six senses should be declared the "six villains." Man was clearly at his greatest when he was the most successful in keeping out of mind all unnecessary reality. (We don't need to go into the fascinating Chinese belief that theory building and the aesthetic life belong together, and therefore the aspiring intellectual should be cautious about becoming emotionally involved in practical affairs.)

There is just no telling how far the Chinese intellectuals might have gone in examining the *li* and ignoring the *ch'i* if history hadn't rudely disrupted their contemplative world. The Western impact was, however, a massive challenge, and Chinese intellectuals came in time to realize that the essence of the challenge was Western science and technology. Now, to make a long story short, once the Chinese began to look into Western science it occurred to them that in their *li-ch'i* approach they were onto the essence of science. Wasn't *li* the same as theory, or abstract generalization, and *ch'i* the same as empirical data? Things therefore couldn't be nearly as bad as they seemed. Like latter-day social scientists, they believe that with time they too might soon be advancing with all the successes of the physical scientists.

The Chinese intellectuals did, however, acknowledge one big difference between the way they had been carrying on and the ways of Western science: science dealt with practical problems and sought to be useful. The Chinese intellectuals quickly decided that they too should try to be useful. With this commitment they felt that they were fully in line with modern science. What actually happened was that in spite of universal declarations that everyone should be useful, nothing really changed. Those inclined to the *li* went back to their categorizing, and those with a new-found interest in the *ch'i* wondered what they should make of reality. The sum effect of all this was that the Chinese intellectuals, egged on by a determination to be useful, went right on doing what they had been doing, fully convinced that they were being essentially scientific in their approach—again, rather reminiscent of trends in contemporary social science.

I suppose the moral of all this is self-evident, but we might as well say it: the Chinese intellectuals not only failed to establish any meaningful relationship between *li* and *ch'i*, between theory and data, but they never got the point that science calls for the systematic putting of questions to *both* data and theory. Consequently they got themselves endlessly wrapped up in controversies about terms, definitions, and statements about the ideal goals of development, and lost track of what precisely were the pressing problems of their society.

THE T'I-YUNG ISSUE, OR HOW THE ENDS-MEANS CALCULUS CAN LEAD TO CLEAR REASONING BUT FUZZY EMOTIONS

Once the Chinese intellectuals reassured themselves that in a fundamental sense they were headed in the right direction, they still had to cope with the disturbingly obvious fact that Western science had somehow produced a powerful technology that, if the Chinese didn't look out, was about to destroy them. To cope with Western material superiority the Chinese philosophers came up with the *t'i* (pronounced "tea")-*yung* dichotomy, which was the granddaddy of all looking-down-of-noses-at-Western-materialism-and-praising-of-native-spiritual-virtues. Briefly, in this dichotomy the *t'i* stands for "substance," "essence," or "fundamental values," while the *yung* represents "function," "utility," or "means." In this formulation the *t'i* was always superior to the *yung*, just as the *li* was superior to the *ch'i*.

The advocates of the *t'i-yung* formula, when faced with the issue of policy toward change, held that traditional Chinese culture was obviously the *t'i*, and the Western technology and methods had to be *yung*. There is even some evidence that Chinese thinkers fell into raucous laughter and vigorous thigh-slapping when they thought about how clever they were going to be in using the very strength of the West to preserve their own cultural values. To illustrate how bluntly they put the matter, it is worth quoting the words of one Confucian worthy: "To control the barbarians through their own superior technology is to drive away the crocodile and to get rid of the whales." (British ships and guns, of course.)

Chinese thinkers initially found it deceptively easy to maintain the *t'i-yung* distinction. They argued along the line that Western knowledge was manifestly *practical*, and hence it was *useful*, which meant that it was merely a *means* and therefore inescapably inferior to ends, which were Chinese values. There is no recorded evidence that any Westerner at the time appreciated this line of Chinese reasoning, or understood that the more the Chinese were presented with evidence on the effectiveness of Western methods, the more the Chinese were confirmed in their reasoning that such knowledge had to be inferior to Chinese values. The latter had to be ultimate ends because they clearly couldn't be means, since they obviously had no practical worth. All this might seem like the foolishness of simple men, were it not so much like the line of reasoning of those contemporary social scientists who are convinced that their work must be scientific because it has no immediate practical value, and it must be of high importance because it will contribute to something practical in the distant future.

By the 1890's a significant body of Chinese intellectuals began to sense that there was something wrong with the *t'i-yung* formulation. Interestingly enough, it was the essentially conservative group that spotted the difficulty. This group insisted that traditional Confucian knowledge represented a way of life, and therefore it was foolish to talk of distinguishing between ends and means. More particularly, they argued that the traditional system of Confucian values could not be preserved once the educational system was permeated with Western science. The reformers, still happy with their *t'i-yung* formulation, came back with the argument that the conservatives were demonstrably fuddy-duddies because their inability to distinguish between ends and means proved that they didn't understand the nature of rationality. The conservatives countered by suggesting that the reformers were excessively fascinated with their notions about science and rationality, and that they were much too naïve to understand the full cultural context of knowledge and wisdom.

The most telling point the conservatives made was that Western science was not merely a bit of clever ingenuity, but was profoundly related to all of Western civilization, and more particularly it was tied to the essentials of the Judaic-Christian tradition.[16] This notion that you couldn't have a simple *t'i-yung* arrangement was profoundly disquieting to the reformers, and the case could easily be made that they were permanently unnerved. In any case, the reformers were compelled to abandon their more simple and optimistic version of *t'i-yung* formulation.

THE SEARCH FOR A CHINESE MARTIN LUTHER AND FOR A MEETING OF EAST AND WEST

As the reformers lost their confidence with the *t'i-yung* formulation, there developed among Chinese intellectuals an ever increasing degree of curiosity about the relationship between cultural and religious traditions on the one hand and rational and scientific thought on the other hand. (We can leave it to other students of intellectual history to explore the interesting fact that Tawney spent a year in the midst of a later revival of this debate in China just before he wrote his "Religion and the Rise of Capitalism.")

For our purposes it is significant that the Chinese intellectuals responded to these developments by increasingly posing the problem of modernization

---

[16] It is hard to explain this surprising wisdom of the Chinese conservatives, especially since they were such manifest fools in so many other matters. Possibly, however, it came from their instinctive appreciation of the nature and dynamics of political legitimacy. They were certainly sensitive to the links between authority and culture, and between action and moral evaluation. For an interesting discussion of how the problem of legitimacy prevented modernization at this period of Chinese history, see S. N. Eisenstadt, "Transformation of Social, Political and Cultural Orders in Modernization," *American Sociological Review*, 30 (October 1965) : 659–73.

and development in terms of the life cycle of total civilizations. Instead of talking about the problem of change as being an issue of values versus techniques, or of tradition versus rationality as they had initially done, and as most social scientists now do, the Chinese intellectuals felt increasingly compelled to talk of the dynamics of Chinese civilization meeting the dynamics of Western civilization. They saw the problem as a massive confrontation of history, which, quite significantly, gave them as representatives of Chinese civilization a new sense of dignity and self-respect.

At this point the more conservative intellectuals were again content with their formulations and saw no need for action. They were all caught up in speculating about the inexorable workings of history. If Chinese civilization was about to be destroyed by Western civilization, that would be a great tragedy but it would also be history: hence Chinese should and could do no more than live up to their traditions even as they went down to defeat. The reformers, however, began to look for new formulations in terms of the laws of the regeneration of civilizations which might still provide hope for the future of the Chinese spirit.

With this development the discourse of Chinese intellectuals began to be loaded down with such terms as "reformation," "renaissance," "reconstruction," "restoration"—all of which implied a rediscovering and revitalizing of Chinese civilization. The spirit of the reformers was no longer that of men borrowing some things from the West; it became a frantic search for the universal laws of the growth cycles of civilizations. For men like K'ang Yu-wei, Chinese history should be exactly like Western history. He proclaimed the doctrine that the papacy killed Christianity in the West and Luther revived it; Confucianism, done to death by the conservative scholars, needed a Luther, too. His disciple and colleague Liang Ch'i-ch'ao clearly got the point, as witness his simple statement: "My teacher is the Martin Luther of Confucianism." It would not, however, require an Erik H. Erikson to demonstrate that K'ang Yu-wei was no Luther, whatever their respective identity crises may have been.

This new approach gave the Chinese a new perspective on their problems: they could now dwell on the fact that the West had had its Dark Ages, and that all civilizations have their ups and downs. Wasn't it a mere curiosity that China had been up when the West was down, and now it was the other way round, but who could tell how they would stand on the next turn of the wheel? About this time World War I came along, and the Chinese intellectuals showed an ill-concealed delight in pointing out how "irrational" and "uncivilized" the West was now behaving. This set in motion the endless search for the "bad spots" in Western performance which became increasingly a national sport, and brought the intellectuals in close touch with the politicians and the more vulgar elements of Chinese society. This may have reduced the gap between elite and mass, but it certainly soured the tone of public life.

The more serious intellectuals continued their search for universal laws of civilization, and before they knew it this led them to a new position:

knowledge and science belong to no particular culture, but rather are a part of a universal or world culture. There could then be a meeting of East and West on the basis of universally valid wisdom and a common denial of all parochialisms. Ts'ai Yüan-p'ei, the great chancellor of Peking National University, and Dr. Hu Shih, China's leading intellectual and close disciple of John Dewey, were the leaders of this argument. Truth was freedom and all peoples throughout the world were engaged in a common quest.

This new search for a meeting of East and West on the basis of universal, nonculture-bound knowledge did give a spark of boldness to Chinese intellectuals. In 1918 Ts'ai did not hesitate to introduce John Dewey to a Peking audience as "a greater thinker than Confucius." Gradually, however, the followers of this approach became mired down in their search for "Chinese" manifestations of variations of universal knowledge. Hu Shih sought to prove that the Chinese did have an empirical tradition and some understanding of logic. In short, the search soon degenerated from a quest for universal knowledge into an effort to find the "West" in Chinese history. Before the Chinese intellectuals knew it, they were back with the li-ch'i business and the problem of the relationship of the universal and the particular, and that was the point where we came in.

As we come back again full cycle with the Chinese intellectuals, we must end this excursion into Chinese intellectual history by drawing attention to two major conclusions that seem to emerge from all this, and which may have relevance for our thinking about the problems of change and modernization in the contemporary world.

The first conclusion is rather startling when first stated, but I am quite convinced it is sound: the Chinese intellectuals were less confused about the character of what we call "modern" than they were about what is "traditional." We have generally tended to assume that transitional peoples are confused because they can't grasp the fundamentals of modern life. To some degree this was certainly true of the Chinese intellectuals, and I wouldn't want to ignore the importance of this difficulty. The point remains, however, that they seemed much more confused, uncertain, and divided in their interpretations of what "tradition" should stand for. Indeed, this is the central finding of Joseph Levenson in his classic study of the Chinese intellectuals.

The explanation of this may be very simple, and at the same time it leads into the complex question of the psychological dynamics of the tension in transitional systems, which does go a bit beyond the bounds of this paper. But it is important enough for a general understanding of the problem of political modernization so I hope you will forgive what must appear to be another slight digression. The point is that in the case of the Chinese intellectuals we can trace very clearly how their concepts of traditional Confucianism constantly changed as they learned more about other things. In short, the old or the traditional was never a constant, for it was always being affected by the context within which it was being interpreted.

After they had been exposed to Western knowledge, those who had strong sentiments for Confucianism were quite different from those who were happy with their Confucianism without any knowledge of other ways. The difference is like that between the American Anglophile who affects British ways and the Englishman who has never left home. Increasingly among the Chinese Confucianists the balance was shifting from those whose feelings toward their traditions were like those of the Englishman at home to those who were like the Anglophile.

I would not want to attempt here to define all the various categories of attitudes one can have toward the traditional. They would run from the extreme of those to whom their tradition makes eminent sense to the other extreme of those who must out of the new build again an old. (I am convinced that the test of "eminent sense" is really a valid one for telling what is traditional for any people; note how nicely this works with respect to distinguishing what "tradition" of social science scholarship one belongs to.)

The fact that all Chinese intellectuals felt compelled to deal with the nature of their tradition brings up the second main conclusion: all knowledge is wedded to a culture, and all cultures have their parochial dimensions, and hence there is no escaping the issue of what is "ours" as against what is "foreign." As much as the Chinese intellectuals may appear to have been engaged in elaborate rationalizations with their *t'i-yung* formulations and their insistence that the spiritual is more important than the material, they were in fact grappling with the essential question behind all experiences in modernization. The issue is one of the spirit and of what can be done to preserve one's sense of spiritual self-respect and dignity. The Chinese intellectuals were clearly engaged in a frantic search for dignity and self-respect, and all the different formulations of the *t'i-yung* issue by conservatives and reformers, by modernists and traditionalists, can be traced back to this fundamental issue.

These conclusions, oddly enough, lead me back to my old view that the problem of modernization and political change is essentially a problem of "identity"—but this is obviously only an idiosyncratic difficulty of someone who is the prisoner of his own "tradition" and who can't get away from what makes "eminent sense" for himself. The more general conclusion I would suggest for others is that this exercise demonstrates the degree to which the real problems of change rest upon the logic of social processes and not on intellectual ones. The problem, in the spirit of the later Chinese "intellectual" whose "thoughts" are now being frantically studied by all 700 million Chinese, is how to get thought and action joined together. This suggests that we should return to the contemporary world, inspired to understand better the relationship between social science theory and policy action.

III. THE DEAD END OF SCIENCE WITHOUT ENGINEERS

In returning from the never-never land of Chinese logic to the cold realism of modern social science, it is appropriate for us to confront directly the issue of the relevance of social science theory for public policy insofar as each must deal with the problem of understanding change. We have already indicated that a basic bias in our concept of science has left social scientists content to remain slightly behind the flow of events that must dominate the thinking of policy-makers. We have also noted that social scientists have tended to be cautious with respect to the risks of being wrong, rejecting in this sphere the ethos of science and taking on that of the statesman, without concurrently taking on the discipline of having to make decisions or assume any responsibilities.

There is, however, another view about the nature of science which is commonplace in the social sciences and which may further limit our capacity to help policy-makers with the problems of dynamic change. This is the problem that arises from our innocent faith in the ultimate utility of all pure science. Arguing largely in terms of what we feel to be an appropriate analogy in the physical sciences, we easily convince ourselves that we are not being insensitive to the problems of the real world if we concentrate only on matters of pure theory, because no matter how utterly irrelevant such concerns may seem at this moment in time, they will ultimately prove to be of profound practical value at some later date. Time can, and thus in our enthusiasm almost certainly will, ensure the utility of the most abstract speculations. If we have any doubts as to where we may be heading, it is only necessary to reflect for a moment on Einstein and the atomic bomb. Needless to say, it doesn't work so well if one thinks about the Chinese and their *t'i-yung* problem, but, of course, we are not Chinese intellectuals. . . .

This faith in the ultimate utility of pure theory has been used to justify a posture of disinterest in the pressing public policy issues of the moment. The pure social scientist does not need to become involved in the problems of policy-makers because he presumably is working in terms of a larger time perspective. Indeed, some social scientists are not defensive but aggressive in this view, and insist that policy-makers should not expect useful knowledge today, but should patiently await the imminent development of a much more powerful social science that will be of overriding value to the world. But again we are reminded of the problem of the Chinese.

There are undoubtedly many reasons why we should carefully protect this faith in our impending successes, and certainly it is not my purpose here to extol skepticism and deride the self-confidence that is necessary for all difficult achievements. What I would like to suggest is that the view of the spontaneous linkage between theory and practical knowledge rests upon a distorted and much too intellectualized view of the nature of the scientific enterprise.

If we reflect for a moment about what goes on in the physical sciences, and look deeper than the Chinese did, it seems clear that there is no spontaneous or inevitable linkage between the pure theorists and the practical achievements of science. Instead these sciences are elaborate sociological processes that involve the interaction of large numbers of people who in varying ways share their knowledge and are constantly sensitive to each other's concerns. Above all, the translation of theoretical developments into practical achievements depends upon the existence of large cadres of engineers and applied scientists whose skill and knowledge only imperceptibly shade off from those of the most advanced theoretical scientists. The great gap that exists between the social scientist and the policy-maker thus has no counterpart in the physical sciences, for it has been filled by the role of the engineer.

Indeed it does seem that the analogy of the relationship of the scientist to the engineer is most useful in trying to understand what may be critical in the ability of the social sciences to help with the problem of change. This is particularly true if you think of the engineers as having two peculiar professional characteristics: (1) a constant concern with decision-making—to build or not to build, to modify the design or not, etc.—and (2) an acceptance of the need to act even when the appropriate theory has not been perfected—and, indeed, even when there is no theory.

It is of course much easier for the physical sciences to maintain this more complicated division of labor because of the massive nature of their enterprise. The numbers of practitioners are still few in the social sciences, and consequently we are probably somewhat more nervous about what it would mean to standards of performance in each of our disciplines if we were to tolerate too pluralistic a view of what we should be engaged in doing. Yet if we ever are to make sure that the results of our theoretical work will be relevant to policy-making, we will have to take it upon ourselves to train people who will have the skills necessary to translate such knowledge into the principles necessary for guiding public policy. We should recognize that this process calls for a high degree of specialized skill and not just the passage of time during which we can make more and more advances in theory. Unless we are prepared to welcome a greater degree of pluralism in our self-image as a discipline, we shall have to continue to pay the very high costs of experiencing frustration and tensions over trying to do the impossible.

11

Political Feasibility

RALPH K. HUITT

If politics is the "art of the possible," as it is often said to be, and the study of it is concerned with "who gets what, when, and how," the question of what is politically feasible would seem to come close to the heart of the matter. But perhaps the empiricism and practicality implicit in these and like definitions suggest why there is little systematic work to suggest what "political feasibility" *is*; it remains the province of the operator, not the theoretician. Pragmatic judgments in politics, as in other human endeavors, nevertheless are based on calculations about how people will behave in certain stable institutional situations, what problems they face, and what resources they can bring to bear on them. If these are largely unconscious and institutional on the part of the operator, they need not be for the student.

It may be that there are certain elements common to "political feasibility" in all political situations, but searching for them would hardly seem to be the way to begin. At first glance it would appear that what is feasible would vary with the enterprise at hand, with the arena in which action must be mounted, in the goals one has in mind, and with the political actor who is deciding what is feasible. The relatively single-minded business of getting elected President of the United States furnishes an example. It clearly is one thing to win primaries, another to capture a national convention—unless, of course, the first is done so successfully that the second is converted into a ratifying device. Mr. Kefauver was eminently proficient at the first but not at the second; Mr. Kennedy and Mr. Goldwater were nominees virtually before their conventions met. Mr. Dewey and his cohorts demonstrated that it is possible to be masters of convention strategy and tactics and still lose two national elections—one when the prospects were poor, it is true, but the other apparently unlosable. This is to say that each stage of the process presents a different "arena," or institutional setting, with its own peculiar requirements of resources, skills, and sense of timing. These differences may make it fairly easy for a candidate and his coterie to succeed at one and impossible to win at another. But even when the auguries are good at each level, it is still possible —to cite the unfortunate Mr. Dewey once more—to bungle the job somewhere.

The two houses of Congress obviously present similar arenas that differ markedly from Presidential electoral arenas. (Perhaps it is not so obvious; more than one gifted senator has failed to recognize it.) The legislative leader learns the mood and rhythm of his house, the kinds of combinations that can be put together on various categories of issues, and the timing necessary to the success of good strategies. It is well established that men who move from state to national legislature, or from House to Senate in Congress, usually are well prepared and content in their new assignments, while former governors often are not.[1] The move from legislator to chief executive surely must entail similar readjustment and socialization, though it probably helps that the incumbent wanted to make the change and probably considers it an advancement.

The question of feasibility in politics also turns upon the goals under consideration. The election of a man to an office is one thing; a change in the drift of national policy clearly is quite another. One is relatively simple, the other enormously complex, requiring skills and good judgment in many arenas. Again, there is the question whether what is wanted is an immediate victory—say, the passage of a bill—or a major change over time. Political education is part of the legislative process, and a succession of defeats may be necessary to prepare the way for an ultimate victory that in retrospect seems inevitable. President Johnson's choice of Independence, Missouri, as the place to sign the Medicare Act, in the presence of Mr. Truman, was acknowledgment that his predecessor had taken the first step toward Medicare when he fought a losing battle for a more sweeping measure almost twenty years earlier. Again, a plan of action which no practical politician would touch might change the climate in which an issue is joined, making feasible what hitherto would have been deemed impossible. The sit-downs in segregated places staged by well-mannered young Negro students a few years ago are a case in point. Much that came later flowed from these simple expressions of courage and dignity, the political feasibility of which at the time could not have been calculated because they were without precedent and because so much depended on the way they were carried out.

A decentralized political system like our own multiplies the actors whose judgments of feasibility significantly affect a policy decision. It would be too much to expect the President and a member of Congress of his party to strike the same balance on an issue affecting their political futures quite differently. A requisite of responsible party government, after all, is to put leaders and rank-and-file as nearly as possible in the same boat. The calculations of the political price to be paid for a course of action, a basic element in a judgment

---

[1] See Donald R. Matthews, *U.S. Senators and Their World* (Chapel Hill: University of North Carolina Press, 1960), pp. 103–9.

of political feasibility, likewise would vary widely. Two senators otherwise similarly situated, for example, might compute cost quite differently if one aspired to the White House and the other did not.

The purpose of this study is to state some of the conditions of political feasibility which seem to be operative in the making of national policy through the executive and legislative branches and the groups associated with them. The courts, active partners though they are, will not be included because they are somewhat isolated, their reaction is delayed, and the behavior appropriate to them is quite different, and because we shall have trouble enough without them. Moreover, it is policy-making in the here and now that we shall be talking about, not the slow evolution of major change.

I. THE PROBLEM

There are Americans who believe that almost any social problem that can be solved with money is within the competence of the U.S. government if only the attack on the problem is sufficiently massive. Indeed, there are many who seem to believe that *all* social problems could be tackled at once with adequate scope, if only the country would withdraw from Vietnam. Even a casual attention to what went on in congressional committees early in 1966 will bear this out. Again and again members decried attempts to hold down expenditures on this or that problem with the simple contention: But more is needed! And so it was. But the first point to be made is this: that for all its affluence, the American system cannot deal adequately with its acknowledged needs; that this is a system in which an allocation of scarce resources must indeed be made, with all the pain that inevitably entails.

No attempt will be made to catalogue the needs. Anyone can make a list in a few minutes which would overtax resources for years to come. Some samples will suffice. Water-pollution control, which has barely begun, could use $100 billion without wasting a cent. Hospital modernization, to replace 260,000 obsolete beds (and the 13,000 annual increment) would take at least $8 billion. Building 375,000 classrooms in the next five years would cost $15 billion. Building really modern urban transportation, re-creating core cities, breaking the poverty cycle of families by using all the health, education, and welfare resources in a coordinated way—each of these would cost immense sums. Put more accurately, each would call for trained manpower and other resources, which already are in short supply, far beyond any present capacity to meet the demand.

This catalogue of needs, some of them almost catastrophic in proportion, is all the more remarkable in the light of the efforts that have been made. The budget of the Public Health Service, for example, increased in twelve years from $250 million to $2.4 billion in fiscal 1967. The Office of Education spent only $539 million in 1961; in fiscal 1967 its budget was about $3.5 billion. Three sessions of Congress (1963–65) enacted twenty pieces of landmark legislation in health, nineteen in welfare.

The requirement that resources be allocated among needs that cannot be met poses the problem of priorities. Which is more important to society, intensive care for high-risk infants (40 percent of children who die in their first year die in their first day) or artificial kidneys to keep productive adults alive (there are facilities now for continuous treatment of 200 to 300 patients of a possible 10,000 who might be saved)? Head-start programs for disadvantaged preschoolers or basic education for disadvantaged adults? The problem is even harder when the claims of cancer research, say, are compared with the desirability of getting to the moon.

This is an academic discussion of little interest until one is forced by experience to realize that decisions on questions like these actually *do* have to be made and actually *are* being made. What happens to various segments of the population next year depends on these decisions. But what really is appalling is to know upon what flimsy data and partial information these choices often are made. It is perfectly possible, for instance, that it may be decided to increase the funds for adult basic education by a certain amount without the slightest notion of how many people have been taught to read, say, under the existing program. This is not said in criticism of anybody; the men who set the priorities feel their burdens heavily and they get the best help they can. The policy system simply is not geared to let them do better.

What considerations enter into the selection of priorities and the specific program designed to meet them? One, inevitably, is "political feasibility." Will it "go" on the Hill? Will the public buy it? Does it have political "sex appeal"? What "can't be done" is likely to get low priority. An administration bill must be passed if possible, and the men who bear the responsibility for that shrink from taking on one that may discredit them. Political columns like to run a Presidential "box score," and there is no place on it for the bill no one expected to pass, the bill that was introduced as part of the educational process necessary to enact the legislation later on. The "box score" mentality is likely to permeate the discussions of men charged with preparing the President's program. What determines political feasibility therefore is a matter of urgent concern.

Political feasibility as a consideration in national policy-making is, so far as I know, a term of art. It is a seat-of-the-pants judgment, based on the experience of the person making it. It may be shrewd indeed, or appear so, if the men pooling their experience are shrewd and artful men. It may be simply a repetition of some long-accepted and untested cliché about what public or politicians will do. For nearly two decades, for instance, many members of Congress have said in private conversations, "I favor recognizing Red China (or admitting her to the UN), but I wouldn't dare say it. It would be political suicide." How did they know? Again, it may be based on what representatives of interest groups have said, probably in all honesty, but from a remoteness from the currents that run in the country which only a man who spends twenty years in Washington can have. Political feasibility as a target will not track. Any consideration of it that gets anywhere must start from some assumptions and limit the task that is undertaken.

Let us begin therefore by assuming that it is possible to confront the policy system with a set of proposals that actually do maximize the benefits the American people can get from the expenditure of a given amount of appropriations—that is, an ideal allocation of scarce resources. As a matter of fact, a process designed to do just that already has been set in motion, a major innovation in the executive branch called Planning-Programming-Budgeting System (PPBS).[2] This system sets out to bring to the conference table where decisions are made an analysis based on the program goals of the government, and the relative success of various programs in achieving them, which will give the decision-makers the materials they need.

PPBS in the federal government originated in the Pentagon, where Secretary McNamara abandoned the old practice of considering a budget for each military service, with the traditional outlays for personnel, operations, equipment, and the like, in favor of a budget based on nine major defense missions. The weapons that could be assigned to each mission were listed without regard to the service that nominally claimed them. All costs of developing, procuring, and operating a weapon were assigned to it and the measure of defense provided by each system was determined. With this kind of information, choices among weapons and systems in terms of their costs and relative effectiveness could be made.

Because the goals of the Defense Department are relatively simple and consistent—deterrence of war, defense of the country, victory in war—PPBS encounters fewer problems there than in departments with many, perhaps conflicting, goals. Nevertheless, in the summer of 1965 President Johnson ordered more than eighty angencies comprising the executive branch to set up staffs capable of establishing the new system. Each agency is to set up broad program goals, with more specific subcategories. All operating programs with similar goals are to be placed in the appropriate category, regardless of the organizational units to which they are attached. If a program goal is stated as "Breaking the Poverty Cycle," for instance, it might require a grouping of programs in education, health, welfare, vocational rehabilitation, poverty, and perhaps others.

The costs of various programs could be established then and measured against specific benefits. The budget would be stated, not in terms of "inputs" —items for personnel, research, planning, etc.—but in the amount of reduction in delinquency, improvement in health or education, and so forth. Thus it would be possible to estimate which programs did more to achieve the goal per dollar expended.

PPBS aims ultimately to do more than help determine which programs contribute most to the same goal. The system would aim in time at measuring one goal against another, so that priorities could be set on the basis of knowledge of comparative benefits.

---

[2] See David Novick, ed., *Program Budgeting . . . Program Analysis and the Federal Budget* (Washington: U.S. Government Printing Office, 1964); *Budgeting for National Objectives* (New York: Committee for Economic Development, 1966); "Planning-Programming-Budgeting System: A Symposium," *Public Administration Review*, 26 (December 1966): 243–310.

I have not attempted to explain PPBS in any detail, but rather to set forth its basic assumptions and suggest how it will work. I wish to accept the most extreme claims that could be made for it—to assume that it could produce clear proof that one goal is socially preferable to another, and one way to reach it better than another; that a budget can be drawn which demonstrably gets the most benefits for the resources expended—as a basis for examining some of the structural arrangements in the political system which would have to be taken into account in putting its findings into effect. Of course, it is not necessary for PPBS to achieve anything like these extreme claims to be a highly useful tool of analysis, capable of introducing more rationality in decision-making. Neither is it necessary to postulate a successful PPBS to pose the problem: if pure social intelligence confronted the system with a program, could the system accept it and put it into effect? In a word, would the program be politically feasible?

II. THE EXECUTIVE BRANCH

The classic solution to decentralized national power is more power concentrated in the President. He is the one official elected by the people. He is the one person charged with, and capable of, thinking about the national interest. It would seem therefore that the social intelligence made available by a perfected PPBS would inevitably strengthen his hand. Perhaps it would. Nevertheless, a few more studies that concentrated on the President himself as a political man, trying to survive and have his way (like Neustadt's *Presidential Power*),[3] studies whose authors are not hypnotized by the many hats he wears, might suggest some difficulties the President will have if and when he is confronted by the national program he (or his predecessor) has caused to be made. I have not made such a study and probably never will, but perhaps I can suggest a couple of places a student might look for the answers such a study would provide.

One is the peculiarly vulnerable political position of the President. He is the one American politician who cannot hide. He must be prepared at all times for whatever ill wind may blow. Moreover, his power depends to some extent at least on never surrendering the initiative for very long—or so it must seem to him. When a competitor threatens to propose something good, the temptation is strong for the President to occupy the field first, or to deluge it with something Presidential in scope if he cannot.[4] If there is a carefully

---

[3] Richard E. Neustadt, *Presidential Power* (New York: John Wiley & Sons, 1960).

[4] An example of the President's need to maintain (or regain) the initiative, especially in an election year, was Mr. Johnson's widely previewed speech in Baltimore on October 10, 1966, asking for changes in the social security system which included a 10 percent benefit increase *in the next session of Congress*. The regular procedures of legislative program-building were bypassed. The Republicans promptly responded by demanding that the changes be made in the 89th Congress, which had less than two weeks of life left to it.

constructed legislative proposal at hand, so much the better. If there is not, something may very well be proposed anyway. If he finds himself in congenial company, he, like other men, may suggest what the country needs. Once it has been said, however casually, the machinery works inexorably. Furthermore, the bill that goes up must be passed if possible. Failure catches on much more quickly than success. (Exceptions might occur in election years, when a proposal that cannot pass might make a good campaign issue.) Finally, it is reasonable to doubt whether a President can be the good shepherd of a program someone else has made, even though it be made by his own people and the very best computers. The drama of leadership, of his awful isolation, of his lonely decisions, is the great weapon in his armory.

The second area worth the student's investigation would be the network of executive staff which can truly be called Presidential. This might be stretched to include the Presidential appointees in the agencies, whose loyalty to him usually is dependable, though their lack of intimate knowledge of much of his business reduces their direct usefulness to him almost to the vanishing point. It certainly would not include the bureaucracy, the source of information both branches perforce rely upon, but which in its multitudinous bureaus, divisions, and offices is no more certainly allied to him than to congressional committees or interest groups—or to nobody. Those that remain —the tiny White House staff and the Bureau of the Budget (an effective staff arm whose political judgment often is affected, alas, by its preoccupation with the budget)—are not really a match for the bureaucracy. They are in the sense that they speak for the President and so may have the last word. They are not in the sense of information and expertise. In having the last word, which they must if the President is to have his way, they often overrule the work of months with judgments made in haste and under pressure. Like Congress, they can deal really effectively with the bureaucracy's expertise only by constructing a bureaucracy of their own. If to the weight of experience and expertise which they now bring to the table the bureaucracy could add the authority of PPBS, what then would the President's people do? It must be remembered, after all, that each agency has its own PPBS. Obviously, it is crucial that the ultimate formulations of PPBS would have to be brought under the President's control, with all the very human intrusions on computerized rationality that implies.

The heart of the matter probably is that no intellectual system—and certainly not PPBS—is designed to produce a single right policy, but rather to present policy alternatives, with analyses of the costs and benefits of each. The President would have the advice of his agency heads based on their choices. In all likelihood he would also have his own staff of professional program specialists who would work with agency counterparts and assist him with his own decisions, as members of the Bureau of the Budget staff do now in their own fields. If their advice sometimes reflected their own policy biases, they would be no more guilty of human frailty than are the agency planners. In a word, there are no insurmountable difficulties in the way of getting to the President the kind of advice PPBS can give; the problem would be to get for

PPBS the kind of political respectability and acceptance that would cause the President to heed it against the other influences that bear upon him.

The character of the bureaucracy presents problems for unified policy, some of which appear, at least, to be insoluble. First there is the inescapable question of the basis upon which an agency should be organized. By function —health, education, welfare—which augments professionalization and promises a high quality of service? By clientele—labor, farmers, commerce—which has a kind of built-in coherence? By ecological unit—the core city, the river basin for water-pollution control—which encompasses a broad array of related problems? By problem—poverty, crime—which calls for the application and coordination of many services? Each has its justification and all are actually used, of course. No single organizational structure will do for all, nor is it judicious to try to apply logical consistency to their division of labor. If all education were to be placed in the Office of Education, for instance, more than fifty agencies would have to surrender programs to it. The Office of Education would have to administer the three military service academies, the Department of State's foreign service school, Agriculture's graduate school, and the in-service training programs of all the agencies of the federal government—to name only a few. It is safe to say that if any large department tried to claim all the programs that might logically be assigned to it, the federal executive branch would grind to a stop.

Needless to say, overlapping and duplication of effort are inevitable, inspiring the continuous demand for "coordination." But coordination is more easily subscribed to than accomplished. Agencies perforce are parochial; they think in terms of their own statutory authority, operating structure, and clientele. Even plans they make for coordination tend to have agency perimeters. One proposal that has won a high degree of acceptance from all the relevant agencies, to give an example, is the so-called "multipurpose" (or "one-stop") neighborhood center, containing under one roof all the services that a family is likely to need. But when agencies submit concrete plans, they usually are *single-agency* "multipurpose" centers.

The problem of parochialism is exaggerated by the occupational immobility of the civil service. It is not uncommon for careers to be spent wholly in one department, perhaps in a single bureau. Transfers within the bureaucracy threaten status and a way of life; when they take employees outside the civil service, even to Capitol Hill, they disturb and may temporarily destroy retirement rights, to mention only one of a host of disabilities. But clearly, if the flexibility and innovation implicit in PPBS are to be exploited, it must be possible to reduce, perhaps eliminate, some organizational entities. This is incredibly difficult where employees have a justifiable vested interest in their jobs, which they are quick to protect. When a thirty-year man in the bureaucracy takes his grievance to Congress (where occupational immobility is perhaps the supreme value), he is sure of a sympathetic hearing from members he has worked with for years. There is much talk about occupational mobility among officials in the bureaucracy, but little more than talk. What is needed, if PPBS or something like it is to succeed, is a genuine career line in the civil service (not in a particular agency) with easy transferability from one agency to another. More than that, genuine mobility requires an easy flow into and out of private employment, with vested rights in retirement and all the other elements of job security. This would seem to be relatively simple with professionals, whose central loyalty tends to be to their own disciplines, but probably very difficult to achieve with nonprofessionals, whose loyalties and habits are agency-oriented.

To the political people who man the President's program, the relationship of civil servants to Congress is perennially troubling. At one extreme, bureaucrats may resist *all* political considerations, rejecting job applications tainted with congressional recommendations, ignoring legislative intent in administering the laws, and refusing to consider the effect of political reactions on the success of their own legislative and appropriation bills. On the other hand, bureaucrats who know full well the transience of their political superiors may build up mutually advantageous relationships with relevant committees which defy the wishes and will of the President himself. In between are the political "volunteers" who gratuitously help with the legislative process, threatening delicate relationships with sadly misplaced self-confidence. Needless to say, each in his way will obstruct or dilute any coherent Presidential program.

III. THE LEGISLATIVE BRANCH

When a programmatic approach to national policy is mentioned, any student of American government with adequate reflexes is bound to say "Congress." The inability of Congress to consider, at any stage of the legislative process, the whole sweep of a program sponsored by the President is notorious, and a fair number of political scientists have made a respectable living emphasizing it.[5] The outlines hardly need repeating. The party leadership is weak. The committee chairmen, selected by seniority, are strong. The result is a kind of confederation of little legislatures, some of them fragmented even further into subcommittees with specialized jurisdictions which have managed to become small feudalities in their own right. This is the system that baffles the champions of responsible party government, and it is this system that has kept Congress strong. One by one, other national legislatures subservient to party leadership (for which read "executive") have been turned into passive parti-

[5] Twenty years after the enactment of the Legislative Reorganization Act of 1946, a joint Committee on the Organization of Congress (one of whose cochairmen was Senator Mike Monroney, who as a member of the House of Representatives had co-authored the 1946 act) tackled anew the problem of congressional reform. Eleven monographs written by political scientists were published by the American Enterprise Institute for Public Policy Research to assist the joint committee. They were later published by American Enterprise under the editorship of Alfred de Grazia as *Congress: The First Branch of Government* (Washington, 1966). Another political science treatise, titled much the same as other books appearing over the two decades, was Roger H. Davidson, David M. Kovenock, and Michael K. O'Leary, *Congress in Crisis: Politics and Congressional Reform* (Belmont, Calif.: Wadsworth Publishing Company, 1966).

sans whose hope of sharing power depends upon their climbing into the
executive themselves. Not so Congress. Committee chairmen often care about
the President's wishes, even when he belongs to the other party. They usually
take an administration bill seriously—even if only as a point of departure,
which it often is when the President's party is in a minority on the committee.
But they cannot be forced by party leadership in either branch. Indeed, when
administration spokesmen go as a matter of courtesy to discuss their programs with congressional party leaders, the latter are polite but not much
interested. They know that their work begins after the committee has reported
a bill.

The organization of Congress around specialized concerns shapes the
entire system that makes legislation. It is fashionable to speak of a "legislative
system," which includes Congress, the interest groups that serve and influence
it, the executive agencies that must deal with it, the press that writes about it,
and the constituencies that reward and punish and occasionally know what is
going on. It is more accurate, I think, to begin with the committees and speak
of the *policy system*, which is focused about each pair of committees that
shares similar, if not identical, jurisdiction. There are interest groups that
have commitments ranging across a broad sweep of the legislative spectrum,
and there are executive departments with similarly large responsibilities. Just
the same, none is likely to deal regularly with more than four or five
committees in either house, and then there probably is specialization on their
legislative staffs. Large newspapers are likely also to develop subject-matter
experts on their staffs. More common than the giants by far are the groups
with a single interest (albeit a broad one, like higher education), and the
executive agency with one or a handful of bills, all of whose business is done
with a single committee in each house. The term "constituency" likewise
begins to make sense when it signifies numerous specialized interests that are
likely to get involved only when those interests are touched. The concept of
the mass constituency is hardly more useful analytically than the notion of a
mass public.

Two points perhaps should be stressed. The first is the relative isolation
that develops around each of these policy systems. They are like planes that
cut each other only at points of decision-making, such as the roll-call vote on
the floor. One reason for the unresponsiveness of Congress to Presidential
pleas for economy in 1966 (in the early days of the session, at least)
undoubtedly was the submersion of each committee and its associates in their
own work, which they knew to be vitally important. The President was right,
of course, but he certainly must have been talking about somebody else. Only
after heroic efforts on the President's part did the message begin to sink in
that he was talking about, and to, everybody. The sense of isolation is less
stark in the Senate, where each member belongs to more than one committee
and several subcommittees. But the result ultimately is the same, or worse.
The burden of many assignments requires the members to rely heavily on
committee staff. Needless to say, these persons are experts if they can be, their

fierce specialization unrelieved by the varied life of chamber and constituency which tends to liberate the minds of their principals.

The second point to be emphasized is the very large measure of control over the business in their charge by each of these policy systems. This too may be demonstrated many times over in the second session of the 89th Congress. After unprecedented success with a huge legislative program the year before, President Johnson decided, because of the Vietnam war and threats of inflation, to make only modest increases in most programs and actual cuts in some. One of the latter was aid to school districts that bore the impact of federal installations, in which he proposed a sharp reduction on the ground that the large sums available under new federal education programs justified it. Roughly 315 congressional districts were affected. The two education committees agreed with the powerful impacted-area lobby that it was not worth discussing—and they did not discuss it. The Secretary of Health, Education, and Welfare was not asked a single question about it in either house. In their own good time the committees increased the authorization.

An incident equally revealing concerned the President's proposal to convert the direct loans to students under the National Defense Education Act to private loans guaranteed by the government. The education subcommittee in the House believed the colleges needed to know what they could count on for the next year, whereupon by a simple unanimous vote in executive session they eliminated that title from the bill. It is significant that the colleges could not know what they could count on then unless they had complete confidence the subcommittee action would stand. The subcommittee never doubted they would have that confidence, and they did.

IV. COMMENTS ON POLITICAL FEASIBILITY

If the foregoing sketch of the policy systems that pool their respective programs to make the national policy is reasonably correct, it should be possible now to make some suggestions about political feasibility at the national level.

What is least feasible is what requires serious, responsible consideration of some unitary conception of national need. Congress does not manage it, does not try to do so, and with its present power structure is virtually incapable of trying. With the President the case is not so clear. He does indeed present his "program" in the early months of the year, in successive unveilings marked by messages to Congress. Viewed uncharitably, they represent an agglomeration of most of the programs the policy systems would have insisted on anyway. Nevertheless, they bear his imprint. The President—in the institutional sense at least and, in what matters most, personally—has considered them all and supplied emphasis. Moreover, his notions of relative weights are expressed in his budget, the only genuinely unitary policy instrument in national life. Congress, it may be said in passing, cannot even pretend to look at national policy whole until it develops an institutional capacity to cope with the concept of a budget. Needless to say, once the budget is delivered to Congress and dismembered among its subcommittees, the President too virtually abandons the unitary view and plays the congressional game: he fights for his bills.

Low feasibility also must be attached to whatever is genuinely new or innovative, especially if it can be successfully labeled as such, and more especially if it rubs an ideological nerve. What is most feasible is what is purely incremental, or can be made to appear so. Paradoxically, it is politically attractive to tout a proposal as "new" so long as it is generally recognized that it is not new at all, but a variation on a familiar theme. But the political art can make feasible what is not feasible by finding halfway houses (what the lawyers might call "quasis") which supply at least part of what is needed under the guise of doing something else. Halfway houses may become so numerous and large they occupy the field; nevertheless, a simple declaration that this is so may cause bitter controversy.

Examples are legion. President Hoover's misfortunes demonstrated for those who could learn that the President must accept, or have thrust upon him, responsibility for the health of the economy. President Roosevelt demonstrated that he had learned the leasson well; his twelve years in the White House were studded with attempts to mend the health and even the structure of the economy. Just the same, a watered-down policy statement of national responsibility for employment had real trouble in Congress as late as 1946. Again, the federal government had been the most important influence in the housing market long before a bill plainly marked "housing" could pass finally in 1949. In education, the three furies—federal interference, racial strife, church and state—never sleep, but they doze; they can be stepped around. Veterans can be helped, federally impacted areas aided, education for national defense fostered, disadvantaged children succored. All this so long as the dread concepts are not invoked by name.

The halfway-house approach comes at a high price, it must be admitted. It cannot face a whole problem frankly and try to do what needs to be done, and usually it cannot deal equitably among respective claimants for federal benefits. Moreover, what is accomplished this way becomes imbedded in law. Beneficiaries may support broader, better laws when the climate is propitious, but they will not let go what they have. The legislative halfway house tends to be as permanent as a temporary government building.

It follows that what is most feasible is what is incremental, what can be made to seem a comfortable next step under a program that has already received the good-conduct medal. Nothing is better than an amendment. A once hated housing law becomes an annual invitation to try to get something else under a respected umbrella, where it may take shelter forevermore. A higher education bill that was killed in conference in 1962 by a telegram and passed with great exertion in 1963 was renewed and extended by the House of Representatives in 1966 under suspension of the rules, without a recorded vote. No one fears the familiar; nothing succeeds like success: in politics the bromides are the best guides.

All of this is not meant to say that the approach to policy represented by PPBS is doomed to futility. Far from it. Even if it is only modestly successful in the kind of analysis it will attempt, its weight in the policy process should not be discounted. Who would deny that the unitary approach represented by the budget has had a real, if incalculable, influence on the conduct of the national government? It is without doubt the most formidable policy tool the President has. So could it be with systematic program planning: a President who can support his values with the authority of science will be a formidable competitor indeed. Rationality is respected, sometimes irrationally, in a democratic society.

The history of the national budget may provide an answer to our original question: if social intelligence could confront the policy system with a program that would maximize the benefits to be received from the exertions of the federal government, could that program ever be made politically feasible? The budget experience suggests it could. The budget was adopted because it had to be; the fiscal system could no longer afford the luxury of irresponsibility. The decentralized policy structure with its many policy systems which has evolved here under our constitutional separation of institutions has many virtues: diversity of skills, creativeness within appointed bounds, easy public access to a multiplicity of decision points, openness in the conduct of public business, hospitality to ideas, continuous political education for those who pay attention, and the enormous stimulation that comes with the opportunity to fashion great careers. Nevertheless, the sheer weight of items on the national agenda will require that choices be made, which in turn could force changes in process and structure to make possible a more coherent approach to the needs of the system.

12

The Social Sciences: Maturity, Relevance, and the Problem of Training*

DAVID B. TRUMAN

The political scientist has a special sort of concern for the substance of public policy. His attention is focused, by convention and by the academic division of labor, upon the forms and processes from which public policies emerge. In consequence and almost inescapably he may feel, and his associates and critics may demand, that he must have something to say about the content of those policies. But the connections between his acknowledged professional competence in matters of form and process and his assumed ability to offer professional recommendations concerning substance are far from simple, as the preceding essays in this volume indicate. Despite his special concerns, however, the political scientist's problems in dealing with the substance of policy are not unique. Most of his intellectual perplexities in this area are shared by the entire community of social scientists. This essay is therefore directed to that larger community and to those whom they may serve, as well as to political scientists and to those who look to political scientists for assistance.

The bearing of the social sciences on public policy is a broad but also a treacherous area. It is, in consequence, often and prudently avoided. To examine it risks, among other things, exposing to view past embarrassments that we would prefer to forget, records of youthful excesses, sources of controversy so recently dispatched as to be menacingly current, and evidences of the gap between our aspirations or pretensions and our performance. Small wonder that on most occasions the problem is exorcised and ignored.

* A revised version of a vice-presidential address delivered before Section K of the American Association for the Advancement of Science, New York City, December 27, 1967, and subsequently published in *Science*, 1968, pp. 508–12.

Despite our strenuous efforts, however, the problem reappears. The data of our concerns, if not the constructs with which we work, are never far from the arena of public decision. Our own motivations, however dominated by intellectual fascination, are often and not obscurely rooted in an early and persistent interest in the public weal. This fact we may suppress, but we cannot dispose so easily of the prudential consideration that if our inquiries, strongly though of course inadequately supported by public and quasi-public funds, are not in some increasing measure pertinent to public and governmental decisions, we can hardly expect such support to be forthcoming indefinitely. An art or a science, any science, must be partly, perhaps even predominantly, an end in itself; basic research, however we may agree to define it, is its own first justification. But an art or a science, if it is to be supported and not merely tolerated by a society, also must be, or give prospect of being, pleasing or instructive or useful. Since we bring pleasure to few beyond our own ranks and since our instructiveness is frequently limited, even among the young, by the propensity for every man to be his own social scientist, we can scarcely afford to reject the value of usefulness.

The problem acquires a current and more serious insistence from the evidence that out of the secondary and tertiary effects of accelerating technological change is emerging a range of problems to which the social sciences are presumptively relevant. New or altered technologies directly and indirectly challenge the adaptive potential of public policy. What is at stake in the quality of emerging public policy is not merely whether means can be found to avoid critical dislocations and destructive reactions to change. At issue also is the more fundamental question that has motivated groups such as the Commission on the Year 2000: Can policy be so taken as to provide moral choices among recognizable alternatives? These policies are not the domain of the social sciences, but it is reasonable to expect that these sciences should be able to offer substantial assistance in defining issues, shaping alternatives, and anticipating consequences. An attempt of this kind and degree of involvement in public policy can hardly be avoided.

Meeting the challenge of relevance, however, cannot be reduced to an act of will or to a collection of well-intentioned commitments to the discharge of a public obligation. It is entangled with aspects of the history of the social sciences, especially in this country, and with features of their development as sciences that seriously complicate the form and quality of their participation in the making of policy. These complications may be in the process of becoming more restrictive. If this is the case, then it may be desirable to reexamine the forms and channels of such participation and reassess the allocation of our collective energies.

I. BACKGROUND INFLUENCES

American social scientists have reason, drawn from the history of their disciplines, for being cautious about assuming the sponsorship of any innovation in public policy. Their institutional memories have not forgotten the first decade or two of this century, when their predecessors with rare exceptions were conspicuously overready to claim for particular "reform" programs and policies the authority of their fields of study. They were a major reliance of the Progressive movement in its various forms and, to a lesser degree, of its adversaries. Less close, perhaps, to points of real influence than are their counterparts today, they made up in certainty of pronouncement what they lacked in power.

The civic motivations underlying these involvements cannot be questioned. Nor can one justifiably, even with the wisdom of hindsight, say that all of the proposals they championed were unsound or counterproductive. One can reasonably argue, however, that in general they were intellectually premature and scientifically innocent. Inadequately supported by empirical data and lacking, for the most part, any but the most simplistic theoretical foundation, they were relevant, as a newspaper editorial may be relevant, but almost entirely lacking in rigor and in anticipation of consequences.

In the years after World War I what might be described as a reaction against this kind of premature relevance developed. Stronger and more needed in some fields than others, and often not explicitly acknowledged as a rejection of the earlier involvements, since its origins were in fact much more complex, it took the form of an increased preoccupation with the several fields as disciplines and with social science as science. This concern was for a time especially marked in a collective search for stronger data and improved research techniques.

Illustrative of and important to the new emphasis was the establishment of the Social Science Research Council in 1924, distinctive, especially in its early years, for its concern with *common* problems intrinsic to research and especially with research techniques. This was a period in which at least the assumption of a joint perspective was at a maximum. It produced at least one seriously regarded manual of methods purporting to cover the whole range of the social sciences.[1] During these years also the first edition of the *Encyclopaedia of the Social Sciences* was conceived, marking a high point of collective and common concern among a large fraction of at least the leaders in most of the social science fields.

II. DEVELOPMENTS BETWEEN THE WARS

If one were to write an adequate history of these disciplines during the quarter century following the First World War, he would likely find himself emphasizing at least two significant developments. In the first place, the period seems to have provided the conditions required for rapid and fruitful advances in the social sciences. Looking only at those influences internal to the American setting—probably the most important, though clearly not the only ones of importance—he would note a strong preoccupation with more

---

[1] Stuart A. Rice, ed., *Methods in Social Science* (Chicago: University of Chicago Press, 1933).

sophisticated and systematic approaches to problems and data, one aspect of the reaction against the naïvely based policy involvements already referred to. He would also record an increase in funds available for research, chiefly from foundations. These were small by current standards, but substantial in comparison with those of any earlier day. Finally, he would have to reckon with the indications that during this period there was actively at work in the United States a sufficient number of social scientists, overall if not in each discipline, to constitute a community. The frequency and the character of the contacts among the members of this community seem to have provided both stimulus and reinforcement to new developments. The significance of this matter of numbers and relationships can scarcely be exaggerated. These three conditions in the United States in the years after World War I were peculiarly favorable to a "takeoff" by the social sciences and to their achievement of greater sophistication and competence.

The second significant development in this period that probably would be emphasized by a historical analysis would be certain aspects of the increased sophistication that grew from these favorable conditions. The growth in skill and technicality was, of course, uneven. Some fields inevitably developed more rapidly and more fruitfully than others, but the general trend was consistent. Paradoxically, however, as such growth took place it was associated with a decline or shift in the common perspectives that marked the beginning of the trend and with some reduction in the concern of the several disciplines for public policy.

An increase in intellectual competence could hardly have occurred if many practitioners in each field had not devoted their energies disproportionately not only to the discipline as such, but also to more or less distinct technical segments of each field. A decline in perspectives common to the several disciplines was thus almost inevitable. One may suspect that this natural tendency has been further encouraged by the rapid increase in numbers of social scientists since 1945, so that an influence that earlier seems to have fostered a collaborative community of social scientists assisted, as numbers grew larger, in later segmenting the social sciences into a series of communities. It would not be a complete exaggeration to say that what these "communities" retained in common were chiefly their problems of "external relations"—the form and volume of governmental support of the social sciences, professional problems concerning the privacy of human subjects, and the like. It seems likely that communication on most other matters affecting the social sciences increasingly has been restricted to the segmented "communities." This tendency presumably had something to do with the skepticism that met proposals in the 1950's to compile a new *Encyclopaedia of the Social Sciences*. Although the enterprise was subsequently undertaken and completed, critics argued that these disciplines had outgrown any such unified compendium and that the utility of an encyclopedia would be restricted by the specialized interests of the prospective users.

An apparently reduced concern of the social sciences for public policy, despite greater sophistication, is a related but more complex matter. If one mark of a developing discipline is that it sets its own agenda in terms of those things that its members as scientists regard as important, then at least a temporary withdrawal from the area of public policy is to be expected as the social science matures. If the preoccupations that in large part define a discipline are being set by the problems of public policy, then in some measure they are not being set by the problems that confront the discipline itself as an intellectual enterprise. The alternatives are in fact usually not as sharply separable as this statement may suggest, but the tendency and its underlying logic seem perfectly clear. Especially given the inclination in all of the sciences to grant the highest prestige to those members whose work is most completely oriented to the discipline, the theoreticians, a turning away from policy concerns as a field matures is scarcely remarkable.

In a very real sense, moreover, a more sophisticated discipline becomes increasingly irrelevant to public policy. Sciences seem to develop in two ways, both of which contribute to this outcome by confining, in effect, their impingements on policy to segments of their enterprise. In the first mode of development, systematic, theoretically valuable work proceeds by successive abstractions from reality or simplifications of reality, portions or aspects of the phenomenal world being postulated, assumed, or controlled in the interests of precision and manageability. Although in various ways complexity can be reintroduced and phenomena brought back from limbo, the science does not reproduce reality. Its bearing on the complex world of public policy therefore remains in some degree segmental. The segment may, of course, be useful in the making of policy, but one suspects that this utility is achieved, when it is, through another process that is not science, though obviously it is related to it. They are perhaps correct who argue that, as a social science reaches a point where its practitioners begin to understand the causal relationships underlying change, pertinent social policy will become more effective. But they seem to ignore or at least underestimate the problems and pitfalls that lie between such sharpened understanding and altered policy.

The second path of scientific development is through specialization and at least to a degree through subspecialization. This is a process that is inherently segmental and even divisive. Its segmental character can be seen readily when a group of specialists is assembled to discuss a policy matter or quasi-policy area that extends beyond any of their individual disciplines. Each participant, following the assumptions and procedures of his specialty, defines the problem differently. If communication occurs and certainly if any sort of joint effort is achieved, either a means of simultaneous translation must be found or one set of participants, drawing on higher disciplinary prestige or on force of personality, must succeed in imposing its formulation on the others. Divisiveness is also illustrated by the difficulty, in this time of rapid growth of information, that the specialist encounters, even if the translation problem is absent, in knowing what is known in closely proximate specialties. His remoteness, and the waste and frustration involved in rediscovering the discovered, lead to what Margaret Mead, in another context, calls "a rebellion of the educated man against a new kind of ignorance . . . not the stimulating ignorance of the unknown, but the ignorance of what is already known."[2]

For the public official the sources of these impediments are of less concern than the fact of apparently limited relevance. The social sciences, for the most part, have not become so esoteric and so specialized that even their presumptive bearing on a policy problem is unclear. Perhaps they never will reach such a point. But they are becoming sufficiently segmental and specialized in character that the public official who turns to them risks either hearing little but noise or receiving "fractional advice to deal with whole policy," as William T. R. Fox expresses the problem presented by the natural scientists.[3]

Some increased isolation of the social sciences from each other and some increased obstacles to a direct pertinence of the social sciences to public policy are clearly unavoidable. A growth in rigor leads inevitably to greater self-consciousness in a discipline, to the setting of priorities and agendas of research in terms of the assumptions and requirements of the discipline—as seen by the practitioners themselves—and consequently to remoteness from each other and from the full, complex reality of problems in the political arena. The contrast, of course, is not between a simpler, less pretentious set of social sciences, fully sensitive and pertinent to the range of policy, on the one hand, and a more sophisticated group of disciplines paradoxically rendered socially impotent by an increase in power that is purely scholastic on the other. It is rather between a set of presciences scarcely distinguishable from the folklore and wisdom operating in the marketplace and a group of sciences or nascent sciences that have attempted to set themselves intellectually manageable problems by abstracting in various degrees from reality, by discarding some of its features, and hence have created the problem of relevance as they have separated themselves from folklore, from each other, and from the totality of the policy complex.

III. POLICY RELEVANCE AS A PROBLEM

The problem of relevance remains, however, and if one is justified in projecting the trends of the past two decades, it will become more visible and probably more troublesome. This relevancy problem, as the forgoing discussion implies, has at least two dimensions. One is the proportion of the research energy of the social sciences that is allocated to the solution of problems that emerge primarily from the needs of the discipline or subdiscipline as an intellectual enterprise. (I use the word "primarily" because I realize that this is a matter far subtler and more complex than the flat statement

---

[2] Margaret Mead, "Conference Behavior," *Columbia University Forum*, 10, no. 2 (Summer 1967) : 16.

[3] William T. R. Fox, "Science in International Politics" (keynote address, eighth annual convention of the International Studies Association, April 14, 1967), mimeographed, p. 12.

suggests.) The second is the degree of effectiveness in focusing or merging the technical elements of these sciences so the gap between them and the policy problem as a complex whole is reduced to minimal and hopefully manageable proportions. I propose to concentrate my attention on the second dimension of the problem, in part because I should expect that if solutions to it can be approximated, the first will take care of itself.

Consideration of this second dimension of the question of relevance—the problem of focusing the elements of the social sciences on a reasonable approximation of the public policy issue—can usefully employ the distinctions proposed by Don K. Price among four broad functions or "estates" in the area of governmental affairs: the scientific, the professional, the administrative, and the political.[4]

Without trying to reproduce his analysis, one may recall that the principal distinction between the scientific and the professional functions is that while the former has progressed by cutting itself off from concern with purpose, "except the abstract purpose of advancing truth and knowledge," the latter is "organized around a combination of a social purpose and a body of knowledge, much of it drawn from science." The administrators, on the other hand, although necessarily and deeply involved with purpose and value, somewhat resemble but are not, in this sense, professionals, since, unlike engineers or physicians, they cannot be identified by a particular social purpose distinguishable from the purposes of their political superiors or by a definite body of knowledge that specified their training and the criteria for admission to their ranks.

The professions, as Price conceives them, are related almost exclusively to the natural sciences. Both these sciences as such and the professions are, of course, in varying degrees directly involved in public affairs. Together, however, they provide a variety and differentiation for the public concerns growing out of natural science that are almost wholly lacking in connection with the social sciences. For perfectly understandable historical reasons, professions drawing their distinctive knowledge from the social sciences have not yet clearly emerged. Even the legal profession, which comes as close as any, does not yet bear the same relation to economics or psychology that the engineering profession does to physics or chemistry. Some aspects of operations research may be developing in this direction, but this is not yet clear.

This lack of functional differentiation means that in policy areas pertinent to the social sciences, the relating of scientific knowledge to political purpose may be attempted by the scientist, but it is more likely to be attempted, unaided, by the administrator. The social scientist's attempts at relating scientific knowledge to political purpose involve an awkward mixture of functions. To be sure, an increasingly sophisticated set of social sciences can contribute to the sharpening of the criteria of judgment and can even identify emerging policy problems with increased speed and precision. But

---

[4] Don K. Price, *The Scientific Estate* (Cambridge: Harvard University Press, 1965), pp. 132ff. See also Chapter 1 above.

these potentialities in themselves are not sufficient to narrow significantly the gap between the sciences and the policy complex. Something more is necessary.

Three kinds of development may provide at least a part of the something more. One is the practice, as yet limited and rather localized, of a frequent but apparently largely unplanned interchange between governmental administrative positions and university positions. This alternation of roles is valuable and probably should be explored and encouraged on a systematic basis. It has limitations on both sides, however. On the governmental side, it brings into the policy arena in any particular instance only one scientific specialty. A merger of specialties, where desirable, is not provided for. Further, such in-and-out arrangements may sacrifice a continuity of administrative experience that may be important in itself. On the science side, prolonged absence from the research arena may retard or even block the scientific accomplishments of the man who attempts so to interchange roles. A second device is the partial interchange of roles that may be accomplished through regular seminars or conferences between social scientists and administrators, in which each program is a carefully designed combination or an alternation of scientific developments and policy problems, unlike the normal consultant relationship. Imaginatively used, these devices can avoid the wasteful limitations of most conferences, with which all of us have had too much experience, and they clearly can help to meet the problem. They are likely, however, to fall short of an effective fusion of specialties. The third device is the familiar multidisciplinary team characteristic of the nonprofit institute working on contract. It clearly can provide flexible combinations of specialties and can, at least under some circumstances, occupy a portion of the gap between scientific knowledge and public purpose. It may, however, depending on qualities of staff, management, and contract arrangements, risk losing its gap-narrowing potential if it moves toward a preoccupation identical with that of either the policy-maker or the scientist, and its distinctiveness may, at least in the area of the social sciences, place it at a crippling distance from both.

IV. TRAINING THE PUBLIC ADMINISTRATOR

The limitations on all these devices plus the essential absence of pertinent professional structures thus indicate that the problem of making social science relevant to public policy is peculiarly a burden upon the public administrator, whether he recognizes it or not. Who he is, what he knows, and what skills he possesses, therefore, not only are matters of general public consequence, but also need to be serious collective concerns of the social sciences.

These concerns the social scientists seem to be neglecting. In fact, there is considerable danger that the very trends that have led to the strengthened competence of the social scientists as such have encouraged and contributed to that neglect. Ironically for a set of disciplines operating primarily from institutions of higher education, the seat of the neglect seems to be in the educational process, and particularly in the college and university. The ability of the administrator to give social science an appropriate relevance to public policy will depend heavily on his education.

This is one aspect of the general problem of how to train governmental administrators, one far broader than that under discussion. Appropriate to the narrower focus, however, is Price's proposition that the education of the administrator "cannot be reduced to a specific discipline or a restricted field," which follows from his conception of the function. If this is the case in general, it surely pertains no less accurately to the education of administrators to make effective and relevant policy use of a set of increasingly specialized and technical disciplines.

The general features of such an education certainly would involve a broad acquaintance with the theories, methods, and problems, including ways of stating problems, that characterize the several disciplines. If it is to be a training that is to be not *about* social science but *in* social science, it must also involve experience sufficiently advanced to include doing some scientific work, as part of a collective enterprise or individually. It is most unlikely that a critical understanding of the difficulties, limitations, and pitfalls of work in any social science can be acquired without really doing some.

These are reasonable and, one suspects, acceptable objectives. The difficulty is that they are not easily compatible with each other, with what appear to be the requirements for a career in one of the disciplines, or with the tendencies of current practice. The visible signs and the underlying pressures overwhelmingly indicate that, for all students, the second objective, technical proficiency in a discipline, is dominant and increasingly so.

Students, especially able students, who are always in short supply, become essentially the property of a department or even an individual professor, not only at the graduate level, but even during the undergraduate years. The requirements of the major at the undergraduate stage and the departmental Ph.D. program in the graduate years take an early and often almost preclusive priority. At its most defensible, and it is defensible, this pattern is aimed at the entirely reasonable goal of bringing the able and motivated student to the highest possible level of technical proficiency with minimal loss of the time, energy, and imagination that are the rapidly wasting assets of those years. This serves, and presumably well serves, the purpose of advancing the discipline and the competence of its practitioners. It is at least questionable, however, whether it meets the need for training public administrators, and incidentally whether it constitutes good education.

It is perhaps appropriate to suggest that influences other than promotion of the discipline also contribute to this pattern of training. A desire to reproduce one's specialized self in one's students is at least unconsciously influential. Appearances suggest also that the rate of production of young specialists is one of the key but unacknowledged counters in the genteel rivalries between departments, institutions, and even individual teachers that are obviously a part, and not necessarily an unhealthful part, of the academic climate.

Collectively these influences gain strength from the inclinations and dilemmas of students themselves, especially at the undergraduate level and particularly among able undergraduates. Despite the considerable amount of nonsense that is being uttered about them, it does seem clear that a large fraction of the ablest feel the need for a kind of closure, for the certainty of a clear objective in a world of multiple options. This many of them can find in a complete preoccupation with the major discipline. They are encouraged in this direction, moreover, not only by approving responses from their instructors, but also by their own estimates, as they contemplate the competition for entrance to a Ph.D. program, of what will do them good in the eyes of a departmental admissions committee. For the admitted graduate student this kind of specialized commitment is not only natural, but almost certainly necessary. It also is desirable in some degree at the undergraduate stage, but in what degree? The prospects for training an adequate number of competent generalist-administrators are likely to turn on how that question is answered.

Another tendency that deserves mention in this general connection is the interdisciplinary competition implicit in most efforts by social scientists to alter the curricula of the secondary schools. Such efforts are not to be deplored. They are long overdue and they have not gone far enough toward correcting the dilution of quality that followed the society's commitment half a century ago to mass education through the high school. What is questionable about these undertakings is that for the most part they have been a matter of each discipline for itself, and the effort has been not merely to improve the quality of teaching materials, but also to stake out a new or enlarged claim for each discipline in the limited time budget of the secondary school. In asserting these claims, little or nothing is asked or said about their proper relations with cognate disciplines. Reconciliation tends to be left to chance, to bargaining, or to the peculiar qualifications of professional curriculum makers.

One should be careful not to exaggerate the seriousness of these problems for education in general or for the training of administrators. The ability of students to educate themselves and one another in spite of the system, and in so doing to devise programs of training nowhere recognized in the catalogues, should never be underestimated. It may even be the case that such informal, chance factors constitute the only way to produce the administrator types that we need. Experience would indicate that it is one way. But the suspicion remains that something more deliberate is needed.

If this is the case, then it will require from active academics a serious, explicit, and continuing concern for education. One can get the impression that departmental and professional gatherings, except as they discuss the particular discipline, are the last places, even after general faculty meetings, in which to encounter serious thought about education. Presidents and deans are expected to pontificate on such matters, and the talk of professional educationists is tolerated if they keep to themselves, but an impression is conveyed that such concerns are not quite respectable for serious scholars. The impression is not accurate, of course, but circumstances give it some appearance of validity.

V. A PROPOSAL

My impression is that a fairly large number of academics retain a more than residual concern for education over a reach broader than the individual discipline. If this impression is correct, then what is characteristically lacking is an appropriate setting in which such concerns can be focused. Especially in the social sciences, which in recent years have concentrated heavily on the development of individual disciplines and consequently have given encouragement to segmental preoccupations, it is understandable that such settings have not been contrived. But perhaps a stage has been reached where it would be possible and fruitful to give some formal consideration to such joint concerns.

An interdisciplinary commission in the social sciences could, if its questions were radical enough, contribute not only to the training of administrators capable of making the social sciences more effective in the formation of policy, but also to education in a broader sense. In fact, to deal effectively with the one, its mandate probably would have to encompass the other. This is not the place to attempt to outline its agenda. It seems clear, however, that such an investigation should look at the patterns of exposure to and immersion in the social sciences at least over the span of the undergraduate and doctoral years. What can or should be the distinctive functions of each of these stages? How early and in what measure is disciplinary specialization essential? How early and how continuously can interdisciplinary problems, including those growing out of policy issues, be confronted without inviting superficiality and the irrelevance of a groundless certainty? How can they be identified?

In the years ahead the problems associated with the bearing of the social sciences on public policy are likely to become more difficult and more complex. That prospect suggests that these disciplines have some joint policy problems of their own. Chance unquestionably will play a major part in whatever solutions or accommodations are reached in both areas. How much is it necessary or wise to leave to chance?